Readings in United States History

Volume I

Seventh Edition

Ron Wright | Larry Watson | Blanche Brick

CENGAGE
Learning·

Australia • Brazil • Japan • Korea • Mexico • Singapore • Spain • United Kingdom • United States

CENGAGE
Learning·

**Readings in United States History: Volume I,
Seventh Edition**

Ron Wright
Larry Watson

Senior Manager, Student Engagement:

Linda deStefano

Janey Moeller

Manager, Student Engagement:

Julie Dierig

Marketing Manager:

Rachael Kloos

Manager, Production Editorial:

Kim Fry

Manager, Intellectual Property Project Manager:

Brian Methe

Senior Manager, Production and Manufacturing:

Donna M. Brown

Manager, Production:

Terri Daley

For product information and technology assistance, contact us at
Cengage Learning Customer & Sales Support, 1-800-354-9706
For permission to use material from this text or product,
submit all requests online at **cengage.com/permissions**
Further permissions questions can be emailed to
permissionrequest@cengage.com

ISBN-13: 9781305026070

ISBN-10: 1305026071

WCN: 01-100-101

Cengage Learning

5191 Natorp Boulevard
Mason, Ohio 45040
USA

Cengage Learning is a leading provider of customized learning solutions with
office locations around the globe, including Singapore, the United Kingdom,
Australia, Mexico, Brazil, and Japan. Locate your local office at:
international.cengage.com/region

Cengage Learning products are represented in Canada by Nelson Education, Ltd.

For your lifelong learning solutions, visit **custom.cengage.com**

Visit our corporate website at **cengage.com**

Printed in the United States of America

CREDITS

Chapter 2. Daniel J. Boorstin, "Paradise Found and Lost," from THE DISCOVERERS by Daniel J. Boorstin, copyright (c) 1983 by Daniel J. Boorstin. Used by permission of Random House, Inc.

Chapter 3. Winthrop, John. "A Modell of Christian Charity." Published in WINTHROP PAPERS, VOLUME II, 1623-1630, pages 282-295. Boston: Massachusetts Historical Society, 1931.

Chapter 4. The New England Quarterly, v. 15, December 1942 for ?Puritans and Sex? by Edmund S. Morgan. Copyright held by The New England Quarterly. Reproduced by permission of the publisher and the author.

Chapter 5. "The Middle Passage" by Malcolm Cowley and Daniel P. Mannix is from February 1962 issue of AMERICAN HERITAGE. Copyright (c) 1962 Daniel P. Mannix.

Chapter 6. "Anne Hutchinson versus Massachusetts" by Wellington Newcomb is from the June 1974 issue of AMERICAN HERITAGE.

Chapter 7. "Sinners in the Hands of an Angry God, 1741" by Jonathan Edwards, 1741.

Chapter 9. Mary Beth Norton, "The Philadelphia Ladies Association" from AMERICAN HERITAGE, 1980. Used by permission of Mary Beth Norton.

Chapter 10. Reprinted by permission fo the publisher from THE ADAMS PAPERS: ADAMS FAMILY COORESPONDENCE, VOLUME I - December 1761 - May 1776, edited by L. H. Butterfield, Cambridge, Mass.: The Belknap Press of Harvard University Press, Copyright (c) 1963 by the Massachusetts Historical Society.

Chapter 10a. Reprinted by permission fo the publisher from THE ADAMS PAPERS: ADAMS FAMILY COORESPONDENCE, VOLUME I - December 1761 - May 1776, edited by L. H. Butterfield, Cambridge, Mass.: The Belknap Press of Harvard University Press, Copyright (c) 1963 by the Massachusetts Historical Society.

Chapter 11. "What is an American?" by Hector St. John de Crevecoeur, 1782.

Chapter 13. Gordon S. Wood, "Hope and Heritage: Myth and Thomas Jefferson," THE WILSON QUARTERLY, Spring, 1993. Used by permission of the author.

Chapter 14. "Dying of Breast Cancer in the 1800s," REFLECTIONS ON THE AMERICAN PAST: A READER edited by Robert Shadle and James S. Olsen, Brandywine Press, pp. 52-60.

Chapter 15. "The Virginia Resolution, 1798" by James Madison.

Chapter 16. "Farewell Addres" by George Washington, 17 September 1796.

Chapter 17. "Thomas Jefferson: First Inaugural Address - 1801"

Chapter 18. Robert V. Remini, "The Jacksonian Revolution: Myth and Reality," WORLD AND I, January 1998. Source: The Washington Times Corp.

Chapter 19. Map on p. 48: "Trail of Tears" from DISINHERITED: THE LOST BIRTHRIGHT OF THE AMERICAN INDIAN by Dale Van Every. Copyright (c) 1966 by Dale Van Every. Reprinted by permission of HarperCollins Publishers, Inc./William Morrow.

Chapter 20. Edward R. Crowther, "Holy Honor: Sacred and Secular in the Old South," JOURNAL OF SOUTHERN HISTORY, November 1992, pp. 619-636. Copyright 1992 by the Southern Historical Association. Reprinted by permission of the Managing Editor.

Chapter 21. Welter, bARBARA. The Cult of True Womanhood, 1820-1831. AMERICAN QUARTERLY 18:2 (1966), pp. 151-174. Copyright (c) The American Studies Association. Reprinted with permission of The Johns Hopkins University Press.

Contents

I

Colonial Period to 1763

1. Paradise Found and Lost

Daniel J. Boorstin

On shipboard off the Azores in mid-February 1493, returning from his first voyage, Columbus wrote his own report of what he thought, and wanted others to think, that he had accomplished. Since it would have been disrespectful for him to address Ferdinand and Isabella directly, he reported to them in a "letter" addressed to Santangel, the crown official who had persuaded Queen Isabella, at the very last moment, to support Columbus' Enterprise of the Indies. Columbus' letter, written in Spanish, was printed in Barcelona about April 1, 1493, then translated into Latin dated April 29, and again printed in Rome in May as an eight-page pamphlet entitled *De Insulis Inuentis*. Frequently and speedily reprinted, by the standards of its day it became a best seller. At Rome there were three further editions in 1493, and six different editions printed at Paris, Basel, and Antwerp in 1493-94. By mid-June 1493 the Latin letter had been translated into a 68-stanza poem (printed in Rome and twice in Florence in 1493) in Tuscan, the dialect of Florence.

Northern Europe only slowly received news of Columbus' exploit. The famous Nuremberg Chronicle, an illustrated world history from the Creation to the present (printed on July 12, 1493), made no mention of the Columbus voyage. Not until late March 1496 do we find word of Columbus in England, and the first German translation of Columbus' letter was printed at Strasbourg in 1497.

What was the news that Columbus brought? The first illustrated Latin edition of his report (Basel, 1493) carried crude woodcuts that had already been used in earlier Swiss books that had no connection with Columbus, the Indies, or the New World. One woodcut purported to show the landing of Columbus in the Indies, in a forty-oared Mediterranean galley; another, supposed to represent the Bahama Islands, could have depicted any south-European seaside village.

Columbus, having convinced himself that a trip across the Western Ocean would take him to the Indies, now set about convincing a wider audience. He had a heavy vested interest in his destination actually being the Indies. In this first public announcement of his momentous voyage, Columbus was careful not to mention disasters or near disasters—the loss of the flagship, *Santa Maria,* the insubordination of Martin Alonso Pinzón, the commander of the *Pinta,* or the mutinous spirit of the crew. Following the national-security regulations of his day, he omitted information on the courses taken or the precise distance covered in order to prevent competitors from following where he had led. While Columbus conceded that he had not actually seen the Great Khan or the court of gold-rich Cipangu, he detailed numerous clues reinforcing his belief that he was just off the coast of China. The resplendent Great Khan, he was confident, would be found just a little farther on, doubtless on the next voyage.

Although Columbus was a hardheaded observer of the winds and waves, on the crucial question of where he had arrived he remained the slave of his hopes. He was determined to find signs everywhere that he had reached the fringes of Asia. Botany, still a vague wilderness whose images were not yet standardized by printing, was his happy hunting ground. From the moment when he first touched the north coast of Cuba on his first voyage, he had no trouble finding the Asiatic flora. A shrub that smelled like cinnamon he eagerly called cinnamon and so made it a hint of untold spice treasures. The aromatic West Indies gumbo-limbo, he insisted, must be an Asiatic form of the mastic tree of the Mediterranean that yielded resin. A small inedible nut, the *nogal de pais*, he hastily mistook for the coconut described by Marco Polo. The ship's surgeon examined some roots that the men had dug up and obligingly pronounced them the valuable medicinal Chinese rhubarb, a strong cathartic drug. Actually it was only the common garden rhubarb that we now use for pies and tarts, *Rheum rhaponticum,* not the pharmacist's *Rheum officinale*. But so many false scents somehow seemed to add up to the authentic odor of the Orient.

In the mind of Columbus such clues quickly clinched the thesis that had secured support for his enterprise of the Indies. Typical of his frame of mind and his exploring techniques was his first expedition into Cuba. On October 28, 1492, Columbus' caravels entered Bah'a Bariay, a beautiful harbor in the Oriente province of Cuba. There the captive San Salvador natives whom he had brought along as interpreters interviewed the local Indians and told Columbus that there was gold at Cubanacan (meaning mid-Cuba) only a short trek inland. Columbus eagerly assumed that they had meant to say "El Gran Can," the Great Khan of China, and at once sent an embassy to meet that Oriental potentate. An Arabic-speaking scholar whom he had brought along for just such missions was put in charge, accompanied by an able seaman who years before had once encountered an African king in Guinea, and so was supposed to know how to deal with exotic royalty. They took along diplomatic paraphernalia—their Latin passport, a letter of credence from their Catholic Majesties to his Chinese Majesty, and a rich gift for the Khan—along with glass beads and trinkets to buy food en route Led on by visions of Cambaluc, which had been named by Marco Polo as the Mongol capital of China where the Khan held his splendid court, they hiked up the valley of the Cocayuguin River. What they found were some fifty palm-thatched huts. The local cacique feasted them as messengers from the sky and the people kissed their feet. But they got no word of the Great Khan.

On the trail back to the harbor, Columbus' two ambassadors did have one epochal encounter. They met a walking party of Taino Indians—"many people who were going to their villages, with a firebrand in the hand, and herbs to drink the smoke thereof, as they are accustomed." The long cigar that they carried would be relighted at every stop by small boys carrying along firebrands, then passed around for each member of the party to take a few drags through his nostrils. After the relaxing interval the Tainos resumed their journey. This was the first recorded European encounter with tobacco. Obsessed by visions of China's gold, Columbus' embassy saw only a primitive custom. Some years later, when the Spaniards had colonized the New World and learned to enjoy tobacco themselves, they introduced it to Europe, Asia, and Africa, where it was to become a source of wealth, delight, and dismay.

Meanwhile, Columbus remained back at the harbor, working up the figures from his dead reckoning to confirm his conviction that Cuba really was Marco Polo's Province of Mangi. He occupied his spare moments gathering the botanical specimens that he believed could not be found anywhere except in Asia.

The conspicuously pious Christian nomenclature that Columbus affixed on the lands he first visited—San Salvador, Navidad, Santa Maria de Guadalupe, S. M. de Monserrate, S. M. la Antigua, S. M. la Redonda, San Martin, San Jorge, Santa Anastasia, San Cristóbal, Santa Crux, Santa Ursula y las xi mil Virgenes, San Juan Bautista—bore witness to his proverbial piety. It was his divinely appointed errand to enlarge the realm of the True Faith with the souls of pagan millions. His confidence as God's messenger had given him strength to bear years of ridicule, to risk mutiny, and would continue to shape his views of world geography.

Columbus' first voyage had many features of a Caribbean cruise, for he mainly enjoyed the sights, sounds and curiosities which he could witness from the coast, with only occasional short excursions inland. He had speedily coursed through the Bahamas, then skirted the northern coasts of eastern Cuba and of Hispaniola. Just three months after he first sighted the land of "the Indies," the island of San Salvador, his caravels set sail on January 16, 1493, from Samaná Bay on the eastern end of the island of Hispaniola to return home.

After only so brief a journey to the peripheral islands, with so little experience of the interior and such ambiguous clues to the Oriental character of the country, Columbus remained undaunted in his faith. His report revealed no doubt that he had reached "the Indies." And he generalized with all the confidence of the quickie tourist. The natives, he asserted, were "so ingenuous and free with all they have, that no one would believe it who has not seen it; of anything that they possess, if it be asked of them, they never say no; on the contrary, they invite you to share it and show as much love as if their hearts went with it, and they are content with whatever trifle be given them, whether it be a thing of value or of petty worth." "In all these islands, I saw no great diversity in the appearance of the people or in their manners and language, but they all understand one another, which is a very singular thing, on account of which I hope that their Highnesses will determine upon their conversion to our holy faith, towards which they are much inclined." The place he chose for La Villa de Navidad was "in the best district for the gold mines and for every trade both with this continent and with that over there belonging to the Gran Can [Grand Khan], where there will be great trade and profit." To their Catholic Highnesses he promised "as much gold as they want if their Highnesses will render me a little help; besides spices and cotton, as much as their Highnesses shall command; and gum mastic, as much as they shall order shipped... and aloe wood, as much as they shall order shipped, and slaves, as many as they shall order, who will be idolators. And I believe that I have found rhubarb and cinnamon, and I shall find a thousand other things of value, which the people whom I have left there will have discovered, for I have not delayed anywhere, provided the wind allowed me to sail..."

During the next twelve years Columbus undertook three more voyages to "the Indies." They were called voyages of discovery, but more precisely they should have been called voyages of confirmation. For someone less committed they might have produced tantalizing puzzles, planting seeds of doubt. When these successive voyages still failed to connect with the Great Khan or to discover Oriental splendors, it became harder to persuade others back home. Although Columbus was ingenious at inventing new strategies of explanation, as his explanations became increasingly farfetched be once again became a butt of ridicule, a casualty of his own faith.

Only six months after returning from his first voyage, Columbus set out again. This time his expedition was on a far grander scale. Instead of three small caravels he had an armada of seventeen vessels and at least twelve hundred men (still no women), now including six priests to oversee the work of conversion, numerous officials to enforce order and keep books, colonists hoping to make their fortunes in the Indies, and, of course, the crews. While the first voyage could have been called merely exploratory, this second voyage was planned to make the exploration pay off. Columbus was now commissioned to set up a trading post in Hispaniola. He was under greater pressure than ever to prove that he had found the fabled treasure trove of the Indies. This time Columbus' feat of seamanship was even more impressive. While crossing the ocean, he managed to keep the seventeen ships together, and, as Samuel Eliot Morison boasts, "Columbus hit the Lesser Antilles at the exact spot recommended by sailing directions for the next four centuries!" His actual discoveries were also significant, for he found the Lesser Antilles, Jamaica, and Puerto Rico, explored the south coast of Cuba, and established the first permanent European settlement on this side of the Atlantic. Still, for Columbus this was not enough. He demanded the shores of Asia.

On this second trip, as Columbus proceeded through countless small islands of the Lesser Antilles he was encouraged by recalling Sir John Mandeville's observation that there were five thousand islands in the Indies. By the time he reached the southern tip of Cuba he was convinced that he had reached the mainland of Asia. As he coasted Cuba westward from the Gulf of Guacanayabo he was confident that he was following the shores of Marco Polo's Mangi in southern China. When he reached Bah'a CortŽs, a point where the coast turns sharply toward the south, he knew that he was at the starting point of the eastern shores of the Golden Chersonese (the Malay Peninsula). If he had not yet found the sea passage that Marco Polo said would lead him to the Indian Ocean, he had found the peninsula at the end of which the sea passage would surely appear. But at this point his caravels were leaking, his ships' rigging tattered, his supplies low, and his crew showing signs of mutiny. Columbus decided to turn beck. A pity. If he had gone only fifty miles farther, he could have discovered that Cuba was an island.

To protect himself against accusations of timidity or cowardice and to "confirm" his geographic ideas, from the officers and crew of all the three ships which he had detached for this exploring sally he extracted sworn depositions. This was not an unprecedented procedure, as Columbus must have known. Only six years earlier, in 1488, Columbus had been at Lisbon when Dias returned and had to justify his reversing course at the critical moment when he had clear sailing to India. As we have seen, Bartholomeu Dias had taken this same precaution to prove that it was his crew that forced him to return. But while Dias' crew had been asked only to certify Dias' courage and seamanship, Columbus' crew was asked also to certify Columbus' geography. The deposition that all were required to sign declared that the coast they had sailed three hundred and thirty-five leagues from east to west was longer than any island they had seen, that therefore they were certain that this coast must be part of a continent, which was obviously Asia, and that if they had sailed farther, they would have encountered "civilized people of intelligence who know the world." Columbus threatened to prove it by continuing the voyage until they had circumnavigated the globe. As an additional argument, Columbus explained that anyone who refused to sign would be fined ten thousand maravedis and have his tongue cut out. If the obstinate sailor happened to be a boy, he would take a hundred lashes on his bare back.

The return of Columbus' ships to Spain in March 1496 was anything but a triumph. He was warmly received at court, but the discovery of islands, of the Indies in the Western Ocean no longer created a sensation. Like a second moon landing, Columbus' feat had somehow been minimized by showing that it could be repeated. Except among a few men of learning word of this voyage was received with indifference. One reason surely was that the commercial payoff for the large investment had been so negligible. Some of his closest collaborators were beginning to doubt that Columbus' "Indies" really were Asia. Juan de la Cosa, who had been master of the *Santa Maria* on Columbus' first voyage and was with him too on the second voyage, had actually signed the required "Cuba no island" deposition. But when La Cosa made his famous world map in 1500, he showed Cuba as an island. Dubious European map-makers for many years showed two Cubas —one an island, the other conforming to the shape of Marco Polo's Mangi as the mainland of south China.

The multiplying doubts of others hardened Columbus' obstinacy. "The Admiral... named the first coast he touched [in Cuba] Alpha and Omega," reported the chronicler Peter Martyr in 1501, "because he thought that there our East ended when the sun set in that island, and our West began when the sun rose...

He expected to arrive in the part of the world underneath us near the Golden Chersonese, which is situated to the east of Persia. He thought, as a matter of fact, that of the twelve hours of the sun's course of which we are ignorant he would have lost only two."

Now it was only with difficulty, and after two full years of promotional activity, that he collected a fleet of six ships for a third voyage to depart on May 30, 1498. New rumors and reports already suggested that a great land mass, perhaps not Asia, might lie somewhere to the west of the islands Columbus had found. But Columbus was not impressed. Instead he was more eager than ever to speedily find the sea passage around the Golden Chersonese into the Indian Ocean and so vindicate his hopes. On this third trip he encountered some geographic conundrums, which led him into fantasies which would discredit him among the best cartographers of his age. The faith of medieval Christian geographers was still very much alive in the mind of Christopher Columbus.

On this voyage his first "discovery" was the island he christened Trinidad in honor of the Holy Trinity. Then he happened into the Gulf of Paria, the bay formed by the delta of the great Orinoco River. Till then, of course, it had been an article of his faith that there could be no land mass down that way. But how explain this great freshwater sea, and the breadth of the freshwater rivers that poured into it? Was there, after all, a land mass not found in Ptolemy, which gathered this great flood of fresh water? "I believe that this is a very great continent, until today unknown," Columbus recorded with surprise in his journal. "And reason aids me greatly because of that so great river and fresh-water sea, and next, the saying of Esdras ... that the six parts of the world arc of dry land, and one of water....Which book of Esdras St. Ambrose approved in bit *Examenon* and so St. Augustine in the passage *morietur filius meus Christus,* as Francisco de Mayrones alleges; and further I am supported by the sayings of many Carib Indians whom I took at other times, who said that to the south of them was mainland...and... that in it there was much gold...and if this be a continent, it is a marvelous thing, and will be so among all the wise, since so great a river flows that it makes a fresh-water sea of 48 leagues."

Columbus the zealot was not unprepared for some grand new revelation about the shape of the planet. "God made me the messenger of the new heaven and the new earth of which he spoke in the Apocalypse by St. John, after having spoken of it by the mouth of Isaiah and he showed me the spot where to find it." This revelation required revision of the orthodox dogmas of the earth:

> I have always read that the world comprising the land and the
> water was spherical, and the recorded experiences of Ptolemy and all
> others have proved this by the eclipses of the moon and other observa-
> tions made from east to west, as well as by the elevation of the pole
> from north to south. But I have now seen so much irregularity that I
> have come to another conclusion respecting the earth, namely that it

is not round as they describe, but of the form of a pear...or like around ball, upon one part of which is a prominence like a woman's nipple, this protrusion being the highest and nearest the sky, situated under the equinoctial line, and at the eastern extremity of this sea where the land and the islands end... [The ancients] had no certain knowledge respecting this hemisphere, but merely vague suppositions, for no one has ever gone or been sent to investigate the matter until now that Your Highnesses have sent me to explore both the sea and the land.

Here, finally, was the actual earthly location of the Scriptural landscape which medieval Christian cosmographers had so long featured at the top of their maps.

I am convinced that it is the spot of the earthly paradise whither no one can go but by God's permission...I do not suppose that the earthly paradise is in the form of a rugged mountain, as the descriptions of it have made it appear, but that it is on the summit of the spot which I have described...I think also that the water I have described [i.e., of the Orinoco] may proceed from it, though it be far off, and that stopping at the place which I have just left, it forms this lake [the Gulf of Paria]. There are great indications of this being the terrestrial paradise, for its site coincides with the opinion of holy and wise theologians, and, moreover, the older evidences agree with the supposition, for I have never either read or heard of fresh water coming so large a quantity in close conjunction with the water of the sea. The idea is also corroborated by the blandness of the temperature; and if the water of which I speak does not proceed from the earthly paradise, it seems to be a still greater wonder, for I do not believe that there is any river in the world so large or so deep.

Columbus' location of the Terrestrial Paradise on this unexpected mainland to the south was no random fantasy but the only rational explanation to reconcile the existence of some vast source of fresh water with his Christian doctrine, with his Ptolemaic geography, with the Asiatic identity of Cuba, and the certainty of a direct sea passage around the Golden Chersonese to the Indian Ocean.

To understand Columbus' problem, and why he sought refuge in his Terrestrial Paradise, we must remind ourselves of the Ptolemaic-Christian view of the lands of the earth. All the habitable parts of the earth were believed to be parts of a single land mass, the Island of the Earth, or *Orbis Terrarum*, including Europe, Asia, and Africa, surrounded by a comparatively small amount of water. The Book of Esdras argued the unity of all land that was not covered by the sea. Another vast land mass like the Americas separated by oceans on two sides from the Island of the Earth would not fit into that picture at all. Such a possibility suggested more water than there could possibly be (ex *hypothesi* on only one-seventh of the planet's surface). Moreover, lands of that sort would block the fulfillment of Columbus' great hope—a straight westward passage to India.

Another serious objection to new continents, from Columbus' orthodox point of view, was that, as we have seen, Christian doctrine refused to admit the possibility of habitable lands below the equator. Detached continents not continuous with the three-continent Island of the Earth, although suggested by pagan authors, were explicitly denied by the Church Fathers. Confronted with the possibility of a vast land mass where Christian doctrine insisted it could not be, the pious Columbus fitted it into his faith as the Terrestrial Paradise. In the best Christian sense that would be, in Columbus' phrase, *orbis alterius* or *otro mundo*—another world or another "island of earth."

Still, Columbus could round out his argument, confirm his Christian faith, and fulfill his obsessive reach for the Indies only by finding the sea passage around Marco Polo's Golden Chersonese. With this specific purpose, the same for which ten years earlier he had undertaken his first voyage, Columbus set out on his fourth and last voyage. With four caravels he left Seville on April 3, 1502. Somewhere between Cuba, which he still believed to be China, and the Terrestrial Paradise to the south he determined to find the strait through which Marco Polo had sailed from China into the Indian Ocean. This time he carried a letter of introduction from their Catholic Majesties to Vasco da Gama, whom he expected to meet in India. Of course, the Pacific Ocean, still unknown to Europe, did not figure in anybody's calculations.

A fair wind carried his four caravels across the Atlantic, from the Canaries to Martinique, in only twenty-one days. Columbus, who was fifty-one years old when he set out, called this fourth voyage *El Alto Viaje*, the High Voyage.

Still not discovering Cuba to be an island, he sailed southwestward from Cuba until he touched the Atlantic littoral of the present Republic of Honduras. He then followed the coast eastward and southward, ever seeking the opening around this imagined Golden Chersonese to the Indian Ocean. He continued to find reassuring clues to the Asiatic character of this land in the form of botanical specimens and rumors of gold mines like those described by Marco Polo. After several disillusions—for example, when he explored Bahia Almirante near the Panama-Costa Rica border—he concluded that there was no sea passage in this area.

Instead of giving up his Asiatic hypothesis, Columbus seems to have concluded that there were actually two Asiatic peninsulas of the Golden Chersonese, one much longer than had been supposed. If only he had gone far enough southward along the coast, he still insisted, he would eventually have found his way around into the Indian Ocean. Perhaps, after all, the Gulf of Paria was not port of a separate *Orbis Terrarum*, but was merely an extension of this part of Asia. Columbus died believing that while he had incidentally found some Asiatic islands and peninsulas that had not yet appeared on the maps, all along he had been following the east coast of Asia.

2. A Modell of Christian Charity

written by John Winthrop
for the Massachusetts Bay Colony, 1630

In the summer of 1630, John Winthrop led a fleet of seventeen ships and about one thousand Puritan men and women across the Atlantic Ocean to Massachusetts Bay. During the passage over, Winthrop delivered the lecture "A Modell of Christian Charity" on board the flagship Arbella. With a blend of logic and Biblical admonition, he reminded them that Massachusetts Bay Colony was a "work" given to them by God. They had a special commission from God while they had entered into a "covenant" with God. The colony was to be a special Christian commonwealth, a "city upon a hill" that the rest of the world would admire and imitate.

Winthrop was a realist. He understood that the colony's success depended on the preservation of the unity of the community of believers. They were to love and care for each other. Winthrop challenged his "fellow members of Christ" to obey God's laws as expressed in the Bible. The covenant they had with God was conditional. If they failed, their colony would suffer God's judgement.

Winthrop invoked the ideas of "mission" and "destiny" together with the idea of "covenant." Later on in American history, many Americans will appropriate some of Winthrop's ideas to declare a belief in America's "manifest destiny." God had chosen this country as a beacon of democracy and freedom.

A MODELL HEREOF

God Almightie in his most holy and wise providence hath soe disposed of the Condicion of mankinde, as in all times some must be rich, some poore, some highe and eminent in power and dignitie others meane and in subjeccion.

THE REASON HEREOF

1. Reason: First, to hold conformity with the rest of his workes being delighted to shewe forthe the glory of his wisdome in the variety and differance of the Creatures and the glory of his power in ordering all these differences for the preservacion and good of the whole; and the glory of his greatnes that as it is the glory of princes to have many officers, soe this great King will have many Stewards, counting himselfe more honoured in dispenceing his gifts to man by man, than if tree did it by his owne immediate hand.

2. Reason: Secondly, That he might have the more occasion to manifest the worke of his Spirit: first, upon the wicked in moderate ing and restraineing them: soe that the riche and mighty should not eate upp the poore, nor the poore and dispised rise upp against their superiours and shake off thiere yoake; secondly in the regenerate in exerciseing his graces in them, as in the greate ones, their love, mercy, gentlenes, temperance, etc., in the poore and inferiour sorte, theire faithe, patience, obedience, etc.

3. Reason: Thirdly, That every man might have need of other, and from hence they might be all knit more nearly together in the Bond of brotherly affeccion: from hence it appeares plainely that noe man is made more honourable than another or more wealthy etc., out of any perticuler and singuler respect to himselfe but for the glory of his Creator and the Common good of the Creature, Man, Therefore God still reserves the propperty of these gifts to himselfe as Ezek: 16.17. he there calls wealthe his gold and his silver, etc. Prov: 3.9 he claimes theire service as his due, honour the Lord with thy riches, etc. All men being thus (by divine providence) ranked into two sortes, riche and poore; under the first, are comprehended all such as are able to live comfortably by theire owne meanes duely improved; and all others are poore according to the former distribution. There are two rules whereby wee are to walke one towards another: JUSTICE and MERCY. These are allwayes distinguished in theire Act and in theire object, yet may they both concurre in the same Subject in eache respect; as sometimes there may be an occasion of shewing mercy to a rich man, in some sudden danger of distresse, and allsoe doeing of meere Justice to a poor man in regard of some perticuler contract, etc. There is likewise a double Lawe by which wee are regulated in our conversacion one towardes another: in both the former respects, the lawe of nature and the lawe of grace, or the morrall lawe or the lawe of the gospel!, to omit the rule of Justice as not propperly belonging to this purpose otherwise than it may fall into consideraction in some perticuler Cases: By the first of these lawes man as he was enabled soe withall [is] commanded to love his neighbour as himselfe. Upon this ground stands all the precepts of the morrall lawe, which concernes our dealings with men. To apply this to the works of mercy this lawe requires two things: first, that every man afford his help to another in every want or distress. Secondly, That hee performe this out of the same affeccion which makes him careful! of his owne good according to that of our Saviour, Math: [7.12] Whatsoever ye would that men should doe to you. This was practiced by Abraham and Lott in entertaineing the Angells and the old man of Gibea.

The Lawe of Grace or the Gospell hath some differance from the former as in these respects: first, the lawe of nature was given to man in the estate of innocency; this of the gospell in the estate of regeneracy. Secondly, the former propounds one man to another, as the same fleshe and Image of god; this as a brother in Christ allsoe, and in the Communion of the same spirit and soe teacheth us to put a diflference betweene Christians and others. Doe good to all, especially to the household of faith; upon this ground the Israelites were to putt a difference betweene the brethren of such as were strangers though not of the Canaanites. Thirdly, the Lawe of nature could give noe rules for dealing with enemies, for all are to be considered as friends in the estate of innocency, but the Gospell commands love to an enemy. Proofe: If thine Enemie hunger feede him; Love your Enemies, doe good to them that hate you Math: 5.44.

This Lawe of the Gospell propoundes likewise a difference of seasons and occasions. There is a tyme when a Christian must sell all and give to the poore, as they did in the Apostles times. There is a tyme allsoe when a Christian (though they give not all yet) must give beyond theire ability, as they of Macedonia. Cor: 2.6. Likewise community of perills calls for extraordinary liberallity and soe cloth Community in some speciall service for the Churche. Lastly, when there is noe other meanes whereby our Christian brother may be relieved in this distresse, wee must help him beyond our ability, rather than tempt God, in putting him upon help by miraculous or extraordinary meanest.

It rests now to make some application of this discourse by the present designe which gave the occasion of writeing of in Herein are four things to be propounded: first, the persons; secondly, the worke; thirdly, the end; fourthly, the meanest

1. For the persons, wee are a Company professing our selves fellow members of Christ, in which respect onely though wee were absent from eache other many miles, and had our imploymentes as farre distant, yet wee ought to account our selves knits together by this bond of love, and live in the exercise of it, if wee would have comforte of our being in Christ. This was notorious in the practice of the Christians in former times, as is testified of the Waldenses from the mouth of one of the adversaries Aeneas Sylvius, mutuo [solent amare] pene antequam norint. They use to love any of theire own religion even before they were acquainted with them.

2. For the worke wee have in hand, it is by a mutuall consent through a special overruleing providence, and a more than an ordinary approbation of the Churches of Christ to seeke out a place of Cohabitation and Consorteshipp under a due forme of Government both civill and ecclesiasticall. In such cases as this the care of the publique must oversway all private respects, by which not onely conscience, but meare Civill pollicy cloth binde us; for it is a true rule that perticuler estates cannott subsist in the ruine of the publique.

3. The end is to improve our lives, to doe more service to the Lord, the comforte and encrease of the body of Christ whereof wee are members, that our selves and posterity may be the better preserved from the Common corrupcions of this evill world, to serve the Lord and worke out our Salvacion under the power and purity of his holy Ordinances.

4. For the meanes whereby this must bee effected, they are twofold, a Conformity with the worke and end wee aime at; these wee see are extraordinary,

therefore wee must not content our selves with usuall ordinary meanest What-soever wee did or ought to have done when wee lived in England, the same must wee doe and more allsoe where wee goe: That which the most in theire Churches mainteine as a truthe in profession onely, wee must bring into familiar and constant practice, as in this duty of love wee must love brotherly without dissimulation, wee must love one another with a pure hearse fervently, wee must beare one anothers burthens, wee must not looke onely on our owne things but allsoe on the things of our brethren, neither must wee think that the lord will beare with such faileings at our hands as tree clothe from those among whome wee have lived.

Thus stands the cause betweene God and us. Wee are entered into Covenant with him for this worke, wee have taken out a Commission the Lord hath given us leave to draw our owne Articles, wee have professed to enterprise these Ac-cions upon these and these ends, wee have hereupon besought him of favour and blessing: Now if the Lord shall please to heare us, and bring us in peace to the place wee desire. then hath tree ratified this Covenant and sealed our Com-mission [and] will expect a strickt performance of the Articles contained in it, but if wee shall neglect the observacion of these Articles which are the ends wee have propounded, and dissembling with our God, shall fall to embrace this pres-ent world and prosecute our carnall intencions seekeing grease things for our selves and our posterity, the Lord will surely breake out in wrathe against us, be revenged of such a perjured people and make us knowe the price of the breache of such a Covenant.

Now the onely way to avoyde this shipwracke and to provide for our poster-ity is to followe the Counsell of Micah, to doe Justly, to love mercy, to walke humbly with our God. For this end, wee must be knit together in this worke as one man, wee must entertaine each other in brotherly Affeccion, wee must be willing to abridge our selves of our superfiuities, for the supply of others necessi-ties, wee must uphold a familiar Commerce together in all meeknes, gentlenes, patience and liberallity, wee must delight in each other, make others Condicions our owne, rejoyce together, mourne together, labour and suffer together, all-wayes haveing before our eyes our Commission and Community in the worke, our Community as members of the same body, soe shall wee keepe the unitie of the spirit in the bond of peace, the Lord will be our God and delight to dwell among us as his owne people and will command a blessing upon us in all our wayes, soe that wee shall see much more of his wisdome, power, goodnes and truthe than formerly wee have beene acquainted with. Wee shall finde that the God of Israell is among us, when ten of us shall be able to resist a thousand of our enemies, when hee shall make us a prayse and glory, that men shall say of succeeding plantacions: the lord make it like that of New England: for wee must Consider that wee shall be as a Citty upon a Hill, the eies of all people are up-pon us; soe that if wee shall deale falsely with our god in this worke wee have undertaken and soe cause him to withdrawe his present help from us, wee shall shame the faces of many of gods worthy servants, and cause theire prayers to be turned into Cursses upon us till wee be consumed out of the good land whither wee are goeing: And to shut upp this discourse with that exhortacion of Moses, that faithfull servant of the Lord in his last farewell to Israell, Deut. 30. Beloved there is now sett before us life, and good, deathe and evill in that wee are Commaunded this day to love the Lord our God, and to love one another, to walke in his wayes and to keepe his Commaundements and his Ordinance, and his lawes, and the Articles of our Covenant with him that wee may live and be multiplied, and that the Lord our God may blesse us in the land whither we goe to possesse it: But if our hearses shall turne away soe that wee will not obey, but shall be seduced and worship . . . other Gods, our pleasures, and proffitts, and serve them; it is propounded unto us this day, wee shall surely perishe out of the good Land whither wee passe over this vast Sea to possesse it;

> Therefore lett us choose life,
> that wee, and our Seede,
> may live; by obeyeing his
> voyce, and cleaveing to him,
> for hee is our life, and
> our prosperity.

3. The Puritans and Sex

Edmund S. Morgan

The stereotype of Puritans as humorless and sexually repressed has been a part of the popular historical imagination for a long time. In the 1920s, H. L. Mencken defined Puritanism as "the haunting fear that someone, somewhere, may be happy." In this article, Edmund Morgan portrays Puritans in a different way than the popular perception. Puritans were extremely religious, yet in their view of sex they were not narrow-minded bigots. Sex was part of God's plan for marriage.

The Anglicans of England were harsh in their disapproval of those who would not follow the Church of England's teachings. Those, such as the Quakers and Puritans, were persecuted and forced to leave the Mother Country and seek asylum in another country or perhaps in the distant New World. John Winthrop led a small group of Puritans to America and in 1630 established the Massachusetts Bay Colony. Here the settlers were determined to put into practice their cherished beliefs and to praise God in their own way. They hoped to build a model community, a "City Upon a Hill," for the rest of the world to witness. They would stress education, a strict work ethic, a limited democracy and utopianism. Their theocratic government would not tolerate moral weaknesses. There would be serious punishment for those who were not hard workers or those who did not practice strict self-denial. There would be severe punishments for those who were guilty of gambling, drunkenness, or enjoying theatrical performances. There was also a long list of sexual crimes that the Puritans must avoid. By studying numerous court cases of the times, it is clear that many of the people succumbed to such vices as fornication, rape, adultery and other weaknesses. And yet, in spite of this strict code of expected behavior, the Puritans broke with their sexual stereotype in the case of spouses and the use of the marriage bed.

Henry Adams once observed that Americans have "ostentatiously ignored" sex. He could think of only two American writers who touched upon the subject with any degree of boldness—Walt Whitman and Bret Harte. Since the time when Adams made this penetrating observation, American writers have been making up for lost time in a way that would make Bret Harte, if not Whitman, blush. And yet there is still more truth than falsehood in Adams' statement. Americans, by comparison with Europeans or Asiatics, are squeamish when confronted with the facts of life. My purpose is not to account for this squeamishness, but simply to point out that the Puritans, those bogeymen of the modern intellectual, are not responsible for it.

At the outset, consider the Puritan's attitude toward marriage and the role of sex in marriage. The popular assumption might be that the Puritans frowned on marriage and tried to hush up the physical aspect of it as much as possible, but listen to what they themselves had to say. Samuel Willard, minister of the Old South Church in the latter part of the seventeenth century and author of the most complete textbook of Puritan divinity, more than once expressed his horror at "that Polish conceit of the Excellence of Virginity." Another minister, John Cotton, wrote that

> Women are Creatures without which there is no comfortable Liv-
> ing for man: it is true of them what is wont to be said of Governments,
> *That bad ones are better than none*: They are a sort of Blasphemers
> then who dispise and decry them, and call them a *necessary Evil*, for
> they are *a necessary* Good.

These sentiments did not arise from an interpretation of marriage as a spiritual partnership, in which sexual intercourse was a minor or incidental matter. Cotton gave his opinion of "Platonic love" when he recalled the case of

> one who immediately upon marriage, without ever approaching the
> *Nuptial Bed*, indented with the *Bride*, that by mutual consent they
> might both live such a life, and according did sequestring themselves
> according to the custom of the times, from the rest of mankind, and af-
> terwards from one another too, in their retired Cells, giving themselves
> up to a Contemplative life; and this is recorded as an instance of no
> little or ordinary Vertue; but I must be pardoned in it, if I can account
> it no other than an effort to blind zeal, for they are the dictates of a
> blind mind they follow therein, and not of that Holy Spirit, which saith
> *It is not good that man should be alone.*

Here is as healthy an attitude as one could hope to find anywhere. Cotton certainly cannot be accused of ignoring human nature. Nor was he an isolated example among the Puritans. Another minister stated plainly the "the Use of the Marriage Bed" is "founded in mans Nature," and that consequently any withdrawal from sexual intercourse upon the part of husband or wife "Denies all reliefe in Wedlock vnto Human necessity: and sends it for supply vnto Beastiality when God gives not the gift of Consistency." In other words, sexual intercourse was a human necessity and marriage the only proper supply for it. These were the views of the New England clergy, the acknowledged leaders of the community, the most Puritanical of the Puritans. As proof that their congregations concurred with them, one may cite the case in which the members of the First Church of Boston expelled James Mattock because, among other offenses, "he denyed Conjugall fellowship vnto his wife for the space of two years together

vpon pretense of taking Revenge upon himself for his abusing of her before mar-
ryage." So strongly did the Puritans insist upon the sexual character of marriage
that one New Englander considered himself slandered when it was reported,
"that he Brock his deceased wife's hart with Greife, that he would be absent from
her three weeks together when he was at home, and wold never come nere her,
and such Like."

There was just one limitation which the Puritans placed upon sexual relations in marriage: sex must not interfere with religion. Man's chief end was to
glorify God, and all earthly delights must promote that end, not hinder it. Love
for a wife was carried too far when it lead a man to neglect his God:

> . . . sometimes a man hath a good affection to Religion, but the love
> of his wife carries him away, a man may bee so transported to his wife,
> that hee dare not bee forward in Religion, lest hee displease his wife,
> and so the wife, lest shee displease her husband, and this is an inordi-
> nate love, when it exceeds measure.

Sexual pleasures, in this respect, were treated like other kinds of pleasure.
On a day of fast, when all comforts were supposed to be foregone in behalf of
religious contemplation, not only were tasty food and drink to be abandoned
but sexual intercourse too. On other occasions, when food, drink and recreation
were allowable, sexual intercourse was allowable too, though of course only between persons who were married to each other. The Puritans were not ascetics;
they never wished to prevent the enjoyment of earthly delights. They merely
demanded that the pleasures of the flesh be subordinated to the greater glory
of God: husband and wife must not become "so transported with affection, that
they look at no higher end than marriage it self." "Let such as have wives," said
the ministers, " look at them not for their own ends, but to be fitted for Gods
service, and bring them nearer to God."

Toward sexual intercourse outside of marriage the Puritans were as frankly
hostile as they were favorable to it in marriage. They passed laws to punish adultery with death, and fornication with whipping. Yet they had no misconceptions
as to the capacity of human beings to obey such laws. Although the laws were
commands of God, it was only natural—since the fall of Adam—for human beings to break them. Breaches must be punished lest the community suffer the
wrath of God, but no offense, sexual or otherwise, could be occasion for surprise
or for hushed tones of voice. How calmly the inhabitants of seventeenth century
New England could contemplate rape or attempted rape is evident in the following testimony offered before the Middlesex County Court of Massachusetts:

> The examination of Edward Wire taken the 7th of october and
> alsoe Zachery Johnson. who sayeth that Edward Wires mayd being sent
> into the towne about busenes meeting with a man that dogd hir from

about Joseph Kettles house to goody marshes. She came into William Johnsones and desired Zachery Johnson to goe home with her for that the man dogd hir. accordingly he went with her and being then as far as Samuel Phips his house the man over tooke them. which man caled himselfe by the name of peter grant would have led the mayd but she oposed itt three times: and coming to Edward Wires house the said grant would have kist hir but she refused itt: wire being at prayer grant dragd the mayd between the said wiers and Nathanill frothinghams house. hee then flung the mayd downe in the streete and got atop hir; Johnson seeing it hee caled vppon the fellow to be sivill and not abuse the mayd then Edward wire came forth and ran to the said grant and took hold of him asking him what he did to his mayd, the said grant asked whether she was his wife for he did nothing to his wife: the said grant swearing he would be the death of the said wire. when he came of the mayd; he swore he would bring ten men to pul down his house and soe ran away and they followed him as far as good[y] phipses house where they mett with John Terry and George Chin with clubs in there hands and soe they went away together. Zachy Johnson going to Constable Heamans, and wire going home. there came John Terry to his house to ask for beer and grant was in the streete but afterward departed into the towne, both Johnson and Wire both aferme that when grant was vppon the mayd she cryed out severall times.

Deborah hadlocke being examined sayth that she mett with the man that cals himselfe peeter grant about good prichards that he dogd hir and followed hir to hir masters and there threw hir down and lay vppon hir but had not the use of hir body but swore several othes that he would ly with hir and gett hir with child before she got home.

Grant being present denys all saying he was drunk and did not know what he did.

The Puritans became inured to sexual offenses, because there were so many. The impression which one gets from reading the records of seventeenth century New England courts is that illicit sexual intercourse was fairly common. The testimony given in cases of fornication and adultery—by far the most numerous class of criminal cases in the records—suggests that many of the early New Englanders possessed a high degree of virility and very few inhibitions. Besides the case of Peter Grant, take the testimony of Elizabeth Knight about the manner of Richard Nevars's advances toward her:

The last publique day of Thanksgiving (in the year 1674) in the evening as I was milking Richard Nevars came to me, and offered me abuse in putting his hand, under my coates, but I turning aside with much adoe, saved myself, and when I was settled to milking he agen took me by the shoulder and pulled me backward almost, but I clapped one hand on the Ground and held fast the Cows teatt with the other hand, and cryed out, and then came to mee Jonathan Abbot one of my Masters Servants, whome the said Never asked wherefore he came, the said Abbot said to look after you, what you doe unto the Maid, but the said Never bid Abbot goe about his businesse but I bade the lad to stay.

One reason for the abundance of sexual offenses was the number of men in the colonies who were unable to gratify their sexual desires in marriage. Many of the first settlers had wives in England. They had come to the new world to make a fortune, expecting either to bring their families after them or to return to England with some of the riches of America. Although these men left their wives behind, they brought their sexual appetites with them; and in spite of the laws which required them to return to their families, they continued to stay, and more continued to arrive, as indictments against them throughout the seventeenth century clearly indicate.

Servants formed another group of men, and of women too, who could not ordinarily find supply for human necessity within the bounds of marriage. Most servants lived in the homes of their masters and could not marry without their consent, a consent which was not likely to be given unless the prospective husband or wife also belonged to the master's household. This situation will be better understood if it is recalled that most servants at this time were engaged by contract for a stated period. They were, in the language of the time, "covenant servants," who had agreed to stay with their masters for a number of years in return for a specified recompense, such a transportation to New England or education in some trade (the latter, of course, were known more specifically as apprentices). Even hired servants who worked for wages were usually single, for as soon as a man had enough money to buy or build a house of his own and to get married, he would set up in farming or trade himself. It must be emphasized, however, that anyone who was not in business for himself was necessarily a servant. The economic organization of seventeenth century New England had no place for the independent proletarian workman with a family of his own. All production was carried on in the household by the master of the family and his servants, so that most men were either servants or masters of servants; and the former, of course, were more numerous than the latter. Probably most of the inhabitants of Puritan New England could remember a time when they had been servants.

Theoretically no servant had a right to a private life. His time, day or night, belonged to his master, and both religion and law required that he obey his master scrupulously. But neither religion nor law could restrain the sexual impulses of youth, and if those impulses could not be expressed in marriage, they had to be given vent outside marriage. Servants had little difficulty in finding the occasions. Though they might be kept at work all day, it was easy enough to slip away at night. Once out of the house, there were several ways of meeting with a maid. The simplest way was to go to her bedchamber, if she was so fortunate as to have a private one of her own. Thus Jock, Mr. Solomon Phipps's Negro man, confessed in court

> that on the sixteenth day of May 1682, in the morning, betweene 12 and one of the clock, he did force open the back doores of the House of Laurence Hammond in Charlestowne, and came in to the House, and went up into the garret to Marie the Negro.
>
> He doth likewise acknowledge that one night the last week he forced into the House the same way, and went up to the Negro Woman Marie and that the like he hath done at severall other times before.

Joshua Fletcher took a more romantic way of visiting his lady:

> Joshua Fletcher . . . doth confesse and acknowledge that three severall nights, after bedtime, he went into Mr. Fiskes Dwelling house at Chelmsford, at an open window by a ladder that he brought with him. the said windo opening into a chamber, whose was the lodging place of Gresill Juell servant to mr. Fiske. and there he kept company with the said mayd. she sometimes having her cloathes on, and one time he found her in her bed.

Sometimes a maidservant might entertain callers in the parlor while the family was sleeping upstairs. John Knight described what was perhaps a common experience for masters. The crying of his child awakened him in the middle of the night, and he called to his maid, one Sarah Crouch, who was supposed to be sleeping with the child. Receiving no answer, he arose and

> went downe the stayres, and at the stair foot, the latch of doore was pulled in. I called severall times and at last said if shee would not open the doore, I would breake it open, and when she opened the doore shee was all undressed and Sarah Largin with her undressed, also the said Sarah went out of doores and Dropped some of her clothes as shee went out. I enquired of Sarah Crouch what men they were, which was with them. Shee made mee no answer for some space of time, but at last shee told me Peeter Brigs was with them, I asked her whether Thomas Jones was not there, but shee would give mee no answer.

In the temperate climate of New England it was not always necessary to seek out a maid at her home. Rachel Smith was seduced in an open field "about nine of the clock at night, being darke, neither moone nor starrs shineing." She was walking through the field when she met a man who asked here where shee lived, and what her name was and shee told him. and then shee asked his name, and he told her Saijing that he was old Good-man Shepards man. Also she saith he gave her strong liquors, and told her that it was not the first time he had been with maydes after his master was in bed.

Sometimes, of course, it was not necessary for a servant to go outside his master's house in order to satisfy his sexual urges. Many cases of fornication are on record between servants living in the same house. Even where servants had no private bedroom, even where the whole family slept in a single room, it was not impossible to make love. In fact many love affairs must have had their consummation upon a bed in which other people were sleeping. Take for example the case of Sarah Lepingwell. When Sarah was brought into court for having an illegitimate child, she related that one night when her master's brother, Thomas Hawes, was visiting the family, she went to bed early. Later, after Hawes had gone to bed, he called to her to get him a pipe of tobacco. After refusing for some time,

at the last I arose and did lite his pipe and cam and lay doune one my one bead and smoaked about half the pip and siting vp in my bead to give him his pip my bead being a trundell bead at the sid of his bead he reached beyond the pip and Cauth me by the wrist and pulled me on the side of his bead but I biding him let me goe he bid me hold my peas the folks wold here me and if it be replyed come why did you not call out I Ansar I was posesed with fear of my mastar least my mastar shold think I did it only to bring a scandall on his brothar and thinking thay wold all beare witnes agaynst me but the things is true that he did then begete me with child at that tim and the Child is Thomas Hauses and noe mans but his.

In his defense Hawes offered the testimony of another man who was sleeping "on the same side of the bed," but the jury nevertheless accepted Sarah's story.

The fact that Sarah was intimidated by her master's brother suggests that maidservants may have been subject to sexual abuse by their masters. The records show that sometimes masters did take advantage of their positions to force unwanted attentions upon their female servants. The case of Elizabeth Dickerman is a good example. She complained to the Middlesex County Court,

against her master John Harris senior for profiring abus to her by way of forsing her to be naught with him: . . . he has tould her that if she tould her dame: what cariag he did show to her shee had as good be hanged and shee replyed then shee would run away and he sayd run the way is befor you: . . . she says if she should liwe ther shee shall be in fear of her lif.

The court accepted Elizabeth's complaint and ordered her master to be whipped twenty stripes.

So numerous did cases of fornication and adultery become in seventeenth century New England that the problem of caring for the children of extra-marital unions was a serious one. The Puritans solved it, but in such a way as to increase rather than decrease the temptation to sin. In 1668 the General Court of Massachusetts ordered:

> that where any man is legally convicted to be the Father of a Bastard childe, he shall be at the care and charge to maintain and bring up the same, by such assistance of the Mother as nature requireth, and as the Court from time to time (according to circumstances) shall meet to Order: and in case the Father of a Bastard, by confession of other manifest proof, upon trial of the case, do not appear to the courts satisfaction, then the Man charged by the Woman to be the father, shee holding constant in it, (especially being put upon the real discovery of the truth of it in the time of her Travail) shall be the reputed Father, and accordingly be liable to the charge of maintenance as aforesaid unless the circumstances of the case and pleas be such, on the behalf of the man charged, as that the Court that have the cognizance thereon shall see reason to acquit him, and otherwise dispose of the Child and education thereof.

As a result of this law a girl could give away to temptation without the fear of having to care for a illegitimate child by herself. Furthermore, she could, by a little simple lying, spare her lover the expense of supporting the child. When Elizabeth Wells bore a child, less than a year after this statute was passed, she laid it to James Tufts, her master's son. Goodman Tufts affirmed that Andrew Robinson, servant to Goodman Dexter, was the real father, and he brought the following testimony as evidence:

> Wee Elizabeth Jefts aged 15 ears and Mary tufts aged 14 ears doe testify that their being one at our house sumtime the last winter who sayed that their was a new law made concerning bastards that If any man wear aqused with a bastard and the woman which had aqused him did stand vnto it in her labor that he should bee the reputed father of it and should mayntayne it Elizabeth Wells hearing of the sayd law she sayed vnto vs that If shee should bee with Child shee would bee sure to lay it vn to won who was rich enough abell to mayntayne it wheather it

wear his or no and shee farder sayed Elizabeth Jefts would not you doe so likewise If it weare your case and I sayed no by no means for right must tacke place: and the sayed Elizabeth wells sayed If it wear my Caus I think I should doe so.

A tragic unsigned letter that somehow found its way into the files of the Middlesex County Court gives more direct evidence of the practice which Elizabeth Wells professed:

> der loue i remember my loue to you hoping your welfar and i hop to imbras the but now i rit to you to let you nowe that i am a child by you and i wil ether kil it or lay it to an other and you shal have no blame at al for I haue had many children and none have none of them . . . [*i. e.*, none of their fathers is supporting any of them.]

In face of the wholesale violation of the sexual codes to which all these cases give testimony, the Puritans could not maintain the severe penalties which their laws provided. Although cases of adultery occurred every year, the death penalty is not known to have been applied more than three times. The usual punishment was a whipping or a fine or both, and perhaps a branding, combined with a symbolical execution in the form of standing on the gallows for an hour with a rope about the neck. Fornication met with a lighter whipping or a lighter fine, while rape was treated in the same way as adultery. Though the Puritans established a code of laws which demanded perfection—which demanded, in other words, strict obedience to the will of God—they nevertheless knew that frail human beings could never live up to the code. When fornication, adultery, rape, or even buggery and sodomy appeared, they were not surprised, nor were they so severe with the offenders as their codes of law would lead one to believe. Sodomy, to be sure, they usually punished with death; but rape, adultery, and fornication they regarded as pardonable human weakness, all the more likely to appear in a religious community, where the normal course of sin was stopped by wholesome laws. Governor Bradford, in recounting the details of an epidemic of sexual misdemeanors in Plymouth, wrote resignedly:

> it may be in this case as it is with waters when their streames are stopped or damned up, when they gett passage they flow with more violence, and make more noys and disturbance, then when they are suffered to rune quietly in their owne chanels. So wickednes being here more stopped by strict laws, and the same more nerly looked unto, so as it cannot rune in a comone road of liberty as it would, and is inclined, it searches every wher, and at last breaks out wher it getts vente.

The estimate of human capacities here expressed led the Puritans not only to deal leniently with sexual offenses but also to take every precaution to prevent such offenses, rather than wait for the necessity of punishment. One precaution was to see that children got married as soon as possible. The wrong way to promote virtue, the Puritans thought, was to "ensnare" children in vows of virginity, as the Catholics did. As a result of such vows, children, "not being able to contain," would be guilty of "unnatural pollutions, and other filthy practices in secret: and too oft of horrid Murthers of the fruit of their bodies," said Thomas Cobbett. The way to avoid fornication and perversion was for parents to provide suitable husbands and wives for their children:

> Lot was to blame that looked not out seasonably for some fit matches for his two daughters, which had formerly minded marriage (witness the contract between them and two men in *Sodom*, called therefore for his Sons in Law, which had married his daughters, (Gen.19.14.) for they seeing no man like to come into them in a conjugall way . . . then they plotted that incestuous course, whereby their Father was so highly dishonoured. . . .

As marriage was the way to prevent fornication, successful marriage was the way to prevent adultery. The Puritans did not wait for adultery to appear; instead, they took every means possible to make husbands and wives live together and respect each other. If a husband deserted his wife and remained within the jurisdiction of a Puritan government, he was promptly sent back to her. Where the wife had been left in England, the offense did not always come to light until the wayward husband had committed fornication or bigamy, and of course there must have been many offenses which never came to light. But where both husband and wife lived in New England, neither had much chance of leaving the other without being returned by order of the county court at its next sitting. When John Smith of Medfield left his wife and went to live with Patience Rawlins, he was sent home poorer by ten pounds and richer by thirty stripes. Similarly Mary Drury, who deserted her husband on the pretense that he was impotent, failed to convince the court that he actually was so, and had to return to him as well as to pay a fine of five pounds. The wife of Phillip Pointing received lighter treatment: when the court thought that she had overstayed her leave in Boston, they simply ordered her "to depart the Towne and goe to Tanton to her husband." The courts, moreover, were not satisfied with mere cohabitation; they insisted that it be peaceful cohabitation. Husbands and wives were forbidden by law to strike one another, and the law was enforced on numerous occasions. But the courts did not stop there. Henry Flood was required to give bond for good behavior because he had abused his wife simply by "ill words calling her whore and cursing of her." The wife of Christopher Collins was presented for railing at her husband and calling him "Gurley gutted divill." Apparently in this case the court thought that Mistress Collins was right, for although the fact was proved by two witnesses, she was discharged. On another occasion the court favored the husband: Jacob Pudeator, fined for striking and kicking his wife, had the sentence moderated when the court was informed that she was a woman "of great provocation."

Whenever there was strong suspicion that an illicit relation might arise between two persons, the authorities removed the temptation by forbidding the two to come together. As early as November, 1630, the Court of Assistants of Massachusetts prohibited a Mr. Clark from "cohabitacion and frequent keepeing company with Mrs. Freeman, vnder paine of such punishment as the Court shall think meete to inflict." Mr. Clark and Mr. Freeman were both bound "in XX£ apeece that Mr. Clearke shall make his personall appearance att the nexte Court to be holden in March nexte, and in the meane tyme to carry himselfe in good behaviour towards all people and especially towards Mrs. Freeman, concerning whome there is stronge suspicion of incontinency."

Forty-five years later the Suffolk County Court took the same kind of measure to protect the husbands of Dorchester from the temptations offered by the daughter of Robert Spurr: Spurr was presented by the grand jury

> for entertaining persons at his house at unseasonable times both by
> day and night to the greife of theire wives and Relations &c The Court
> haveing heard what was alleaged and testified against him do Sentence
> him to bee admonish't and to pay Fees of Court and charge him upon
> his perill not to entertain any married men to keepe company with his
> daughter especially James Minott and Joseph Belcher.

In like manner Walter Hickson was forbidden to keep company with Mary Bedwell, "And if at any time hereafter hee be taken in company of the saide Mary Bedwell without other company to bee forthwith apprehended by the Constable and to be whip't with ten stripes." Elizabeth Wheeler and Joanna Peirce were admonished "for theire disorderly carriage in the house of Thomas Watts being married women and founde sitting in other mens Laps with theire Arms about theire Necks." How little confidence the Puritans had in human nature is even more clearly displayed by another case, in which Edmond Maddock and his wife were brought to court "to answere to all such matters as shalbe objected against them concerning Haarkwoody and Ezekiell Euerells being at their house at unseasonable tyme of the night and her being up with them after her husband was gone to bed." Haarkwoody and Everell had been found "by the Constable Henry Bridgehame about tenn of the Clock at night sitting by the fyre at the house being on sleepe [sic] on the bedd." A similar distrust of human ability to resist temptation is evident in the following order of the Connecticut Particular Court:

James Hallett is to returne from the Correction house to his master Barclyt, who is to keepe him to hard labor, and course dyet during the pleasure of the Court provided that Barclet is first to remove his daughter from his family, before the sayd James enter therein.

These precautions, as we have already seen, did not eliminate fornication, adultery, or other sexual offenses, but they doubtless reduced the number from what it would otherwise have been.

In the sum, the Puritan attitude toward sex, though directed by a belief in absolute, God-given moral values, never neglected human nature. The rules of conduct which the Puritans regarded as divinely ordained had been formulated for men, not for angels and not for beasts. God had created mankind in two sexes; He had ordained marriage as desirable for all, and sexual intercourse as essential to marriage. On the other hand, He had forbidden sexual intercourse outside of marriage. These were the moral principles which the Puritans sought to enforce in New England. But in their enforcement they took cognizance of human nature. They knew well enough that human beings since the fall of Adam were incapable of obeying perfectly the laws of God. Consequently, in the endeavor to enforce those laws they treated offenders with patience and understanding, and concentrated their efforts on prevention more than on punishment. The result was not a society in which most of us would care to live, for the methods of prevention often caused serious interference with personal liberty. It must nevertheless be admitted that in matters of sex Puritans showed none of the blind zeal or narrow-minded bigotry which is too often supposed to have been characteristic of them. The more one learns about these people, the less do they appear to have resembled the sad and sour portraits which their modern critics have drawn of them.

4. The Middle Passage

Daniel Mannix and Malcolm Cowley

To Europeans like William Byrd, America offered an environment of unparalleled freedom and stimulation; for those of lesser fortune, as the historical record shows, it supplied only somewhat less opportunity for self-expression and improvement. But for Africans—roughly ten percent of all the colonists by the middle of the eighteenth century—America meant the crushing degradation of slavery. Until recently, without excusing or justifying slavery, most historians have tended not so much to ignore as to compartmentalize (one is almost tempted to say "segregate") the history of African Americans from the general stream of American development. When generalizing about American "free institutions," "opportunity," and "equality," the phrase "except for blacks" needs always to be added if the truth is to be told.

Historical arguments have developed about the condition of slaves in America, about the differences between the British-American and Latin-American slave systems, and about other aspects of the history of blacks in the New World. But there has been only unanimity among historians about the horrors associated with the capture of blacks in Africa and with the dread "middle passage" over which the slaves were shipped to the Americas. In this essay the literary critic Malcolm Cowley and the historian Daniel Mannix combine their talents to describe what it meant to be wrenched from one's home and native soil, herded in chains into the foul hold of a slave ship, and dispatched across the torrid mid-Atlantic into the hell of slavery.

Long before Europeans appeared on the African coast, the merchants of Timbuktu were exporting slaves to the Moorish kingdoms north of the Sahara. Even the transatlantic slave trade had a long history. There were Negroes in Santo Domingo as early as 1503, and the first twenty slaves were sold in Jamestown, Virginia, about the last week of August, 1619, only twelve years after the colony was founded. But the flush days of the trade were in the eighteenth century, when vast supplies of labor were needed for the sugar plantations in the West Indies and the tobacco and rice plantations on the mainland. From 1700 to 1807, when the trade was legally abolished by Great Britain and the United States, more than seventy thousand Negroes were carried across the Atlantic in any normal year. The trade was interrupted by wars, notably by the American Revolution, but the total New World importation for the century may have amounted to five million enslaved persons.

Most of the slaves were carried on shipboard at some point along the four thousand miles of West African coastline that extend in a dog's leg from the

Sahara on the north to the southern desert. Known as the Guinea Coast, it was feared by eighteenth century mariners, who died there by hundreds and thousands every year.

Contrary to popular opinion, very few of the slaves—possibly one or two out of a hundred—were free Africans kidnapped by Europeans. The slaving captains had, as a rule, no moral prejudice against manstealing, but they usually refrained from it on the ground of its being a dangerous business practice. A vessel suspected of manstealing might be "cut off" by the natives, its crew killed, and its cargo of slaves offered for sale to other vessels.

The vast majority of the Negroes brought to America had been enslaved and sold to the whites by other Africans. There were coastal tribes and states, like the Efik kingdom of Calabar, that based their whole economy on the slave trade. The slaves might be prisoners of war, they might have been kidnapped by gangs of black marauders, or they might have been sold with their whole families for such high crimes as adultery, impiety, or, as in one instance, stealing a tobacco pipe. Intertribal wars, the principal source of slaves, were in many cases no more than large scale kidnapping expeditions. Often they were fomented by Europeans, who supplied both sides with muskets and gunpowder—so many muskets or so much powder for each slave that they promised to deliver on shipboard.

The ships were English, French, Dutch, Danish, Portuguese, or American. London, Bristol, and finally Liverpool were the great English slaving ports. By 1790 Liverpool had engrossed five eighths of the English trade and three sevenths of the slave trade of all Europe. Its French rival, Nantes, would soon be ruined by the Napoleonic wars. During the last years of legal slaving, Liverpool's only serious competitors were the Yankee captains of Newport and Bristol, Rhode Island.

Profits from a slaving voyage, which averaged nine or ten months, were reckoned at thirty percent, after deducting sales commissions, insurance premiums, and all other expenses. The Liverpool merchants became so rich from the slave trade that they invested heavily in mills, factories, mines, canals, and railways. That process was repeated in New England, and the slave trade provided much of the capital that was needed for the industrial revolution.

A slaving voyage was triangular. English textiles, notions, cutlery, and firearms were carried to the Guinea Coast, where they were exchanged for slaves. These were sold in America or the West Indies, and part of the proceeds was invested in colonial products, notably sugar and rice, which were carried back to England on the third leg of the voyage. If the vessel sailed from a New England port, its usual cargo was casks of rum from a Massachusetts distillery. The rum was exchanged in Africa for slaves—often at the rate of two hundred gallons per man—and the slaves were exchanged in the West Indies for molasses, which was carried back to New England to be distilled into rum. A slave ship or Guineaman was expected to show a profit for each leg of its triangular course. But the base of the triangle, the so-called Middle Passage from Africa to the New World with a black cargo, was the most profitable part of the voyage, at the highest cost in human suffering. Let us see what happened in the passage during the flush days of the slave trade.

As soon as an assortment of naked slaves was carried aboard a Guineaman, the men were shackled two by two, the right wrist and ankle of one to the left wrist and ankle of another; then they were sent below. The women—usually regarded as fair prey for the sailors—were allowed to wander by day almost anywhere on the vessel, though they spent the night between decks, in a space partitioned off from that of the men. All the slaves were forced to sleep without covering on bare wooden floors, which were often constructed of unplanned boards. In a stormy passage the skin over their elbows might be worn away to the bare bones.

William Bosman says, writing in 1701, "You would really wonder to see how these slaves live on board; for though their number sometimes amounts to six or seven hundred, yet by the careful management of our masters of ships"—the Dutch masters, in this case—"they are so regulated that it seems incredible: And in this particular our nation exceeds all other Europeans; for as the French, Portuguese and English slave-ships are always foul and stinking; on the contrary ours are for the most part clean and neat."

Slavers of every nation insisted that their own vessels were the best in the trade. Thus, James Barbot, Jr., who sailed on an English ship to the Congo in 1700, was highly critical of the Portuguese. He admits that they made a great point of baptizing the slaves before taking them on board, but then, "It is pitiful," he says, "to see how they crowd those poor wretches, six hundred and fifty or seven hundred in a ship, the men standing in the hold ty'd to stakes, the women between decks and those that are with child in the great cabin and the children in the steeridge which in that hot climate occasions an intolerable stench." Barbot adds, however, that the Portuguese provided the slaves with coarse thick mats, which were "softer for the poor wretches to lie upon than the bare decks . . . and it would be prudent to imitate the Portuguese in this point." The English, however, did not display that sort of prudence.

There were two schools of thought among the English slaving captains, the "loose-packers" and the "tight-packers." The former argued that by giving the slaves a little more room, better food, and a certain amount of liberty, they reduced the death rate and received a better price for each slave in the West Indies. The tight-packers answered that although the loss of life might be greater on each of their voyages, so too were the net receipts from a larger cargo. If many of the survivors were weak and emaciated, as was often the case, they could be fattened up in a West Indian slave yard before being offered for sale.

The argument between the two schools continued as long as the trade itself, but for many years after 1750 the tight-packers were in the ascendant. So great was the profit on each slave landed alive that hardly a captain refrained from loading his vessel to its utmost capacity. Says the Reverend John Newton, who was a slaving captain before he became a clergyman:

> The cargo of a vessel of a hundred tons or a little more is calculated to purchase from 220 to 250 slaves. Their lodging rooms below the deck which are three (for the men, the boys, and the women) besides a place for the sick, are sometimes more than five feet high and sometimes less; and this height is divided toward the middle for the slaves to lie in two rows, one above the other, on each side of the ship, close to each other like books upon a shelf. I have known them so close that the shelf would not easily contain one more.
>
> The poor creatures, thus cramped, are likewise in irons for the most part which makes it difficult for them to turn or move or attempt to rise or to lie down without hurting themselves or each other. Every morning, perhaps, more instances than one are found of the living and the dead fastened together.

Newton was writing in 1788, shortly before a famous parliamentary investigation of the slave trade that lasted four years. One among hundreds of witnesses was Dr. Alexander Falconbridge, who had made four slaving voyages as a surgeon. Falconbridge testified that "he made the most of the room," in stowing the slaves, "and wedged them in. They had not so much room as a man in his coffin either in length or breadth. When he had to enter the slave deck, he took off his shoes to avoid crushing the slaves as he was forced to crawl over them." Falconbridge "had the marks on his feet where the slaves bit and pinched him."

Captain Parrey of the Royal Navy was sent to measure the slave ships at Liverpool and make a report to the House of Commons. That was also in 1788. Parrey discovered that the captains of many slavers possessed a chart showing the dimensions of the half deck, lower deck, hold, platforms, gunroom, orlop, and great cabin, in fact of every crevice into which slaves might be wedged. Miniature black figures were drawn on some of the charts to illustrate the most effective method of packing in the cargo.

On the *Brookes*, which Parrey considered to be typical, every man was allowed a space six feet long by sixteen inches wide (and usually about two feet seven inches high); every woman, a space five feet ten inches long by sixteen inches wide; every boy, five feet by fourteen inches; every girl, four feet six inches by twelve inches. The *Brookes* was a vessel of 320 tons. By a new law passed in 1788 it was permitted to carry 454 slaves, and the chart, which later became famous, showed where 451 of them could be stowed away. Parrey failed to see how the captain could find room for three more. Nevertheless, Parliament was told by reliable witnesses, including Dr. Thomas Trotter, formerly surgeon of the

Brookes, that before the new law she had carried 600 slaves on one voyage and 609 on another.

Taking on slaves was a process that might be completed in a month or two by vessels trading in Lower Guinea, east and south of the Niger delta. In Upper Guinea, west and north of the delta, the process was longer. It might last from six months to a year or more on the Gold Coast, which supplied the slaves most in demand by the English colonies. Meanwhile the captain was buying Negroes, sometimes one or two a day, sometimes a hundred or more in a single lot, while haggling over each purchase.

Those months when a slaver lay at anchor off the malarial coastline were the most dangerous part of her voyage. Not only was her crew exposed to African fevers and the revenge of angry natives; not only was there the chance of her being taken by pirates or by a hostile man-of-war; but there was also the constant threat of a slave mutiny. Captain Thomas Phillips says, in his account of a voyage made in 1693–94:

> When our slaves are aboard we shackle the men two and two, while we lie in port, and in sight of their own country, for 'tis then they attempt to make their escape, and mutiny; to prevent which we always keep centinels upon the hatchways, and have a chest full of small arms, ready loaden and prim'd, constantly lying at hand upon the quarterdeck, together with some granada shells; and two of our quarterdeck guns, pointing on the deck thence, and two more out of the steerage, the door of which is always kept shut, and well barr'd; they are fed twice a day, at ten in the morning, and four in the evening, which is the rime they are aptest to mutiny, being all upon the deck; therefore all that time, what of our men are not employ'd in distributing their victuals to them, and settling them, stand to their arms; and some with lighted matches at the great guns that yaun upon them, loaden with partridge, till they have done and gone down to their kennels between decks.

In spite of such precautions, mutinies were frequent on the Coast, and some of them were successful. Even a mutiny that failed might lead to heavy losses among the slaves and the sailors. Thus, we read in the Newport, Rhode Island, *Mercury* of November 18, 1765:

> By letters from Capt. Hopkins in a Brig belonging to Providence arrived here from Antigua from the Coast of Africa we learn That soon after he left the Coast, the number of his Men being reduced by Sickness, he was obliged to permit some of the Slaves to come upon Deck to assist the People: These Slaves contrived to release the others, and

the whole rose upon the People, and endeavored to get Possession of the Vessel: but was happily prevented by the Captain and his Men, who killed, wounded and forced overboard, Eighty of them, which obliged the rest to submit.

There are scores of similar items in the colonial newspapers.

William Richardson, a young sailor who shipped on an English Guineaman in 1790, tells of going to the help of a French vessel on which the slaves had risen while it was at anchor. The English seamen jumped into the boats and pulled hard for the Frenchman, but by the time they reached it there were "a hundred slaves in possession of the deck and others tumbling up from below." The slaves put up a desperate resistance. "I could not but admire," Richardson says, "the courage of a fine young black who, though his partner in irons lay dead at his feet, would not surrender but fought with his billet of wood until a ball finished his existence. The others fought as well as they could but what could they do against fire-arms?"

There are fairly detailed accounts of fifty-five mutinies on slavers from 1699 to 1845, not to mention passing references to more than a hundred others. The list of ships "cut off" by the natives—often in revenge for the kidnapping of free Africans—is almost as long. On the record it does not seem that Africans submitted tamely to being carried across the Atlantic like chained beasts. Edward Long, the Jamaican planter and historian, justified the cruel punishments inflicted on slaves by saying, "The many acts of violence they have committed by murdering whole crews and destroying ships when they had it in their power to do so have made these rigors wholly chargeable on their own bloody and malicious disposition which calls for the same confinement as if they were wolves or wild boars." For "wolves or wild boars" a modern reader might substitute "men who would rather die than be enslaved."

With the loading of the slaves, the captain, for his part, had finished what he regarded as the most difficult part of his voyage, Now he had to face only the ordinary perils of the sea, most of which were covered by his owners' insurance against fire, shipwreck, pirates and rovers, letters of mart and counter-mart, barratry, jettison, and foreign men-of-war. Among the risks not covered by insurance, the greatest was that of the cargo's being swept away by disease. The underwriters refused to issue such policies, arguing that they would expose the captain to an unholy temptation. If insured against disease among his slaves, he might take no precautions against it and might try to make his profit out of the insurance.

The more days at sea, the more deaths among his cargo, and so the captain tried to cut short the next leg of his voyage. If he had shipped his slaves at Bonny, Old Calabar, or any port to the southward, he might call at one of the Portuguese islands in the Gulf of Guinea for an additional supply of food and fresh water, usually enough, with what he had already, to last for three months. If he had traded to the northward, he made straight for the West Indies. Usually he had from four to five thousand nautical miles to sail—or even more, if the passage was from Angola to Virginia. The shortest passage—that from the Gambia River to Barbados—might be made in as little as three weeks, with favoring winds. If the course was much longer, and if the ship was becalmed in the doldrums or driven back by storms, the voyage might take more than three months, and slaves and sailors would be put on short rations long before the end of the Middle Passage.

On a canvas of heroic size, Thomas Stothard, Esquire, of the Royal Academy, depicted *The Voyage of the Sable Venus from Angola to the West Indies*. His painting is handsomely reproduced in the second volume of Bryan Edwards's *History of the British Colonies in the West Indies* (1793), where it appears beside a poem on the same allegorical subject by an unnamed Jamaican author, perhaps Edwards himself.

The joint message of the poem and the painting is simple to the point of coarseness: that slave women are preferable to English girls at night, being passionate and accessible; but the message is embellished with classical details, to show the painter's learning.

Meanwhile the Sable Venus, if she was a living woman carried from Angola to the West Indies, was roaming the deck of a ship that stank of excrement; as was said of any slaver, "You could smell it five miles down wind." She had been torn from her husband and her children, she had been branded on the left buttock, and she had been carried to the ship bound hand and foot, lying in the bilge at the bottom of a dugout canoe. Now she was the prey of the ship's officers.

Here is how she and her shipmates spent the day.

If the weather was clear, they were brought on deck at eight o'clock in the morning. The men were attached by their leg irons to the great chain that ran along the bulwarks on both sides of the ship; the women and half-grown boys were allowed to wander at will. About nine o'clock the slaves were served their first meal of the day. If they were from the Windward Coast—roughly, the shoreline of present-day Liberia and Sierra Leone—the fare was boiled rice, millet, or corn meal, sometimes cooked with a few lumps of salt beef abstracted from the sailors' rations. If they were from the Bight of Biafra, at the east end of the Gulf of Guinea, they were fed stewed yams, but the Congos and the Angolas preferred manioc or plantains. With the food they were all given half a pint of water, served out in a pannikin.

After the morning meal came a joyless ceremony called "dancing the slaves." "Those who were in irons," says Dr. Thomas Trotter, surgeon of the *Brookes* in 1783, "were ordered to stand up and make what motions they could, leaving a passage for such as were out of irons to dance around the deck." Dancing was prescribed as a therapeutic measure, a specific against suicidal melancholy, and also against scurvy—although in the latter case it was a useless torture for men with swollen limbs. While sailors paraded the deck, each with a cat-o'-nine-tails in his right hand, the men slaves "jumped in their irons" until their ankles were bleeding flesh. Music was provided by a slave thumping on a broken drum or an upturned kettle, or by an African banjo, if there was one aboard, or perhaps by a sailor with a bagpipe or a fiddle. Slaving captains sometimes advertised for "A person that can play on the Bagpipes, for a Guinea ship." The slaves were also told to sing. Said Dr. Claxton after his voyage in the *Young Hero*, "They sing, but not for their amusement. The captain ordered them to sing, and they sang songs of sorrow. Their sickness, fear of being beaten, their hunger, and the memory of their country, etc., are the usual subjects."

While some of the sailors were dancing the slaves, others were sent below to scrape and swab out the sleeping rooms. It was a sickening task, and it was not well performed unless the captain imposed an iron discipline. James Barbot, Sr., was proud of the discipline maintained on the *Albion-Frigate*. "We were very nice," he says, "in keeping the places where the slaves lay clean and neat, appointing some of the ship's crew to do that office constantly and thrice a week we perfumed betwixt decks with a quantity of good vinegar in pails, and red-hot iron bullets in them, to expel the bad air, after the place had been well washed and scrubbed with brooms." Captain Hugh Crow, the last legal English slaver, was famous for his housekeeping. "I always took great pains," he says, "to promote the health and comfort of all on board, by proper diet, regularity, exercise, and cleanliness, for I considered that on keeping the ship clean and orderly, which was always my hobby, the success of our voyage mainly depended." Certainly he lost fewer slaves in the Middle Passage than the other captains, some of whom had the filth in the hold cleaned out only once a week.

At three or four in the afternoon the slaves were fed their second meal, often a repetition of the first. Sometimes, instead of African food, they were given horse beans, the cheapest provender from Europe. The beans were boiled to a pulp, then covered with a mixture of palm oil, flour, water, and red pepper, which the sailors called "slabber sauce." Most of the slaves detested horse beans, especially if they were used to eating yams or manioc. Instead of eating the pulp, they would, unless carefully watched, pick it up by handfuls and throw it in each other's faces.

That second meal was the end of their day. As soon as it was finished they were sent below, under the guard of sailors charged with stowing them away on their bare floors and platforms. The tallest men were placed amidships, where the vessel was widest; the shorter ones were tumbled into the stern. Usually there was only room for them to sleep on their sides, "spoon fashion." Captain William Littleton told Parliament that slaves in the ships on which he sailed might lie on their backs if they wished—"though perhaps," he conceded, "it might be difficult all at the same time."

After stowing their cargo, the sailors climbed out of the hatchway, each clutching his cat-o'-nine-tails; then the hatchway gratings were closed and barred. Sometimes in the night, as the sailors lay on deck and tried to sleep, they heard from below "an howling melancholy noise, expressive of extreme anguish." When Dr. Trotter told his interpreter, a slave woman, to inquire about the cause of the noise, "she discovered it to be owing to their having dreamt they were in their own country, and finding themselves when awake, in the hold of a slave ship."

More often the noise heard by the sailors was that of quarreling among the slaves. The usual occasion for quarrels was their problem of reaching the latrines. These were inadequate in size and number, and hard to find in the darkness of the crowded hold, especially by men who were ironed together in pairs.

In squalls or rainy weather, the slaves were never brought on deck. They were served their two meals in the hold, where the air became too thick and poisonous to breathe. Dr. Falconbridge writes:

> For the purpose of admitting fresh air, most of the ships in the slave-trade are provided, between the decks, with five or six airports on each side of the ship, of about six inches in length and four in breadth; in addition to which, some few ships, but not one in twenty, have what they denominate wind-sails [funnels made of canvas and so placed as to direct a current of air into the hold]. But whenever the sea is rough and the rain heavy, it becomes necessary to shut these and every other conveyance by which the air is admitted . . . . The negroes' rooms very soon become intolerably hot. The confined air, rendered noxious by the effluvia exhaled from their bodies and by being repeatedly breathed, soon produces fevers and fluxes which generally carry off great numbers of them.

Dr. Trotter says that when tarpaulins were thrown over the gratings, the slaves would cry, "Kickeraboo, kickeraboo, we are dying, we are dying." Falconbridge gives one instance of their sufferings:

> Some wet and blowing weather having occasioned the portholes to be shut and the grating to be covered, fluxes and fevers among the negroes ensued. While they were in this situation, I frequently went down among them till at length their rooms became so extremely hot as to be only bearable for a very short time. But the excessive heat was not the only thing that rendered their situation intolerable. The deck, that is, the floor of their rooms, was so covered with the blood and mucus which had proceeded from them in consequence of the flux, that it resembled a slaughter-house.

While the slaves were on deck they had to be watched at all times to keep them from committing suicide. Says Captain Phillips of the *Hannibal*, "We had about twelve negroes did wilfully drown themselves, and others starv'd themselves to death; for," he explained, "'tis their belief that when they die they return home to their own country and friends again.'"

This belief was reported from various regions, at various periods of the trade, but it seems to have been especially strong among the Ibos of eastern Nigeria. In 1788, nearly a hundred years after the *Hannibal's* voyage, Dr. Ecroide Claxton was the surgeon who attended a shipload of Ibos. Some, he testified,

> wished to die on an idea that they should then get back to their own country. The captain in order to obviate this idea, thought of an expedient viz. to cut off the heads of those who died intimating to them that if determined to go, they must return without heads. The slaves were accordingly brought up to witness the operation. One of them by a violent exertion got loose and flying to the place where the nettings had been unloosed in order to empty the tubs, he darted overboard. The ship brought to, a man was placed in the main chains to catch him which he perceiving, made signs which words cannot express expressive of his happiness in escaping. He then went down and was seen no more.

Dr. Isaac Wilson, a surgeon in the Royal Navy, made a Guinea voyage on the *Elizabeth*, the captain of which, John Smith, . . . was said to have been very humane. Nevertheless, Wilson was assigned the duty of flogging the slaves. "Even in the act of chastisement," Wilson says, "I have seen them look up at me with a smile, and, in their own language, say 'presently we shall be no more.'" One woman on the *Elizabeth* found some rope yarn, which she tied to the armorer's vise; she fastened the other end round her neck and was found dead in the morning.

On the *Brookes* when Thomas Trotter was her surgeon, there was a man who, after being accused of witchcraft, had been sold into slavery with all his family. During the first night on shipboard he tried to cut his throat. Dr. Trotter sewed up the wound, but on the following night the man not only tore out the stitches but tried to cut his throat on the other side. From the ragged edges of the wound and the blood on his fingers, he seemed to have used his nails as the only available instrument. His hands were then tied together, but he refused all food, and he died of hunger in eight or ten days.

Besides the propensity for suicide, another deadly scourge of the Guinea cargoes was a phenomenon called "fixed melancholy." Even slaves who were well fed, treated with kindness, and kept under relatively sanitary conditions would often die, one after another, for no apparent reason; they had simply lost the will to live. Dr. Wilson believed that fixed melancholy was responsible for the loss of two thirds of the slaves who died on the *Elizabeth*. "No one who had it was ever cured," he says, "whereas those who had it not and yet were ill, recovered. The symptoms are a lowness of spirits and despondency. Hence they refuse food.

This only increases the symptoms. The stomach afterwards got weak. Hence the belly ached, fluxes ensued, and they were carried off." But in spite of the real losses from despair, the high death rate on Guineamen was due to somatic more than to psychic afflictions.

Along with their human cargoes, crowded, filthy, undernourished, and terrified out of the wish to live, the ships also carried an invisible cargo of microbes, bacilli, spirochetes, viruses, and intestinal worms from one continent to another; the Middle Passage was a crossroad and market place of diseases. From Europe came smallpox, measles (somewhat less deadly to Africans than to American Indians), gonorrhea, and syphilis (which last Columbus' sailors had carried from America to Europe). The African diseases were yellow fever (to which the natives were resistant), dengue, blackwater fever, and malaria (which was not specifically African, but which most of the slaves carried in their blood streams). If anopheles mosquitoes were present, malaria spread from the slaves through any new territories to which they were carried. Other African diseases were amoebic and bacillary dysentery (known as "the bloody flux"), Guinea worms, hookworm (possibly African in origin, but soon endemic in the warmer parts of the New World), yaws, elephantiasis, and leprosy.

The particular affliction of the white sailors after escaping from the fevers of the Guinea Coast was scurvy, a deficiency disease to which they were exposed by their monotonous rations of salt beef and sea biscuits. The daily tot of lime juice (originally lemon juice) that prevented scurvy was almost never served on merchantmen during the days of the legal slave trade, and in fact was not prescribed in the Royal Navy until 1795. Although the slaves were also subject to scurvy, they fared better in this respect than the sailors, partly because they made only one leg of the triangular voyage and partly because their rough diet was sometimes richer in vitamins. But sailors and slaves alike were swept away by smallpox and "the bloody flux," and sometimes whole shiploads went blind from what seems to have been trachoma.

Smallpox was feared more than other diseases, since the surgeons had no way of curing it. One man with smallpox infected a whole vessel, unless—as sometimes happened—he was tossed overboard when the first scabs appeared. Captain Wilson of the *Briton* lost more than half his cargo of 375 slaves by not listening to his surgeon. It was the last slave on board who had the disease, say Henry Ellison, who made the voyage. "The doctor told Mr. Wilson it was the small-pox," Ellison continues. "He would not believe it, but said he would keep him, as he was a fine man. It soon broke out amongst the slaves. I have seen the platform one continued scab. We hauled up eight or ten slaves dead of a morning. The flesh and skin peeled off their wrists when taken hold of, being entirely mortified."

But dysentery, though not so much feared, probably caused more deaths in the aggregate. Ellison testified that he made two voyages on the *Nightingale*. On the first voyage the slaves were so crowded that thirty boys "messed and slept

in the long boat all through the Middle Passage, there being no room below";
and still the vessel lost only five or six slaves in all, out of a cargo of 270. On the
second voyage, however, the *Nightingale* buried "about 150, chiefly of fevers and
flux. We had 250 when we left the coast."

The average mortality in the Middle Passage is impossible to state accurately
from the surviving records. Some famous voyages were made without the loss of
a single slave. On one group of nine voyages between 1766 and 1780, selected
at random, the vessels carried 2,362 slaves and there were no epidemics of disease. The total loss of slaves was 154, or about 6.5 percent. That figure is to be
compared with the losses on a list of twenty voyages compiled by Thomas Clark-
son, the abolitionist, in which the vessels carried 7,904 slaves with a mortality of
2,053, or twenty-six percent. Balancing high and low figures together, the English Privy Council in 1789 arrived at an estimate of 12.5 percent for the average
mortality among slaves in the Middle Passage. To this figure it added 4.5 percent
for the deaths of slaves in harbors before they were sold, and thirty-three percent for deaths in the so-called "seasoning" or acclimatizing process, making a
total of fifty percent. If these figures are correct, only one slave was added to the
New World labor force for every two purchased on the Guinea Coast.

To keep the figures in perspective, it might be said that the mortality among
slaves in the Middle Passage was possibly no greater than that of white inden-
tured servants or even of free Irish, Scottish, and German immigrants in the
North Atlantic crossing. On the better-commanded Guineamen it was probably
less, and for a simple economic reason. There was no profit on a slaving voyage
until the Negroes were landed alive and sold; therefore the better captains took
care of their cargoes. It was different on the North Atlantic crossing, where even
the hold and steerage passengers paid their fares before coming aboard, and
where the captain cared little whether they lived or died.

After leaving the Portuguese island of São Tomé—if he had watered there—
a slaving captain bore westward along the equator for a thousand miles, and then
northwestward toward the Cape Verde Islands. This was the tedious part of the
Middle Passage. "On leaving the Gulf of Guinea," says the author of a *Universal
Geography* published in the early nineteenth century, ". . . that part of the ocean
must be traversed, so fatal to navigators, where long calms detain the ships under
a sky charged with electric clouds, pouring down by torrents of rain and of fire.
This sea of thunder, being a focus of mortal diseases, is avoided as much as possible, both in approaching the coasts of Africa and those of America." It was not
until reaching the latitude of the Cape Verde Islands that the vessel fell in with
the-northeast trades and was able to make a swift passage to the West Indies.

Dr. Claxton's ship, the *Young Hero*, was one of those delayed for weeks before
reaching the trade winds. "We were so straightened for provisions," he testified,
"that if we had been ten more days at sea, we must either have eaten the slaves
that died, or have made the living slaves *walk the plank*," a term, he explained,
that was widely used by Guinea captains. There are no authenticated records of

cannibalism in the Middle Passage, but there are many accounts of slaves killed for various reasons. English captains believed that French vessels carried poison in their medicine chests, "with which they can destroy their negroes in a calm, contagious sickness, or short provisions." They told the story of a Frenchman from Brest who had a long passage and had to poison his slaves; only twenty of them reached Haiti out of five hundred. Even the cruelest English captains regarded this practice as Latin, depraved, and uncovered by their insurance policies. In an emergency they simply jettisoned part of their cargo.

Often a slave ship came to grief in the last few days of the Middle Passage. It might be taken by a French privateer out of Martinique, or it might disappear in a tropical hurricane, or it might be wrecked on a shoal almost in sight of its harbor. On a few ships there was an epidemic of suicide at the last moment.

These, however, were exceptional disasters, recounted as horror stories in the newspapers of the time. Usually the last two or three days of the passage were a comparatively happy period. All the slaves, or all but a few, might be released from their irons. When there was a remaining stock of provisions, the slaves were given bigger meals—to fatten them for market—and as much water as they could drink. Sometimes on the last day—if the ship was commanded by an easy-going captain—there was a sort of costume party on deck, with the women slaves dancing in the sailors' castoff clothing. Then the captain was rowed ashore, to arrange for the disposition of his cargo.

This was a problem solved in various fashions. In Virginia, if the vessel was small, it might sail up and down the tidal rivers, bartering slaves for tobacco at private wharves. There were also public auctions of newly imported slaves, usually at Hampton, Yorktown, or Bermuda Hundred. In South Carolina, which was the great mainland slave market, the cargo was usually consigned to a commission merchant, who disposed of the slaves at auction, then had the vessel loaded with rice or indigo for its voyage back to England.

In the smaller West Indian islands, the captain sometimes took charge of selling his own slaves. In this case he ferried them ashore, had them drawn up in a ragged line of march, and paraded them through town with bagpipes playing, before exposing them to buyers in the public square. In the larger islands, commission merchants took charge of the cargo, and the usual method of selling the slaves at retail was a combination of the "scramble"—to be described in a moment—with the vendue or public auction "by inch of candle."

First the captain, with the commission merchant at his side, went over the cargo and picked out the slaves who were maimed or diseased. These were carried to a tavern and auctioned off, with a lighted candle before the auctioneer; bids were received until an inch of candle had burned. The price of so-called "refuse" slaves sold at auction was usually less than half of that paid for a healthy Negro. "I was informed by a mulatto woman," Dr. Falconbridge says, "that she purchased a sick slave at Grenada, upon speculation, for the small sum of one dollar, as the poor wretch was apparently dying of the flux." There were some slaves so diseased and emaciated that they could not be sold for even a dollar, and these might be left to die on the wharves.

The healthy slaves remaining after the auction were sold by "scramble," that is, at standard prices for each man, each woman, each boy, and each girl in the cargo. The prices were agreed upon with the purchasers, who then scrambled for their pick of the slaves. During his four voyages Falconbridge was present at a number of scrambles. "In the *Emilia*," he says,

> at Jamaica, the ship was darkened with sails, and covered round. The men slaves were placed on the main deck, and the women on the quarter deck. The purchasers on shore were informed a gun would be fired when they were ready to open the sale. A great number of people came on board with tallies or cards in their hands, with their own names upon them, and rushed through the barricado door with the ferocity of brutes. Some had three or four handkerchiefs tied together, to encircle as many as they thought fit for their purposes.

For the slaves, many of whom believed that they were about to be eaten, it was the terrifying climax of a terrifying voyage.

The parliamentary investigations of 1788–1791 presented a complete picture of the Middle Passage, with testimony from everyone concerned except the slaves, and it horrified the English public. Powerful interests in Parliament, especially those representing the Liverpool merchants and the West Indian planters, prevented the passage of restrictive legislation at that time. But the Middle Passage was not forgotten, and in 1807 Parliament passed a law forbidding any slaver to sail from a British port after May 1 of that year. At about the same time, Congress prohibited the importation of slaves into American territory from and after January 1, 1808. All the countries of Europe followed the British and American example, if with some delay. During the next half century, however, reformers would learn that the trade was difficult to abolish in fact as well as in law, and that illegal slaving would continue as long as slavery itself was allowed to flourish.

5. Anne Hutchinson versus Massachusetts

Wellington Newcomb

"An individualist in an authoritarian age."

Massachusetts in the 1630s was a rather uncivilized place: sparsely settled, under siege from an often unforgiving environment and the ever-present native population. John Winthrop and his small group of religious dissenters, the Puritans, nonetheless chose to stake their future and, so they thought, the future of mankind, there.

A few years after its founding, cracks became visible in Winthrop's theocracy. Not everyone agreed with the Winthrop version of heaven on earth. Anne Hutchinson, a woman of iron will and a clear sense of religious destiny, dramatically exposed the flaws and prejudices within the Puritan doctrine. Her gruesome fate serves as a reminder that freedom of religion is often hard to come by, and it has not come cheap.

How does her story illustrate the gender divisions in Puritan society? Why were people reluctant to defend her? How can Winthrop's view of the case be defended? In what ways was Hutchinson to blame for her own fate? How is freedom of religion different than tolerance of religious beliefs?

It would have been no pleasant thing for any defendant to hear John Winthrop, governor of the Massachusetts colony, declaim the serious charges brought against Anne Hutchinson at her trial in 1637. In the Puritan society of early Massachusetts they were among the gravest that could be imagined. As recorded by the court reporter, they seem to evoke the gravity with which John Winthrop must have delivered them:

Mrs. Hutchinson, you are called here as one of those that have troubled the peace of the commonwealth and the churches here. You are known to be a woman that hath had a great share in the promoting and divulging of those opinions that are causes of this trouble. . . . You have spoken divers things, as we have been informed, very prejudicial to the honour of the churches and ministers thereof. And you have maintained a meeting and an assembly in your house that hath been condemned by the general assembly as a thing not tolerable nor comely in the sight of God nor fitting for your sex.

Anne Hutchinson, forty-five years old, stood listening to these charges on a November day when the New England fall had turned to its bleakest season. She faced her adversaries in the somber meetinghouse in Newtown, later to be called Cambridge. It was a square, rude building with small windows admitting little light. The grays, browns, and blacks of Mrs. Hutchinson's surroundings were relieved only by the pallor of earnest English faces all focussed on her. But despite the severity of the setting, the meetinghouse was crowded to capacity with people eager to see how this woman, who had stirred the greatest storm yet in the young colony, would acquit herself. For people who eschewed the theatre as sinful the Newtown meetinghouse had become the stage for an exciting performance.

From what we know of Anne Hutchinson, she probably did not flinch for a moment upon hearing the charges against her. She was a woman of keen intelligence and strong personality, possessed of stubborn convictions not the least of which was that she had found direct favor with God. Even Winthrop, writing in his journal, begrudgingly described her as "a woman of a ready wit and bold spirit," and he had good reason to know. But nowhere in his writings did it ever occur to him to describe what she looked like. Puritans were like that.

The daughter of a clergyman, Anne Hutchinson had been born Anne Marbury in Lincolnshire, England. By the time of her trial she had borne her husband, William Hutchinson, thirteen children; she was now expecting her fourteenth. Husband, wife, and children had arrived in Boston in September, 1634, on the ship *Griffin*, and Anne had been the motivating force that had started them on the long and arduous voyage to the New World. She had felt the need to follow their former minister, the Reverend John Cotton, to Massachusetts. His departure had caused a spiritual crisis in her life, for there had been no other minister in England whom she felt she could trust to preach the Word without adulteration. Once her beloved Mr. Cotton had left their native land, there had been no doubt in her mind that she must join him in the New World.

Her journey had taken her now to stand before the Great and General Court of Massachusetts to be accused of traducing the ministry, as sure an act of sedition as could be imagined in a community where the church was, in effect, the government. It appears, though not conclusively, that the ministers who were to be witnesses against her were also her judges, and they must have constituted a fearsome and awesome presence.

John Winthrop continued to recite his statement. "We have thought good to send for you to understand how things are, that if you be in an erroneous way, we may reduce you that so you may become a profitable member here among us. Otherwise, if you be obstinate . . . then the court may take such course that you may trouble us no further." The defendant paid close attention to him, as did, presumably, everyone in the room.

Among the listeners was the Reverend Mr. Cotton. He was a man of fifty-two whose light curly hair fell to his shoulders, framing a benign countenance. He was an eloquent preacher and had the reputation of being one of the greatest of Puritan scholars; it had been a momentous event to welcome him to the Bay Colony in 1633. The Reverend John Wilson was already pastor of the Boston church when he arrived; Cotton had been called to be its "teacher." It was an equally important position and gave broad scope to his preaching. In his journal Winthrop described Cotton's almost immediate success: "It pleased the Lord to give special testimony of his presence in the church of Boston, after Mr. Cotton was called to office there. More were converted and added to that church, than to all the other churches in the bay. . . . Divers profane and notorious evil persons came and confessed their sins, and were comfortably received into the bosom of the church." But as much as Anne Hutchinson, too, admired Cotton's preaching, the one uncertainty that may have disturbed her as her trial opened was the question of what role her idol might play in it.

Cotton had long admired Mrs. Hutchinson. He thought she too did great good works for the Christian faith. When, after her arrival in Boston, she had experienced some trouble in being admitted to church membership, Cotton quickly smoothed matters over. By no means unaware of her intense esteem of him, Cotton had been truly glad to see her near at hand once again. Yet the troubles leading to her trial were related to that esteem.

As well as having a sharp mind and tongue, Mrs. Hutchinson was a woman of practical bent. She had borne many children herself, and she knew how to help other women through their confinements. An accomplished herbalist, she seems to have known as much about medicine as anyone in those times. And, together with her other virtues, this talented woman knew how to speak the language of religious comfort to the sick. This all played its part in her growing influence in the nascent town of Boston.

But whatever its causes, her influence grew to surprising proportions. Winthrop credited her with gathering at least sixty women at the weekly meetings she began to hold in her house. And, as she admitted at her trial (with no little danger to herself, for women were not considered fit to teach men), some males had attended meetings in her house. All in all, according to Winthrop, "she had more resort to her for counsel about matter of conscience, and clearing up men's spiritual estates, than any minister . . . in the country."

At first these gatherings were nothing more than discussions about the sermons of the week, a "godly" activity much encouraged in a Puritan society. But with Anne Hutchinson discussion became commentary, and commentary became criticism. In short, she began to attack the clergy, only the Reverend John Cotton and her own brother-in-law, the Reverend John Wheelwright, being excepted.

Mistress Hutchinson was an individualist living in an authoritarian age. Given her make-up, it was perhaps inevitable that she would attack the orthodoxy on those very matters of faith which constituted the foundation of the state. The concrete issue of Anne Hutchinson's trial was whether she had accused the clergy of preaching "a covenant of works" instead of "a covenant of grace." It was by raising this charge at her meetings that Mrs. Hutchinson had "troubled the peace of the commonwealth and the churches here." To accuse the ministry of preaching a covenant of works was, in the temper of the time and place, to destroy it if the accusation stuck.

The Puritans adhered to the Calvinist doctrine that sinful man was saved by God's grace alone. No man could do a thing, no matter how worthy or wonderful, to effect his own salvation. To stress the point that God saved whomsoever He desired with no help from man or church was, in essence, to preach a covenant of grace. A "covenant of works" was the contemptuous Puritan term for the antithesis of Calvinist teaching—the doctrine that a man by his own good works could achieve the salvation of God. To the Puritans (Anne Hutchinson included) this was blasphemy, for it detracted from that all-sovereign and perfect will of God by which He had in the beginning predetermined the entire future of the universe. To put it bluntly, the Calvinist doctrine of predestination held that you were already either saved or damned and that, in either case, there was nothing you could do about it.

Not only was this doctrine somewhat less than comforting to anyone who had doubts about his state of grace; it also left something to be desired from a social point of view. What incentive was there to live a moral and useful life if one had already been picked, willy-nilly, for heaven or hell? The town drunk might in the end turn out to be among the saved, and the governor among the damned. The Puritan divines, who were also the colony's rulers, therefore devised a system that, although it left the statement of the doctrine intact, reduced its formidable practical impact. They decided that they could look to the outward signs of a man's life—among which would be his good works—as the evidence, or lack of evidence, of his salvation by God's grace. Thus in Massachusetts the clergy, among their other duties, became the earthly arbiters to decide what people had in fact been saved by God's grace. When a person applied for church membership, he was examined at great length to determine whether his behavior suggested a state of grace. If the clergy and the laity of the church agreed that the applicant had been saved, he was thereupon admitted to membership. It was this feature of Puritan practice in Massachusetts that Anne Hutchinson denounced as in effect preaching a covenant of works.

But she went even further. Not only did she accuse the ministers of preaching a covenant of works, but she also asserted that they were incapable of preaching a covenant of grace. It is little wonder that these leaders, being thus called both deluded and incompetent, responded as they did. Mrs. Hutchinson's accusations also robbed church members of their hard-earned assurances of salvation. In a commonwealth founded on the rock of a ministry supposed to know its business, this was highly subversive.

In contrast to the ordained clergy, Anne Hutchinson told her adherents, she herself preached a pure covenant of grace. She claimed she received direct revelations from the Holy Ghost, which, as the horrified Winthrop later reported it, gave her infallible knowledge of the salvation of her followers. "If she had but one half hour's talk with a man, she would tell whether he were elect or not." In a day when hell gaped beneath the feet of every mortal, every man and woman longed to hear of his salvation from the highest authority available. Here then was Anne Hutchinson's tremendous message: if the ministry could not honestly give the people knowledge of their salvation, she could.

Being a clergyman's daughter, a keen Bible scholar, and a "student" of Mr. Cotton as well as a brilliant woman, Anne Hutchinson was able to offer a mass of theological argument to support her heavenly credentials. The extensiveness of her doctrine may be judged from the fact that the synod that had been convened at Newtown in the summer of 1637 to deal with her heresies condemned no fewer than "eighty opinions, some blasphemous, others erroneous, and all unsafe." It also condemned her meetings as disorderly "where sixty or more did meet every week, and one woman (. . . by resolving questions of doctrine, and expounding scripture) took upon her the whole exercise."

As her chief points of doctrine Mrs. Hutchinson denied that sanctification (that is, a good life) was any proof of salvation, and she asserted instead that only the indwelling of the Holy Ghost constituted such proof. With the very first mention of her name in his journal these were the items listed by Winthrop as her "two dangerous errors." It is not hard to see why. If good works, or a good life, were not the outward evidence of a person's salvation, what objective basis was left in the Puritan scheme of things?

Men, as well as women, became Mrs. Hutchinson's adherents. Among them were some of the colony's notables, including William Aspinwall, John Coggeshall, and William Coddington, who was at one time treasurer of the commonwealth. But the most eminent of her adherents had been the young Sir Henry Vane, son of a privy councillor to King Charles and easily the foremost aristocrat of the colony. Although he was later to play a most important role in the Puritan Revolution in England, it was his connection with royalty that led to his being elected governor within seven months after his arrival in October, 1635. Such prominent people as these, together with others like the Reverend John Wheelwright, constituted Anne Hutchinson's faction—a faction that, Winthrop felt, threatened the power of the established order.

This was the background of the struggle that had now crowded the meetinghouse at Newtown with anxious spectators. As John Winthrop finished making his long statement their eyes were now fastened upon the person of the accused. One may well imagine that as Winthrop himself stared at her the aristocratic features of his face—the thin lips and pointed nose and beard—appeared colder than usual. He had labored selflessly to build this Puritan commonwealth on the firm foundation of the Word. To him this pestilential woman, this emissary from the underworld, was doing her utmost to ensnare the people in an evil trap and thereby overthrow that foundation.

But Mrs. Hutchinson was unimpressed. With that histrionic sense common to many religious leaders, which she abundantly possessed, she probably waited so that the room would become perfectly quiet. Then she calmly replied: "I am called here to answer before you, but I hear no things laid to my charge."

It was a simple but brilliant opening. It jolted Winthrop by its effrontery, and he spluttered back, "I have told you some already and more I can tell you."

"Name one, sir," was Mrs. Hutchinson's quick challenge.

"Why! for your doings, this: you did harbour and countenance those that are parties in this faction that you have heard of. . . . "

"What law have I broken?"

"Why, the fifth commandment. . . . "

"Wherein?"

"Why, in entertaining them."

"What breach of law is that, sir?"

"Why, dishonoring of parents!" (By this, Winthrop meant to say that she had dishonored the fathers of the state and the elders of the church.)

"But put the case, sir," she replied, "that I do fear the Lord and my parents. May not I entertain them that fear the Lord [just] because my parents will not give me leave?"

Winthrop had no answer except to burst out, "We do not mean to discourse with those of your sex." The defendant had piqued his masculine vanity, and the depth of it may be judged by another of his outbursts, which followed shortly. "We do not call you to teach the court but to lay open yourself." To make her "lay open herself"—to confess her sins—was the main purpose of the trial.

After more fruitless argument with the accused, Winthrop made another statement. "Your course is not to be suffered. . . . It is to seduce many honest persons that are called to those meetings. . . . We see no rule of God for this. We see not that any should have authority to set up any other exercises besides what authority hath already set up. And so what hurt comes of this, you will be guilty of and we for suffering you."

"Sir, I do not believe that to be so."

"Well, we see how it is. We must therefore put it away from you or restrain you from maintaining this course."

"If you have a rule for it from God's word, you may."

"We are your judges and not you ours," Winthrop exploded, "and we must compel you to it."

Governor Winthrop was, for a Puritan, a man of magnanimous spirit. He also possessed great ability. Yet so far he had made little headway with Anne Hutchinson. It was probably with great relief that he allowed his cantankerous deputy governor to assume direction of the trial. The mean and petty-minded Thomas Dudley was soon to display a much greater capacity for the unpleasant business at hand.

Dudley, with telling succinctness, restated the charges against Mrs. Hutchinson: " . . . About three years ago, we were all in peace. Mrs. Hutchinson from that time she came hath made a disturbance. . . . But now it appears by this woman's meeting that Mrs. Hutchinson hath so forestalled the minds of many by their resort to her meeting that now she hath a potent party in the country. . . . And if she in particular hath disparaged all our ministers in the land that they have preached a covenant of works, and only Mr. Cotton a covenant of grace, why! this is not to be suffered."

This was the first mention made in the trial of the two covenants. It is surprising that Winthrop had said nothing about them. But Anne Hutchinson remained confident and challenged Dudley as boldly as she had Winthrop. "I pray, sir, prove it that I said they preached nothing but a covenant of works. . . . Did I ever say they preached a covenant of works then?"

"If they do not preach a covenant of grace—clearly, then they preach a covenant of works."

"No sir. One may preach a covenant of grace more clearly than another. So I said."

Thomas Dudley had fared no better than John Winthrop in making the defendant "lay open herself." But at least he had framed the most important issue of the trial, and the accused had been forced to reveal the nature of her defense somewhat earlier than she probably wanted to.

Now the deputy governor put a question that seemed to contain the nub of the whole case. "I do but ask you this: when the ministers do preach a covenant of works, do they preach a way of salvation?" But it was really an ambiguous question, and Anne did the only thing she could do: she refused to answer. "I did not come hither to answer questions of that sort," she proclaimed.

There was nothing else for him to do but to present his evidence, and he did so. Apparently—or so Mrs. Hutchinson made it seem—it came as a surprise to her when he called as witnesses six ministers who had, the year before, remonstrated with her about her meetings. She claimed that their discussion with her was to be held in confidence. But Winthrop quickly ruled that there had been no basis for any confidence. What the six ministers had to state was more than sufficient evidence for the charges against her. The gist of their testimony was that she had told them that only the Reverend John Cotton preached a covenant of grace; that they preached a covenant of works; that they were not able ministers of the New Testament; and that they *could not* preach a covenant of grace because they were not sealed of the Holy Spirit to do so. She might just as well have called them Pharisees. The trial had taken an ugly turn against the woman who had had the indiscretion to give such vent to her convictions about the ministers.

Anne Hutchinson did her best to deny what she could of this testimony. But for her to prevail required more than denying the testimony of—as Winthrop put it— "six undeniable ministers." Although the day had started badly, Winthrop was pleased with its outcome. With evident satisfaction he said, "Mrs. Hutchinson, the court you see hath laboured to bring you to acknowledge the error of your way that so you might be reduced. The time now grows late. We shall therefore give you a little more time to consider of it and therefore desire that you attend the court again in the morning."

Back from Newtown, across the tidal basin and mud flats of the Charles River, back upon the small and hilly cape of land that held the town of Boston—dotted only here and there with a few feeble lights in the autumn darkness—back in the temporary sanctuary of her home, there was much indeed that Anne Hutchinson could "consider of." By the flame of a candle she must have pored over whatever papers she had that concerned her trial. As she did so it could not have failed to remind her of all the events of her three years in Boston.

She could have wished that young Sir Harry Vane were still there, but he had returned to England. If he had still been governor, her good "Brother Wheelwright" would not have been tried and sentenced to banishment for a fiery sermon he had preached in January. And after his trial those men who had signed a petition asking mercy for him found that Winthrop would deal with them, too. Aspinwall, Coddington, Coggeshall, and Captain John Underhill were all being called to account.

But there was one ominous event by which Anne Hutchinson doubtless was baffled. It concerned the Reverend John Cotton, who in her eyes was incapable of wrongdoing. At first Cotton had refused to join in the condemnation of all eighty errors attributed to her by the synod. And those he balked at condemning included some of the most objectionable. But Cotton finally adopted the synod's statement of condemned errors completely. Probably he did so because he felt that Anne was sure to be found guilty, and he could no longer afford to be regarded as her mentor. Too intelligent a man not to know what he was doing, he well understood the blow he had thus dealt his admirer.

But whatever her thoughts about past events Mrs. Hutchinson found time that night to deal with her immediate problem. Although the ministers' testimony against her had been damaging in the extreme, it had not been given under oath, and she now plotted a way around it. The next morning, back in court, she boldly stated, "The ministers come in their own cause. Now the Lord hath said that an oath is the end of all controversy. Though there be a sufficient number of witnesses, yet they are not according to the Word. Therefore, I desire they may speak upon oath."

Winthrop tried to ignore her demand. But this woman was no one to be brushed aside. She went on to say, "I have since I went home perused some notes out of what Mr. Wilson did then write and I find things not to be as hath been alledged." She was referring to notes that Wilson had written after the occasion of the ministers' remonstrance. Although neither she nor the Reverend John Wilson had the notes in court, the effect of it all was to throw doubt on the ministers' testimony. In these circumstances her demand for the oath loomed large.

One Simon Bradstreet pointed out that if by chance the ministers had misunderstood Anne's doctrines, "You would make them to sin if you urge them to swear." But this was precisely the pressure she wanted the ministers subjected to, pressure to make them hedge their testimony and destroy its effect. She insisted upon the oath. "If they accuse me, I desire it may be upon oath." Then she struck from the other flank: "There are some that will take their oaths to the contrary." She was gaining ground; she had pushed the ministers into a tight spot.

There was a growing commotion in her favor in the court after Winthrop called out, "Let those that are not satisfied in the court speak." The transcript reads "Many say:—We are not satisfied." Ever a realist, Winthrop decided to give way. "I would speak this to Mrs. Hutchinson. If the ministers shall take an oath, will you sit down satisfied?"

Having virtually forced this concession from the unwilling Winthrop, Anne made a mistake. Her reply was "I can't be—notwithstanding oaths—satisfied against my own conscience." This seemed to be the answer of a person whose self-assurance had become an arrogant contempt of those not in agreement with her, and it weakened the effect of her demand for an oath.

After some further argument it was decided to first call the witnesses appearing on behalf of Mrs. Hutchinson. No oath was administered to them. The first, John Coggeshall, did his ineffective best. As he was already under the threat of banishment for having disturbed the peace, his state of mind may easily be imagined. But having been present at her meeting with the ministers, he stated that the accused had not said all that they had charged against her. Whereupon one of the ministers, Hugh Peter—later a chaplain in Cromwell's army—exclaimed, "How dare you look into the court to say such a word."

"Mr. Peter takes upon him to forbid me," Coggeshall said. "I shall be silent." And he was.

The next witness was Thomas Leverett. A ruling elder of the Boston church, he had also been present at the meeting of Mrs. Hutchinson and the ministers. He stated that she had merely said the other ministers did not preach a covenant of grace so clearly as did Mr. Cotton. If that could have been substantiated, Anne Hutchinson might have overcome the prejudgment of the court against her. But even Leverett's testimony, standing alone, was hardly sufficient to refute that of six "godly elders."

Now came the most important witness of all, John Cotton. A prudent man, Cotton opened his testimony by laying out his line of retreat in case he should find himself in trouble: "I did not think I should be called to bear witness in this cause, and therefore did not labour to call to remembrance what was done." He went on to say he was sorry that the comparison between his brethren and him had ever been made. But on the important issue he did stand by the accused. "And I must say that I did not find her saying they were under a covenant of works, nor that she said they did preach a covenant of works."

That the ministers were concerned by this testimony was demonstrated when Peter began to cross-examine Cotton. Some of the theological points they argued along the way are obscure, but Cotton seems to have held his own. One wonders what was going on in the mind of the defendant all this while. Certainly she failed to realize that things were going her way. Had it been otherwise, she would not have intervened at this point to make her second and final mistake.

Dudley had just restated the charge that Anne had disparaged the ministers as unable to rightly preach the New Testament; Cotton had replied that he did not remember it. Had Anne Hutchinson been able to content herself with renewing her demand for the ministers' oath, she might well have walked out of the court a free woman. But she chose this moment to declaim a confession of faith. The Lord had given her to see, she said, that those who did not rightly preach the covenant of grace had the spirit of Antichrist, and "upon this he did discover the ministry unto me and ever since, I bless the Lord, he hath let me see which was the clear ministry and which the wrong. . . . Now if you do condemn me for speaking what in my conscience I know to be truth, I must commit myself unto the Lord."

Dudley, who had sized up the defendant more shrewdly than anyone else, immediately pressed his advantage. He began to taunt her, driving this now overwrought woman into traps that she had previously avoided with great skill. When she claimed she could distinguish between right and wrong ministries by an immediate revelation, he encouraged her to go on by asking, "How! an immediate revelation?"

With that, Mistress Hutchinson launched into a tirade bordering on hysteria. She called on Scripture to support her claims and compared herself to Daniel in the lions' den. It was an apt comparison but hardly one to charm the court. She closed by screaming, "You have power over my body but the Lord Jesus hath power over my body and soul. And assure yourselves thus much: you do as much as in you lies to put the Lord Jesus Christ from you. And if you go on in this course you begin, you will bring a curse upon you and your posterity! And the mouth of the Lord hath spoken it."

In the shocked silence that followed this outburst, Dudley turned to the court and asked sarcastically: "What is the Scripture she brings?" Then Israel Stoughton, who earlier had favored administering the oath to the ministers, declared: "Behold, I turn away from you." The tide of opinion was now running against Anne Hutchinson.

John Winthrop now triumphantly addressed the court: "We have been hearkening about the trial of this thing and now the mercy of God by a providence hath answered our desires and made her to lay open her self and the ground of all these disturbances to be by revelations. . . . And that is the means by which she hath very much abused the country that they shall look for revelations and are not bound to the ministry of the Word, but God will teach them by immediate revelations. And this has been the ground of all these tumults and troubles, and I would that all those were all cut off from us that trouble us." And after further unflattering remarks Winthrop summed up: "I am persuaded that the revelation she brings forth is delusion." The transcript then reads "All the court but some two or three ministers cry out, 'We all believe it—we all believe it.'"

However unnecessary it may now have been, there was one remaining scruple to be satisfied. Winthrop asked the ministers to take the oath. The transcript reads "Here now was a great whispering among the ministers. Some drew back, others were animated on." Three of them then took the oath and testified to more or less the same effect as before. The heresy of Anne Hutchinson, which had been presumed throughout, was now officially established.

William Coddington, beseeching the court not "so to force things along," courageously maintained her defense until the end. "No man may be a judge and an accuser too," he cried out. But his efforts were useless. All but three members of the court voted to banish her.

John Winthrop solemnly pronounced the sentence of the court: "Mrs. Hutchinson . . . you are banished from out of our jurisdiction as being a woman not fit for our society, and are to be imprisoned till the court shall send you away."

It was not possible to banish Anne Hutchinson immediately. First she had to be excommunicated, and this raised an inconvenient complication. The power of excommunication, by established New England practice, was held by the whole congregation. But since Anne Hutchinson still had a considerable following in the Boston church, it was a good question whether the congregation actually would do the job. The ministers, fully recognizing the challenge they faced, made their preparations with great care.

Anne was confined in a house in Roxbury (out of the reach of her Boston following), where, as Winthrop put it, "divers of the elders and others resorted to her." This went on for more than three months, and the visitations seem to have succeeded in breaking down her resistance. On March 15, 1638, a defeated and debilitated Anne Hutchinson was called before the congregation of the church in Boston. As teacher of the Boston church the Reverend John Cotton presided.

Various of her "errors" were read to her, and she was asked whether she would renounce them or not. Although she still showed faint signs of her old fire, she seemed to have given up. It must have been a crushing experience for her to hear John Cotton say, " . . . let me warn you . . . the dishonour you have brought unto God by these unsound tenets of yours is far greater than all the honour you have brought to him, and the evil of your opinions doth outweigh all the good of your doings. Consider how many poor souls you have misled."

Winthrop, who was present and who took a minor part in these proceedings, wrote in his journal, "Mr. Cotton pronounced the sentence of admonition with great solemnity, and with much zeal and detestation of her errors and pride of spirit." When the great John Cotton turned against her, Anne Hutchinson's last hope was extinguished.

On March 22, 1638, Anne Hutchinson stated to the congregation of the church of Boston, "As my sin hath been open, so I think it needful to acknowledge how I came to fall into these errors. Instead of looking upon myself I looked at men. . . . I spake rashly and unadvisedly. I do not allow [that is, sanction] the slighting of ministers, nor of the Scriptures, nor any thing that is set up by God."

This confession did make an impression on John Cotton, and perhaps he briefly hoped that Anne might be spared excommunication after all. When it was asked if her confession could be repeated for those who had not heard it, he said, "The sum of what she said is this: . . . She doth utterly disallow herself and condemn herself for [her] carriage. And she confesseth the root of all was the height and pride of her spirit. [As] for her slighting the ministers, she is heartily sorry for it . . . and desires all that she hath offended to pray to God for her to give her a heart to be more truly humbled." Any good this might have done, however, was quickly wiped out by Anne herself. With a flash of her old stubbornness she spoke up and said: "My judgment is not altered, though my expression alters."

This gave the ministers exactly what they needed. One after the other, while the great Cotton remained silent, they all stated their opinions. What they had to say is best summed up by the words of the Reverend Thomas Shepard: "Yea, this day she hath showed herself to be a notorious imposter. It is a trick of as notorious subtlety as ever was held in the church to say . . . that she all this while hath not altered her judgment, but only her expressions." And the Reverend John Wilson pointedly added that it would be a sin against God not to rid themselves of a woman who could tell such a lie.

John Cotton saw what was expected of him, and he remained silent no longer. Whatever Anne Hutchinson may have been to him, he now joined the majority of the ministers. "I see this pride of heart is not healed but is working still," he said. "God hath let her fall into a manifest lie, yea, to make a lie. And . . . I think we are bound upon this ground to remove her from us and not to retain her any longer, seeing that she doth prevaricate in her words, as that her judgment is one thing and her expression another."

As the sin of telling a lie was considered a matter of practice rather than doctrine, Cotton turned the proceedings over to Pastor Wilson, who wasted no further time. Before any member of the church could express dissent, the pastor quickly pronounced the sentence of excommunication, calling her a heathen, a publican, and a leper.

The transcript of Anne Hutchinson's second trial comes to an end with the pastor's command to her to depart. Writing of this moment at a later time, Winthrop related the following: "In her going forth, one standing at the door said, 'The Lord sanctify this unto you,' to whom she made answer, 'The Lord judgeth not as man judgeth. Better to be cast out of the church than to deny Christ.'"

Two or three days after her excommunication Governor Winthrop sent Anne a warrant ordering her departure from the jurisdiction before the end of the month. Anne Hutchinson sailed to what is now Quincy and thence walked overland through the wilderness to Roger Williams' Providence Plantations. With her family and a number of her followers she settled on the island of Aquidneck in what is now Portsmouth, Rhode Island. The faithful Coddington became governor of her colony.

But the strain of her prosecution and the hardship of her journey in her pregnant condition had been too much for her. She fell sick, and when the time of her delivery came, she had a stillbirth. Rumors quickly spread that the still-born child was "a monster."

The "monstrous birth" of Anne Hutchinson's child became the instrument for a sharp attack upon her. Even Cotton preached two sermons on the subject. The story was bruited about Massachusetts for the rest of the century, so that impressionable minds could not fail to draw the desired moral: God had punished Anne for her heresy. Long after the child had been buried, it lived as a ghost to haunt all would-be nonconformists.

Mrs. Hutchinson never fully recovered from the shocks of her experience. Although surrounded by her family, followers, and friends in the colony and presumably enjoying some happiness, she left Rhode Island after her husband's death in 1642 and went to the New Netherlands. Her tragedy was soon to run its full course. Finally settling near the present limits of New York City (her name is perpetuated by the Hutchinson River Parkway), she and five of her children were massacred there by Native Americans in 1643. Writing of her death, the Reverend Thomas Welde asserted that the Native Americans had gone to more barbaric lengths than usual: "And therefore God's hand is the more apparently seene herein, to pick out this wofull woman, to make her and those belonging to her, an unheard of heavie example of their cruelty above al others."

John Winthrop later described Anne as an "American Jezebel." He could not have failed to think that like Ahab's wicked wife, who had led another chosen people in the way of false worship, Mrs. Hutchinson had also met a violent end as part of God's judgment. In any event, the trial and banishment of Anne Hutchinson were only the beginning of the Puritan theocracy's repression of religious and social deviation. Her punishment was relatively mild, but it foreshadowed the fate of the unhappy "witches" who were to die by hanging in the hysteria that swept over the colony at the end of the seventeenth century; and it was to be another hundred years before true freedom of conscience would be tolerated in Massachusetts.

June 1974

6. A Time To Be Born

George Marsden

Jonathan Edwards (October 5, 1703 – March 22, 1758) was a Puritan preacher, philosopher, and theologian. He was also considered to be one of America's greatest intellectuals of the 18th century. Edwards played a critical role in shaping the First Great Awakening, and oversaw some of the first revivals in 1733–35 at his church in Northampton, Massachusetts.

He was acquainted with George Whitefield and later would serve as a missionary to the native Indian tribes in western Massachusetts. This fact is especially significant in understanding the complicated and sometimes violent relationship that existed in Massachusetts as indicated by the events covered in this article during the time of his youth.

Edwards died from a smallpox inoculation shortly after beginning the presidency at the College of New Jersey (Princeton). He was the grandfather of Aaron Burr, the third Vice President of the United States.

God accomplished his blessings with warning of his judgments. Solomon Stoddard, pastor of the river town of Northampton, Massachusetts, knew that well and preached it often. Although he was the most renowned man in the promising valley of the Connecticut River, he knew that no mortal could guarantee the survival of the English on this beleaguered frontier . In 1703 the little towns stretched out along the river were not the peaceful New England villages of later postcards. Many of them looked more like armed garrisons, especially from Northampton north to Deerfield, the region most vulnerable to Indian attacks. Part of Northampton itself was surrounded by a stockade wall and the town was divided into "military divisions." Some families picketed their homes as well, creating an ominous effect almost the reverse of the next century's white picket fences.

Stoddard often served as a spokesman for the western half of Massachusetts. According to legend, the witticism in this hyper-Protestant land was that Stod-dard aspired to be the "pope" of the Connecticut Valley. He was at least a for-midable presence. Every year he traveled 120 miles to Boston, the capital city, a horseback journey of two-and-a-half days, often preaching at a major public event, either the Harvard commencement or election day. Stoddard was a large, impressive man and a powerful preacher famed for speaking without notes. Sixty years old in 1703, he had come of age in Boston when Oliver Cromwell ruled in England, and he still dressed in the austere Puritan manner. Stoddard disdained the modern fashion of gentlemen wearing wigs. Some of Boston's Congrega-tional clergy now affected such English manners. To him their wigs made them look "as if they were more disposed to court a maid, than to bear upon their hearts the weighty concernments of God's Kindom." Yet Stoddard was also a man of affairs: his brother was a leading Boston merchant, the influential Judge Samuel Sewall was a close friend and the governors sought his advice on matters concerning the western regions of the colony.

On May 26, 1703, election day, Stoddard preached "before his excellency, the governour, the honoured Council and Assembly," and his fellow clergy on "The way for a People to Live Long in the Land that God have Given Them." The subject was survival. The text was the Fifth Commandment; "Honour thy father and thy mother, that thy days may be long upon the land which the Lord thy God giveth thee" (Exodus 20:12). The commandment taught, as the Puritans had conventionally argued, to honor not only parents but "all who are in authority," including civil rulers and clergy. These were God's representatives on earth. To honor them was to honor God. Survival and prosperity depended on honoring God.

The latest threats to New England arose because England was, for the second time in a decade, at war with France. Queen Anne's War renewed two deadly conflicts for the colonists. Most monumental in New Englanders' minds was the contest with Roman Catholicism, with the Antichrist. Under Louis XIV, Catholic France was at its zenith, and New France was on New England's borders. The Sun King revoked the Edict of Nantes in 1685 and drove French Protestants from their homeland. Huguenot refugees in the Boston audience were ready with tales of Catholic cruelty. England, too, it was feared, could revert to becoming a Catholic domain. Although Protestants had ousted the openly Catholic James II in 1688, the question of succession was still in turmoil. Parliament had declared in 1701 that only Protestants might succeed to the throne, but Queen Anne (r. 1702-14), a Protestant daughter of James, had no surviving children, and Louis XIV supported James' Catholic son, James III, or the "Pretender"," as the rightful "King of Great Britain and Ireland." In New England, heirs to the Puritans knew that their liberty and their destiny as a people depended on the triumph of the Protestant cause.

War with France also renewed the more immediate deadly threat of Indian attacks on the colonial frontiers. The New Englander's most conspicuous failure was their relationship to the natives they were displacing. King Philip's War of 1675-76, the most destructive war in losses per capita in American history, ended early hopes for peaceful relations and successful missions. Many of the surviving Indians were driven into the arms of the French and–worse–their Jesuit missionaries. The 15,000 French residents of New France would have been little threat to the far more numerous New Englanders, except for their Indian allies. Because the French population was small, it had not displaced Indians from their lands, making relations with the natives generally more harmonious and missionary work more effective.

In this wartime setting Stoddard's message to the royal governor and the Massachusetts legislators was what would become classic advice from the Amer-ican west: keep taxes low and defenses strong. "Do not lay unnecessary burdens on the people, yet be willing to expand what is necessary." "People are in a bad condition" when those who are "to preserve them" are "pillaging of them themselves" when their shepherds prove like evening wolves." Yet at the same time the government "may not decline any necessary [expense for] the safety of the land," lest New England go the way of Carthage and Constantinople, which were lost "through the penuriousness of the people."

The far deeper problem, Stoddard declared, was moral and spiritual. God was punishing New England because its people violated his commandments. The evidence was clear. "God has had a great controversy with the country for many years," Stoddard warned in familiar terms. Stoddard, who could have been a businessman himself, had calculated the economic consequences of God's judgments. "I do judge that a third part of that income, that the country had or might with an ordinary blessing have had, has been taken away by the judg-ments of God." The only solution was "the work of reformation." "We live in a corrupt age, and multitudes of men take a licentious liberty, in their drinking and   apparel, and company, and recreations, and unsavory discourses," Stoddard warned in vintage style. Perhaps with a glance at the powdered wigs among the assembled clergy, he added ominously, "and ministers living in an infectious air, are in danger o be infected also." Many people of the land made a "profession of godliness." The clergy must now "labour after their sincere conversion" more effectively."

Stoddard believed that God had brought these people to this promising land with an eternal purpose. God had designed all their earthly blessings and punish-ments, promises and warnings, to teach them of their need for a higher citizen-ship, to accept God's free gift of an eternal kingdom. New Englanders should thank God for their temporal blessings, yet they must always bear in mind that they were no better than the people of Old Testament Israel. God, like a lov-ing father, taught them by chastisements as much as by blessings. Israel, New England's model, had lost its land and been carried into captivity.

Northampton, October 1703

Solomon Stoddard knew well, then, how he should interpret the juxtapo-sition of earthly emotions that confronted him in early October 1703. Within a week he heard the news from down river, from East Windsor, Connecticut, that his daughter Esther Stoddard had borne a child–finally a son after four daughters–and he also received an alarming report that threatened family mem-bers closer to home. At Deerfield, just fifteen miles to the north, Indians had ambushed two young men and carried them captive into Canada. John Wil-liams, Deerfield's pastor and the Stoddards' son-in-law, had narrowly escaped a similar fate.

Deerfield was in a panic. Stoddard wrote to Governor Joseph Dudley urging further protection and tax relief for the already overburdened town. He also proposed a controversial innovation that was later widely adopted: the colonial government might authorize the training of dogs to help track Indians, who were skilled at disappearing into the woods.

Stoddard had a deep personal stake in the protection of Deerfield in the winter of 1702-4. His stepdaughter, Eunice Mather Williams, had grown up in Stoddard's household after he had married Esther Warham Mather, the widow of Eleazar Mather, Solomon's predecessor at the church in Northampton. Her husband, John Williams, was a leading ministerial ally and a member of the most influential clan in the region. He and Eunice had seven children whom Solomon regarded as his own grandchildren.

Deerfield, February 1704

John Stoddard was probably as brave as any Harvard graduate was likely to be. Unlike an older brother and many of his classmates who had entered the ministry, the multitalented twenty-two-year-old son of Solomon Stoddard was now a young soldier heading toward a career in which he would eventually become commander of the military and the leading magistrate of the region. Whatever his bravery, when he was startled awake before dawn on February 29, 1704, he knew that the better part of valor was to run. No sooner did he hear the desperate call of his brother-in-law, the Reverend John Williams, than he realized that the house was overrun with Indian warriors–perhaps twenty. He must escape. Grabbing only his greatcoat, he was out the back, barefoot, in two feet of snow. Once he made his way across the Deerfield River, he stopped long enough to cut off the bottom of his coat to cover his nearly frozen feet. He arrived completely exhausted at Hatfield, more than ten miles to the south, with the first news confirming the attack. The river towns had already sounded their alarms when they saw the sky ominously aglow with the fires at Deerfield.

The militia roused to aid the beleaguered town returned with grisly news. The Indians and their French officers killed 39 of Deerfield's some 300 residents and carried away another 112 through the deep snows as captives to Canada. For the Stoddards, the news, when it was all pieced together, was especially grim. In the early assault the Indians killed two of the William's children, six-week-old Jerusha and six-year-old John Jr. in front of their horrified parents. Their mother, Eunice (the Stoddards' daughter), recovering from childbirth and now further burdened by inexpressible grief, faltered and fell crossing a river on the second day of the trek to Canada. An Indian warrior put her out of her misery "with his hatchet at one stroke." The Reverend John Williams and his surviving children were taken as captives to Canada.

The attack on Deerfield–to New Englanders, a terrorist massacre of innocents (even if the displaced Indians saw it as a justified act of war) –was the defining event of the era, especially for families of the victims, such as the Stod-dards. Over a year later Esther Mather Stoddard was still reeling from images of the slaughter of her daughter and two grandchildren. These losses were com-pounded by the sudden death of a son and by more recent news that another close family member, taken captive at sea, had died in France. "What shall I say?" she wrote to her daughter Esther Stoddard Edwards in East Windsor. "It becomes me Aaron-like to hold my peace. God grant that I may, with Job, come as gold out of the fire when I have been tried." The mother went on to remind her daughter to be prepared for death at any moment. "The time is short, and it may be very short to us that remains, as was to your sister and brother. One day made a great change in my dear daughter's condition." Her best consolation was that her son-in-law the Reverend John Williams, though still in captivity, had sent a letter assuring the family of her spiritual condition of his slain wife. "Son Williams is satisfied that she is now in glory."

East Windsor: Later That Same Era

Jonathan Edwards' earliest memories were shaped in this wartime setting. Although East Windsor, a small river town near Hartford, Connecticut, was far enough from the frontier to be safe from attack, the continuing war was ever present in defining who he, his family, and his people were. The family gathered for prayers several times a day. In their repeated entreaties he learned not only of distant conflicts, but also that the encounters were not simply among the English, the French, and their Indian allies. The real war was among spiritual powers, a nation God had favored with true religion versus peoples in Satan's grip, Catholics and pagans.

Retellings of the Deerfield massacre vividly reinforced this understanding of the cosmic significance of the international struggles. Since before Jonathan could remember, family prayers included petitions for his Uncle Williams of Deerfield and cousins, captive in Canada. After Williams and two of his three remaining captive children returned in fall 1706, petitions continued for the one remaining child, Eunice (aged seven at the time of her capture), still with the Indians and, far worse, reportedly under Romish delusions.

By the time the precocious Jonathan was old enough to read, he would have discovered that one of the most fascinating books in his father's library was his uncle's The Redeemed Captive, Returning to Zion. John Williams' best-selling narrative vividly recounted the horrors of the Indian attack, the agony of seeing two children killed and losing his wife, and the pain of his long captivity among the Indians and French in Canada. Williams' story highlighted the deviltry of the inventions of Rome, the judgment of God on papal superstitions, and the awful plight of the souls of the poor Indians subject to the deceptions of the Antichrist.

Queen Anne's War (which lasted until 1713) touched the Edwards family di-rectly and almost disastrously. In summer 1711, when Jonathan was in his eighth year, his father, the Reverend Timothy Edwards, set out from home to serve as a chaplain for a colonial military expedition against Canada. Timothy Edwards was an extraordinarily meticulous, careful man, always concerned to control ev-ery detail. He was not suited for military life. Almost immediately he fell ill with a nervous stomach. He started to keep a campaign diary, but he soon became so preoccupied with the symptoms of his illness and his spiritual well-being that he recorded little about the campaign. By the time the army reached its staging ground in Albany, he was too ill to go on and feared he might die. Eventually he was shipped by wagon back to East Windsor where he soon recovered.

Although the Reverend Timothy Edwards' time "in the queen's service" was less than glorious, he was a formidable figure in his own domains–his home and his church. Jonathan, his only son, followed closely in his father's footsteps. One might think of Leopold and Wolfgang Amadeus Mozart, later in the century, for a partial analogy. The father was accomplished in his own right and controlling. The son was precocious and eventually out-shown his father, but his achievements were also a tribute to the father's careful tutelage and continuing looming influence.

The Edwards Household

Timothy Edwards' letters home while he was serving as chaplain in 1711 provide our best picture of the Edwards household. The first of these letters, written to his wife, Esther, within a week of leaving home, is filled with admonitions. At the top of the list is the instruction for Jonathan's schooling: "I desire you to take care that Jonathan don't lose what he has learned but that as he has got the accidence, and above two sides of propria Quae moribus by heart so that he keep what he has got." The older sisters were helping in the Latin lessons and learning that language, which usually set apart the class of educated men, primarily for their brother's benefit. So their father continues, "I would therefore have him say pretty often to the girls; I would also have the girls keep what they have learned of the grammar, and get by heart as far as Jonathan has learned: he can help them to read as far as he has learned: and would have both him and them keep their writing, and therefore write much oftener than they did when I was at home."

The scene that this letter depicts reminds us also that, while Timothy Edwards was unquestionably the head of the household, Jonathan was growing up in a home that was, practically speaking, a world of women. In addition to his mother, he had four older sisters in 1711 and three younger. Eventually he would have six younger sisters. All eleven children would, remarkably, survive childhood. Timothy Edwards, who was more given to witticisms than the son, later referred to them as his "sixty-feet f daughters." Even allowing room for exaggeration, this was a tall family in an era when the average heights were far less than today. Jonathan, who would grow to be over six feet but strikingly thin as an adult, was probably spindly as a child.

We can only speculate as to what effect living in such a feminine environment had on Jonathan. He did have several male cousins, including one his age, living next door, and there were many other boys in East Windsor, a village of close to a hundred households of large families. Nevertheless, he seems to have been close to his sisters. They were an accomplished group.

New England's elite encouraged their daughters to develop their intellectual gifts as these were use-ful for religion. The biblical figure of Mary who listened to Jesus; discourses, rather than helping her sister Martha in the kitchen, was a favorite Puritan mod-el for women's learning–even though the care of family and home was their pri-mary calling. Collegiate education was reserved strictly for men, yet in a pastor's household girls might be encouraged to learn all they could appropriate to their station. The Edwardses also sent all but one of Jonathan's sisters to Boston for finishing school. The eldest daughter, Esther, apparently wrote a satirical piece called "The Soul," which was long attributed to Jonathan. A younger sister, Jerusha, was said to have great delight in books and especially in theology. An-other younger sister, Hannah, who did not marry until her thirties, remarked that women may find the single state a great advantage "if they can make reli-gion and knowledge their chief end." One of the other younger sisters, Martha, apparently was not so easy to get along with. When a clergyman suitor asked Timothy for her hand, the father warned him of her temperament. The suitor persisted, pointing out that he had heard Martha had received God's converting grace. "Oh yes, yes," Timothy replied, "Martha is a good girl but… the grace of God will dwell where you or I cannot!"

While we would like to know more about the sisters, especially about the older girls who took care of Jonathan, we can be sure that as the family's only boy in a culture where males had many prerogatives, he was doted over and soon deferred to. One of the overarching rules of life was that everyone must respect God-ordained orders of society. Puritans did insist on the spiritual equality of all before God, but they carefully limited the applications of that potentially revolutionary doctrine in their social relationships. They also stressed the bonds of affection between superiors and inferiors. The affections and piety of some of his sisters may have been early lessons in his own cultivation of such sensibili-ties. Many commentators on Edwards have remarked on how often, in his later accounts of true religious affections and remarkable piety, he used women or girls to illustrate his point.

Jonathan's mother, Esther Stoddard Edwards, was a formidable presence in her own right, but it is symptomatic of those times that we know little about her. What we do know is largely from what was culled from much later in her life (she outlived both her husband and her son by twelve years). East Windsor villagers remembered her as "tall, dignified and commanding in appearance" yet "affable and gentle in her manners: and as of impressive intelligence, learning, and theo-logical acumen. Solomon Stoddard had sent his daughter to finishing school in Boston. As a young mother Esther assisted her husband in teaching their chil-dren and those of the town in a small school that occupied one of the two large downstairs rooms in their farmhouse. As an old woman, after her husband died, she remained an avid reader and teacher. Until she was in her nineties, women of East Windsor regularly came to afternoon sessions in the old parlor-school room for readings of the Bible and theological writers punctuated by her acute commentary.

Nevertheless, whatever the talents of Solomon Stoddard's daughter, it went without saying that Esther was a subordinate in Timothy Edwards' household. For Puritans, as for almost everyone else, the axiom that the world was hierarchical was as unquestionable as that the sun rose in the east. Fathers were the heads of their households and their rule was law. The household was also an economy in which everyone shared. The Edwardses farmed a number of acres of land to supplement their income. They used some of this land for orchards and some for crops such as flax, which the women could make into linen yarn, and they kept some cattle. Hospitality was an important virtue and the crowded household often included guests.

To help with this work, the Edwardses always had an African slave. Household slaves were particularly common among New England clergy, both because of a pastor's social status and because the head of the house was not primarily engaged in physical labor. The enslavement of Africans could take root in seventeenth-century New England not only because even the most pious were not exempt from human cupidity but also because other sorts of enslavements had been common for so long and were taken for granted in Scripture. Even so, by 1700 at least some whites recognized the unusual inequities of African slavery. Solomon Stoddard's Boston friend Judge Samuel Sewall raised the issue most forcefully in The Selling of Joseph: a Memorial (Boston, 1700). Yet Sewall's unusual views created only a ripple. Cotton Mather, whom Timothy Edwards knew and admired, probably represented the majority when he justified slavery as an opportunity for converting Africans to the Gospel. Mather also campaigned for treating slaves kindly as fellow humans. If some New England slave owners had uneasy consciences, their most common way of dealing with the subject was to avoid it; so the topic received little more public discussion until the era of the American Revolution.

In household economy where family members shared many tasks, Puritan fathers –as Timothy Edwards' wartime letters suggests–played a significant role in overseeing the discipline and spiritual nurture of the children. Children's natural selfishness, greed, and disobedience were everyday reminders that the human race was corrupt, inheriting sinful natures from their first parents, Adam and Eve. Likely the elder Edwardses subscribed to the principle of suppressing any signs of willfulness, although Puritan practices of childrearing varied and often included more displays of warm affection than is sometimes depicted. For those whose first concern was to prepare their children for salvation, the most loving thing a parent could do was to teach children the disciplines that would open them to receive a truly submissive spirit. Ultimately that could come only through the regenerating grace of God, but habits of obedience to God's commands could pave the way. As John Wesley, who was also born in 1703 and reared with similar rigor in an English parsonage, put it, "Break their wills that you may save their souls."

Timothy's wartime letters reveal that Jonathan at age seven was not the perfect child. "I hope you will take special care of Jonathan," Timothy urged Esther, "that he doesn't learn to be rude and naughty[y] etc. of which you and I have lately discoursed. I wouldn't have you venture him to ride out into the woods with Tim. "This same letter is especially revealing of some characteristics of the father that shaped the son. No detail is too small to escape Timothy's attention and advice. "Let care be taken that the cattle don't get into the orchard and wrong the trees. And that the barn door ben't left open to the cattle." Be sure the "dung be carried out and laid in the orchard where there is most need before winter and that the flax be not spoiled." And so on and so forth. One suspects the family had heard these admonitions before. Or that, "if any of the children should at any time go over the river to meeting I would have them be exceed-ingly careful, how they sit or stand in the boat lest they should fall in the river." Even what we might assume would be his wife's domain comes under his pur-view: "And let Esther and Berry [the two oldest girls] take their powders as soon as the dog days are over, and if they don't help Esther, talk further with the doc-tor about her.... Something also should be done for Anne who as thou knowest is weakly: and take care of thyself, and don't suckle little Jerusha too long."

If such advice suggest overmanaging, even in matters that might be thought Esther's domain, it also reveals an affectionate father who is homesick and is thinking about everyone. Timothy's letters are filled with expressions of deep love for Esther and the children. In one he writes, "Remember my love to each of the children," and then mentions each of the first seven by name, "Esther , Elizabeth, Anne, Mary, Jonathan, Eunice and Abigail." He goes on: "The Lord have mercy on and eternally save them all, with our dear little Jerusha. The Lord bind up their souls with thine and mine in the bundle of life. "Ask the children," he continues, "if they desire to see their father again, to pray daily for me in se-cret; and above all things to seek the grace and favor of God in Christ, and that while they are young." In a later sermon Timothy preached that a husband's love for his wife should be a "singular peculiar thing," that displayed the "honor and respect" she deserved. He should "not act magisterial or lordly, but in a loving manner with due respect to his wife."

At the same time the loving father was not indulgent to his children. After his own father died in 1718, Timothy made the best of his grief by writing privately for his "soul's profit and comfort" an eighty-eight-page tribute and spiritual biography. He observed approvingly that his father did not "favor" his children: "Yea his spirit (though he loved them dearly) was more stirred against that which is evil in them than in such as were by neighbors." Everything we know about Timothy Edwards suggests an intensely disciplined perfectionist, a worrier about details, a firm authoritarian who was nonetheless capable of good humor and warm affections toward his family. Jonathan Edwards never entirely escaped the hold this demanding yet affectionate father had over him. He followed closely in his father's footsteps and, except for greater reserve, closely resembled his father in standards and attitudes.

It is not hard to guess one source of the family's perfectionist discipline. Timothy had learned from his father to use exacting discipline to overcome adversity. Timothy's great-grandfather had been a clergyman in Wales and then rector of a school in England, but his death in 1625 had brought the family into poverty. In 1635 the family migrated to Massachusetts and settled in Hartford, joining Thomas Hooker's migration to the new western colony. Timothy's father, Richard, born in Hartford in 1647, brought the family back to some financial success, turning a cooper's trade into a prosperous merchant business.

Timothy's mother, however, was a scandal and a disgrace. Three months after she married Richard Edwards, in 1667, Elizabeth Tuthill (or Tutle) revealed that she was pregnant by another man. Richard nonetheless protected her by paying the fine for fornication himself and arranging to have the child raised by her parents. The problem proved to be much deeper. Elizabeth was afflicted with a serious psychosis. She was given to fits of perversity "too grievous to forget and too much here to relate," repeated infidelities, rages, and threats of violence, including the threat to cut Richard's throat while he was asleep. The Tuthill family was evidence that New England was not the staid place that we might imagine, but rather one where humans suffered the same horrors found in any era. One of Elizabeth's sisters murdered her own child, and a brother killed another sister with an ax. Jonathan Edwards is sometimes criticized for having too dim a view of human nature but it may be helpful to be reminded that his grandmother was an incorrigible profligate, his great-aunt committed infanticide, and his great-uncle was an ax-murderer.

Elizabeth Tuthill Edwards' condition worsened with the burden of bearing six children to Richard, of whom Timothy was the eldest. Eventually she deserted her family for a number of years, staying away from Richard's bed when she returned. By 1688 her behavior became so erratic that Richard did something almost unheard of in new England: he sued for divorce. He had suffered, he told the court, from "afflictions, discontents, jealousies, the rage of man, with horrible confusions, distractions, with intricate, heart-breaking miseries, the most pinching pressures of spirit that have been my meat day and night."

Despite these agonizing circumstances, the court refused Richard's request. After more years of suffering, he presented his case again, and this time the court relented, granting the divorce on the advice of a council of ministers. From then on Richard's situation improved dramatically. He joined the Hartford church. Still in his forties, he married a second wife, who bore him six more children. Richard, always a man of learning as well as of piety, read law and in 1708 was appointed "Queen's attorney." He became particularly noted for some cases he pleaded for the Pequot Indians.

In the meantime Timothy, who came by his apprehensive disposition honestly, had been groomed by his father to go to college to prepare for the ministry. He entered Harvard in 1686. Early in 1688 he left the college, apparently expelled. All we know is that an "ominous" mark was entered next to his name in the "Severe Punishments" column of the Harvard records. The best guess is that this had something to do with his father's first divorce proceedings, which began about the same time. Everything else we know about Timothy is of a meticulously disciplined perfectionist, and this episode did not ruin his reputation in the long run or divert him from his plans for a ministerial career. He continued his studies under the private tutelage of the Reverend Peletiah Glover in Spring--field, Massachusetts, just north of Hartford. Timothy was a most able student, and in 1694 Harvard recognized his accomplishments by granting him both his belated B.A. and a M.A. (the latter a degree routinely granted for three years of some study, usually on one's own, beyond the four-year B.A.).

Timothy was proving himself to all who knew him and fast overcoming any stigma that may have been attached to his family background or the Harvard episode. Puritans were strict, but they were also strictly forgiving if the circumstances warranted. Timothy's dramatic rise in status came with the imprimatur of none other than Solomon Stoddard, who in 1967 granted him permission to marry his second daughter, Esther. By this time the Stoddards knew Timothy well because he was teaching school in Northampton. Everything quickly fell into place for the promising young man: Harvard granted him his degrees, and a new parish, called Windsor Farms or East Windsor, across the Connecticut River from Windsor and not far from his native Hartford, called him to be its pastor.

Esther, the new bride, was the granddaughter of John Warham, well remembered as the sometimes controversial first pastor in Windsor, so she was already part of one of the leading families of the original town. Richard Edwards, who must have been delighted not only to have his children settled nearby but also with this second great upturn in the family's position, gave the new couple farmlands and a very adequate house. Their home stood along the one long road of East Windsor, paralleling the Connecticut and overlooking the fertile floodplain, the river in the distance and the roofs of Windsor beyond that. Soon there were grandchildren much the same age as Richard's second family. Timothy and Esther named Jonathan after the first son of Richard's second marriage, a child who had died in infancy.

II

Era of Revolution: 1763–1783

7. Patriot Father, Loyalist Son

Benjamin and William Franklin
Sheila L. Skemp

The American Revolution was a civil war as well as a struggle for independence from Great Britain. John Adams, the staunch Massachusetts patriot and second president of the United States, famously estimated that one–third of Americans were "loyalists" (that is, remained loyal to England), one–third were "rebels" (or patriots), and another third were neutral. Historians continue to debate the issue. But it is clear that during the War for Independence, a sizable portion of the white population either opposed independence or declared a "plague on both your houses" by choosing neither side during the conflict.

For example, regional affiliations mattered: perhaps 90 percent of New England adhered to the patriot cause; it is possible, however, that the majority of Americans who lived in the recently settled, more thinly populated western regions of the colonies were either loyalist or neutral. Religion could be an issue. In Pennsylvania and Delaware, most Presbyterians supported rebellion against England, but the majority of Quakers in those colonies— whose religious values prohibited participation in war—were "passive loyalists," in the words of one historian. Loyalists could come from any social or economic group. For instance, when Massachusetts banished 300 loyalists in 1778, only one–third of them could be described as well-off, well-educated "gentlemen." Two-thirds of the banished Massachusetts loyalists were middling farmers, unskilled laborers, artisans, and owners of small shops. Rebels and loyalists, then, could hail from almost every region, social status or ethnic group.

The attitudes of nonwhite Americans toward independence were important as well. At the start of the conflict, most Native American tribes declared their intention to remain neutral. In the end, however, many Indians realized that land–hungry Americans were a greater threat to their future well–being than the continued dominion of Great Britain. The vast majority of Indians who fought during the war, therefore, sided with the British. This was true of African Americans as well, who hoped that a British victory would spell the end of slavery. But many more enslaved black Americans took advantage of the chaos created by the war to flee their owners than fought for either side. Thomas Jefferson estimated that in one year alone—1778—more than 30,000 Virginia slaves ran to freedom.

The War for Independence sometimes divided families as well. The most famous example was Benjamin Franklin and his son William, described by Sheila L. Skemp in the next essay. Benjamin Franklin was the most renowned and perhaps most revered American of his time—his "rags to riches" American journey continues to fascinate numerous biographers and millions of Americans. Franklin's son William was illegitimate—born of an illicit affair between Benjamin Franklin and an unknown woman. The elder Franklin was not particularly attentive to family matters. His affair with William's unknown mother may have occurred the same year he married his wife, Deborah, in 1730. But it appears that he and William were very close. Young William helped Benjamin conduct his famous experiments on electricity. His father sponsored William Franklin's training as a lawyer, and in 1763 the elder Franklin's political connections helped secure William's appointment as Royal Governor of New Jersey.

Benjamin Franklin had a deep affection for the British Empire and, like many colonists, was slow to embrace the idea of American Independence. Once committed to rebellion, however, Franklin pursued it passionately and played a crucial role in its ultimate success. But William Franklin, like most other Royal appointees in the colonies, never veered from his loyalty to the Crown. The result was a gradual and ultimately bitter split between father and son.

There is an additional aspect of the Revolution that relates to private issues such as fathers, sons, and family that has an interesting twist in the case of the Franklins. A number of historians, including Skemp, have suggested that the American Revolution was not only a political rebellion against a king who was viewed by rebels as a tyrant; it was also symbolic revolt against the king as a father figure by rebellious sons intent upon living their own lives in their own way. In other words, the Revolution was a revolt against patriarchy. It was a declaration of independence by American sons who longed for a degree of personal autonomy that was incompatible with traditional notions of obedience and deference toward paternal authority. And it didn't matter whether that authority sat on a throne, in a palace or in a rocking chair at home.

How does this play out in the case of Benjamin and William Franklin? William certainly rebelled against his biological father, but not against the king-as-father-figure, to whom he remained deeply loyal. Could William's status as in illegitimate child who did not know his mother help account for his decision to remain loyal to England? Perhaps his loyalty to England—known as the "Mother Country" to the colonists—mattered as much or more to William as his connection to his biological father. For William, loyalty to king and mother country may have enabled him to retain a father figure, while giving him the "mother" he never knew.

Whatever the metaphorical meaning of the Revolution in terms of fathers and sons, the rebellion itself was a very complex matter. It cannot be explained simply by looking at the disagreement between a father and his son in one elite American family such as the Franklins. But what Skemp does show is that the major issues of the Revolutionary era, such as the Stamp Act crisis and the Boston Tea Party, were more than important political events. They also affected people in the most intimate areas of their lives. Her essay demonstrates how *public issues affect private lives.*

The Boston Tea Party set the stage for a series of events that ultimately separated America from England. Those same events led Benjamin and William Franklin to choose opposite sides in a war that both men would have preferred to avoid. By the middle of 1774 the two men simply quit discussing political issues, and by the end of 1775 they no longer communicated at all.

After Parliament passed the legislation that became known as the Coercive Acts in 1774, both Franklins attempted to find some way to resolve the issues that were tearing the empire apart. This time they operated from very different perspectives. Benjamin urged the colonists to cut off all commercial intercourse with England, arguing that if the mother country had backed down before in the face of colonial unity, it would surely do so again. William was convinced that England would not retreat. He insisted that the colonists had to exhibit a willingness to compromise if they seriously wanted a rapprochement. Ironically, he relied on his own father to work out the detail of such a compromise.

While the two men surely realized that their political views were diverging in the early 1770s, they continued to try to nurture the personal side of their relationship. Benjamin purchased English goods for the governor and his wife, taking care that every tea urn and every mahogany chair that he sent to America met his son's exacting standards. Whenever he could, he called William's achievements to the attention of the ministry.... For his part, William continued to support his father, even as he grew uneasy about his politics. He worried about Benjamin's health, urging him to come home before old age caught up with him. He refused to criticize his father, no matter how great the temptation might have been. When William Stratham wrote to warn him that Benjamin was out of touch "with the [British] Ministry in general," telling him that some people assumed he held "the same political opinions with [his] father," William's reply was circumspect, although he did put some distance between himself and the elder Franklin. There was, he insisted, "no reason (other than the natural connexion between us) to imagine that I entertain the same political opinions with my father. My sentiments are really in many respects different from those which have been published on either side of the question." He knew that he often suffered from his "natural connexion" with Benjamin, but he refused to repudiate a man whose affection he cherished.

Yet despite their best intentions, an aura of animosity increasingly pervaded the letters between father and son in the years before the Revolution.

That this should have been the case is hardly surprising. Both men were deeply embroiled in the controversies of the day, and while they both tried to avoid an argument, neither could resist the temptation to lash out from time to time.

As Benjamin grew disenchanted with the ministry, he tried to convey his mood to his son. Generally, he engaged in reasoned discourse, but on occasion he abandoned his pose of disinterested equanimity altogether.... Apparently forgetting that he had once helped launch William's career as a Crown servant and that he had also sought royal preferment for himself, he now insisted that he "rather wish[ed] to see all I am connected with in an Independent Station, supported by their own Industry." Whenever Benjamin discussed [grandson] Temple's prospects with William, he implied that he hoped the boy would not follow in his father's footsteps. Independence, not royal patronage, should be the key to Temple's success. Above all, he thundered, "I would have him a Free Man."

Such comments must have made William wince, for their message was unmistakable. Still, he generally refrained from striking back or even acknowledging his father's pointed barbs. And he remained stubbornly convinced that Benjamin had both the will and the ability to find the magic solution that would reconcile the differences between England and America. He thought his father was the one colonial agent whose opinion Whitehall [the seat of the British government] respected...

William's faith in his father was not as naïve as it appears in hindsight. He knew Benjamin had always harbored a deep and abiding love for the empire. True, the elder Franklin's criticisms of Parliament and the ministry had grown harsh over the years. But William had endured enough of his own quarrels with Whitehall to know that the ministry was capable of making serious errors. Moreover, he had sworn obedience to the king, not to Parliament. So long as his father remained loyal to the Crown, William did not foresee the possibility that he and Benjamin would go their separate ways.

Unfortunately for William, Benjamin Franklin's views of the king's role in imperial affairs was beginning to change. In this instance, he was ahead of most of his American compatriots. The colonists had always insisted that their quarrel was with a Parliament that had been corrupted by a venal ministry. At least in public, they refused to blame the king for their differences with the mother country. By the summer of 1773, however, Benjamin Franklin was finding it increasingly difficult to maintain a belief in the king's innocence. He was also beginning to argue that the colonists owed no absolute obedience to the monarch. When the first settlers came to America, he said, they voluntarily agreed to obey the English sovereign. It went without saying that their decedents had the right to reverse that voluntary decision to obey the king should circumstances warrant it. Even worse from William's perspective, Franklin blamed the king himself for the colonists' continued differences with England. "Between you and I," he confided to his son, speaking especially of the Tea Act, "the late Measures have been, I suspect, very much the King's own."

It is easy to imagine William Franklin groaning aloud when he read these comments, but it would be a mistake to assume that he comprehended their full import. Indeed, for a long time Benjamin himself was not prepared to follow his own arguments to their logical conclusion. Moreover, so long as the vast majority of Americans retained their loyalty to the king, and so long as the elder Franklin kept his darkest thoughts to himself, William did not think he needed to worry unduly about their consequences.

In 1774, however, after his ordeal before the [English Ministry's] Privy Council [where he was wrongly accused of inciting the Boston Tea Party and other acts of rebellion in that city], Benjamin's mood changed dramatically.... He was angered even more when the government stripped him of his post office position. To most people, even to his sister Jane, he hid his anger behind a mask of bland indifference. But when he wrote to William, just two days after he had been fired, Benjamin revealed his pain. It was a terse message, for he was too distraught to discuss his experience in any detail. Nevertheless, his expectation was clear. He assumed that William would resign his position as governor to protest his father's treatment. William now had no chance of being promoted, he pointed out, and his present position was poorly funded and likely to remain so. "I wish," he said, "you were settled on your Farm. 'Tis an honester and a more honourable because a more independent Employment."

While William sympathized with his father, he had no intention of leaving a position that was his sole source of income, identity, and purpose. Moreover, he was not a man who abandoned his obligations lightly...Benjamin's letter came as a shock. It revealed how far his father had moved from England's corridors of power. Not only had the elder Franklin's usefulness to the governor come to an end, but he could now prove to be a detriment. Still, William had no more desire to turn his back on his father than he did to abandon the king. Thus, he simply did nothing....

When news of the Boston Tea Party reached London, the government re-acted harshly, displaying its determination to flex its muscles and reassert its authority in Massachusetts. At the end of March 1774, Parliament passed the Boston Port Act, closing Boston Harbor to all shipping until the East India Company had been reimbursed for its losses. News of the Port Act reached America in May, and the Massachusetts committee of correspondence responded immediately, asking the other colonies to suspend all trade with England. Merchants in New York and Philadelphia, however, did not view the proposed boycott with enthusiasm. They favored an inter-colonial meeting where delegates from all the colonies could discuss their differences with England. While Boston's political leaders were unhappy with what they saw as a delaying tactic, they reluctantly agreed to support the proposal for a continental congress. William tried to use the prospect of the congress to lure his father home [from England]. Everyone, he said, valued Franklin's experience and wanted him to attend. Unfortunately, in the same letter, William discussed his views of the Boston Tea Party, suggest-ing that the Bay Colony would be wise to pay the East India Company for the damages it had sustained. Not only would such compensation accord with the principles of "strict Justice," but it would be smart politics as well. It made sense for Massachusetts inhabitants to "do Justice before they ask it of others. Their making reparations to those whom they have injured would besides give greater Weight to their Representatives and do Credit to their Cause."

In September, when Benjamin replied to William's letters, he exploded. In a less contentious time, he had called his son a "thorough government man." But then, he had promised to make no attempt to "convert" him. He was no longer able to maintain a philosophical attitude toward his son's politics. He was deeply hurt by William's apparent indifference to his own public humiliation and pained by the implication that he had outlived his usefulness in London. The fact that the governor seemed more disturbed by Boston's rioters than he was by England's attack on colonial rights also disturbed the elder Franklin.

Thus, he lashed out. "I do not," he wrote with obvious sarcasm, "so much as you do, wonder that the Massachusetts have not offered Payment for the Tea." Although he himself had once proposed that Boston reimburse the East India Company for its losses, he now claimed that America owed England nothing. Rather, Parliament owed the colonies money for the "many Thousand Pounds" it had "extorted" from America over the years. But "you," he said in a tone that revealed the width of the chasm separating him from his son, "who are a thorough Courtier, see every thing with Government Eyes."

Clearly, Franklin had no immediate plans to return to America. To the contrary, despite his occasional fulminations and bitter outbursts, he still entertained some hope that he might be of use in persuading Parliament to soften its stance toward the colonists. Until Parliament passed the Boston Port Act, Franklin had remained surprisingly optimistic about the prospects for reconciliation.... But when the government began to take measures to punish the Bay Colony, Franklin's position hardened. The Port Act had been bad enough. Even worse were the three reform bills that Parliament passed in late May and early June. Known collectively, with the Port Act, as the Coercive Acts, the legislation envisioned a total restructuring of Massachusetts' government. Parliament directed local authorities to find convenient quarters for royal troops and allowed the governor the right to transfer trials to England or to another colony if he thought local juries would be prejudiced against the government's case. It also gave the governor the right to appoint his council and to appoint or remove sheriffs and judges at his own discretion. Finally, it allowed the governor to forbid all town meetings except the annual one to elect officers.... In effect, Massachusetts existed under martial law...

Franklin's on again, off again contacts with various government emissaries lasted through the first part of March 1775. But at least by the middle of February, it was clear that Whitehall would not consider any limitations on Parliament's right to legislate for or to tax the colonies, nor would the ministry abdicate its power to alter colonial governments at will. That being the case, there really was nothing more to say. Franklin lost his normally cheery perspective. He was having a hard time sleeping. And he began to worry that nothing, not even the colonial boycott, would force the ministry to back down....

Benjamin Franklin did not realize the extent of his son's commitment to the king.... The governor did more to help the ministry than offer his suggestions for solving the imperial crisis. As early as June 1774, he began systematically to compile and forward all news about events in New Jersey to Whitehall. By September, as the Continental Congress got under way, he started to amass information abut colonial disorders everywhere. He sent [Lord] Dartmouth [President other the Ministry's Board of Trade] letters bulging with newspaper clippings describing the activities of the various committees of correspondence. He documented colonial attempts to organize committees of correspondence. He documented colonial attempts to organize extralegal provincial assemblies. He also enclosed Joseph Galloway's descriptions of the activities of the Continental Congress, whose meetings were held in secret. Franklin was, for all intents and purposes, acting a self-appointed spy for the English government. He was fully aware of the implications of his activities. Much of the news came from sources who trusted his discretion, men who had no idea that their conversations ended up in Dartmouth's hands. It was just as well they didn't know, Franklin explained candidly, "lest they might be deterred from giving me Information." There were still many colonists who did not know how committed to serving the king he was, and William obviously needed to keep it that way.... He remembered all too well how [Massachusetts Royal Governor] Thomas Hutchinson had suffered when the contents of his private letters had been revealed to the public. The stakes were higher now, and he had no wish to incur the hostility that would surely accompany a public airing of his own letters. Thus he marked early every letter he sent to London "secret and confidential."

With each letter he sent, Franklin reiterated what would become a constant theme of all loyalists until the end of the Revolutionary war. The Continental Congress, he maintained, did not speak for most colonists. To the contrary, nearly everyone privately decried the actions of those radicals who had somehow seized the reins of power and were running roughshod over the moderate majority. "Few," he insisted, "have the Courage to declare their Disapprobation pubickly, as they well know, if they do not conform, they are in Danger of becoming Objects of popular Resentment." Franklin, like loyalist leaders throughout the continent, did not recognize the depth or breadth of American anger. Moreover, he found it impossible to imagine that honest men might disagree with him. Thus, by definition, he believed that opposition leaders had their own agenda, an agenda that did not serve the interests of the people they so insidiously claimed to represent.

Had Benjamin Franklin known what his son was doing, he would have been devastated. At the beginning of 1775, Benjamin had written to Joseph Galloway. Rumor had it, he warned, that both Galloway and John Jay, a delegate to the Continental Congress from New York, were acting as spies for England. "I do not believe this," he said, "but I thought it a Duty of Friendship to acquaint you with the Report." He would have been incredulous had he known that his own son was involved with what, from his perspective, was a dishonorable business.

He would have been equally angry by the contents of William's letters. For years he had railed against Americans who claimed that colonial opposition to English policy was the province of a "small Fraction." Indeed, he had often written to William arguing that the colonists' "discontents were really general and their Sentiments concerning their Rights unanimous, and not the Fiction of a few Demagogues, as their Governors us'd to represent them here." He professed to believe that these false depictions of colonial sentiment were largely responsible for the ministry's refusal to heed American demands. So long as English leaders believed that America was divided, that support for Boston was confined to a few well-organized and noisy hotheads, they would stand firm....

When Benjamin Franklin sailed for home in the spring of 1775, he was nearly seventy years old. Angry and bitter, he had probably already accepted the reality that few other Americans were willing to face. Independence was inevitable. Only the timing was at issue. In America he began a round of activities that would have exhausted anyone half his age. He knew, he explained, that he was on old man whose most productive years were behind him. What fortune he possessed would have to support him for the rest of his life. He no longer expected to make any contribution to the world of science that would compare with the day he and William had brought the lightning from the skies. He intended to devote what time he had left to preserving his country's liberties. He only hoped that he could persuade his son to join him in his last adventure.

William was waging his own war for the hearts and minds of New Jersey's legislators when his father arrived in America. He was trying to hold his colony together and to fend off—or at least ignore—all extralegal committees and congresses that were taking over the country and turning his own world upside down. He was also fighting for his very life, as he began to fear that he would be captured by his enemies and led "like a Bear through the Country." As he saw other governors abandon their posts, fleeing to the safety provided by the king's troops, he occasionally considered following their example. But like his father, William Franklin was a stubborn man. Benjamin had often declared that he would never voluntarily relinquish any position. "I shall never ask, never refuse, nor ever resign an Office," he said. For, as he had once observed to his son, "One may make something of an Injury, nothing of a Resignation." Thus both Franklins stuck to their respective positions, refusing even to sit out the growing controversy on the sidelines. Neither man would shrink from his duty as he saw it. King and country, father and son, were about to go their separate ways....

Benjamin and William Franklin did not meet again until after the Revolution. [In June 1776, William was removed as governor of New Jersey] and remained a prisoner at Connecticut for more than two years, first at Wallingford and then at Middletown. At first, his accommodations were tolerable, and as a gentleman he was allowed to roam the countryside at will. Unfortunately, he used his freedom to render covert aid to the British army, granting pardons to the farmers he met on those not so innocent rides on the outskirts of town. Consequently, at the beginning of May 1777, the defiant prisoner was removed from his lodgings in Middletown and marched forty miles to Litchfield, where he remained in solitary confinement for nearly eight months. There, in his cramped and dirty lodgings, his captors watched him constantly, denying him the use of pen or paper and allowing him almost no contact with the outside world. By this time, most colonial leaders saw Franklin as a threat to their cause.

Benjamin did not lift a hand to secure his son's freedom or even to make his imprisonment more comfortable. Rather, he viewed William's predicament with singular detachment and only reluctantly offered his daughter-in-law [Elizabeth] any financial support. Indeed when he sent Elizabeth sixty dollars to help meet her barest expenses, he brusquely reminded her that many other suffered more than she did. By now he had only two passions. He wanted to win the independence that America had declared in July 1776. And he was determined to keep [his grandson] Temple from embracing the loyalist doctrines that permeated the air the boy breathed whenever he visited [Elizabeth].... Benjamin Franklin devoted the war years to the service of his country. His universal reputation as a scientist and political philosopher preceded him to Paris, and he was treated with respect, even awe, by some of France's most renowned luminaries. So long as he remained in France [as American ambassador], Franklin played the role of modest republican for all it was worth. Still, he lived a life of opulence that would have surprised, even disappointed, many of the leaders whose cause he so ably represented. In fact, Franklin was perfectly suited to his new role. A seasoned politician who was adept at the gamesmanship that characterized diplomatic activity in the eighteenth century, he enjoyed the intrigue in which he was involved even while he was a shrewd, indeed tough, bargainer.

For William Franklin, the American Revolution was neither so pleasant nor so rewarding. He was finally released from Litchfield jail in October 1778, at the age of forty-eight. He emerged a bitter man. His wife had died while he was in captivity.... Franklin left Connecticut for the protection of British-controlled New York at the end of October 1778. His property had been confiscated, his salary discontinued, his health nearly broken. He had already paid a heavier price for his loyalty than any other colonial governor. Still, he did not yet join the some eighty thousand loyalists who fled the country.

Instead, Franklin became an unofficial spokesman for all loyal Americans, speaking out against [British] General Henry Clinton's lethargic war effort, seeking help for needy refugees, and interceding on behalf of loyalist prisoners of war. In 1780, he became president of the Board of Associated Loyalists, an American paramilitary outfit that organized and equipped loyalist units and planned guerrilla raids on rebel strongholds. After the defeat of General Cornwallis at Yorktown in 1781, the war for all practical purposes was over. Lord North resigned from the ministry to be replaced by the Earl of Rockingham. Parliament began to press for negotiations that would bring an end to the hostilities between England and its former colonies. William Franklin's Associated Loyalists tried to keep those hostilities alive, ordering the capture and execution of rebel officer Joshua Huddy in a vain effort to disrupt peace negotiations between the British and American forces. Benjamin, from his post in France, worked with John Jay and John Adams to negotiate to end the war.... Perhaps not surprisingly, it was Benjamin Franklin who fought hardest against the British request that the new American government compensate the former loyalists for the losses they sustained as a result of the war.

While Benjamin celebrated his and America's victory, his son left his native land in the fall of 1782 for the life of an exile in England, the cloud cast by the execution of Joshua Huddy still hanging over his head. Once in England, he tried to influence the peace negotiations, lobbying especially hard for provisions that would benefit American loyalists. In this, as in so many other efforts in these years, he was basically unsuccessful. Only after the Peace of Paris had been signed did William make an effort to patch up the differences between him and his father. The war was over. He had lost. Now it was time to let bygones be bygones, to "revive that affectionate intercourse and Connection which till the Commencement of the late Troubles had been the Pride and Happiness of [his] life." He refused to apologize for his part in the war. "I uniformly acted from a Strong Sense of what I conceived my Duty to my King and Regard to my Country." he said... Still, he begged his father for a "personal interview," hoping that now that he had "broken the ice," he and Benjamin might be friends once more.

Benjamin was unmoved. "Nothing," he said, "has hurt me so much and affected me with such keen Sensations as to find myself deserted in my old Age by my only Son; and not only deserted, but to find him taking up Arms against me, in a Cause wherein my good Fame, Fortune and Life were all at Stake." Had William taken a neutral position, he might have forgiven his son. He could not tolerate an active loyalist.

The two men saw one another only once after the war. In 1785, as Benjamin was preparing to leave for home... they met briefly at Southampton [in England]. The hurried visit was not cordial. Benjamin persuaded William to sell Temple his New Jersey lands for a paltry two thousand pounds sterling. He also insisted that he turn over some property he owned in New York in lieu of a debt of fifteen hundred pounds he still owed his father. His business with William at an end, Benjamin returned to America. This would be the last time he would cross the Atlantic.

8. Equal Rights and Equal Men, 1774–76

Edmund Morgan

Fifty-five men rode into Philadelphia in September, 1774, and began at once to take each other's measure, at dinner parties and breakfasts as well as on the floors of Carpenter's Hall. John Adams sized them all up: John Rutledge of South Carolina ("his appearance is not very promising"); William Livingston of New Jersey ("nothing elegant or genteel about him...but very sensible and learned"); and Charles Thomson ("the Sam Adams of Philadelphia"), who was elected Secretary of the Congress at its first meeting even though he was not a delegate.

While John Adams was ticking off the members in this fashion, his cousin, the real Sam Adams, was already at work pulling the wires he had learned to manage so dexterously in Boston. Those delegates who had hoped the Congress would take a humble tone were dismayed to see how quickly his influence made itself felt. "He eats little," observed Joseph Galloway of Pennsylvania, "drinks little, sleeps little, thinks much, and is most decisive and indefatigable in the pursuit of his objects." Skillfully prodded by Adams, the Congress began its work by approving the "Suffolk Resolves"—so called because they had been adopted September 6 by a convention in Suffolk County, Massachusetts—which daringly declared that no obediance was due to the Coercive Acts.

With the members already committed to so radical a position it was a foregone conclusion that they would adopt the non-importation, non-exportation, non-consumption agreement they had met to consider. They did so on October 20, but first they engaged in a more significant activity, a reassessment of their relation to the mother country. In the debates on this subject they discovered how far they had traveled in the nine years since the Stamp Act Congress. The delegates to that meeting had agreed that Parliament had no right to tax Americans, but only the rashest proposed to set limits on its legislative authority. Now the question was whether Parliament had any authority in the colonies at all. Many Americans had arrived long since at the conclusion that it did not.

They had reached this point with the aid of Parliament itself. Englishmen had derided and denounced their distinction between legislation and taxation, and Parliament convincingly demonstrated that their liberty could be destroyed as easily by the one as by the other. What no one showed them (and few attempted) was why Parliament should have a right to either. Grenville had once claimed that Americans were subject to Parliament because they were "virtually" represented in it, but this argument was reduced to rubble by Daniel Dulany. Nothing had since been offered to take its place except the Declaratory act, in which the members of Parliament assured themselves that they had the authority by announcing that they had it. If anyone thereafter wanted to know where it came from it came from the announcement!

Faced with this impenetrable assumption of omnipotence, the colonists gradually reacted with an equally absolute but somewhat more rational denial. Parliament, they believed from the beginning, had no authority to tax them, because they were unrepresented. By the same token, if legislation and taxation were indivisible, Parliament had no right to legislate, and so no authority at all over them.

How the claim of absolute authority generated its opposite may be seen at closer range in Massachusetts. When the committees of correspondence in the various towns there began to list their grievances, Governor Hutchinson was alarmed to see how extensively they denied the validity of Parliamentary legislation. He decided to recall them to their senses by another affirmation of their total subordination, with more arguments than Parliament itself had hitherto deigned to offer.

In January, 1773, he read the House of Representatives a long lecture on the subject. "I know of no line that can be drawn," he told them, "between the supreme authority of Parliament and the total independence of the colonies." Hutchinson was the learned author of a history of the colony; and well aware of the American reverence for historical precedent, he drew upon his authority as a scholar to demonstrate that the founders of the colony had always acknowledged the supremacy of Parliament. But Hutchinson was up against a sharper wit and a keener mind than his own.

The House in drafting its answer called upon John Adams, a lawyer from Braintree, more learned in the law than his cousin Samuel and quite as learned in history as the governor. With his assistance an argument was prepared which showed that the founders of the colony had supposed themselves beyond the control of Parliament—and showed it by citations from Hutchinson's own history. With devilish ingenuity Adams even pointed out how the very King who granted the colony's first charter had supposed the same thing. The King, of course, was Charles I, who tried to do away with Parliament altogether! From here the answer went on with relentless logic to turn the governor's own words against him:

"Your Excellency tells us," it said, "you know of no line that can be drawn between the supreme authority of Parliament and the total independence of the colonies. If there be no such line, the consequence is, either that the colonies are the vassals of the Parliament, or that they are totally independent. As it cannot be supposed to have been the intention of the parties in the compact, that we should be reduced to a state of vassalage, the conclusion is, that it was their sense, that we were thus independent." Independent, of course, meant independent of Parliament, not of the King.

Hutchinson had maintained that if the colonies threw off Parliamentary supremacy, they would form distinct kingdoms like England and Scotland. "Very true, may it please your Excellency," replied the committee, "and if they interfere not with each other, what hinders, but that being united in one head and common Sovereign [the King], they may live happily in that connection, and mutually support and protect each other?" When the House of Representatives adopted this reply to the governor as their own, they committed the whole province to the very position that Hutchinson had hoped to forestall, that Parliament had no authority in the colonies whatever.

Hutchinson and the Adamses, in their different ways, brought Massachusetts to this point in 1773. Other Americans reached it in other ways and at other times. Benjamin Franklin got there as early as 1766 and waited quietly for his countrymen to catch up. Another Pennsylvanian, James Wilson, found his way to it in 1770 but refrained from saying so until he heard of the Coercive Acts. Then in a persuasive pamphlet he pointed out the short and easy route to others: the arguments against Parliamentary taxation would apply with equal force to all its legislation.

At Philadelphia in 1774 many of the delegates had followed one route or another to a total repudiation of Parliament, but for some the question of trade regulation remained an obstacle. They felt that for the benefit of the whole empire and of England in particular, as mother country and protector of the seas, there ought to be some central direction of imperial trade and that Parliament was entitled to the job. Others, like Galloway, thought a total reorganization of the empire was necessary, with an American Parliament, subsidiary to the English Parliament, empowered to oversee all intercolonial matters. The Congress, after considering Galloway's plan for a day, voted to table it (and on the last day of the meetings rejected it). Instead they defined their relationship to Parliament in an ambiguously worded resolution worked out by James Duane of New York and by John Adams.

> That the foundation of English liberty, and of all free government, is a right in the people to participate in their legislative council: and as the English colonies are not represented, and from their local and other circumstances, cannot properly be represented in the British Parliament, they are entitled to a free and exclusive power of legislation in their several provincial legislatures, where their right of representation can alone be preserved, in all cases of taxation and internal polity, subject only to the negative of their sovereign, in such manner as has been heretofore used and accustomed. But, from the necessity of the case, and a regard to the mutual interest of both countries, we cheerfully consent to the operation of such Acts of the British Parliament, as are bona fide restrained to the regulation of our external for the purpose of securing the commercial advantages of the whole empire to the mother country, and the commercial benefits of its respective members; excluding every idea of taxation, internal or external, for raising a revenue on the subjects in American without their consent.

In this equivocal declaration the members with one breath denied the right of Parliament to legislate for them and with the next volunteered to abide by that wonderful old state of things that existed in 1763. In such a mood of reluctant defiance they broke up on October 26, 1774, after providing for another congress in the following spring.

As they prepared to cast off the authority of Parlaiment, Americans were genuinely eager to keep their grip on the Past. They had ransacked English and colonial history for precedents to justify their constitutional position, to show that they were still true to the traditions of Englishmen; and they had been remarkably successful in finding the precedents they wanted. But while they clung so persistently to the past, they were actually moving, if only half-consciously and unwillingly, away from it. They were in fact on a the verge of a discovery that would turn history in a new direction, a discovery that is still reverberating among us and liberating us from our past as it was soon to liberate them, in spite of themselves, from theirs.

This discovery was nothing more or less than the principle of human equality. In 1774 the Americans may not have realized how close they were to it, but there were others who perceived, however dimly, that the whole course of their resistance to Parliament was leading them in that direction. As early as 1767 the French chargé d'affaires in London, following closely the British family quarrel, remarked that the Americans did not aspire to independence but simply to equality of rights with the mother country. The Frenchman's analysis was correct, but he did not dream how far beyond this the demand for equality might carry a people. Lord North was more perceptive. "I can never acquiesce" he said in 1770, "in the absurd opinion that, all men are equal." He was talking at the time about the pretensions of the London rabble in petitioning Parliament, but he rightly sensed what that absurd opinion could do to the authority of Parliament, whether in England or America.

The colonists had not voiced such an opinion, even to themselves, when Lord North spoke, and with tactful treatment they might still have been prevented from reaching it. By 1774 they were perilously near it. As long as they stopped their objections to Parliament's authority short of a wholesale rejection, they were accepting a smaller degree of freedom than their brethren in England; but when they repudiated Parliament altogether, they elevated their own assemblies to equal rank with it and themselves to an equality with all the King's subjects in Great Britain. From this position it would be only a short step to the absurd opinion that Lord North so rightly feared.

Lord North, if he had known how, would have liked nothing better than to return to 1763, as the colonists themselves were urging. And his new Secretary of State for the Colonies, the Earl of Dartmouth (who replaced Hillsborough in 1772), felt the same way. But the road back, as these statesmen saw it, was barred by colonial denials of Parliamentary authority, denials not merely in words but in flagrant resistance. What was worse, the colonists were busy building more road blocks. The very meeting of the Continental Congress appeared as a challenge to Parliament, and congressional measures, however hesitant, as outright treason.

Inside Parliament only Pitt and his small following would question the authority to tax, and even Pitt was strong for Parliament's legislative authority. The only conciliatory gesture that North could prevail upon himself and the other members to make was a proposal, passed in February, 1775, that the colonists tax themselves in lieu of a Parliamentary tax. This was merely a repetition of the gesture that Grenville had made in advance of the stamp tax, and it was still as vague and undefined, still as unacceptable, as it had been then.

After pausing for this futile aside, Parliament pressed ahead with its catastrophic instruction of the colonists in the meaning of its authority. With enthusiastic majorities it passed a bill to restrain the entire trade of New England and exclude her from the Newfoundland fisheries. And as the members debated further educational devices, the New Englanders bought gunpowder. On April 19, 1775 they used a good deal of it on the road from Concord to Boston.

The men who faced the British at Lexington Green that morning were part of the Massachusetts militia. Every colony trained its able-bodied men in a militia system for defense against Indians or foreign invasion. When no danger was in the offing, training day was a boisterous holiday, accompanied by light talk, heavy drinking, and precious little training. After Parliament passed the Coercive Acts, the festivities gave way to serious marching and maneuvers. In Massachusetts special companies of "minute-men" were formed to assemble at a moment's notice against the danger that threatened not from the Indians but from the troops that were guarding what was left of England's authority in Boston. The danger materialized on April 19, 1775, when the British marched to Concord, intent on seizing powder and guns, stored there by the Americans. Shooting began, almost by accident, at Lexington, but the shots that started the British on their way back from Concord were nobody's mistake. Minute-men and militia closed in on the line of march from all sides and peppered the British columns as they reeled toward Boston. After the last redcoat entered the city, the militia encamped outside it, and the siege of Boston began.

When the Second Continental Congress assembled on May 10, 1775 the members found themselves conducting a war and voted to raise a regular army, of which it was hoped the forces encircling Boston would form the nucleus. To command this "Continental Army" Congress chose not a New Englander but a Virginian, George Washington, and he hurried off to Massachusetts to take charge. Even before he arrived, the militiamen gave the soldiers in Boston one of the worst days in the history of the British Army. On the night of June 16 the Americans invaded Breed's Hill, adjacent to Bunker Hill in Charlestown, overlooking Boston. When the British decided to remove them the next day, the result was an unbelievable slaughter of the redcoats who came marching up the hill in close order. In the Battle of Bunker Hill, as it was called, the British showed a courage that wiped out the stain of their hurried retreat from Concord two months before; they kept coming until the Americans ran out of ammunition, and when the day was over the English regiments held the hill. But it would be a long time before they attempted another frontal assault on the raw militia whom they had thought to topple so easily.

Gunpowder is a great equalizer, and after the Americans had matched their muskets against the British, they were more confident than before in denying the authority of Parliament. But there still existed among the members of Congress a forlorn hope that the situation might somehow be retrieved. Though they had had enough of Parliament, and would fight rather than submit to its laws, some of them thought that it might be possible to maintain loyalty and subordination to the King. If their assemblies could be recognized as co-ordinate with Parliament, Americans might still join with Englishmen in subjection to a common sovereign. In this hope, while they prepared to seek foreign aid and organized for an extended war, the members addressed a last petition to George III—the Olive Branch Petition, it was called—urging him to prevent the efforts of Parliament under a corrupt ministry to enslave them.

The Americans did not yet realize that the King was an Englishman of only moderate abilities and a vision that reached no farther than that of his ministers and his Parliament. In the preceding ten or twelve years the members of parliament had demonstrated that they were unfit to rule an empire. They were, in fact, what the most recent historical scholarship has shown them to be: parochial and provincial. Though in theory each member was supposed to represent the whole kingdom (Grenville had said the whole empire), actually they were wedded to local interests in their particular boroughs and counties. They did not even have a sufficiently large vision to associate in political parties on a national scale. The whole business of parliament seldom rose above the level of logrolling.

The man who kept the logs rolling was the King. In the absence of any better politician it was he who brought miscellaneous factions together to form a working majority for whatever measures he and they could agree on. George III was good at the job, but he was no bigger than the men he managed. In order to play the role the colonists assigned him, he would have been obliged to abandon the one he was engaged in and stand entirely above Parliament. It might even have been necessary for him to resume the veto power and disallow bills in which Parliament sought to legislate for the colonies.

Had he wished to do this, he could scarcely have succeeded, and the few friends of the Americans in Parliament would have been the first to denounce the attempt as a resumption of Stuart tyranny. George III, however, had no such wish. Though he wanted desperately to keep his American colonies, he was wholeheartedly committed to the supremacy of Parliament and ready to go to any length to defend it against his rebellious subjects. While the Continental Congress prepared its last appeal to him, his ministers negotiated for 20,000 Russian mercenaries to accomplish what the regular troops in Boston seemed unable to do. When the Czarina refused to hire out her subjects, the ministers satisfied themselves with Hessians instead. The King himself treated the Olive Branch Petition with contempt. Two days after its arrival in August, 1775, he issued a proclamation declaring the colonies in rebellion, and in December he agreed to an act of Parliament prohibiting all intercourse with them and commanding the seizure of their ships on the high seas. Americans would evidently have to choose between their rights and their King, and in spite of everything the King had done or failed to do, the choice was not easy. While they were gathering their courage to make it, a new voice spoke out in words that imparted all the courage needed—the voice of Thomas Paine, an Englishman who had appeared in Philadelphia less than a year before Bunker Hill. In January, 1776, he published a piece called *Common Sense* which was immediately read throughout the colonies. It was read because it said superbly all the things that Americans were waiting to be told.

The colonists were only fooling themselves, Paine said, if they hoped to enjoy freedom under George III. Not only was the King as bad as his ministers and his Parliament; he was worse; he was the author of their troubles.

The ruler Paine described may not have been the real George III. It may be, as modern scholars have emphasized, that George was playing the only role a responsible monarch could play in the existing situation of politics in Great Britain. But if British politics demanded such a monarch, it was high time for the colonies to cut loose. If Paine misconstrued the motives of the King, he did not misconstrue the facts: there was simply no room in the existing British Empire for people who wanted the rights that Americans demanded.

Paine, however, did not deliver his message in sadness; his mission was not simply to destroy a lingering faith in the House of Hanover but to liberate Americans from the very idea of monarchy. Hitherto the demand for equality had found expression in assertions that equated Americans with Englishmen. Englishmen were taxed only by consent; therefore Americans must be. Englishmen had a right to be represented in their own legislative body; therefore Americans should have such a right and their assemblies be co-ordinate with Parliament. But Paine made bold to extend the inquiry. Why, he asked, should any man be exalted above others as a king was? "Male and female," he said, "are the distinctions of nature, good and bad the distinctions of Heaven; but how a race of men [hereditary kings] came into the world so exalted above the rest, and distinguished like some new species, is worth inquiring into, and whether they are the means of happiness or of misery to mankind." The result of his inquiry was to show that the only basis for hereditary monarchy is usurpation. "The plain truth," he announced, "is that the antiquity of English monarchy will not bear looking into," or for that matter any monarchy. Nothing but misery had come from kings.

Paine's boldness was breathtaking, and many colonists drew back in horror from the abyss of anarchy toward which his conclusions seemed to lead them. There were in 1776, as there always are, conservative men who thought the overthrow of a government, however evil, must entail worse consequences than submission. They had come this far in seeking what they considered their legal and constitutional rights, but to go where Paine was leading was to abandon both law and constitution and risk all in the untried and unrigged ship of "natural" rights. Rather than board such a vessel they would give up the contest and accept whatever King and Parliament chose to give them.

Many Americans, however, had learned from history that governments deserve no such reverence. In the 1640's Englishmen deposed their king, and in 1688 they did it again. After the first deposition a political philosopher, James Harrington, explained what had happened in his *Oceana,* a book that Americans still studied. In Oceana, (England) most of the property, originally in the hands of the king and his nobility, had gradually passed into the hands of a much larger segment of the population. And whoever owns the property, Harrington taught, will sooner or later own the government. In 1649, as Harrington saw it, the people who owned the property of England deposed the king and began to take charge of the government.

Their action proved premature. Monarchy and aristocracy turned out to be stronger than Harrington had supposed, but he gave the people (or at least those who owned property) the nerve to think that they might own their own government. And they vindicated his judgment in 1688 when they again got rid of a king and replaced him with one who would understand that he governed only with their consent. By this time Harrington was dead (after years of imprisonment), but another philosopher, John Locke, in a book that became even more popular than Harrington's, explained to his countrymen why they had every right to fashion their own government.

Men, Locke said, are by nature free, equal, and independent of each other. In a "state of nature" each man began with the possession only of his own body. But by applying the labor of his body to the land, each transformed what was formerly common into his own private property. In order to protect themselves and their hard-won possessions from attack by wicked individuals, men would agree in a social compact to end the complete independence that existed in the state of nature and to form a society under the supervision of government. Government therefore is instituted by consent of the governed for a definite purpose, and if any particular government fails to fulfill that purpose, it should be replaced by one that will.

Harrington and Locke were popular reading in America, perhaps more so than in England, because what they said made more sense in America. When Locke described his state of nature, he could explain it most vividly by saying that "in the beginning all the World was America." And indeed many Americans had had the actual experience of applying labor to wild land and turning it into their own. Some had even participated in social compacts, setting up new governments in wilderness areas where none had previously existed. And if Harrington was right in thinking that the wide distribution of property in England was what gave the people of England control of their government, Americans knew that their property was much more widely distributed; and in their representative assemblies they let it be known that they expected government to stick to its proper business of protecting them and their property.

During the years of controversy from 1763 to 1776 the colonists studied Locke and Harrington closely (along with subsequent writers like Thomas Gordon, John Trenchard, and James Burgh, who carried on the tradition of Locke and Harrington). And as they tried to define the constitutional limits of British authority, they had ever in mind the elemental principles by which the political philosophers taught them to measure a government's performance.

They regarded the rights they demanded not simply as constitutional rights but as natural rights which it was the very purpose of government to protect. They made their demands both as men and as Englishmen, for the English government had been the pattern for Locke's study; and hitherto, at least, Englishmen and English colonists almost alone among the peoples of the world actually did enjoy the rights which Locke believed all men were entitled to.

When the Americans prepared to resist rather than submit to a government that had exceeded its authority, elemental principles became increasingly relevant. As early as the Stamp Act crisis, colonial writers began discussing the process of dissolving government, and the Sons of Liberty prepared to put the ideas into practice. The group at New London, Connecticut, for example, resolved on December 10, 1765: "1st. That every Form of Government rightfully founded, originates from the Consent of the People. 2d. That the Boundaries set by the People in all Constitutions, are the only Limits within which any Officer can lawfully exercise Authority. 3d. That whenever those Bounds are exceeded, the People have a Right to reassume the exercise of that Authority which by Nature they had, before they delegated it to Individuals."

Ten years later, after fighting began, while they continued to hope against hope that England would recognize and restore their constitutional rights, Americans were talking more about the state of nature, the origin of government, the limits of authority, and the rights of man. All these ideas were fused in Thomas Paine's denunciation of monarchy. At one stroke he propelled Americans into the great discovery of a human equality toward which they had been moving unwittingly ever since they first denied Parliament's right to tax.

There is an exaltation, an excitement, about *Common Sense* that conveys the very uncommon sense of adventure Americans felt as they moved toward independence. With it would come new perils, but also new opportunities, new freedoms. They knew they were on the threshold of a great experience not only for themselves but perhaps for the whole world. "The cause of America," Paine told them, "is in a great measure the cause of all mankind." And they believed him.

On May 15, 1776, the Virginia House of Burgesses voted to instruct its delegates in Congress to propose independence, and on the same day the Congress adopted a resolution sponsored by John Adams, advising the various colonies to assume the complete powers of government within themselves. On June 7 Richard Henry Lee, following the instructions of his Virginia constituents, moved a resolution formally declaring the colonies independent. On July 2 this resolution was adopted and two days later the famous declaration to the world, drafted by Thomas Jefferson.

The Declaration did not go as far as Paine had gone: it was directed only against the "present" King of Great Britain and would not have precluded a monarchical form of government for the United States or for any of its constituent parts. But the Declaration, like *Common Sense*, was much more than a repudiation of George III. It put into words, even more effectively than Paine did, the principle which had been forming in the American mind, "that all men are created equal." The only immediate application was the assertion that Americans were entitled to "a separate and equal station" among the nations of the earth, but the words were phrased in the form of a sacred creed and with an elemental eloquence that has been moving men ever since. The declaration that all men were created equal might mean for the moment that Americans should have the same independence as a nation that other peoples enjoyed. What else it might mean remained to be seen. During the exciting years that lay ahead, as they took their new and independent way, Americans would begin to find out.

Meanwhile they had a job to do.

III

New Nation: 1783–1815

9. What is an American?

J.H.S. de Crévecoeur

Michel Guillaume Jean de Crevecoeur (December 31, 1795 – November 12, 1813), naturalized in New York as John Hector St. John, was a French-American writer. He was born in Caen, Normandy, France to the Comte and Comtesse de Crevecoeur (Count and Countess of Crevecoeur).

In 1755 he immigrated to New France in North America. There, he served in the French and Indian War as a surveyor in the French Colonial Militia, rising to the rank of lieutenant. Following the British defeat of the French Army in 1759 he moved to New York State, then the Province of New York, where he took out citizenship, adopted the English-American name of John Hector St. John, and in 1770 married an American woman, Mehitable Tippet. He bought a sizable farm in Orange County, N.Y., where he prospered as a farmer and took up writing about life in the American colonies and the emergence of an American society. In 1779, during the American Revolution, the faltering health of his father forced him to travel to Europe. Accompanied by his son, he crossed British-American lines to enter British-occupied New York City, where he was imprisoned as an American spy for three months without being heard. Eventually he was able to leave Britain.

In 1782, in London, he published a volume of narrative essays entitled Letters from an American Farmer. The book quickly became the first literary success by an American author in Europe and turned Crevecoeur into a celebrated figure. He was the first writer to describe to Europeans – employing many American English terms – the life on the American frontier and to explore the concept of the American Dream, portraying American society as characterized by the principles of equal opportunity and self-determination. His work provided useful information and understanding of the "New World" that helped to create an American identity in the minds of Europeans by describing an entire country rather than another regional colony. The writing celebrated American ingenuity and its uncomplicated lifestyle and spelled out the acceptance of religious diversity in a melting pot being created from a variety of ethnic and cultural backgrounds.

From Britain, he sailed for France, where he was briefly reunited with his father. When the United States had been recognized by Britain following the Treaty of Paris in 1783, Crevecoeur returned to New York City. He learned that, in his absence, his wife had died, his farm had been destroyed, and his children were now living with neighbors. Eventually, he was able to regain custody of his children. For most of the 1780's Crevecoeur lived in New York City where he now served as the French consul for New York, New Jersey and Connecticut. In 1784, he published a two-volume version of his Letters from an American Farmer, enlarged and completely rewritten in French. A three-volume version followed in 1787. On Letters from an American Farmer III, he wrote "What is an American?"

What attachment can a poor European emigrant have for a country where he had nothing? The knowledge of the language, the love of a few kindred as poor as himself, were the only cords that tied him. His country is now that which gives him his land, bread, protection, and consequence . . .What then is the Amercan, this new man? He is neither a European nor the descendant of a European; hence that strange mixture of blood which you will find in no other country. I could point out to you a family whose grandfather was an Englishman, whose wife was Dutch, whose son married a French woman, and whose present four sons have now four wives of different nations. He is an American who, leaving behind him all his ancient prejudices and manners, receives new ones from the new mode of life he has embraced, the new government he obeys, and the new rank he holds. He becomes an American by being received in the broad lap of our great alma mater. Here individuals of all nations are melted into a new race of men whose labors and posterity will one day cause great changes in the world. Americans are the western pilgrims, who are carrying along with them the great mass of arts, sciences, vigor, and industry which begin long since in the East. They will finish the great circle. The Americans were once scattered all over Europe. Here they are incorporated into one of the finest systems of population which has ever appeared and which will hereafter become distinct by the power of the different climates they inhabit. The American ought therefore to love this country much better than that in which either he or his forefathers were born. Here the rewards of his industry follow with equal steps the progress of his labor. His labor is founded on the basis of nature, self-interest: can it want a stronger allurement? Wives and children, who before in vain demanded of him a morsel of bread, now, fat and frolicsome, gladly help their father to clear those fields whence exuberant crops are to rise, to feed and to clothe them all, without any part being claimed either by despotic prince, a rich abbot, or a mighty lord. Here religion demands but little of him—a small voluntary salary to the minister, and gratitude to God—can he refuse these? The American is a new man who acts on new principles; he must therefore entertain new ideas and form new opinions. From involuntary idleness, servile dependence, penury, and useless labor, he has passed to toils of a very different nature, rewarded by ample subsistence.

This is an American.

10. Farewell Address
September 17, 1796

George Washington

The letter was originally prepared in 1792 with the help of James Madison as Washington prepared to retire following a single term in office. However, he set aside the letter and ran for a second term after his Secretary of the Treasury, Alexander Hamilton, and his Secretary of State, Thomas Jefferson, convinced him that the growing divisions between the newly formed Federalist and Democratic-Republican parties, along with the current state of foreign affairs, would tear the country apart in the absence of his leadership.

For years later, as his second term came to a close, Washington revisited the letter and with the help of Hamilton prepared a revision of the original draft to announce his intention to decline a third term in office; to reflect the emerging issues of the American political landscape in 1796; to offer his parting advice to his fellow Americans, to express his support for the government eight years following the adoption of the Constitution; and to defend his administration's record.

The letter was written by Washington after years of exhaustion due to his advanced age, years of service to his country, the duties of the presidency, and increased attacks by his political opponents. It was published almost two months before the Electoral College cast their votes in the 1796 presidential election.

To the People of the United States.

FRIENDS AND FELLOW-CITIZENS:

The period for a new election of a citizen, to administer the executive goverment of the United States, being not far distant, and the time actually arrived, when your thoughts must be employed designating the person, who is to be clothed with that important trust, it appears to me proper, especially as it may conduce to a more distinct expression of the public voice, that I should now apprize you of the resolution I have formed, to decline being considered among the number of those out of whom a choice is to be made.

I beg you at the same time to do me the justice to be assured that this resolution has not been taken without a strict regard to all the considerations appertaining to the relation which binds a dutiful citizen to his country; and that in withdrawing the tender of service, which silence in my situation might imply, I am influenced by no diminution of zeal for your future interest, no defi ciency of grateful respect for your past kindness, but am supported by a full conviction that the step is compatible with both.

The acceptance of, and continuance hitherto in, the office to which your suffrages have twice called me, have been a uniform sacrifi ce of inclination to the opinion of duty, and to a deference for what appeared to be your desire. I constantly hoped, that it would have been much earlier in my power, consistently with motives, which I was not at liberty to disregard, to return to that retirement, from which I had been reluctantly drawn. The strength of my inclination to do this, previous to the last election, had even led to the preparation of an address to declare it to you; but mature reflection on the then perplexed and critical posture of our affairs with foreign nations, and the unanimous advice of persons entitled to my confi dence impelled me to abandon the idea.

I rejoice, that the state of your concerns, external as well as internal, no longer renders the pursuit of inclination incompatible with the sentiment of duty, or propriety; and am persuaded, whatever partiality may be retained for my services, that, in the present circumstances of our country, you will not disapprove my determination to retire.

The impressions, with which I first undertook the arduous trust, were explained on the proper occasion. In the discharge of this trust, I will only say, that I have, with good intentions, contributed towards the organization and administration of the government the best exertions of which a very fallible judgment was capable. Not unconscious, in the outset, of the inferiority of my qualifi cations, experience in my own eyes, perhaps still more in the eyes of others, has strengthened the motives to diffi dence of myself; and every day the increasing weight of years admonishes me more and more, that the shade of retirement is as necessary to me as it will be welcome. Satisfi ed, that, if any circumstances have given peculiar value to my services, they were temporary, I have the consolation to believe, that, while choice and prudence invite me to quit the political scene, patriotism does not forbid it.

In looking forward to the moment, which is intended to terminate the career of my public life, my feelings do not permit me to suspend the deep acknowledgment of that debt of gratitude, which I owe to my beloved country for the many honors it has conferred upon me; still more for the steadfast confi dence with which it has supported me; and for the opportunities I have thence enjoyed of manifesting my inviolable attachment, by services faithful and persevering, though in usefulness unequal to my zeal. If benefi ts have resulted to our country from these services, let it always be remembered to your praise, and as an instructive example in our annals, that under circumstances in which the passions, agitated in every direction, were liable to mislead, amidst appearances sometimes dubious, vicissitudes of fortune often discouraging, in situations in which not unfrequently want of success has countenanced the spirit of criticism, the constancy of your support was the essential prop of the efforts, and a guarantee of the plans by which they were effected. Profoundly penetrated with this idea, I shall carry it with me to my grave, as a strong incitement to unceasing vows that Heaven may continue to you the choicest tokens of its benefi cence; that your union and brotherly affection may be perpetual; that the free constitution, which is the work of your hands, may be sacredly maintained; that its adminis- tration in every department may be stamped with wisdom and virtue; than, in fine, the happiness of the people of these States, under the auspices of liberty, may be made complete, by so careful a preservation and so prudent a use of this blessing, as will acquire to them the glory of recommending it to the applause, the affection, and adoption of every nation, which is yet a stranger to it.

Here, perhaps I ought to stop. But a solicitude for your welfare which cannot end but with my life, and the apprehension of danger, natural to that solicitude, urge me, on an occasion like the present, to offer to your solemn contempla- tion, and to recommend to your frequent review, some sentiments which are the result of much reflection, of no inconsiderable observation, and which appear to me all-important to the permanency of your felicity as a people. These will be offered to you with the more freedom, as you can only see in them the disin- terested warnings of a parting friend, who can possibly have no personal motive to bias his counsel. Nor can I forget, as an encouragement to it, your indulgent reception of my sentiments on a former and not dissimilar occasion.

Interwoven as is the love of liberty with every ligament of your hearts, no recommendation of mine is necessary to fortify or confirm the attachment.

The unity of Government, which constitutes you one people, is also now dear to you. It is justly so; for it is a main pillar in the edifice of your real independence, the support of your tranquillity at home, your peace abroad; of your safety; of your prosperity; of that very Liberty, which you so highly prize. But as it is easy to foresee, that, from different causes and from different quarters, much pains will be taken, many artifices employed, to weaken in your minds the conviction of this truth; as this is the point in your political fortress against which the batteries of internal and external enemies will be most constantly and actively (though often covertly and insidiously) directed, it is of infinite moment, that you should properly estimate the immense value of your national Union to your collective and individual happiness; that you should cherish a cordial, habitual, and immovable attachment to it; accustoming yourselves to think and speak of it as of the Palladium of your political safety and prosperity; watching for its preservation with jealous anxiety; discountenancing whatever may sug- gest even a suspicion, that it can in any event be abandoned; and indignantly frowning upon the fi rst dawning of every attempt to alienate any portion of our country from the rest, or to enfeeble the sacred ties which now link together the various parts.

For this you have every inducement of sympathy and interest. Citizens, by birth or choice, of a common country, that country has a right to concentrate your affections. The name of american, which belongs to you, in your national capacity, must always exalt the just pride of Patriotism, more than any appella- tion derived from local discriminations. With slight shades of difference, you have the same religion, manners, habits, and political principles. You have in a common cause fought and triumphed together; the Independence and Liberty you possess are the work of joint counsels, and joint efforts, of common dangers,sufferings, and successes.

But these considerations, however powerfully they address themselves to your sensibility, are greatly outweighed by those, which apply more immediately to your interest. Here every portion of our country finds the most commanding motives for carefully guarding and preserving the Union of the whole.

The North, in an unrestrained intercourse with the South, protected by the equal laws of a common government, finds, in the productions of the latter, great additional resources of maritime and commercial enterprise and precious materials of manufacturing industry. The South, in the same intercourse, benefi ting by the agency of the North, sees its agriculture grow and its commerce expand. Turning partly into its own channels the seamen of the North, it finds its particular navigation invigorated; and, while it contributes, in different ways, to nourish and increase the general mass of the national navigation, it looks forward to the protection of a maritime strength, to which itself is unequally adapted. The East, in a like intercourse with the West, already finds, and in the progressive improvement of interior communications by land and water, will more and more find, a valuable vent for the commodities which it brings from abroad, or manufactures at home. The West derives from the East supplies requisite to its growth and comfort, and, what is perhaps of still greater consequence, it must of necessity owe the secure enjoyment of indispensable outlets for its own productions to the weight, influence, and the future maritime strength of the Atlantic side of the Union, directed by an indissoluble community of interest as one nation. Any other tenure by which the West can hold this essential advantage, whether derived from its own separate strength, or from an apostate and unnatural connexion with any foreign power, must be intrinsically precarious.

While, then, every part of our country thus feels an immediate and particular interest in Union, all the parts combined cannot fail to find in the united mass of means and efforts greater strength, greater resource, proportionably greater security from external danger, a less frequent interruption of their peace by foreign nations; and, what is of inestimable value, they must derive from Union an exemption from those broils and wars between themselves, which so frequently afflict neighbouring countries not tied together by the same governments, which their own rivalships alone would be sufficient to produce, but which opposite foreign alliances, attachments, and intrigues would stimulate and embitter. Hence, likewise, they will avoid the necessity of those overgrown military establishments, which, under any form of government, are inauspicious to liberty, and which are to be regarded as particularly hostile to Republican Liberty. In this sense it is, that your Union ought to be considered as a main prop of your liberty, and that the love of the one ought to endear to you the preservation of the other.

These considerations speak a persuasive language to every reflecting and virtuous mind, and exhibit the continuance of the union as a primary object of Patriotic desire. Is there a doubt, whether a common government can embrace so large a sphere? Let experience solve it. To listen to mere speculation in such a case were criminal. We are authorized to hope, that a proper organization of the whole, with the auxiliary agency of governments for the respective subdivisions, will afford a happy issue to the experiment. It is well worth a fair and full experiment. With such powerful and obvious motives to Union, affecting all parts of our country, while experience shall not have demonstrated its impracticability, there will always be reason to distrust the patriotism of those, who in any quarter may endeavour to weaken its bands.

In contemplating the causes, which may disturb our Union, it occurs as matter of serious concern, that any ground should have been furnished for characterizing parties by Geographical discriminations, Northern and Southern, Atlantic and Western; whence designing men may endeavour to excite a belief, that there is a real difference of local interests and views. One of the expedients of party to acquire influence, within particular districts, is to misrepresent the opinions and aims of other districts. You cannot shield yourselves too much against the jealousies and heart-burnings, which spring from these misrepresentations; they tend to render alien to each other those, who ought to be bound together by fraternal affection. The inhabitants of our western country have lately had a useful lesson on this head; they have seen, in the negotiation by the Executive, and in the unanimous ratification by the Senate, of the treaty with Spain, and in the universal satisfaction at that event, throughout the United States, a decisive proof how unfounded were the suspicions propagated among them of a policy in the General Government and in the Atlantic States unfriendly to their interests in regard to the Mississippi; they have been witnesses to the formation of two treaties, that with Great Britain, and that with Spain, which secure to them every thing they could desire, in respect to our foreign relations, towards confirming their prosperity. Will it not be their wisdom to rely for the preservation of these advantages on the union by which they were procured? Will they not henceforth be deaf to those advisers, if such there are, who would sever them from their brethren, and connect them with aliens?

To the efficacy and permanency of your Union, a Government for the whole is indispensable. No alliances, however strict, between the parts can be an adequate substitute; they must inevitably experience the infractions and interruptions, which all alliances in all times have experienced. Sensible of this momentous truth, you have improved upon your first essay, by the adoption of a Constitution of Government better calculated than your former for an intimate Union, and for the efficacious management of your common concerns. This Government, the offspring of our own choice, uninfluenced and unawed, adopted upon full investigation and mature deliberation, completely free in its principles, in the distribution of its powers, uniting security with energy, and containing within itself a provision for its own amendment, has a just claim to your confidence and your support. Respect for its authority, compliance with its laws, acquiescence in its measures, are duties enjoined by the fundamental maxims of true Liberty. The basis of our political systems is the right of the people to make and to alter their Constitutions of Government. But the Constitution which at any time exists, till changed by an explicit and authentic act of the whole people, is sacredly obligatory upon all. The very idea of the power and the right of the people to establish Government presupposes the duty of every individual to obey the established Government.

All obstructions to the execution of the Laws, all combinations and associations, under whatever plausible character, with the real design to direct, control, counteract, or awe the regular deliberation and action of the constituted authorities, are destructive of this fundamental principle, and of fatal tendency. They serve to organize faction, to give it an artificial and extraordinary force; to put, in the place of the delegated will of the nation, the will of a party, often a small but artful and enterprising minority of the community; and, according to the alternate triumphs of different parties, to make the public administration the mirror of the ill-concerted and incongruous projects of faction, rather than the organ of consistent and wholesome plans digested by common counsels, and modified by mutual interests.

However combinations or associations of the above description may now and then answer popular ends, they are likely, in the course of time and things, to become potent engines, by which cunning, ambitious, and unprincipled men will be enabled to subvert the power of the people, and to usurp for themselves the reins of government; destroying afterwards the very engines, which have lifted them to unjust dominion.

Towards the preservation of your government, and the permanency of your present happy state, it is requisite, not only that you steadily discountenance irregular oppositions to its acknowledged authority, but also that you resist with care the spirit of innovation upon its principles, however specious the pretexts. One method of assault may be to effect, in the forms of the constitution, alterations, which will impair the energy of the system, and thus to undermine what cannot be directly overthrown. In all the changes to which you may be invited, remember that time and habit are at least as necessary to fix the true character of governments, as of other human institutions; that experience is the surest standard, by which to test the real tendency of the existing constitution of a country; that facility in changes, upon the credit of mere hypothesis and opinion, exposes to perpetual change, from the endless variety of hypothesis and opinion; and remember, especially, that, for the efficient management of our common interests, in a country so extensive as ours, a government of as much vigor as is consistent with the perfect security of liberty is indispensable. Liberty itself will find in such a government, with powers properly distributed and adjusted, its surest guardian. It is, indeed, little else than a name, where the government is too feeble to withstand the enterprises of faction, to confine each member of the society within the limits prescribed by the laws, and to maintain all in the secure and tranquil enjoyment of the rights of person and property.

I have already intimated to you the danger of parties in the state, with particular reference to the founding of them on geographical discriminations. Let me now take a more comprehensive view, and warn you in the most solemn manner against the baneful effects of the spirit of party, generally.

This spirit, unfortunately, is inseparable from our nature, having its root in the strongest passions of the human mind. It exists under different shapes in all governments, more or less stifled, controlled, or repressed; but, in those of the popular form, it is seen in its greatest rankness, and is truly their worst enemy.

The alternate domination of one faction over another, sharpened by the spirit of revenge, natural to party dissension, which in different ages and countries has perpetrated the most horrid enormities, is itself a frightful despotism. But this leads at length to a more formal and permanent despotism. The disorders and miseries, which result, gradually incline the minds of men to seek security and repose in the absolute power of an individual; and sooner or later the chief of some prevailing faction, more able or more fortunate than his competitors, turns this disposition to the purposes of his own elevation, on the ruins of Public Liberty.

Without looking forward to an extremity of this kind, (which nevertheless ought not to be entirely out of sight,) the common and continual mischiefs of the spirit of party are sufficient to make it the interest and duty of a wise people to discourage and restrain it.

It serves always to distract the Public Councils, and enfeeble the Public Administration. It agitates the Community with ill-founded jealousies and false alarms; kindles the animosity of one part against another, foments occasionally riot and insurrection. It opens the door to foreign influence and corruption, which find a facilitated access to the government itself through the channels of party passions. Thus the policy and the will of one country are subjected to the policy and will of another.

There is an opinion, that parties in free countries are useful checks upon the administration of the Government, and serve to keep alive the spirit of Liberty. This within certain limits is probably true; and in Governments of a Monarchical cast, Patriotism may look with indulgence, if not with favor, upon the spirit of party. But in those of the popular character, in Governments purely elective, it is a spirit not to be encouraged. From their natural tendency, it is certain there will always be enough of that spirit for every salutary purpose. And, there being constant danger of excess, the effort ought to be, by force of public opinion, to mitigate and assuage it. A fire not to be quenched, it demands a uniform vigilance to prevent its bursting into a flame, lest, instead of warming, it should consume.

It is important, likewise, that the habits of thinking in a free country should inspire caution, in those intrusted with its administration, to confine themselves within their respective constitutional spheres, avoiding in the exercise of the powers of one department to encroach upon another. The spirit of encroachment tends to consolidate the powers of all the departments in one, and thus to create, whatever the form of government, a real despotism. A just estimate of that love of power, and proneness to abuse it, which predominates in the human heart, is sufficient to satisfy us of the truth of this position. The necessity of reciprocal checks in the exercise of political power, by dividing and distributing it into different depositories, and constituting each the Guardian of the Public Weal against invasions by the others, has been evinced by experiments ancient and modern; some of them in our country and under our own eyes. To preserve them must be as necessary as to institute them. If, in the opinion of the people, the distribution or modification of the constitutional powers be in any particular wrong, let it be corrected by an amendment in the way, which the constitution designates. But let there be no change by usurpation; for, though this, in one instance, may be the instrument of good, it is the customary weapon by which free governments are destroyed. The precedent must always greatly overbalance in permanent evil any partial or transient benefit, which the use can at any time yield.

Of all the dispositions and habits, which lead to political prosperity, Religion and Morality are indispensable supports. In vain would that man claim the tribute of Patriotism, who should labor to subvert these great pillars of human happiness, these firmest props of the duties of Men and Citizens. The mere Politician, equally with the pious man, ought to respect and to cherish them. A volume could not trace all their connexions with private and public felicity. Let it simply be asked, Where is the security for property, for reputation, for life, if the sense of religious obligation desert the oaths, which are the instruments of investigation in Courts of Justice? And let us with caution indulge the supposition, that morality can be maintained without religion. Whatever may be conceded to the influence of refined education on minds of peculiar structure, reason and experience both forbid us to expect, that national morality can prevail in exclusion of religious principle.

It is substantially true, that virtue or morality is a necessary spring of popular government. The rule, indeed, extends with more or less force to every species of free government. Who, that is a sincere friend to it, can look with indifference upon attempts to shake the foundation of the fabric ? It is substantially true, that virtue or morality is a necessary spring of popular government. The rule, indeed, extends with more or less force to every species of free government. Who, that is a sincere friend to it, can look with indifference upon attempts to shake the foundation of the fabric ?

Promote, then, as an object of primary importance, institutions for the general diffusion of knowledge. In proportion as the structure of a government gives force to public opinion, it is essential that public opinion should be enlightened.

As a very important source of strength and security, cherish public credit. One method of preserving it is, to use it as sparingly as possible; avoiding occasions of expense by cultivating peace, but remembering also that timely disbursements to prepare for danger frequently prevent much greater disbursements to repel it; avoiding likewise the accumulation of debt, not only by shunning occasions of expense, but by vigorous exertions in time of peace to discharge the debts, which unavoidable wars may have occasioned, not ungenerously throwing upon posterity the burthen, which we ourselves ought to bear. The execution of these maxims belongs to your representatives, but it is necessary that public opinion should cooperate. To facilitate to them the performance of their duty, it is essential that you should practically bear in mind, that towards the payment of debts there must be Revenue; that to have Revenue there must be taxes; that no taxes can be devised, which are not more or less inconvenient and unpleasant; that the intrinsic embarrassment, inseparable from the selection of the proper objects (which is always a choice of difficulties), ought to be a decisive motive for a candid construction of the conduct of the government in making it, and for a spirit of acquiescence in the measures for obtaining revenue, which the public exigencies may at any time dictate.

Observe good faith and justice towards all Nations; cultivate peace and harmony with all. Religion and Morality enjoin this conduct; and can it be, that good policy does not equally enjoin it? It will be worthy of a free, enlightened, and, at no distant period, a great Nation, to give to mankind the magnanimous and too novel example of a people always guided by an exalted justice and benevolence. Who can doubt, that, in the course of time and things, the fruits of such a plan would richly repay any temporary advantages, which might be lost by a steady adherence to it ? Can it be, that Providence has not connected the permanent felicity of a Nation with its Virtue? The experiment, at least, is recommended by every sentiment which ennobles human nature. Alas! is it rendered impossible by its vices ?

In the execution of such a plan, nothing is more essential, than that permanent, inveterate antipathies against particular Nations, and passionate attachments for others, should be excluded; and that, in place of them, just and amicable feelings towards all should be cultivated. The Nation, which indulges towards another an habitual hatred, or an habitual fondness, is in some degree a slave. It is a slave to its animosity or to its affection, either of which is sufficient to lead it astray from its duty and its interest. Antipathy in one nation against another disposes each more readily to offer insult and injury, to lay hold of slight causes of umbrage, and to be haughty and intractable, when accidental or trifling occasions of dispute occur. Hence frequent collisions, obstinate, envenomed, and bloody contests. The Nation, prompted by ill-will and resentment, sometimes impels to war the Government, contrary to the best calculations of policy. The Government sometimes participates in the national propensity, and adopts through passion what reason would reject; at other times, it makes the animosity of the nation subservient to projects of hostility instigated by pride, ambition, and other sinister and pernicious motives. The peace often, sometimes perhaps the liberty, of Nations has been the victim.

So likewise, a passionate attachment of one Nation for another produces a variety of evils. Sympathy for the favorite Nation, facilitating the illusion of an imaginary common interest, in cases where no real common interest exists, and infusing into one the enmities of the other, betrays the former into a participation in the quarrels and wars of the latter, without adequate inducement or justification. It leads also to concessions to the favorite Nation of privileges denied to others, which is apt doubly to injure the Nation making the concessions; by unnecessarily parting with what ought to have been retained; and by exciting jealousy, ill-will, and a disposition to retaliate, in the parties from whom equal privileges are withheld. And it gives to ambitious, corrupted, or deluded citizens, (who devote themselves to the favorite nation,) facility to betray or sacrifice the interests of their own country, without odium, sometimes even with popularity; gilding, with the appearances of a virtuous sense of obligation, a commendable deference for public opinion, or a laudable zeal for public good, the base or foolish compliances of ambition, corruption, or infatuation.

As avenues to foreign influence in innumerable ways, such attachments are particularly alarming to the truly enlightened and independent Patriot. How many opportunities do they afford to tamper with domestic factions, to practise the arts of seduction, to mislead public opinion, to influence or awe the Public Councils! Such an attachment of a small or weak, towards a great and powerful nation, dooms the former to be the satellite of the latter.

Against the insidious wiles of foreign influence (I conjure you to believe me, fellow-citizens,) the jealousy of a free people ought to be constantly awake; since history and experience prove, that foreign influence is one of the most baneful foes of Republican Government. But that jealousy, to be useful, must be impartial; else it becomes the instrument of the very influence to be avoided, instead of a defence against it. Excessive partiality for one foreign nation, and excessive dislike of another, cause those whom they actuate to see danger only on one side, and serve to veil and even second the arts of influence on the other. Real patriots, who may resist the intrigues of the favorite, are liable to become suspected and odious; while its tools and dupes usurp the applause and confidence of the people, to surrender their interests.

The great rule of conduct for us, in regard to foreign nations, is, in extending our commercial relations, to have with them as little political connexion as possible. So far as we have already formed engagements, let them be fulfilled with perfect good faith. Here let us stop.

Europe has a set of primary interests, which to us have none, or a very remote relation. Hence she must be engaged in frequent controversies, the causes of which are essentially foreign to our concerns. Hence, therefore, it must be unwise in us to implicate ourselves, by artificial ties, in the ordinary vicissitudes of her politics, or the ordinary combinations and collisions of her friendships or enmities.

Our detached and distant situation invites and enables us to pursue a different course. If we remain one people, under an efficient government, the period is not far off, when we may defy material injury from external annoyance; when we may take such an attitude as will cause the neutrality, we may at any time resolve upon, to be scrupulously respected; when belligerent nations, under the impossibility of making acquisitions upon us, will not lightly hazard the giving us provocation; when we may choose peace or war, as our interest, guided by justice, shall counsel.

Why forego the advantages of so peculiar a situation? Why quit our own to stand upon foreign ground? Why, by interweaving our destiny with that of any part of Europe, entangle our peace and prosperity in the toils of European ambition, rivalship, interest, humor, or caprice?

It is our true policy to steer clear of permanent alliances with any portion of the foreign world; so far, I mean, as we are now at liberty to do it; for let me not be understood as capable of patronizing infidelity to existing engagements. I hold the maxim no less applicable to public than to private affairs, that honesty is always the best policy. I repeat it, therefore, let those engagements be observed in their genuine sense. But, in my opinion, it is unnecessary and would be unwise to extend them.

Taking care always to keep ourselves, by suitable establishments, on a respectable defensive posture, we may safely trust to temporary alliances for extraordinary emergencies.

Harmony, liberal intercourse with all nations, are recommended by policy, humanity, and interest. But even our commercial policy should hold an equal and impartial hand; neither seeking nor granting exclusive favors or preferences; consulting the natural course of things; diffusing and diversifying by gentle means the streams of commerce, but forcing nothing; establishing, with powers so disposed, in order to give trade a stable course, to define the rights of our merchants, and to enable the government to support them, conventional rules of intercourse, the best that present circumstances and mutual opinion will permit, but temporary, and liable to be from time to time abandoned or varied, as experience and circumstances shall dictate; constantly keeping in view, that it is folly in one nation to look for disinterested favors from another; that it must pay with a portion of its independence for whatever it may accept under that character; that, by such acceptance, it may place itself in the condition of having given equivalents for nominal favors, and yet of being reproached with ingratitude for not giving more. There can be no greater error than to expect or calculate upon real favors from nation to nation. It is an illusion, which experience must cure, which a just pride ought to discard.

In offering to you, my countrymen, these counsels of an old and affectionate friend, I dare not hope they will make the strong and lasting impression I could wish; that they will control the usual current of the passions, or prevent our nation from running the course, which has hitherto marked the destiny of nations. But, if I may even flatter myself, that they may be productive of some partial benefit, some occasional good; that they may now and then recur to moderate the fury of party spirit, to warn against the mischiefs of foreign intrigue, to guard against the impostures of pretended patriotism; this hope will be a full recompense for the solicitude for your welfare, by which they have been dictated.

How far in the discharge of my official duties, I have been guided by the principles which have been delineated, the public records and other evidences of my conduct must witness to you and to the world. To myself, the assurance of my own conscience is, that I have at least believed myself to be guided by them.

In relation to the still subsisting war in Europe, my Proclamation of the 22d of April 1793, is the index to my Plan. Sanctioned by your approving voice, and by that of your Representatives in both Houses of Congress, the spirit of that measure has continually governed me, uninfluenced by any attempts to deter or divert me from it.

After deliberate examination, with the aid of the best lights I could obtain, I was well satisfied that our country, under all the circumstances of the case, had a right to take, and was bound in duty and interest to take, a neutral position. Having taken it, I determined, as far as should depend upon me, to maintain it, with moderation, perseverance, and firmness.

The considerations, which respect the right to hold this conduct, it is not necessary on this occasion to detail. I will only observe, that, according to my understanding of the matter, that right, so far from being denied by any of the Belligerent Powers, has been virtually admitted by all.

The duty of holding a neutral conduct may be inferred, without any thing more, from the obligation which justice and humanity impose on every nation, in cases in which it is free to act, to maintain inviolate the relations of peace and amity towards other nations.

The inducements of interest for observing that conduct will best be referred to your own reflections and experience. With me, a predominant motive has been to endeavour to gain time to our country to settle and mature its yet recent institutions, and to progress without interruption to that degree of strength and consistency, which is necessary to give it, humanly speaking, the command of its own fortunes.

Though, in reviewing the incidents of my administration, I am unconscious of intentional error, I am nevertheless too sensible of my defects not to think it probable that I may have committed many errors. Whatever they may be, I fervently beseech the Almighty to avert or mitigate the evils to which they may tend. I shall also carry with me the hope, that my Country will never cease to view them with indulgence; and that, after forty-five years of my life dedicated to its service with an upright zeal, the faults of incompetent abilities will be consigned to oblivion, as myself must soon be to the mansions of rest.

Relying on its kindness in this as in other things, and actuated by that fervent love towards it, which is so natural to a man, who views it in the native soil of himself and his progenitors for several generations; I anticipate with pleasing expectation that retreat, in which I promise myself to realize, without alloy, the sweet enjoyment of partaking, in the midst of my fellow-citizens, the benign influence of good laws under a free government, the ever favorite object of my heart, and the happy reward, as I trust, of our mutual cares, labors, and dangers.

11. Dying of Breast Cancer in the 1800s

Robert Shadle and James S. Olson

For many women in contemporary America, few fears are more visceral than the fear of breast cancer. The disease has terrified women for countless generations. For thousands of years, it was cancer. Unlike most malignancies, which were internal, invisible, and inscrutable, breast cancer's ravages were visible to the naked eye. Greeks called them "cancers" (karkinos) because of their "crablike" tenacity, their ability to invade surrounding tissues and recur again and again regardless of the potions applied and the spells cast. Breast cancer was the "dread disease." During the Middle Ages, clerics and physicians knew of a high incidence of breast cancer among Roman Catholic nuns, and they speculated on that phenomenon, wondering whether a lack of sexual intercourse predisposed women to the disease. Questions about the relationship between sexuality and illness, gender and destiny, are central to understanding the history of breast cancer. But the fear of breast cancer had as much to do with the cure as with the disease. For several centuries now, the treatment of choice has been the mastectomy—amputation of the breast. In a society which has idealized the breast as the primary symbol of beauty and eroticism, many women view the cure as worse than the disease. In the following original essay, historian James S. Olson describes an early nineteenth century case of breast cancer.

It was just a tiny dimple. On a man's chin it would have looked rugged and distinguished. On a woman's cheek it might have been called a "beauty mark." But this was a different dimple, a killer dimple. It was on her left breast and "Nabby" Smith wondered what it was. She had never noticed it before, nor had her husband William. Perhaps it was just another physical sign of age, they thought, an indicator that she was not a young woman anymore. It was a sign, to be sure, but not of old age. The dimple was as much a symbol of premature death as a skull and crossbones, and within a few years, it would turn Nabby into a virtual skeleton before killing her in a pain-wracked stupor. Actually the dimple itself was not really the problem. Beneath the dimple, buried an inch below the skin, a small malignant tumor was attaching itself to surface tissues and drawing them in. like a sinking ship pulling water down its own whirlpool. It was 1808 and Nabby was forty-four years old. She had a husband and three children but she did not have much of a life left.

At first Nabby did not give it much thought, only noticing it now and when she bathed or dressed in the morning. Nor did she talk about it. Nabby Smith was a shy and somewhat withdrawn woman, quiet and cautious in the expression of ideas, more comfortable with people who guarded their feelings than with those who exposed them. She blushed easily and rarely laughed out loud, allowing only a demure, half-smile to crease her face when she was amused. She had a pleasant disposition and a mellow temperament, both of which endeared her to family and friends. Nabby was a beautiful woman. blessed with long, red hair, a round face, deep-blue eyes, and a creamy, porcelain complexion. She commanded respect, not because of an aggressive personality but simply because of the quality of her mind and a powerful sense of personal dignity.

At least some of that dignity came from her background. Nabby Smith was a member of one of the most distinguished families in the United States. She was born in Quincy, Massachusetts, in 1766. Her parents named her Abigail Adams. They began calling her "Nabby" when she was little. Nabby had an extraordinary childhood. Her father was John Adams, the future president of the United States, and her mother was Abigail Adams, the most prominent woman in early American society. Her little brother John Quincy was destined to become president of the United States. From the time of her birth, Nabby's parents were busily engaged in colonial politics, eventually playing leading roles in the American Revolution and the War for American Independence. They raised her on a steady diet of dinner table and parlor political talk—animated discussions of freedom, liberty, rights, despotism, war, and foreign policy. Nabby absorbed it all; political philosophy in her family was not a mere abstraction. Her position in the family was secure.

She was the apple of their eyes. As an only daughter, Nabby enjoyed the special attentions of her father, who felt the need to protect her and pamper her. Abigail had always doted upon her, dressing her up in the latest fashions when she was little and counseling her when she was an adolescent. When Nabby grew up their relationship quickly evolved into a deep friendship. In spite of the devoted attentions of her parents, Nabby took it all in stride, never becoming spoiled or self-indulgent. She was even-handed, thick-skinned, and not afraid of responsibility—the daughter every parent dreamed of having.

When the War for Independence ended in 1783, Nabby was just seventeen years old, but she was in for an adventure. Congress appointed her father to serve as the first United States minister to England, and in 1785 the family crossed the Atlantic and took up residence in a house on Grosvener Square in London. They were immediately caught up in the social and political life of the world's greatest city, meeting King George 111 at court and other prominent politicians and attending the whirlwind of parties, meetings, banquets, and festivals common to the life of an ambassador.

For the first few months in London, Nabby was somewhat depressed, mostly because of homesickness but also because she had left behind a boyfriend who soon quit writing letters. Her mood caught her parents offguard—it was uncharacteristic of her—and they tried to reassure her that soon she would be feeling better. They were right. Soon Nabby had noticed a young man who was part of the American diplomatic staff in London. Colonel William Smith, a young veteran of the Continental Army and secretary to the American legation in London, had also noticed Nabby.

Smith was a dashing and handsome figure, racing around London in a two-seated carriage, something equivalent to a sports car today. He dressed well— a weakness for silk coats and shirts—and kept company with a variety of people in London's expatriate community, especially with Latin American liberals and radicals interested in securing independence from Spain. He was bold and impetuous, inspired by courage and limited by poor judgement. Because of his work with the American legation in London, and his role as secretary to Minister John Adams, Smith saw a great deal of the Adams family, and Nabby fell secretly in love with him. It was not long before he felt the same way, drawn to Nabby's beauty, grace, and intelligence. He proposed late in 1785 and they were married in June 1786, after a courtship which John and Abigail Adams felt was too short. They excused it because "a soldier is always more expeditious in his courtships than other men."

But Colonel William Smith was a soldier without a war, a dinosaur at the age of twenty-eight, and Nabby was in for a difficult life, an innocent victim of what her brother John Quincy called "fortune's treacherous game." Colonel Smith was not cruel. In fact, he always loved and cared for Nabby, and they had three children. With a stoicism that would have made the most devout Puritan proud, Nabby was more than willing to accept her financial fate and make a life for her family wherever Smith settled. The problem was that Smith never really settled down. He wasted his life away, always searching but never finding a place for himself, winning and losing political appointments, dabbling in Latin American *coup d'etats* and revolutions, dragging Nabby and the kids back and forth between New York and London trying to influence a new power broker or close another deal. He spent far more money than he ever earned, and Nabby was forever worrying about the bills and their reputation. By the early 1800s, Smith was trying to make his fortune in shady real estate schemes, hoping to profit from the desire of so many Americans to move west and get their own land, but he lost everything he had. He was bold but not shrewd enough for the life of an entrepreneur. In 1808, when Nabby first noticed the dimple, they were living on the edge of the frontier, in a small farmhouse along the Chenango River in western New York, where he spent the days behind an iron plow and a mule working a small plot of land. The Smiths were a long way, economically and geographically, from the heady world of Boston and London politics.

During the next year the dimple became more pronounced and more worrisome to Nabby, but it was not until late in 1809 that she felt a hard lump beneath the skin. Nabby Adams was an intelligent, well-informed woman, and throughout her adult life the Adams family had been close friends with Dr. Benjamin Rush, the country's most prominent physician. Breast cancer was as much the dreaded disease in the early 1800s as it is today, something educated woman knew about and feared. Well-informed people had been aware of breast cancer for two thousand years, since Greek physicians first called it *karkinos* (carcinoma), or crab, because of its tenacious ability to hold on, to defy all attempts to cure it or cut it out. In fact, breast cancer in women was really the first cancer human beings ever identified, probably because it was more visible than other deadly tumors. And they knew breast cancer started with a hard lump. No records exist describing Nabby Smith's initial reaction to the lump in her breast, but it is safe to say that the intermittent, low-key concern about the dimple was instantly transformed into a chronic, persistent worry that would never quite go away.

Like so many women then and today, Nabby tried to ignore the lump, hoping that in the daily, busy routines of running a small farm and household she would not have time to think about it. But cancer has a way of asserting itself, finally obliterating even the most elaborate attempts at procrastination and denial. Nabby's cancer was no exception. The lump underwent an ominous growth, in spite of the efforts of local healers who prescribed a dizzying variety of external salves and potions. She wrote home to John and Abigail Adams in February 1811 that her doctor had discovered "a cancer in my breast." As soon as they received the letter, her parents began urging their daughter to come to Boston for medical advice. Some things do not change. Even today, people suffering from cancer often head to the major cities where comprehensive cancer centers can treat them.

In June 1811, with the lump now visible to the naked eye, a desperate Nabby returned to Massachusetts. As soon as she arrived in Quincy, Massachusetts, Nabby wrote to Benjamin Rush in Philadelphia, describing her condition and seeking his advice. When Abigail Adams first looked at her daughter's breast, she found the condition "allarming." The tumor was large enough to distend the breast into a misshapen mass. John and Abigail took Nabby to see several physicians in Boston—Drs. Holbrook and Welsh and Tufts and Johnson—and they were cautiously reassuring, telling her that the situation and her general health were "so good as not to threaten any present danger." They prescribed hemlock pills to "poison the disease."

Soon after that round of reassuring examinations, however, the Adams family received a more ominous reply from Dr. Benjamin Rush. In her initial letter, Nabby told the famous physician that the tumor was large and growing, but that it was "movable"—not attached to the chest wall. Rush found the news encouraging, as do most cancer specialists today. Malignant tumors which are "movable" are better candidates for surgery, since it is more likely that the surgeon can get what is termed a "clean margin"—a border of non-cancerous tissue surrounding the tumor—reducing the chances that the cancer will recur or spread.

Knowing that Nabby had already travelled from western New York to Boston to seek more medical advice and to be cared for by her parents, Rush wrote a letter to John and Abigail Adams, telling them to gently break his news to Nabby. Dr. Rush wrote:

> I shall begin my letter by replying to your daughter's. I prefer giving my opinion and advice in her case in this way. You and Mrs. Adams may communicate it gradually and in such a manner as will be least apt to distress and alarm her.
>
> After the experience of more than 50 years in cases similar to hers, I must protest against all local applications and internal medicines for relief. They now and then cure, but in 19 cases out of 20 in tumors in the breast they do harm or suspend the disease until it passes beyond that time in which the only radical remedy is ineffectual. This remedy is the knife. From her account of the moving state of the tumor, it is now in a proper situation for the operation. Should she wait till it suppurates or even inflames much, it may be too late... I repeat again, let there be no delay in flying to the knife. Her time of life calls for expedition in this business... I sincerely sympathize with her and with you and your dear Mrs. Adams in this family affliction, but it will be but for a few minutes if she submit to have it extirpated, and if not, it will probably be a source of distress and pain to you all for years to come. It shocks me to think of the consequences of procrastination in her case.

Benjamin Rush knew that there were no home remedies or folk cures for breast cancer; Nabby Adams needed surgery—a mastectomy—and she needed it immediately.

Rush wrote to John and Abigail Adams, rather than replying directly to Nabby's inquiry, because he wanted them to break the news to her gently, to help her in overcoming the initial terror she was going to feel about going "under the knife." Surgery in the early nineteenth century was a brutal affair. Cutting instruments were crude and there was no such thing as anasthesia. Patients were wide awake during the operation, and they had to be belted down and restrained from moving or screaming. It was not at all uncommon for sick people to choose death rather than "the knife." And if they survived the surgery, they then faced the threat of massive infections. Nobody understood the principle of microscopic life, of germs which cause disease, or how careful, antiseptic procedures could prevent infections. Patients ran the risk of dying of massive infections within days of the operation. Surgery was always a last resort. But Benjamin Rush was convinced that Nabby's condition had reached the desperate point, and he wanted John and Abigail to talk her into it, to let her know that "the pain of the operation is much less than her fears represent it to be." Amputation of the diseased breast was her only chance.

They first had to convince their son-in-law. Fear of the "dread disease" had pushed William Smith into an advanced state of denial. When he learned of Rush's recommendation, he reacted indignantly, heading for libraries to learn whatever he could about the disease and its prognosis, hoping against hope to spare Nabby the operation. He talked and talked, trying to convince himself that maybe the tumor would just go away, that Nabby could probably live with it, that it was not so bad. Abigail Adams's mother had more faith in Rush and wrote to Smith: "If the operation is necessary as the Dr. states it to be, and as I fear it is, the sooner it is done the better provided Mrs. Smith can bring herself along, as I hope she will consent to it." She even asked her son-in-law, if Nabby agreed to the surgery, to be with "Nabby through the painful tryal." Smith finally acquiesced to Rush's opinion and Abigail's persistence. Nabby was also convinced that surgery was her only chance. They scheduled the operation for October 8, 1811.

There was nothing new about amputating a cancerous breast. Some surgeons in Europe had been performing the operation for more than a century, and the surgery was well known among Boston physicians. In 1728 Dr. Zabdiel Boylston amputated the breast of Sarah Winslow to remove a malignant tumor. The patient survived the surgery and lived another thirty-nine years, dying in 1767 of old age, and local physicians were convinced that the operation had brought about the cure. Amputation was not, however, the treatment of choice for breast cancer in the late-1700s and early-1800s because the surgery itself was so harrowingly painful and the outcomes so problematic. Most patients undergoing surgery in the nineteenth century had to deal with the problem of massive, post-operative infections. Surgery was always a last resort.

Nabby and William Smith, along with their daughter Caroline, and Abigail Adams travelled from Quincy to Boston the day before the operation. Late in the afternoon, they met with John Warren, widely considered to be the city's most skilled surgeon. Warren gave Nabby a brief physical examination and told her what to expect. It was hardly reassuring. In fact, his description of the surgery, of what Nabby was about to go through, was nightmarishly terrifying, enough to make Nabby, William, Abigail, and Caroline rethink the decision. But Rush's warning—"It shocks me to think of the consequences of procrastination in her case"—reverberated through all of their minds. Nabby had no choice if she ever hoped to live to see her grandchildren.

The operation was as bad as they had feared. John Warren was assisted by his son Joseph, who was destined to become a leading physician in his own right, and several other doctors who had examined Nabby back in July. Warren's surgical instruments, laying in a wooden box on a table, were quite simple. One was a large fork with two, six-inch prongs sharpened to a needle point. He also had a wooden-handled razor. A pile of compress bandages was in the box as well. In the corner of the room there was a small oven, full of red-hot coals, into which a flat, thick, heavy iron spatula bad been inserted.

Nabby came into the room dressed for a Sunday service. She was a proper woman from the best family, and she felt obligated to act the part. The doctors were in professional attire—frock coats, with shirts and ties. Modesty demanded that Nabby unbutton only the top of her dress and slip it off her left shoulder, exposing the diseased breast but little else. She remained fully clothed. Since they knew nothing of bacteria in the early 1800s, there were no gloves or surgical masks, no need for Warren to scrub his hands or wash Nabby's chest before the operation or cover his own hair and beard. Warren had her sit down and lean back in a reclining chair. He belted her waist, legs, feet, and right arm to the chair and had her raise her left arm above her head so that the pectoralis major muscle would push the breast up. One of the physicians took Nabby's raised arm by the elbow and held it, while another stood behind her, pressing her shoulders and neck to the chair. Warren told Nabby to shut her eyes, grit her teeth, and get ready. Abigail, Caroline, and William stood off to the side to witness the ordeal.

Warren then straddled Nabby's knees, leaned over her semi-reclined body, and began his work. Like a father carving a Thanksgiving turkey, he took the two-pronged fork and thrust it deep into Nabby's breast. With his left hand, he held onto the fork and raised up on it, lifting the breast from the chest wall. He reached over for the large razor and started slicing into the base of the breast, moving from the middle of her chest toward her left side. When the breast was completely severed, Warren lifted it away from Nabby's chest with the fork. But the tumor was larger and more widespread then he had anticipated. Breast cancer often spreads to regional lymph nodes, and Warren discovered that Nabby already had visible tumor tissue in the nodes of her axilla—under her left armpit. He took the razor in there as well and with his fingers pulled out nodes and tumor.

There was a real premium on speed in early nineteenth surgery. No wonder. Nabby was grimacing and groaning, flinching and twisting in the chair, with blood staining her dress and Warren's shirt and pants. Her hair was soon matted in sweat. Abigail, William, and Caroline had to turn their faces and eyes away from the gruesome struggle. With the patient writhing in pain and her family eyewitnessing the spectacle, Warren wanted to get the job done as quickly as possible. To stop the bleeding, he pulled the red-hot spatula from the oven and applied it several times directly to the wound, cauterizing the worst bleeding points. With each touch, steamy wisps of smoke hissed into the air and filled the room with the distinct smell of burning flesh. Warren then sutured the wounds together, bandaged them, stepped back from Nabby, and mercifully told her that it was over. The whole procedure had taken less than twenty-five minutes. Abigail and Caroline quickly went to the surgical chair and helped Nabby pull her dress back over her left shoulder. Modesty demanded it. William helped her out of the chair and they all walked outside to the carnage. The two-hour ride to Quincy proved to be agony of its own for Nabby, with each bump in the road sending spasms of pain throughout her body.

Nabby had a long recovery from the surgery. Miraculously, she did not suffer from any serious post-surgical infections, but for months after the operation she was weak and feeble, barely able to get around. She could not use her left arm at all, and left it in a sling. Going back to the wilds of western New York was out of the question, so she stayed in Quincy with her mother, hoping to regain the strength she needed to return home. What sustained all of them during the ordeal of Nabby's recovery was the faith that the operation had cured the cancer. Within two weeks of the surgery, Dr. Benjamin Rush wrote John Adams congratulating him "in the happy issue of the operation performed upon Mrs. Smith's breast... her cure will be radical and durable. I consider her as rescued from a premature grave." Abigail wrote to a friend that although the operation had been a "furnace of affliction... what a blessing it was to have extirpated so terrible an enemy." In May 1812, seven months after the surgery, Nabby Adams felt well again. She returned home to the small farm along the Chenango River in western New York.

But Nabby Adams was not cured. Even today, breast cancer victims whose tumors have already spread to the lymph node do not have very good survival rates, even with modern surgery, radiation treatments, and chemotherapy. In Nabby's case, long before Dr. Warren performed the mastectomy, the cancer had already spread throughout her body. She was going to die, no matter what, and the horrific surgery in 1811 had served no purpose. Nabby suspected something was wrong within a few weeks of arriving home in New York. She began to complain of headaches and severe pain in her spine and abdomen. A local physician attributed the discomfort to rheumatism. The diagnosis relieved some of Nabby's anxiety, since she was already worried that the pain had something to do with cancer. Cancer patients grasp at straws, hoping against hope that there is an alternative explanation for their distress, something simple and common, like a cold or the flu or rheumatism, anything but a recurrence of the dread disease.

For Nabby Adams, however, it was not the flu or "the rhemuatism." The cancer was back. That became quite clear in 1813 when she suffered a local recurrence of the tumors. When Warren amputated her breast and excised tissues from her axilla, he thought he had "gotten it all," removing the visible tumor tissue. But cancer is a cellular disease, and millions of invisible, microscopically tiny-malignant cancers were left behind. Some of them had grown into tumors of their own by the spring of 1813—visible tumors below the scar where Nabby's breast had once been and on the skin as well. Nabby's doctor in New York then changed his diagnosis: her headaches and now excruciating body pains were not rheumatism. The cancer was back and had spread throughout her body. Nabby Adams was terminal. She was going to die in a matter of months.

Nabby declined steadily in the late spring, finally telling her husband that she "wanted to die in her father's house." William Smith wrote John and Abigail Adams in May that the cancer had returned and that Nabby wanted "to spend her state of convalescence within the vortex of your kindness and assiduities than elsewhere." The colonel was back into denial, refusing to voice the certainty that his wife was going to die. Since the country was in the midst of the War of 1812, Smith told his in-laws, he had to go to Washington, D.C. to obtain a military appointment, and that he would return to Quincy, Massachusetts, as soon as the congressional session was over. John and Abigail prepared Nabby's room and waited for her arrival.

The trip was unimaginably painful—more than 300 miles in a carriage, over bumpy roads where each jolt meant stabbing pain. Her son John drove the carriage. When Nabby finally reached Quincy on July 26, she was suffering from grinding, constant, multiple-site pain. John and Abigail were shocked when they saw her. She was gaunt and thin, wracked by a deep cough, and her eyes had a moist, rheumy look to them. She groaned and sometimes screamed every time she moved. Huge, dark circles shadowed her cheeks, and a few minutes after she settled into bed, the smell of death was in the air. Cancer cells not only divide rapidly, they also die rapidly, and when a patient has a body full of tumors, the body is also full of an increasing volume of dead, necrotic tissue. Those tissues are rancid and rotten, full of bacteria, and they give off a foul odor. Scientists today call the condition "cachexia"—the body seems to be feeding on itself—but in the early 1800s it was known as "the odor of death."

Nabby's pain was so unbearable, and her misery so unmitigated, that Abigail went into a depression of her own, a depression so deep she could not stand even to visit her daughter's room. It was her husband John Adams, the second president of the United States, who ministered to his dying daughter, feeding her, cleaning her and seeing to her personal needs, combing her hair and holding her hand. He tried to administer several recommended pain killers, but nothing seemed to help, not until she lapsed into a pain-numbing coma. Her husband returned from Washington, D.C., and the deathwatch began. On the morning of August 9, Nabby's breathing became more shallow and the passage of time between breaths more extended. The family gathered around her bedside. She took her last breath early in the afternoon. A few days later, in a letter to Thomas Jefferson, John Adams wrote: "Your Friend, my only Daughter, expired, Yesterday Morning in the Arms of Her Husband, her Son, her Daughter, her Father and Mother, her Husbands two Sisters and two of her Nieces, in the 49th. Year of Age, 46 of which She was the healthiest and firmest of Us all: Since which, She has been a monument to Suffering and to Patience."

Except for a chosen few victims, breast cancer was a death sentence in the early nineteenth century, and the surgical treatment for it was almost as bad as the disease. From the moment she first noticed the lump, Nabby was doomed. During the rest of the century, physicians learned about anesthesia, which dramatically eased the trauma of surgery. They also learned about bacteria and started washing their hands before putting the scalpel to a patient's breast. They discovered that all tissue was composed of tiny cells, and that cancer was a disease process involving those cells. Around 1900, when surgeons developed the radical mastectomy—a new surgical procedure for removing a cancerous breast—patient survival rates increased. Seventy-five years after Nabby Adams died of breast cancer, women with the disease had a better chance of survival.

But even today, nearly 170 years after Nabby's death, breast cancer remains a frighteningly unpredictable disease. More limited surgical procedures, radiation therapy, and chemotherapy provide new treatments, but nearly 50,000 American women die of breast cancer every year. According to statistics released in 1993, one out of eight American women—a total of nearly 17 million people—will develop breast cancer during their lifetime. And according to existing survival rates, approximately forty percent of them will die from it. The only real answer is early detection, hopefully from a mammogram examination when the cancer is tiny and curable. Nabby Adams did not have that option. We do.

12. Hope and Heritage:
Myth and Thomas Jefferson

Gordon S. Wood

Americans seem to have forgotten nothing about Thomas Jefferson, except that he was once a living, breathing human being. Throughout our history, Jefferson has served as a symbol of what we as a people are, someone invented, manipulated, turned into something we like or dislike within ourselves—whether it is populism or elitism, agrarianism or racism, atheism or liberalism. We continually ask ourselves whether Jefferson still survives, or what still lives in his thought, and we quote him on nearly every side of every major question in our history. No figure in our past has embodied so much of our heritage and so many of our hopes.

In his superb *The Jefferson Image in the American Mind* (1960), Merrill Peterson showed that American culture has always used Jefferson as "a sensitive reflector . . . of America's troubled search for the image of itself." The symbolizing, the image mongering, and the identifying of Jefferson with America has not changed a bit since Peterson's book was published, even though the level of professional historical scholarship has never been higher. If anything the association of Jefferson with America has become more complete. During the past three turbulent decades many people, including some historians, have concluded that something is seriously wrong with America and, therefore, that something has to be wrong with Jefferson.

The opening blast in this criticism of Jefferson was probably Leonard Levy's *Jefferson and Civil Liberties: The Darker Side* (1963). No subtle satire, no gentle mocking of the ironies of Jefferson's inconsistencies and hypocrisies, Levy's book was a prosecutor's indictment. Levy ripped off Jefferson's mantle of libertarianism to expose his "darker side": his passion for partisan persecution, his lack of concern for basic civil liberties, and a self-righteousness that became at times out-and-out ruthlessness. Far from being the skeptical enlightened intellectual, allowing all ideas their free play, Jefferson was portrayed by Levy and others as something of an ideologue, eager to fill the young with his political orthodoxy while censoring all those books he did not like.

Not only did Jefferson lack an original or skeptical mind; he could in fact be downright doctrinaire, an early version of a "knee-jerk liberal." In this respect he was very different from his more skeptical and inquisitive friend James Madison. Jefferson, for example, could understand the opening struggles of the French Revolution only in terms of a traditional liberal antagonism to an arrogant and overgrown monarchy. He supported the addition of a bill of rights to the federal

Constitution not because he had thought through the issue the way Madison had but largely because he believed that a bill of rights was what good governments were supposed to have. All of his liberal aristocratic French friends said so; indeed, as he told his fellow Americans, "the enlightened part of Europe have given us the greatest credit for inventing this instrument of security for the rights of the people, and have been not a little surprised to see us so soon give it up." One almost has the feeling that Jefferson advocated a bill of rights in 1787–88 out of concern for what his liberal French associates would think. One sometimes has the same feeling about his antislavery statements, many of which seem to have been shaped to the expectations of enlightened foreigners.

It is in fact his views on black Americans and slavery that have made Jefferson most vulnerable to modern censure. If America has turned out to be wrong in its race relations, then Jefferson had to be wrong too. Samuel Johnson with his quip, "How is it that we hear the loudest yelps for liberty from the drivers of Negroes?" had nothing on modern critics. Who could not find the contrast between Jefferson's great declarations of liberty and equality and his life-long ownership of slaves glaringly inconsistent? Jefferson undoubtedly hated slavery and believed that the self-evident truths that he had set forth in 1776 ought eventually to doom the institution in the United States. Early in his career he tried unsuccessfully to facilitate the manumission of slaves in Virginia, and in the 1780s he worked hard to have slavery abolished in the new western territories. But unlike George Washington, he was never able to free all of his slaves. More than that, as recent historians have emphasized, he bought, bred, and flogged his slaves, and he hunted down fugitives in much the same way his fellow Virginia planters did—all the while declaring that American slavery was not as bad as that of the ancient Romans.

Some recent historians even claim that Jefferson's attitudes and actions toward blacks were so repugnant that identifying the Sage of Monticello with antislavery discredits the reform movement. Jefferson could never truly imagine freed blacks living in a white man's America, and throughout his life he insisted that the emancipation of the slaves be accompanied by their expulsion from the country. He wanted all blacks sent to the West Indies, or Africa, or anywhere out of the United States. In the end, it has been said, Jefferson loaded such conditions on the abolition of slavery that the antislavery movement could scarcely get off the ground. In response to the pleas of younger men that he speak out against slavery, he offered only excuses for delay.

His remedy of expulsion was based on racial fear and antipathy. While he had no apprehensions about mingling white blood with that of the Indian, he never ceased expressing his "great aversion" to miscegenation between blacks and whites. When the Roman slave was freed, Jefferson wrote, he "might mix with, without staining the blood of his master." When the black slave was freed, however, he had "to be removed beyond the reach of mixture." Although Jefferson believed that the Indians were uncivilized, he always admired them and made all sorts of environmental explanations for their differences from whites. Yet he was never able to do the same for the African American. Instead, he lastingly clung to the view that blacks were inherently inferior to whites in both body and mind.

It has even been suggested that Jefferson's obsession (shared by so many other Americans) with black sensuality was largely a projection of his own repressed—and, perhaps in the case of his attractive mulatto slave Sally Hemings, not so repressed—libidinal desires. The charge that Jefferson maintained Hemings as his mistress for decades and fathered several children by her was first made by an unscrupulous newspaperman, James Callender, in 1802. Since then, historians and others have periodically resurrected the accusation. In fact, in the most recent study of Jefferson's political thought, political scientist Garrett Ward Sheldon treats Jefferson's "keeping of a black mistress" as an established fact, a "common transgression of his class."

In her 1974 psychobiography of Jefferson the late Fawn Brodie made the most ingenious and notorious use of Callender's accusation, building up her case for the passionate liaison between Jefferson and his mullato slave largely through contrived readings of evidence and even the absence of evidence. In accord with our modern soap-opera sensibilities, Brodie naturally turned the relationship into a secret love affair. Brodie's suggestion of a love match aroused a great deal of controversy, perhaps because so many people believed it or at least were titillated by it. A novel based on Brodie's concoctions was written, and there was even talk of a TV movie.

These may seem like small and silly matters, but they are not—not where Jefferson is involved—for the nature of American society itself is at stake. The relationship with Sally Hemings may be implausible to those who know Jefferson's character intimately. He was, after all, a man who never indulged his passions but always suppressed them. But whether he had a relationship with Hemings, there is no denying that Jefferson presided over a household in which miscegenation took place, a miscegenation that he believed was morally repugnant. Thus any attempt to make Jefferson's Monticello a model patriarchal plantation is compromised at the outset.

Everyone, it seems, sees America in Jefferson. When Garry Wills in his *Inventing America* (1978) argued that Jefferson's Declaration of Independence owed less to the individualism of John Locke and more to the communitarian sentiments of the Scottish moralist Francis Hutcheson, one critic accused Wills of aiming "to supply the history of the Republic with as pink a dawn as possible." So too the shame and guilt that Jefferson must have suffered from his involvement in slavery and racial mixing best represents the shame and guilt that white Americans feel in their tortured relations with blacks. Where Jefferson for Vernon Louis Parrington and his generation of the 1920s, '30s, and '40s had been the solution, Jefferson for this present generation has become the problem. The Jefferson that emerges out of much recent scholarship therefore resembles the America that many critics have visualized in the past three decades—self-righteous, guilt-ridden, racist, doctrinaire, and filled with liberal pieties that under stress are easily sacrificed.

Quite clearly, no historical figure can bear this kind of symbolic burden and still remain a real person. Beneath all the images, beneath all the allegorical Jeffersons, there once was a human being with very human frailties and foibles. Certainly Jefferson's words and ideas transcended his time, but he himself did not.

The human Jefferson was essentially a man of the eighteenth century, a very intelligent and bookish slaveholding southern planter, enlightened and progressive no doubt, but like all human beings possessing as many weaknesses as strengths, inclined as much to folly as to wisdom. Like most people caught up in fast-moving events and complicated changing circumstances, the human Jefferson was as much a victim as he was a protagonist of those events and circumstances. Despite all his achievements in the Revolution and in the subsequent decades, he was never in control of the popular forces he ostensibly led; indeed, he never even fully comprehended these forces. It is the ultimate irony of Jefferson's life, in a life filled with ironies, that he should not have understood the democratic revolution that he himself supremely spoke for.

It is true that much of Jefferson's thinking was conventional, although, as historian William Freehling points out, he did have "an extraordinary gift of lending grace to conventionalities." He had to be conventional or he could never have had the impact he had on his contemporaries. His writing of the Declaration of Independence, he later correctly recalled, was "not to find out new principles, or new arguments, never before thought of . . . ; but to place before mankind the common sense of the subject, in terms so plain and firm as to command their assent, and to justify ourselves in the independent stand we are compelled to take."

Jefferson's extraordinary impressionability, learning, and virtuosity were the source of his conventionality. He was very well-read and extremely sensitive to the avant-garde intellectual currents of his day. And he was eager to discover just what was the best, most politically correct, and most enlightened in the world of the eighteenth century. It was his insatiable hunger for knowledge and his remarkable receptivity to all that was new and progressive that put him at the head of the American Enlightenment.

The eighteenth century Enlightenment represented the pushing back of the boundaries of darkness and what was called Gothic barbarism and the spreading of light and knowledge. This struggle occurred on many fronts. Some saw the central battle taking place in natural science and in the increasing understanding of nature. Some saw it occurring mostly in religion, with the tempering of enthusiasm and the elimination of superstition. Others saw it happening mainly in politics—in driving back the forces of tyranny and in the creating of new free governments. Still others saw it in the spread of civility and refinement and in the increase in the small, seemingly insignificant ways that life was being made easier, politer, more comfortable, more enjoyable for more and more people. In one way or another, the Enlightenment activities involved the imposition of order and reason on the world. To contemplate aesthetically an ordered universe and to know the best that was thought and said in the world—that was enlightenment.

Jefferson participated fully in all aspects of the eighteenth century Enlightenment. He was probably the American Revolutionary leader most taken with the age's liberal prescriptions for enlightenment, gentility, and refinement. He was born in 1743 the son of a wealthy but uneducated and ungenteel planter from western Virginia. He attended the College of William and Mary, the first of his father's family to attend college. Like many of the Revolutionary leaders who were also the first of their family to acquire a liberal arts education in college, he wanted a society led by an aristocracy of talent and taste. For too long men had been judged by who their fathers were or whom they had married. In a new enlightened republican society they would be judged by merit and virtue and taste alone.

Jefferson was not one to let his feelings show, but even today we can sense beneath the placid surface of his autobiography, written in 1821 at the age of seventy-seven, some of his anger at all those Virginians who prided themselves on their genealogy and judged men by their family background.

In its opening pages Jefferson tells us that the lineage of his Welsh father was lost in obscurity: He was able to find in Wales only two references to his father's family. His mother, on the other hand, was a Randolph, one of the distinguished families of Virginia. The Randolphs, he said with about as much derision as he ever allowed himself, "trace their pedigree far back in England and Scotland, to which let everyone ascribe the faith and merit he chooses." He went on to describe his efforts in 1776 in Virginia to bring down that "distinct set of families" who had used several legal devices to confine the inheritance of property both to the eldest son (primogeniture) and to special lines of heirs (entail) so as to form themselves "into a Patrician order, distinguished by the splendor and luxury of their establishments." Historians have often thought Jefferson exaggerated the power of primogeniture and entail and this "Patrician order." Not only was the setting aside of entails very common in Virginia; the "Patrician order" seemed not all that different from its challengers. But Jefferson clearly saw a difference, and it rankled him. The privileges of this "aristocracy of wealth," he wrote, needed to be destroyed "to make an opening for the aristocracy of virtue and talent"—of which he considered himself a prime example.

To become a natural aristocrat, one had to acquire the attributes of a natural aristocrat—enlightenment, gentility, and taste. We will never understand the young Jefferson until we appreciate the intensity and earnestness of his desire to become the most cosmopolitan, the most liberal, the most genteel, and the most enlightened gentleman in all of America. From the outset he was the sensitive provincial quick to condemn the backwardness of his fellow colonials. At college and later in studying law at Williamsburg he played the violin, learned French, and acquired the tastes and refinements of the larger world. At frequent dinners with Governor Francis Fauquier and his teachers, William Small and George Wythe, Jefferson said he "heard more good sense, more rational and philosophical conversations than in all my life besides." Looking back, he called Williamsburg "the finest school of manners and morals that ever existed in America." Although as a young man he had seen very few works of art, he knew from reading and conversation what was considered good; and in 1771 he wrote a list, ranging from the Apollo Belvedere to a Raphael cartoon, of those celebrated paintings, drawings, and sculptures that he hoped to acquire in copies. By 1782, "without having left his own country," this earnest autodidact with a voracious appetite for learning had become, as the French visitor Chevalier de Chastellux noted, "an American who . . . is at once a musician, a draftsman, an astronomer, a geometer, a physicist, a jurist and a statesman."

In time Jefferson became quite proud of his gentility, his taste, and his liberal brand of manners. In fact, he came to see himself as a kind of impresario for America rescuing his countrymen from their "deplorable barbarism" by introducing them to the finest and most enlightened aspects of European culture. When Americans in the 1780s realized that a statue of Washington was needed, "there could be no question raised," he wrote from Paris, "as to the Sculptor who should be employed, the reputation of Monsr. Houdon of this city being unrivalled in Europe." No American could stand up to his knowledge. When Washington timidly expressed misgivings about Houdon's doing the statue in Roman style, he quickly backed down in the face of Jefferson's frown, unwilling, as he said, "to oppose my judgment to the taste of Connoisseurs."

Jefferson's excitement over the sixteenth century Italian, Andrea Palladio, whose *Four Books of Architecture* was virtually unknown in America, was the excitement of the provincial discovering the cosmopolitan taste of the larger world. He became ashamed of the "gothic" Georgian architecture of his native Virginia, and he sought in Monticello to build a house that would do justice to those models that harked back to Roman antiquity. In the 1780s he badgered his Virginia colleagues into erecting as the new state capitol in Richmond a magnificent copy of the Maison Carrée, a Roman temple from the first century A.D. at Nimes, because he wanted an American public building that would be a model for the people's "study and imitation" and "an object and proof of national good taste." Almost singlehandedly he became responsible for making America's public buildings resemble Roman temples.

No American knew more about wine than Jefferson. During his trips around Europe in 1787–88 he spent a great deal of time investigating French, Italian, and German vineyards and wineries and making arrangements for the delivery of wine to the United States. Everyone in America acknowledged his expertise in wine, and three presidents sought his advice about what wine to serve at presidential dinners. In everything—from gardening and food to music, painting, and poetry—Jefferson wanted the latest and most enlightened in European fashion.

It is easy to make fun of Jefferson and his parvenu behavior. But it would be a mistake to dismiss Jefferson's obsession with art and good taste merely as a trivial affectation, or as the simple posturing and putting on of airs of an American provincial who would be the perfect gentleman. Jefferson might have been more enthusiastic about such matters than the other Revolutionary leaders, but he was by no means unique in his concern for refining his own sensibilities as well as those of other American citizens. This was a moral and political imperative of all of the Founding Fathers. To refine popular taste was in fact a moral and political imperative of all the enlightened of the eighteenth century.

The fine arts, good taste, and even good manners had political implications. As the English philosopher Lord Shaftesbury had preached, morality and good taste were allied: "The science of virtuosi and that of virtue itself become, in a manner, one and the same." Connoisseurship, politeness, and genteel refinement were connected with public morality and political leadership. Those who had good taste were enlightened, and those who were enlightened were virtuous.

But note: *virtuous in a modern, not an ancient, manner*. Politeness and refinement tamed and domesticated the severe classical conception of virtue. Promoting social affection was in fact the object of the civilizing process. This new social virtue was less Spartan and more Addisonian, less the harsh self-sacrifice of antiquity and more the willingness to get along with others for the sake of peace and prosperity. Virtue in the modern manner became identified with politeness, good taste, and one's instinctive sense of morality. As the eighteenth century Scottish philosopher Lord Kames said, "a taste in the fine arts goes hand in hand with the moral sense, to which indeed it is nearly allied."

Indeed, there was hardly an educated person in all of eighteenth century America who did not at one time or another try to describe people's moral sense and the natural forces of love and benevolence holding society together. Jefferson's emphasis on the moral sense was scarcely peculiar to him.

This modern virtue that Jefferson and others extolled was very different from that of the ancient republican tradition. Classical virtue had flowed from the citizen's participation in politics; government had been the source of his civic consciousness and public spiritedness. But modern virtue flowed from the citizen's participation in society, not in government, which the liberal-minded increasingly saw as the source of the evils of the world. "Society," said Thomas Paine in a brilliant summary of this common enlightened separation, "is produced by our wants and government by our wickedness; the former promotes our happiness positively by uniting our affections, the latter negatively by restraining our vices. The one encourages intercourse, the other creates distinctions." It was society— the affairs of private social life—that bred sympathy and the new domesticated virtue. Mingling in drawing rooms, clubs, and coffeehouses—partaking of the innumerable interchanges of the daily comings and goings of modern life—created affection and fellow-feeling, which were all the adhesives really necessary to hold an enlightened people together. Some of Jefferson's contemporaries even argued that commerce, that traditional enemy of classical virtue, was in fact a source of modern virtue. Because it encouraged intercourse and confidence among people and nations, commerce, it was said, actually contributed to benevolence and fellow-feeling.

Jefferson could not have agreed more with this celebration of society over government. Indeed, Paine's conventional liberal division between society and government was the premise of Jefferson's political thinking—his faith in the natural ordering of society, his belief in the common moral sense of ordinary people, his idea of minimal government. "Man," said Jefferson, "was destined for society. His morality, therefore, was to be formed to this object. He was endowed with a sense of right and wrong, merely relative to this . . . The moral sense, or conscience, is as much a part of a man as his leg or arm . . . ." All human beings had "implanted in our breasts" this "love of others," this "moral instinct"; these "social dispositions" were what made democracy possible.

The importance of this domesticated modern virtue to the thinking of Jefferson and of other Americans can scarcely be exaggerated. It laid the basis for all reform movements of the nineteenth century and for all subsequent liberal thinking. We still yearn for a world in which everyone will love one another.

Probably no American leader took this belief in the natural sociability of people more seriously than Jefferson. His scissors-and-paste redoing of the New Testament in the early years of the nineteenth century stemmed from his desire to reconcile Christianity with the Enlightenment and at the same time to answer all of those critics who said that he was an enemy of all religion. Jefferson discovered that Jesus, with his prescription for each of us to love our neighbors as ourselves, actually spoke directly to the modern enlightened age. Jefferson's version of the New Testament offered a much-needed morality of social harmony for a new republican society.

Jefferson's faith in the natural sociability of people also lay behind his belief in minimal government. In fact, Jefferson would have fully understood the Western world's present interest in devolution and localist democracy. He believed in nationhood but not the modern idea of the state. He hated all bureaucracy and all the coercive instruments of government, and he sometimes gave the impression that government was only a device by which the few attempted to rob, cheat, and oppress the many. He certainly never accepted the modern idea of the state as an entity possessing a life of its own, distinct from both rulers and ruled. For Jefferson there could be no power independent of the people, in whom he had an absolute faith.

Although he was not a modern democrat, assuming as he did that a natural aristocracy would lead the country, he had a confidence in the capacity and the virtue of the people to elect that aristocracy that was unmatched by any other of the Founding Fathers. Jefferson like the other Founding Fathers had doubts about all officials in government, even the popularly elected representatives in the lower houses of the legislatures ("173 despots would surely be as oppressive as one"); but he always thought that the people, if undisturbed by demagogues or Federalist monarchists, would eventually set matters right. It was never the people but only their elected agents that were at fault.

Not only did Jefferson refuse to recognize the structure and institutions of a modern state; he scarcely accepted the basic premise of a state, namely, its presumed monopoly of legitimate control over a prescribed territory. For him during his first presidential administration (1801–1804) the United States was really just a loosely bound confederation, not all that different from the government of the former Articles of Confederation. Hence his vision of an expanding empire of liberty over a huge continent posed no problems for his relaxed idea of a state. As long as Americans continued to believe certain things, they remained Americans. Jefferson could be remarkably indifferent to the possibility that a western confederacy might break away from the eastern United States. What did it matter? he asked in 1804. "Those of the western confederacy will be as much our children and descendants as those of the eastern."

It was Jefferson's extraordinary faith in the natural sociability of people as a substitute for the traditional force of government that made the Federalists and especially Alexander Hamilton dismiss him as a hopeless pie-in-the-sky dreamer. The idea that, "as human nature shall refine and ameliorate by the operation of a more enlightened plan," government eventually "will become useless, and Society will subsist and flourish free from its shackles" was, said Hamilton in 1794, a "wild and fatal . . . scheme," even if its "votaries" like Jefferson did not always push such a scheme to the fullest.

Jefferson and other Revolutionary leaders believed that commerce among nations in international affairs was the equivalent to affection among people in domestic affairs. Both were natural expressions of relationships that needed to be freed of monarchical obstructions and interventions. Hence in 1776 and in the years following, Jefferson and other Revolutionary idealists hoped to do for the world what they were doing for the society of the United States—change the way people related to one another. They looked forward to a rational world in which corrupt monarchical diplomacy and secret alliances, balances of power, and dynastic rivalries would be replaced by the natural ties of commerce. If the people of the various nations were left alone to exchange goods freely among themselves, then international politics would become republicanized and pacified, and war itself would be eliminated. Jefferson's and the Republican party's "candid and liberal" experiments in "peaceful coercion"—the various efforts of the United States to use nonimportation and ultimately Jefferson's disastrous Embargo of 1807–09 to change international behavior—were the inevitable consequences of this sort of idealistic republican confidence in the power of commerce.

Conventional as Jefferson's thinking might often have been, it was usually an enlightened conventional radicalism that he espoused. So eager was he to possess the latest and most liberal of eighteenth century ideas that he could easily get carried away. He, like "others of great genius," had "a habit," as Madison gently put it in 1823, "of expressing in strong and round terms impressions of the moment." So he alone of the Founding Fathers was unperturbed by Shays's rebellion in 1786–1787. "I like a little rebellion now and then," he said. "It is like a storm in the Atmosphere." It was too bad that some people were killed, but "the tree of liberty must be refreshed from time to time with the blood of patriots and tyrants. It is its natural manure." Similar rhetorical exaggeration accompanied his response to the bloody excesses of the French Revolution. Because "the liberty of the whole earth" depended on the success of the French Revolution, he wrote in 1793, lives would have to be lost. "Rather than it should have failed, I would have seen half the earth desolated. Were there but an Adam and an Eve left in every country, and left free, it would be better than as it now is." Unlike Coleridge and Wordsworth and other disillusioned European liberals, Jefferson remained a champion of the French Revolution to the end.

He saw it, after all, as a movement on behalf of the rights of man that had originated in the American Revolution. And to the American Revolution and the rights of man he remained dedicated until his death. In the last letter he wrote he described the American Revolution as "the signal of arousing men to burst the chains under which monkish ignorance and superstitution had persuaded them to bind themselves, and to assume the blessings and security of self-government."

Yet during Jefferson's final years in retirement these expressions of confidence in the future progress of the Enlightenment came fewer and farther between. The period between Jefferson's retirement from the presidency in 1809 and his death in 1826 was a tumultuous one in American history—marked by war with the British and Indians, a severe commercial panic, the rapid growth of democracy and evangelical religion, and the Missouri crisis over the spread of slavery. It was also not a happy time for Jefferson. To be sure, there was the Sage of Monticello relaxing among his family and friends and holding court on top of his mountain for scores of visiting admirers. There was his reconciliation with John Adams and the wonderful correspondence between the two old revolutionaries that followed. And there was his hard-fought establishment of the University of Virginia. But there was not much else to comfort him.

The world around him, the world he helped to create, was rapidly changing, and changing in ways that Jefferson found bewildering and sometimes even terrifying. The American Revolution was unfolding with radical and unexpected developments. American society was becoming more democratic and more capitalistic, and Jefferson was not prepared for either development. By the end of his life Jefferson had moments of apprehension that the American Revolution, to which he had devoted his life, was actually in danger of failing. In response his speech and action often did not accord with what we now like to think of as Jeffersonian principles. He turned inward and began spouting dogmas in a manner that many subsequent historians and biographers have found embarrassing and puzzling.

After Jefferson retired from public life in 1809, he became more narrow-minded and localist than he had ever been in his life. He had always prided himself on his cosmopolitanism, yet upon his retirement from the presidency he returned to Virginia and never left it. In fact, he virtually never again lost sight of his beloved Blue Ridge. He cut himself off from many of the current sources of knowledge of the outside world, and became, as one of his visitors George Ticknor noted, "singularly ignorant and insensible on the subjects of passing politics." He took only one newspaper, the Richmond *Enquirer*, and seemed to have no strong interest in receiving his mail. In all this he differed remarkably from his friend and neighbor James Madison. Madison, said Ticknor, "receives multitudes of newspapers, keeps a servant always in waiting for the arrival of the Post—and takes anxious note of all passing events."

Jefferson's turn inward was matched by a relative decline in the place of Virginia in the union. Decay was everywhere in early nineteenth century Virginia, and Jefferson felt it at Monticello. Despite his life-long aversion to public debts, his private debts kept mounting, and he kept borrowing, taking out new loans to meet old ones. He tried to sell his land, and when he could not he sold slaves instead. He feared that he might lose Monticello and complained constantly of his debts, but he refused to cut back on his lavish hospitality and expensive wine purchases.

Unable to comprehend the economic forces that were transforming the country and destroying the upper South, Jefferson blamed the banks and the speculative spirit of the day for both his and Virginia's miseries. It is true that he accepted the existence of commerce and, after the War of 1812, even some limited manufacturing for the United States. But the commerce he accepted was tame and traditional stuff compared to the aggressive commerce that was taking over northern America in the early nineteenth century. Jefferson's idea of commerce involved little more than the sale abroad of agricultural staples—wheat, tobacco, and cotton. His commerce was not the incessant trucking and trading, the endless buying and selling with each other, that was coming to characterize the emerging northern Yankee world. That kind of dynamic domestic commerce and all the capitalistic accouterments that went with it—banks, stock markets, liquid capital, paper money—Jefferson feared and despised.

He did indeed want comforts and prosperity for his American farmers, but like some modern liberals he had little or no appreciation of the economic forces that made such prosperity and comforts possible. He had no comprehension of banks and thought that the paper money issued by banks was designed "to enrich swindlers at the expense of the honest and industrious part of the nation." He could not understand how "legerdemain tricks upon paper can produce as solid wealth or hard labor in the earth." As far as he was concerned, the buying and selling of stocks and the raising of capital were simply licentious speculation and wild gambling—all symptoms of "commercial avarice and corruption."

The ultimate culprit in the degeneration of America, he thought, was the corrupt and tyrannical course of the national government. The Missouri Crisis of 1819–1820, provoked by northern efforts to limit the spread of slavery in the West, was to Jefferson "a fire bell in the night," a threat to the union and to the Revolutionary experiment in republicanism. He believed that the federal government's proposed restriction on the right of the people of Missouri to own slaves violated the Constitution and threatened self-government. Only each state, he said, had the "exclusive right" to regulate slavery. If the federal government arrogated to itself that right, then it would next declare all slaves in the country free, "in which case all the whites within the United States south of the Potomac and Ohio must evacuate their States, and most fortunate those who can do it first."

Jefferson became a bitter critic of the usurpations of the Supreme Court and a more strident defender of states' rights than he had been even in 1798 when he penned the Kentucky Resolution justifying the right of a state to nullify federal laws. While his friend Madison remained a nationalist and upheld the right of the Supreme Court to interpret the Constitution, Jefferson lent his support to the most dogmatic, impassioned, and sectional-minded elements in Virginia, including the arch states'-rightists Spencer Roane and John Randolph. He became parochial and alarmist, and his zeal for states' rights, as even his sympathetic biographer Dumas Malone admits, "bordered on fanaticism."

For someone as optimistic and sanguine in temperament as Jefferson usually was, he had many gloomy and terrifying moments in these years between 1809 and 1826. What happened? What accounts for these moments of gloom and these expressions of fanaticism? How can we explain Jefferson's uncharacteristic but increasingly frequent doubts about the future?

Certainly his personal troubles, his rising debts, the threat of bankruptcy, the fear of losing Monticello, were part of it, but they are not the whole explanation. Something more is involved in accounting for the awkwardness of his years of retirement than these outside forces, and that something seems to lie within Jefferson himself—in his principles and outlook, in his deep and long held faith in popular democracy and the future.

No one of the Revolutionary leaders believed more strongly in progress and in the capacity of the American people for self-government than did Jefferson. And no one was more convinced that the Enlightenment was on the march against the forces of medieval barbarism and darkness, of religious superstition and enthusiasm. So sure was he of the future progress of American society that he was intellectually and emotionally unprepared for what happened in the years following his retirement from public office. He was unprepared for the democratic revolution that he himself had inspired. In the end Jefferson was victimized by his overweening confidence in the people and by his naive hopefulness in the future. The Enlightenment and the democratic revolution he had contributed so much to bring about and his own liberal and rosy temperament finally did him in.

Jefferson's sublime faith in the people and the future is the source of that symbolic power he has had for succeeding generations of Americans. He was never more American than when he told John Adams in 1816 that he liked "the dreams of the future better than the history of the past." He was always optimistic; indeed, he was a virtual Pollyanna about everything. His expectations always outran reality, whether they concerned French aristocrats who turned out to be less liberal than his friend Lafayette, or garden vegetables that never came up, or misbehaving students at the University of Virginia who violated their honor code, or an American Revolution that actually allowed people to pursue their pecuniary happiness. He was the pure American innocent. He had little understanding of man's capacity for evil and had no tragic sense whatsoever.

Through his long public career, while others were wringing their hands, Jefferson remained calm and hopeful. He knew slavery was a great evil, but he believed his generation could do little about it. Instead he counseled patience and a reliance on the young who would follow. When one of those younger men, Edward Coles, actually called on Jefferson in 1814 to lend his voice in the struggle against slavery, he could only offer his confidence in the future "The hour of emancipation is advancing, in the march of time. It will come . . . ."

It was the same with every difficulty. In one way or other he expected things to work out. In 1814 he saw his financial troubles coming at him and his household like "an approaching wave in a storm; still I think we shall live as long, eat as much, and drink as much, as if the wave had already glided under the ship. Somehow or other these things find their way out as they come in, and so I suppose they will now." Was not progress on the march, and were not science and enlightenment everywhere pushing back the forces of ignorance, superstition, and darkness? The future, he felt, was on his side and on the side of the people. A liberal democratic society would be capable of solving every problem, if not in his lifetime, then surely in the coming years.

But Jefferson lived too long, and the future and the coming generation were not what he had expected. Although he continued in his public letters, especially to foreigners, to affirm that progress and civilization were still on the march, in private he became more and more apprehensive of the future. He sensed that American society, including Virginia, might not be getting better after all, but actually going backward. The American people were not becoming more refined, more polite, and more sociable; if anything, he believed, they were more barbaric and factional. Jefferson was frightened by the divisions in the country and by the popularity of Andrew Jackson, whom he regarded as a man of violent passions and unfit for the presidency. He felt overwhelmed by the new paper-money business culture that was sweeping through the country and never appreciated how much his democratic and egalitarian principles had contributed to its rise.

Ordinary people, in whom he placed so much confidence, more certainly than his friend Madison had, were not becoming more enlightened. In fact, superstition and bigotry, which Jefferson identified with organized religion, were actually reviving, released by the democratic revolution he had led. He was temperamentally incapable of understanding the deep popular strength of the evangelical forces that were seizing control of American culture in these early decades of the nineteenth century. He became what we might call a confused secular humanist in the midst of real moral majorities. While Jefferson in 1822 was still predicting that there was not a young man now alive who would not die a Unitarian, Methodists and Baptists and other evangelicals were gaining adherents by the tens of thousands in the Second Great Awakening. In response all Jefferson could do was blame the defunct New England Federalists and an equally bewildered New England clergy for spreading both capitalism and evangelical Christianity throughout the country.

Jefferson's solution to this perceived threat from New England and its "pious young monks from Harvard and Yale" was to hunker down in Virginia and build a university that would perpetuate true republican principles. "It is in our seminary," he told Madison, "that that vestal flame is to be kept alive." Yet even building the university brought sorrow and shock. The Virginia legislature was not as eager to spend money for higher education as he had expected. His support of the university became more of a political liability in the legislature than an asset.

The people in fact seemed more sectarian and less rational than they had been at the time of the Revolution. They did not seem to know who he was, what he had done. Was this the new generation on which he rested all his hopes? During the last year of his life, at a moment, says his biographer Malone, of "uneasiness that he had never known before," Jefferson was pathetically reduced to listing his contributions during sixty-one years of public service in order to justify a legislative favor. No wonder he sometimes felt cast off. "All, all dead!" he wrote to an old friend in 1825, "and ourselves left alone midst a new generation whom we know not, and who knows not us."

These were only small cracks in his optimism, only tinges of doubt in his democratic faith, but for an innocent like him these were enough. Jefferson went further in states' rights principles and in his fears of federal consolidation than his friend Madison did because he had such higher expectations of the Revolution and the people. He had always invested so much more of himself intellectually and emotionally in the future and in popular democracy than Madison had. Jefferson was inspired by a vision of how things could and should be. Madison tended to accept things as they were. Madison never lost his dark foreboding about the America yet to come, and he never shed his skepticism about the people and popular majorities. But Jefferson had nothing but the people and the future to fall back on; they were really all he ever believed in. That is why we remember Jefferson, and not Madison.

13. Thomas Jefferson:
First Inaugural Address, 1801

Henry Steele Commager, ed.

On March 4, 1801, the first real transfer of political power took place in the new nation as Thomas Jefferson succeeded John Adams as President. During the 1790s, opposition to Hamilton's financial policies and controversy over foreign policy had created partisan division between the Federalists, led by Hamilton and Adams, and the Republicans, organized by Madison and Jefferson. Adams defeated Jefferson for the Presidency when Washington stepped down in 1796, but his administration witnessed growing bitterness and dissension as the pro-English Federalists entered into an undeclared naval war with France. Vindictive Federalists in Congress passed the repressive Alien and Sedition Acts, and the Adams administration used them in an effort to silence Republican critics. President Adams finally undercut the Federalist cause by arranging for peace with France over Hamilton's furious objections. In the election of 1800, Jefferson won a narrow but decisive victory, thus ending the Federalist control of the government and ushering in a new era of political harmony.

Jefferson was the first President to take office in the new capital city of Washington—described by a contemporary visitor as "a place with a few bad houses, extensive marshes, hanging on the skirts of a to thinly peopled, weak and barren country." The executive mansion, gleaming with a fresh coat of whitewash, was ready; but at the other end of Pennsylvania Avenue, which was no more than a broad clearing cut through the trees and swamps, the Capitol stood awkwardly unfinished. The north wing was complete, but the rest of the building was still under construction, with the rotunda open to the sky. Jefferson, who had been staying at a nearby boarding house, walked through the mud to the Senate chamber in the north wing on the fourth of March to take the oath of office. John Adams, in a fit of pique, had left the capital that morning, leaving John Marshall, the Chief Justice, to preside at the inauguration. After taking the oath, Jefferson, who was ill at ease as always before an audience, read his carefully prepared speech. Few in the packed hall could hear his mumbled words, but printed copies were quickly made available. The inaugural address proved immensely popular, reassuring the anxious Federalists and confirming Republican faith in Jefferson's greatness.

Friends and Fellow-Citizens:

Called upon to undertake the duties of the first executive office of our country, I avail myself of the presence of that portion of my fellow-citizens which is here assembled to express my grateful thanks for the favor with which they have been pleased to look toward me, to declare a sincere consciousness that the task is above my talents, and that I approach it with those anxious and awful presentiments which the greatness of the charge and the weakness of my powers so justly inspire. A rising nation, spread over a wide and fruitful land, traversing all the seas with the rich productions of their industry, engaged in commerce with nations who feel power and forget right, advancing rapidly to destinies beyond the reach of mortal eye—when I contemplate these transcendent objects, and see the honor, the happiness, and the hopes of this beloved country committed to the issue, and the auspices of this day, I shrink from the contemplation, and humble myself before the magnitude of the undertaking. Utterly, indeed, should I despair did not the presence of many whom I here see remind me that in the other high authorities provided by our Constitution I shall find resources of wisdom, of virtue, and of zeal on which to rely under all difficulties. To you, then, gentlemen, who are charged with the sovereign functions of legislation, and to those associated with you, I look with encouragement for that guidance and support which may enable us to steer with safety the vessel in which we are all embarked amidst the conflicting elements of a troubled world.

During the contest of opinion through which we have passed the animation of discussions and of exertions has sometimes worn an aspect which might impose on strangers unused to think freely and to speak and to write what they think; but this being now decided by the voice of the nation, announced according to the rules of the Constitution, all will, of course, arrange themselves under the will of the law, and unite in common efforts for the common good. All, too, will bear in mind this sacred principle, that though the will of the majority is in all cases to prevail, that will to be rightful must be reasonable; that the minority possesses their equal rights, which equal law must protect, and to violate would be oppression. Let us, then, fellow-citizens, unite with one heart and one mind. Let us restore to social intercourse that harmony and affection without which liberty and even life itself are but dreary things. And let us reflect that, having banished from our land that religious intolerance under which mankind so long bled and suffered, we have yet gained little if we countenance a political intolerance as despotic, as wicked, and capable of as bitter and bloody persecutions. During the throes and convulsions of the ancient world, during the agonizing spasms of infuriated man, seeking through blood and slaughter his long-lost liberty, it was not wonderful that the agitation of the billows should reach even this distant and peaceful shore; that this should be more felt and feared by some and less by others, and should divide opinions as to measures of safety. But every difference of opinion is not a difference of principle. We have called by different names brethren of the same principle. We are all Republicans, we are all Federalists. If there be any among us who would wish to dissolve this Union or to change its republican form, let them stand undisturbed as monuments of the safety with which error of opinion may be tolerated where reason is left free to combat it. I know, indeed, that some honest men fear that a republican government can not be strong, that this Government is not strong enough; but would the honest patriot, in the full tide of successful experiment, abandon a government which has so far kept us free and firm on the theoretic and visionary fear that this Government, the world's best hope, may by possibility want energy to preserve itself? I trust not. I believe this, on the contrary, the strongest Government on earth. I believe it the only one where every man, at the call of the law, would fly to the standard of the law, and would meet invasions of the public order as his own personal concern. Sometimes it is said that man can not be trusted with the government of himself. Can he, then, be trusted with the government of others? Or have we found angels in the forms of kings to govern him? Let history answer this question.

Let us, then, with courage and confidence pursue our own Federal and Republican principles, our attachment to union and representative government. Kindly separated by nature and a wide ocean from the exterminating havoc of one quarter of the globe; too high-minded to endure the degradations of the others; possessing a chosen country, with room enough for our descendants to the thousandth and thousandth generation; entertaining a due sense of our equal right to the use of our own faculties, to the acquisitions of our own industry, to honor and confidence from our fellow-citizens, resulting not from birth, but from our actions and their sense of them; enlightened by a benign religion, professed, indeed, and practiced in various forms, yet all of them inculcating honesty, truth, temperance, gratitude, and the love of man; acknowledging and adoring an overruling Providence, which by all its dispensations proves that it delights in the happiness of man here and his greater happiness hereafter—with all these blessings, what more is necessary to make us a happy and a prosperous people? Still one thing more, fellow-citizens—a wise and frugal Government, which shall restrain men from injuring one another, shall leave them otherwise free to regulate their own pursuits of industry and improvement, and shall not take from the mouth of labor the bread it has earned. This is the sum of good government, and this is necessary to close the circle of our felicities.

About to enter, fellow-citizens, on the exercise of duties which comprehend everything dear and valuable to you, it is proper you should understand what I deem the essential principles of our Government, and consequently those which ought to shape its Administration. I will compress them within the narrowest compass they will bear, stating the general principle, but not all its limitations. Equal and exact justice to all men, of whatever state or persuasion, religious or political; peace, commerce, and honest friendship with all nations, entangling alliances with none; the support of the State governments in all their rights, as the most competent administrations for our domestic concerns and the surest bulwarks against antirepublican tendencies; the preservation of the General Government in its whole constitutional vigor, as the sheet anchor of our peace at home and safety abroad; a jealous care of the right of election by the people—a mild and safe corrective of abuses which are lopped by the sword of revolution where peaceable remedies are unprovided; absolute acquiescence in the decisions of the majority, the vital principle of republics, from which is no appeal but to force, the vital principle and immediate parent of despotism; a well-disciplined militia, our best reliance in peace and for the first moments of war, till regulars may relieve them; the supremacy of the civil over the military authority; economy in the public expense, that labor may be lightly burthened; the honest payment of our debts and sacred preservation of the public faith; encouragement of agriculture, and of commerce as its handmaid; the diffusion of information and arraignment of all abuses at the bar of the public reason; freedom of religion; freedom of the press, and freedom of person under the protection of the habeas corpus, and trial by juries impartially selected. These principles form the bright constellation which has gone before us and guided our steps through an age of revolution and reformation. The wisdom of our sages and blood of our heroes have been devoted to their attainment. They should be the creed of our political faith, the text of civic instruction, the touchstone by which to try the services of those we trust; and should we wander from them in moments of error or of alarm, let us hasten to retrace our steps and to regain the road which alone leads to peace, liberty, and safety.

I repair, then, fellow-citizens, to the post you have assigned me. With experience enough in subordinate offices to have seen the difficulties of this the greatest of all, I have learnt to expect that it will rarely fall to the lot of imperfect man to retire from this station with the reputation and the favor which bring him into it. Without pretensions to that high confidence you reposed in our first and greatest revolutionary character, whose preeminent services had entitled him to the first place in his country's love and destined for him the fairest page in the volume of faithful history, I ask so much confidence only as may give firmness and effect to the legal administration of your affairs. I shall often go wrong through defect of judgment. When right, I shall often be thought wrong by those whose positions will not command a view of the whole ground. I ask your indulgence for my own errors, which will never be intentional, and your support against the errors of others, who may condemn what they would not if seen in all its parts. The approbation implied by your suffrage is a great consolation to me for the past, and my future solicitude will be to retain the good opinion of those who have bestowed it in advance, to conciliate that of others by doing them all the good in my power, and to be instrumental to the happiness and freedom of all.

Relying, then, on the patronage of your good will, I advance with obedience to the work, ready to retire from it whenever you become sensible how much better choice it is in your power to make. And may that Infinite Power which rules the destinies of the universe lead our councils to what is best, and give them a favorable issue for your peace and prosperity.

1801

IV

National Expansion: 1815–1860

14. The Jacksonian Revolution:
Myth and Reality

Robert V. Remini

"What?" cried the outraged North Carolina lady when she heard the dreadful news. "Jackson up for president? *Jackson? Andrew* Jackson? The Jackson that used to live in Salisbury? Why, when he was here, he was such a rake that my husband would not bring him into the house! It is true, he *might* have taken him out to the stable to weigh horses for a race, and might drink a glass of whiskey with him *there*. Well, if Andrew Jackson can be president, anybody can!"

Indeed. After forty years of constitutional government headed by presidents George Washington, John Adams, Thomas Jefferson, James Madison, James Monroe, and John Quincy Adams, the thought of Gen. Andrew Jackson of Tennessee—"Old Hickory" to his devoted soldiers—succeeding such distinguished statesmen came as a shock to some Americans in 1828. And little did they know at the time that Old Hickory would be followed in succession by the Little Magician, Tippecanoe and Tyler too, Young Hickory, and then Old Rough and Ready.

What had happened to the American political process? How could it come about that the Washingtons, Jeffersons, and Madisons of the world could be replaced by the Van Burens, Harrisons, Tylers, and Taylors? What a mockery of the political system bequeathed by the Founding Fathers!

The years from roughly 1828 to 1848 are known today as the Age of Jackson or the Jacksonian era. To many contemporaries, they initiated a "revolution," a shocking overthrow of the noble republican standards of the founders by the "common people," who in 1828 preferred as president a crude frontiersman like Andrew Jackson to a statesman of proven ability with a record of outstanding public service like John Quincy Adams.

Over the forty years following the establishment of the American nation under the Constitution, the United States had experienced many profound changes in virtually all phases of life. Following the War of 1812, the industrial revolution took hold and within thirty years all the essential elements for the creation of an industrial society in America were solidly in place. At the same time, a transportation revolution got underway with the building of canals, bridges, and turnpikes, reaching a climax of sorts in the 1820s with the coming of the railroads. The standard of living was also improved by numerous new inventions. Finally, many of the older eastern states began to imitate newer western states by democratizing their institutions, for example, amending their constitutions to eliminate property qualifications for voting and holding office, thereby establishing universal white manhood suffrage.

The arrival of many thousands of new voters at the polls in the early nineteenth century radically changed American politics. In the past, only the wealthy and better educated were actively involved in government. Moreover, political parties were frowned upon by many of the Founding Fathers. Parties stood for factions or cliques by which greedy and ambitious men, who had no interest in serving the public good, could advance their private and selfish purposes. John Adams spoke for many when he declared that the "division of the republic into two great parties . . . is to be dreaded as the greatest political evil under our Constitution."

But times had changed. An entirely new generation of politicians appeared at the outbreak of the War of 1812, men like Henry Clay, John C. Calhoun, Martin Van Buren, and Daniel Webster, who regarded political parties more favorably. Indeed, the party structure that had emerged before the end of President Washington's administration had been their corridor to power, since none of them could offer to their constituents a public record to match what the founders had achieved. None had fought in the Revolution. None had signed the Declaration or participated in the debates leading to the writing and adoption of the Constitution. Some of them—Martin Van Buren is probably the best example—actually considered parties to be beneficial to the body politic, indeed essential to the proper working of a democratic society. Through the party system, Van Buren argued, the American people could more effectively express their will and take measures to ensure that that will was implemented by their representatives. "We must always have party distinctions," he wrote, "and the old ones are the best. . . . Political combinations between the inhabitants of the different states are unavoidable and the most natural and beneficial to the country is that between the planters of the South and the plain Republicans of the North."

In supporting Andrew Jackson for the presidency in 1828 and trying to win support from both planters and plain Republicans, Van Buren affirmed his belief in the American need for a two-party system. Jackson's election, he told Thomas Ritchie, editor of the Richmond *Enquirer*, "as the result of his military services without reference to party, and, as far as he alone is concerned, scarcely to principle, would be one thing. His election as the result of combined and concerted effort of a political party, holding in the main, to certain tenets and opposed to certain prevailing principles, might be another and far different thing."

Van Buren eventually formed an alliance with John C. Calhoun and a number of other southern politicians, and led the way in structuring a political organization around the presidential candidacy of Andrew Jackson. That organization ultimately came to be called the Democratic Party. Its leaders, including Jackson, Van Buren, Calhoun, and Thomas Hart Benton, claimed to follow the republican doctrines of Thomas Jefferson. Thus they opposed both a strong central government and a broad interpretation of the Constitution, and they regarded the states, whose rights must be defended by all who cared about preserving individual liberty, as a wholesome counterweight to the national government. Many of them opposed the idea of the federal government sponsoring public works, arguing that internal improvements dangerously inflated the power of the central government and jeopardized liberty. As president, Andrew Jackson vetoed the Maysville road bill and contended that the national government should avoid internal improvements as a general practice, except for those essential to the national defense.

The political philosophy these Democrats espoused was fundamentally conservative. It advocated economy in operating the government because a tight budget limited government activity, and Jackson swore that if ever elected president he would liquidate the national debt. True to his word, he labored throughout his administration to cut expenditures by vetoing several appropriations bills he tagged as exorbitant, and he finally succeeded in obliterating the national debt altogether in January 1835—a short-lived accomplishment.

The organization of the Democratic Party in its initial stages included a central committee, state committees, and a national newspaper located in Washington, D.C., the *United States Telegraph*, which could speak authoritatively to the party faithful. In time it was said that the Democratic organization included "a chain of newspaper posts, from the New England States to Louisiana, and branching off through Lexington to the Western States." The supporters of Jackson's election were accused by their opponents of attempting to regulate "the popular election by means of organized clubs in the States, and organized presses everywhere."

Democrats took particular delight in celebrating the candidacy of Andrew Jackson. They found that Old Hickory's personality and military accomplishments made him an attractive and viable candidate for the ordinary voter. Indeed his career and personality stirred the imagination of Democratic leaders around the country and they devised new methods, or improved old ones, to get across the message that Andrew Jackson was a "man of the people." "The Constitution and liberty of the country were in imminent peril, and he has preserved them both!" his supporters boasted. "We can sustain our republican principles . . . by calling to the presidential chair . . . ANDREW JACKSON."

Jackson became a symbol of the best in American life—a self-made man, among other things—and party leaders adopted the hickory leaf as their symbol. Hickory brooms, hickory canes, hickory sticks shot up everywhere—on steeples, poles, steamboats, and stage coaches, and in the hands of all who could wave them to salute the Old Hero of New Orleans. "In every village, as well as upon the corners of many city streets," hickory poles were erected. "Many of these poles were standing as late as 1845," recorded one contemporary, "rotten momentoes [*sic*] of the delirium of 1828." The opponents of the Democratic Party were outraged by this crude lowering of the political process. "Planting hickory trees!" snorted the Washington *National Journal* on May 24, 1828. "Odds nuts and drumsticks! What have hickory trees to do with republicanism and the great contest?"

The Democrats devised other gimmicks to generate excitement for their ticket. "Jackson meetings" were held in every county where a Democratic organization existed. Such meetings were not new, of course. What was new was their audience. "If we go into one of these meetings," declared one newspaper, "of whom do we find them composed? Do we see there the solid, substantial, moral and reflecting yeomanry of the country? No . . . . They comprise a large portion of the dissolute, the noisy, the discontented, and designing of society." The Democratic press retorted with the claim that these so called dissolute were actually the "bone and muscle of American society. They are the People. The real People who understand that Gen. Jackson is one of them and will defend their interests and rights."

The Jacksonians were also very fond of parades and barbecues. In Baltimore a grand barbecue was scheduled to commemorate the successful defense of the city when the British attacked during the War of 1812. But the Democrats expropriated the occasion and converted it into a Jackson rally. One parade started with dozens of Democrats marching to the beat of a fife and drum corps and wearing no other insignia save "a twig of the sacred [hickory] tree in their hats." Trailing these faithful Jacksonians came "gigantic hickory poles," still live and crowned with green foliage, being carted in "on eight wheels for the purpose of being planted by the democracy on the eve of the election." These poles were drawn by eight horses, all decorated with "ribbons and mottoes." Perched in the branches of each tree were a dozen Democrats, waving flags and shouting, "Hurrah for Jackson!"

"Van Buren has learned you know that the *Hurra Boys* were for Jackson," commented one critic, "and to my regret they constitute a powerful host." Indeed they did. The number of voters in the election of 1828 rose to 1,155,340, a jump of more than 800,000 over the previous presidential election of 1824.

The Hurra Boys brought out the voters in 1828, but at considerable cost. The election set a low mark for vulgarity, gimmickry, and nonsensical hijinks; Jackson's mother was accused of being a prostitute brought to America to service British soldiers, and his wife was denounced as an "adulteress" and bigamist. "Ought a convicted adulteress and her paramour husband to be placed in the highest offices of this free and Christian land?" asked one editor. But the Democrats were no better, accusing John Quincy Adams of pimping for the czar of Russia.

The tone and style of this election outraged many voters who feared for the future of American politics. With so many fresh faces crowding to the polls, the old republican system was yielding to a new democratic style and that evolution seemed fraught with all the dangers warned against by the Founding Fathers. Jackson's subsequent victory at the polls gave some Americans nightmares of worse things to come.

At his inauguration people came from five hundred miles away to see General Jackson, wrote Daniel Webster, "and they really seem to think that the country is rescued from some dreadful danger." They nearly wrecked the White House in their exuberance. Their behavior shocked Joseph Story, an associate Justice of the Supreme Court, and sent him scurrying home. "The reign of KING MOB seemed triumphant," he wailed. But a western newspaper disagreed. "It was a proud day for the people," reported the *Argus of Western America*. "General Jackson is *their own* President."

Jackson himself was fiercely committed to democracy. And by democracy he meant majoritarian rule. "The people are the government," he wrote, "administering it by their agents; they are the Government, the sovereign power." In his first message to Congress as president, written in December 1829, Jackson announced: "The majority is to govern." To the people belonged the right of "electing their Chief Executive." He therefore asked Congress to adopt an amendment that would abolish the College of Electors. He wanted all "intermediary" agencies standing between the people and their government swept away, whether erected by the Founding Fathers or not. "The people are sovereign," he reiterated. "Their will is absolute."

So committed was Jackson to the principle of popular self-rule that he told historian-politician George Bancroft that "every officer should in his turn pass before the people, for their approval or rejection." And he included federal judges in this sweeping generalization, even justices of the Supreme Court. Accordingly, he introduced the principle of rotation, which limited government appointments to four years. Officeholders should be regularly rotated back home and replaced by new men, he said. "The duties of all public officers are . . . so plain and simple that men of intelligence may readily qualify themselves for their performance." Otherwise abuse may occur. Anyone who has held office "a few years, believes he has a life estate in it, a vested right, & if it has been held twenty years or upwards, not only a vested right, but that it ought to descend to his children, & if no children then the next of kin—This is not the principles of our government. It is rotation in office that will perpetuate our liberty." Unfortunately, hack politicians equated rotation with patronage and Jackson's enemies quickly dubbed his principle "the spoils system."

But it was never meant to be a spoils system. Jackson wanted every office of government, from the highest to the lowest, within the reach of the electorate, arguing that "where the people are everything . . . there and there only is liberty." Perhaps his position was best articulated by Alexis de Tocqueville, the French visitor in the 1830s whose *Democracy in America* remains one of the most profound observations about American life in print. "The people reign in the American political world," declared Tocqueville, "as the Deity does in the universe. They are the cause and aim of all things; everything comes from them, and everything is absorbed in them." The "constant celebration" of the people, therefore, is what Jackson and the Democratic Party provided the nation during his eight years in office. It is what Jacksonian Democracy was all about.

As president, Jackson inaugurated a number of important changes in the operation of government. For example, he vetoed congressional legislation more times than all his predecessors combined, and for reasons other than a bill's presumed lack of constitutionality. More importantly, by the creative use of his veto power he successfully claimed for the chief executive the right to participate in the legislative process. He put Congress on notice that they must consider his views on all issues before enacting them into law or run the risk of a veto. In effect he assumed the right to initiate legislation, and this essentially altered the relationship between the executive and the Congress. Instead of a separate and equal branch of the government, the president, according to Jackson, was the head of state, the first among equals.

Jackson also took a dim view of the claim that the Supreme Court exercised the final and absolute right to determine the meaning of the Constitution. When the court decided in *McCulloch v. Maryland* that the law establishing a national bank was constitutional, Jackson disagreed. In his veto of a bill to recharter the Second National Bank in 1832, he claimed among other things that the bill lacked authority under the Constitution, despite what the high court had decided. Both the House and the Senate, as well as the president, he continued, must decide for themselves what is and what is not constitutional before taking action on any bill. The representatives of Congress ought not to vote for a bill, and the president ought not to sign it, if they, in their own good judgment, believe it unconstitutional. "It is as much the duty of the House of Representatives, of the Senate, and of the President to decide upon the constitutionality of any bill or resolution which may be presented to them for passage or approval as it is of the supreme judges when it may be brought before them for judicial decision." Jackson did not deny the right of the Supreme Court to judge the constitutionality of a bill. What he denied was the presumption that the Court was the final or exclusive interpreter of the Constitution. All three branches should rule on the question of constitutionality, Jackson argued. In this way the equality and independence of each branch of government is maintained. "The authority of the Supreme Court," he declared, "must not, therefore, be permitted to control the Congress, or the Executive when acting in their legislative capacities, but to have only such influence as the force of their reasoning may deserve." What bothered Jackson was the presumption that four men could dictate what fifteen million people may or may not do under their constitutional form. To Jackson's mind that was not democratic but oligarchic. But that was precisely the intention of the Founding Fathers: to provide a balanced mix of democratic, oligarchic, and monarchical forms in the Constitution.

Of course Jackson was merely expressing his own opinion about the right of all three branches to pass on the constitutionality of all legislation, an opinion the American people ultimately rejected. The great fear in a democratic system—one the Founding Fathers knew perfectly well—was the danger of the majority tyrannizing the minority. Jackson would take his chances. He believed the American people were virtuous and would always act appropriately. "I for one do not despair of the republic," he wrote. "I have great confidence in the virtue of a great majority of the people, and I cannot fear the result. The republic is safe, the main pillars [of] virtue, religion and morality will be fostered by a majority of the people." But not everyone shared Jackson's optimism about the goodness of the electorate. And in time—particularly with the passage of the Fourteenth Amendment—it fell to the courts to guard and maintain the rights of the minority.

Jackson summed up his assertion of presidential rights by declaring that he alone—not Congress, as was usually assumed—was the sole representative of the American people and responsible to them. After defeating Henry Clay in the 1832 election, he decided to kill the Second National Bank by removing federal deposits because, as he said, he had received a "mandate" from the people to do so. The Senate objected and formally censured him, but Jackson, in response, merely issued another statement on presidential rights and the democratic system that had evolved over the last few years.

By law, only the secretary of the treasury was authorized to remove the deposits, so Jackson informed his secretary, William Duane, to carry out his order. Duane refused pointblank. And he also refused to resign as he had promised if he and the president could not agree upon a common course of action with respect to the deposits. Thereupon, Jackson sacked him. This was the first time a cabinet officer had been fired, and there was some question whether the president had this authority. After all, the cabinet positions were created by Congress and appointment required the consent of the Senate. Did that not imply that removal also required senatorial consent—particularly the treasury secretary, since he handled public funds that were controlled by Congress? The law creating the Treasury Department never called it an "executive" department, and it required its secretary to report to the Congress, not the president. None of this made a particle of difference to Andrew Jackson. All department heads were *his* appointees and they would obey *him* or pack their bags. The summary dismissal of Duane was seen by Jackson's opponents as a presidential grab for the purse strings of the nation. And in fact presidential control over all executive functions gave the chief executive increased authority over the collection and distribution of public funds.

By the close of 1833 many feared that Andrew Jackson was leading the country to disaster. Henry Clay regularly pilloried the president on the Senate floor. On one occasion he accused Jackson of "open, palpable and daring usurpation" of all the powers of government. "We are in the midst of a revolution," Clay thundered, "hitherto bloodless, but rapidly tending towards a total change of the pure republican character of the Government."

A "revolution"—that was how the opposition Whig Party characterized Jackson's presidency. The nation was moving steadily away from its "pure republican character" into something approaching despotism. What the nation was witnessing, cried Clay, was "the concentration of all power in the hands of one man." Thereafter Whig newspapers reprinted a cartoon showing Jackson as "King Andrew the First." Clad in robes befitting an emperor he was shown wearing a crown and holding a scepter in one hand and a scroll in the other on which was written the word "veto."

Democrats, naturally, read the "revolution" differently. They saw it as the steady progress of the country from the gentry republic originally established by the Founding Fathers to a more democratic system that mandated broader representation in government and a greater responsiveness to popular will.

Andrew Jackson did not take kindly to Clay's verbal mauling. "Oh, if I live to get these robes of office off me," he snorted at one point, "I will bring the rascal to a dear account." He later likened the senator to "a drunken man in a brothel," reckless, destructive, and "full of fury."

Other senators expressed their opposition to this "imperial" president and seconded Clay's complaints. John C. Calhoun, who by this time had deserted to the enemy camp, adopted the Kentuckian's "leading ideas of revolution" and charged that "a great effort is now making to choke and stifle the voice of American liberty." And he condemned Jackson's insistence on taking refuge in democratic claims. The president "tells us again and again with the greatest emphasis," he continued, "that he is the immediate representative of the American people! What effrontery! What boldness of assertion! Why, he never received a vote from the American people. He was elected by electors . . . who are elected by Legislatures chosen by the people."

Sen. Daniel Webster and other Whigs chimed in. "Again and again we hear it said," rumbled Webster, "that the President is responsible to the American people! . . . And this is thought enough for a limited, restrained, republican government! . . . I hold this, Sir, to be a mere assumption, and dangerous assumption." And connected with this "airy and unreal responsibility to the people," he continued, "is another sentiment . . . and that is, that the President is the direct representative of the American people." The sweep of his language electrified the Senate. And "if he may be allowed to consider himself as the sole representative of all the American people," Webster concluded, "then I say, Sir, that the government . . . has already a master. I deny the sentiment, and therefore protest against the language; neither the sentiment nor the language is to be found in the Constitution of this Country."

Jackson's novel concept that the president served as the people's tribune found immediate acceptance by the electorate, despite the warnings of the Whigs. In effect, he altered the essential character of the presidency. He had become the head of government, the one person who would formulate national policy and direct public affairs. Sighed Senator Benjamin W. Leigh of Virginia: "Until the President developed the faculties of the Executive power, all men thought it inferior to the legislature—he manifestly thinks it superior—and in his hands [it] . . . has proved far stronger than the representatives of the States."

From Jackson's own time to the present, disagreement and controversy over the significance of his presidency have prevailed. In the twentieth century the disagreements intensified among historians. Confusion over the meaning of Jacksonian Democracy, varying regional support for democratic change, and the social and economic status of the Democrats and Whigs have clouded the efforts of scholars to reach reliable conclusions about the Old Hero and the era that bears his name.

Andrew Jackson himself will always remain a controversial figure among historians. That he can still generate such intense partisan feeling is evidence of his remarkable personality. He was an aggressive, dynamic, charismatic, and intimidating individual. And although modern scholars and students of history either admire or dislike him intensely, his rating as president in polls conducted among historians over the past thirty years varies from great to near great. He carries an enormous burden in winning any popularity contest because of his insistence on removing the eastern Indians west of the Mississippi River and on waging a long and vicious war against the Second National Bank of the United States.

His first biographer, James Parton, wrote a three-volume *Life of Andrew Jackson* (1859,1860), and came away with mixed feelings about the man and his democracy. At times Parton railed against the mindless mob "who could be wheedled, and flattered, and drilled," but at other times he extolled democracy as the mark of an enlightened society. What troubled Parton particularly was the spoils system. Rotation, he wrote, is "an evil so great and so difficult to remedy, that if all his other public acts had been perfectly wise and right, this single feature of his administration would suffice to render it deplorable rather than amiable."

William Graham Sumner's *Andrew Jackson* (1882) was relentlessly critical of his subject, deploring in particular Jackson's flawed moral charter and emotional excesses. Sumner and other early historians, such as Herman von Holst and James Schouler, constituted what one student of the Jacksonian age called a "liberal patrician" or "Whig" school of history. These individuals came from European middle or upper middle-class families with excellent backgrounds of education and public service. Because their class had been ousted from political power, these historians were biased against Jacksonian Democracy, and their books reflect their prejudice.

The interpretation of Old Hickory and his adherents took a sharp about-face with the appearance in 1893 of the vastly influential article by Frederick Jackson Turner, "The Significance of the Frontier in American History." Turner argued that American democracy emerged from the wilderness, noting that universal white manhood suffrage guaranteed by the new western states became something of a model for the older, eastern states. Naturally Jackson and his followers were seen as the personification of this frontier democracy. The thesis was advanced and sometimes amplified by Charles A. Beard, Vernon L. Parrington, and other western and southern historians of the early twentieth century who were caught up in the reform movement of the Progressive era. They dubbed the Jacksonian revolution an age of egalitarianism that produced the rise of the common man. Jackson himself was applauded as a man of the people. Thus the liberal patrician school of historiography gave way to the Progressive school.

This interpretation dovetailed rather well with the views of Tocqueville. During his visit, Tocqueville encountered a widespread belief in egalitarianism but worried that majoritarian rule could endanger minority rights. There are so many sharp and accurate insights into American society and institutions in *Democracy in America* that it ought to be the first book anyone reads in attempting to understand the antebellum period of American history. Among other things, he catches the American just as he is emerging from his European and colonial past and acquiring many of the characteristics [that] are generally regarded as typically American today.

Tocqueville's democratic liberalism, augmented by the works of the Progressive historians—especially Turner, Beard and Parrington—dominated historical thought about the American past for the next fifty years or more. Almost all the Progressive historians stressed the role of geographic sections in the nation, and Turner at one point even denied any class influence in the formation of frontier democracy. The only important negative voice concerning Jackson during this period came from Thomas P. Abernethy, whose *From Frontier to Plantation in Tennessee: A Study in Frontier Democracy* (1932) insisted that Jackson himself was a frontier aristocrat, an opportunist, and a land speculator who strongly opposed the democratic forces in his own state of Tennessee.

The virtual shattering of the Progressive school's interpretation of Jacksonian Democracy came with the publication of one of the most important historical monographs ever written concerning American history: *The Age of Jackson* (1945), by Arthur M. Schlesinger, Jr. This classic work virtually rivals in importance the frontier thesis of Frederick Jackson Turner. It is a landmark study and represents the beginning of modern scholarship on Jackson and his era.

Schlesinger argued that class distinctions rather than sectional differences best explain the phenomenon of Jacksonian Democracy. He interpreted Jackson's actions and those of his followers as an effort of the less fortunate in American society to combat the power and influence of the business community. The working classes in urban centers as well as the yeoman farmers, he argued, were the true well-springs of the Jacksonian movement. Jacksonian Democracy evolved from the conflict between classes and best expressed its goals and purposes in the problems and needs facing urban laborers. Schlesinger singled out the bank war as the most telling example of the conflict and as the fundamental key to a fuller understanding of the meaning of Jacksonian Democracy. What attracted many historians to this path-breaking study, besides its graceful and majestic style, was Schlesinger's perceptive definition of Jacksonian Democracy and a precise explanation of its origins.

The reaction to Schlesinger's work was immediate and dramatic. It swept the historical profession like a tornado, eliciting both prodigious praise and within a relatively short time, fierce denunciations from Bray Hammond, in a series of articles as well as his *Banks and Politics in America from the Revolution to the Civil War* (1957), and Richard Hofstadter, in his *The American Political Tradition and the Men Who Made It* (1948), contended that the Jacksonians were not the champions of urban workers or small farmers but rather ambitious and ruthless entrepreneurs principally concerned with advancing their own economic and political advantage. They were "men on the make" and frequently captains of great wealth. According to Hofstadter, the Jacksonians were not so much hostile to business as they were hostile to being excluded from entering the confined arena of capitalists. Where Schlesinger had emphasized conflict in explaining the Jacksonian era, Hofstadter insisted that consensus best characterized the period. The entrepreneurial thesis, as it was called, found strong support among many young scholars who constituted the Columbia University school of historians. In a series of articles and books produced by these critics, Jackson himself was described as an inconsistent opportunist, a strikebreaker, a shady land speculator, and a political fraud. Marvin Meyers, in his *The Jacksonian Persuasion* (1957), provides a slight variation on the entrepreneurial thesis by arguing that Jacksonians did indeed keep their eyes on the main chance but yearned for the virtues of a past agrarian republic. They hungered after the rewards of capitalism but looked back reverentially on the blessings of a simpler agrarian society.

A major redirection of Jacksonian scholarship came with the publication of Lee Benson's *The Concept of Jacksonian Democracy: New York as a Test Case* (1961). This work suggested a whole new approach to the investigation of the Jacksonian age by employing the techniques of quantification to uncover solid, factual data upon which to base an analysis. Moreover, Benson emphasized social questions and found that such things as ethnicity and religion were far more important than economics in determining how a person voted or which party won his allegiance. He dismissed Jacksonian rhetoric about democracy and the rights of the people as "claptrap" and contended that local issues in elections meant more to the voters than national issues. Andrew Jackson himself was dismissed as unimportant in understanding the structure and meaning of politics in this period. In time, some college textbooks virtually eliminated Jackson from any discussion of this period except to mention that he opposed social reforms and that his removal of the Indians was one of the most heinous acts in American history.

An ethnocultural school of historical writing soon emerged that rejected class difference as an important factor in political determinism. German and Irish Catholics, for example, were more likely to vote Democratic because of their ethnicity and religion than anything else. Besides, some argued, Whigs were not materially richer than Democrats. Edward Pessen, in a series of books and articles took the argument one step further and insisted that Jacksonian America was not particularly egalitarian in terms of wealth, as Tocqueville had stated. He rejected the argument that the common man politically came into his own during the Jacksonian age. In a nice turn of phrase concluding his *Jacksonian America: Society, Personality, and Politics* (1969), Pessen declared that there was only *"seeming* deference to the common man by the uncommon men [the rich and powerful] who actually ran things."

By the end of the 1970s the ethnocultural approach had quieted down and was replaced by newer kinds of social analyses, most particularly by cultural Marxists who reemphasized class conflict in understanding voter preference. Other historians took a different approach and sought to describe what might be called a "political culture" for the period. However, many of the insights of Benson and the other students of the ethnocultural school have been incorporated into the whole to form a more sophisticated analysis. Joel Silbey, Sean Wilentz, Harry L. Watson, and others have shown that the electorate normally develops a wide set of values based on class, religion, nationality, family, residence, and several other factors and then invariably votes to safeguard those values as they perceive them. Watson particularly has demonstrated by his study of North Carolina politics that national issues did in fact matter in general elections. Even Jackson has been somewhat restored to his former importance, if not his former heroic stature. My own three-volume life of Old Hickory, *Andrew Jackson and the Course of American Empire, 1767–1821; Andrew Jackson and the Course of American Freedom, 1822–1832; Andrew Jackson and the Course of American Democracy, 1833–1845* (1977, 1981, 1984) highlights Schlesinger's findings and Jackson's faith and commitment to liberty and democracy. I contend that Jackson was in fact a man of the people, just as the Progressive historians had argued, and that he actively attempted to advance democracy by insisting that all branches of government, including the courts, reflect the popular will. I also tried to show that, for a number of reasons, the president's policy of Indian removal was initiated to spare the Indian from certain extinction. And Francis Paul Prucha has argued persuasively that Indian removal was probably the only policy possible under the circumstances.

The study of the Jacksonian era is essential for any serious examination of the evolution of the American presidency. This has been widely recognized since the avalanche of articles and books triggered by the appearance of Schlesinger's monumental work. Jackson himself has never lost his ability to excite the most intense passions and interest among students of American history. No doubt scholars and popular writers will continue to debate his role as a national hero and as an architect of American political institutions.

15. Trail of Tears

Dale Van Every

History records the sufferings of innumerable peoples whose country was over-run and possessed by alien invaders. There have been relatively fewer recorded occasions, as in the instance of the Babylonian Captivity of the Jews, of an entire people being compelled to abandon their country. This has been universally regarded as the ultimate catastrophe that can befall a people inasmuch as it deprives them of the roots which sustain their identity. Upon the exiles has been pronounced a sentence that by its nature denies all hope of reprieve or relief. To Indians, with their inherited conception of the land of their birth as the repository of those spiritual links to their ancestors which were holy and therefore indissoluble, the prospect of expulsion was clothed with added dreads beyond human evaluation.

The threat was in all its aspects so monstrous that in the spring of 1838 the bewildered masses of the Cherokee people, homeless, hungry, destitute, still remained incredulous that so fearful a fate could actually impend. Outrageously as they had been harassed for the past ten years by Georgia and Alabama white men, they still clung to their trust that most white men wished them well. This was a confidence instilled in them by the reports of John Ross [a respected Cherokee chief] who had been made more conversant with the apparent truth by his wide travels across the immense white nation stretching beyond the Cherokee horizon. They had been further prepared to accept his judgment on the inherent goodness of the white race by their own experience with the many white men who had lived among them as teachers, missionaries and counselors, sharing their struggles and tribulations. Their more recent experience with [General John] Wool and his officers and with [General R. G.] Dunlap and his Tennesseans had strengthened their impression that the white race could not be wholly committed to their destruction.

Ross was still in Washington engaged in a final frantic effort, with some dawning hope of success, to wring from the administration a temporary postponement of removal. His followers were continuing to obey his injunction that they persist in their nonviolent resistance. Most continued to refuse even to give their names or a list of their belongings to the agents commissioned to organize the details of the migration. May 23, two years from the date of the President's proclamation of the Senate's ratification of the treaty, was the day, as all had for months been warned, when their residence in the east would become illegal but they still could not believe that a development so frightful could be given reality by that day's sunrise. Even after five regiments of regulars and 4,000 militia and volunteers from adjacent states began pouring into their country they still could not believe.

Major General [Winfield] Scott arrived May 8 to take command of the military operation. His May 10, 1838 address to the Cherokee people proclaimed the terrible reality in terms no Cherokee could longer mistake:

> Cherokees—The President of the United States has sent me with a powerful army, to cause you, in obedience to the treaty of 1835, to join that part of your people who are already established in prosperity on the other side of the Mississippi. Unhappily, the two years which were allowed for the purpose, you have suffered to pass away without following, and without making preparations to follow, and now, or by the time this solemn *address* shall reach your distant settlements, the emigration must be commenced in haste, but, I hope, without disorder. I have no power, by granting a farther delay, to correct the error that you have committed. The full moon of May is already on the wane, and before another shall have passed away, every Cherokee man, woman, and child . . . must be in motion to join their brethren in the far West. . . . My troops already occupy many positions in the country that you are to abandon, and thousands and thousands are approaching from every quarter, to tender resistance and escape alike hopeless . . . Chiefs, head men, and warriors—Will you then, by resistance, compel us to resort to arms? God forbid. Or will you, by flight, seek to hide yourself in mountains and forests, and thus oblige us to hunt you down? Remember that, in pursuit, it may be impossible to avoid conflicts. The blood of the white man, or the blood of the red man, may be spilt, and if spilt, however accidentally, it may be impossible for the discreet and humane among you, or among us, to prevent a general war and carnage. Think of this, my Cherokee brethren. I am an old warrior, and have been present at many a scene of slaughter; but spare me, I beseech you, the horror of witnessing the destruction of the Cherokees.

Scott sincerely hoped that the enforced removal could be accomplished not only without bloodshed but without undue hardship inflicted upon the unfortunate thousands being ejected at bayonet's point from their homes. He had been impressed by Ross during conferences with him in Washington and like most professional soldiers of his time had developed a genuine regard for Indians. In his May 17 general orders to his troops he sternly admonished them to practice restraint:

> Considering the number and temper of the mass to be removed together with the extent and fastnesses of the country occupied, it will readily occur that simple indiscretions, acts of harshness, and cruelty on the part of our troops, may lead, step by step, to delays, to impatience, and exasperation, and, in the end, to a general war and carnage;

a result, in the case of these particular Indians, utterly abhorrent to the generous sympathies of the whole American people. Every possible kindness, compatible with the necessity of removal, must, therefore, be shown by the troops; and if, in the ranks, a despicable individual should be found capable of inflicting a wanton injury or insult on any Cherokee man, woman, or child, it is hereby made the special duty of the nearest good officer or man instantly to interpose, and to seize and consign the guilty wretch to the severest penalty of the laws. The major-general is fully persuaded that this injunction will not be neglected by the brave men under his command, who cannot be otherwise than jealous of their honor and that of their country.

Scott's intentions were humane but the larger portion of his army were state levies unaccustomed to discipline and without his professional susceptibilities. The nature of the operation required the army's dispersion in scattered detachments over a wide area. Most of the Cherokee to be removed were inhabitants of Georgia and their apprehension was conducted by Georgia militia who had long as a matter of policy been habituated to dealing harshly with Indians. Prison stockades had been erected at assembly and embarkation points in which the Cherokee were to be herded and confined while awaiting transportation west. There was little or no likelihood of attempted resistance. Most had been disarmed during Wool's regime and the irresistible military power that had been brought to bear was self-evident. The classic account of what next transpired is that recorded by James Mooney. His contribution to the Bureau of American Ethnology, eventually published in the Nineteenth Annual Report in 1900 under the title *Myths of the Cherokee*, included a history of the Cherokee based upon years of field work. His narrative of the 1838 expulsion was drawn from personal interviews with survivors, white officers as well as Cherokee victims, and had therefore much of the vitality of an eyewitness report:

> The history of this Cherokee removal of 1838, as gleaned by the author from the lips of actors in the tragedy, may well exceed in weight of grief and pathos any other passage in American history. Even the much-sung exile of the Acadians falls far behind it in its sum of death and misery. Under Scott's order the troops were disposed at various points throughout the Cherokee country, where stockade forts were erected for gathering in and holding the Indians preparatory to removal. From these, squads of troops were sent to search out with rifle and bayonet every small cabin hidden away in the coves or by the sides of mountain streams, to seize and bring in as prisoners all the occupants, however or wherever they might be found. Families at dinner were startled by the sudden gleam of bayonets in the doorway and rose up to be driven with blows and oaths along the weary miles of trail that led to

the stockade. Men were seized in their fields or going along the road, women were taken from their wheels and children from their play. In many cases, on turning for one last look as they crossed the ridge, they saw their homes in flames, fired by the lawless rabble that followed on the heels of the soldiers to loot and pillage. So keen were these outlaws on the scent that in some instances they were driving off the cattle and other stock of the Indians almost before the soldiers had fairly started their owners in the other direction. Systematic hunts were made by the same men for Indian graves, to rob them of the silver pendants and other valuables deposited with the dead. A Georgia volunteer, afterward a colonel in the confederate service, said: "I fought through the civil war and have seen men shot to pieces and slaughtered by thousands, but the Cherokee removal was the cruelest work I ever knew." To prevent escape the soldiers had been ordered to approach and surround each house, so far as possible, so as to come upon the occupants without warning. One old patriarch, when thus surprised, calmly called his children and grandchildren around him, and, kneeling down, bid them pray with him in their own language, while the astonished onlookers looked on in silence. Then rising he led the way into exile. A woman, on finding the house surrounded, went to the door and called up the chickens to be fed for the last time, after which, taking her infant on her back and her two other children by the hand, she followed her husband with the soldiers.

Within days nearly 17,000 Cherokee had been crowded into the stockades. Sanitation measures were inadequate in those makeshift concentration camps. Indian families, accustomed to a more spacious and isolated existence, were unable to adapt to the necessities of this mass imprisonment. Hundreds of the inmates sickened. The Indian was by his nature peculiarly susceptible to the depressions produced by confinement. Many lost any will to live and perceiving no glimmer of hope, resigned themselves to death. Those who had become converts found some comfort in the ministrations of their white and native pastors. In every stockade hymn singings and prayer meetings were almost continuous.

All physical preparations had been carefully planned in advance by the federal authorities in charge of the migration so that little time might be lost in getting the movement under way. In the first and second weeks of June two detachments of some 800 exiles were driven aboard the waiting fleets of steamboats, keelboats and flatboats for the descent of the Tennessee. They passed down the storied waterway by the same route taken by the first white settlers of middle Tennessee under John Donelson in 1780. In the shadow of Lookout Mountain they could survey the wilderness vastnesses from which for twenty years bands of their immediate forebears had sallied to devastate the white frontier, some of them commanded by war chiefs who had lived to be condemned to this exile.

Then, at Muscle Shoals there came an ironic contrast between the past and the future as Indians being driven from their ancient homeland were committed to transportation by the white man's newest invention. They disembarked from their boats to clamber, momentarily diverted, aboard the cars drawn by the two puffing little locomotives of the railroad recently constructed to move freight and passengers around the rapids. Returning to other boats, they resumed their seemingly interminable journey in the debilitating heat of an increasingly oppressive summer. The attendant army officers, however sympathetic, were helpless against the waves of illnesses. Scott, moving new contingents toward embarkation, was appalled by the reports he received of the mounting death rate among those who had already been dispatched.

The troops assembled for Cherokee expulsion had been by considered governmental design so numerous as to present a show of military power so overwhelming as to provide no faintest invitation to Indian resistance. By the army's first pounce more than nine tenths of the population had been rounded up and driven into the stockades. There remained only a handful of the wilder and more primitive residents of the higher mountains still at large. This handful, however, represented a problem causing Scott serious concern. Were they provoked to resist they might among their remote and cloud-wreathed peaks prove as difficult to apprehend as were the Seminole in their swamps. From this tactical threat sprang the one heroic action to gleam across the otherwise unrelieved despondency of the removal scene.

Tsali was an hitherto undistinguished mountain Cherokee who suddenly soared to an eminence in Cherokee annals comparable to the homage accorded an Attakullaculla, an Old Tassel, a Sequoyah or a John Ross. The stories of his inspired exploit, drawn from eyewitnesses, survivors and references in contemporary official records, vary in detail and have become encrusted by legend but coincide in most essentials. According to the more generally accepted version, a young Cherokee woman upon being assaulted by two soldiers killed both with a hatchet. Tsali hid the weapon under his shirt and assumed responsibility for his kinswoman's act. Scott could not permit the death of his soldiers to remain unpunished and served notice on the band of mountain Cherokee of which Tsali was a member that a scapegoat must be produced. The band felt that it had a reasonable chance to elude pursuit indefinitely but its councils were impressed by the advice of a white trader, William Thomas, a friend of his native customers in the notable tradition of Ludovic Grant, Alexander Cameron and John Mc-Donald. Thomas pointed out the advantage that could be taken of Scott's demand. Tsali was prepared to offer his life for his people. His fellow tribesmen thereupon notified Scott that he would be turned over to American justice in return for American permission to remain unmolested in their mountains. Scott, eager to escape the uncertainties of a guerrilla campaign in so difficult a terrain, agreed to recommend this course to Washington. Tsali was brought in, the voluntary prisoner of his compatriots. His Cherokee custodians were required to serve as the firing squad by which he, his brother and his eldest son were executed. The story became one of the few Indian stories with a happy ending. Thomas continued for years to interest himself in the prolonged negotiations with the governments of the United States and North Carolina which eventually resulted in federal and state recognition of Cherokee title to their mountain holdings. Tsali's sacrifice had permitted this fraction of the nation to become the remnant of the East Cherokee [and] to cling to their homeland where they still are colorful inhabitants of the North Carolina mountains.

Aside from the Tsali episode the roundup of the Cherokee proceeded without interruption. By June 18 General Charles Floyd, commanding the Georgia militia engaged in it, was able to report to his governor that no Cherokee remained on the soil of Georgia except as a prisoner in a stockade. Scott was able to discharge his volunteers June 17 and two days later to dispatch three of his five regular regiments to sectors where military needs were more pressing, two to the Canadian border and one to Florida.

Meanwhile so many migrants were dying in the drought and heat to which the initial removal was subjected that Scott was constrained to lighten the inexorable pressures. The Cherokee Council, which though technically illegal still spoke for the Cherokee people, begged for a postponement to the more healthful weather of autumn. Scott agreed. In July Ross returned and in conferences with Scott worked out a further agreement under which the Cherokee would cease passive resistance and under his supervision undertake a voluntary migration as soon as weather permitted. Scott was glad to be relieved of further need to use military force. The administration was glad to be offered some defense against the storm of northern criticism. Even Georgia made no serious protest, inasmuch as the Cherokee had already been removed from their land to stockades and there remained no questioning of the state's sovereignty. The one remonstrance, aside from the complaints of contractors, was voiced by the aging [Andrew] Jackson from his retirement at The Hermitage in a letter of August 23, 1838 to Felix Grundy, Attorney General of the United States:

> . . . The contract with Ross must be arrested, or you may rely upon it, the expense and other evils will shake the popularity of the administration to its center. What madness and folly to have anything to do with Ross, when the agent was proceeding well with the removal . . . The time and circumstances under which Gen'l Scott made this contract shows that he is no economist, or is, *sub rosa*, in league with [Henry] Clay & Co. to bring disgrace on the administration. The evil is done. It behooves Mr. [President Martin] Van Buren to act with energy to throw it off his shoulders. I enclose a letter to you under cover, unsealed, which you may read, seal, and deliver to him, that you may aid him with your views in getting out of this real difficulty.
>
> Your friend in haste,

Andrew Jackson

PS. I am so feeble I can scarcely wield my pen, but friendship dictates it and the subject excites me. Why is it that the scamp Ross is not banished from the notice of the administration?

Ross, having at last recognized the inevitable, gave to his preparations for the voluntary removal the same driving energy and attention to detail he had until then devoted to resisting removal. All phases of the organization of the national effort were gathered into his hands. All financial arrangements were under his supervision, including the disbursement of the basic federal subsistence allowance of sixteen cents a day for each person and forty cents a day for each horse. For convenience in management en route the 13,000 Cherokee remaining in the stockades were divided into detachments of roughly a thousand to head each of which he appointed a Cherokee commander. At a final meeting of the Cherokee Council it was provided that the constitution and laws of the Nation should be considered equally valid in the west.

The first detachment set out October 1, 1838 on the dreaded journey over the route which in Cherokee memory became known as The Trail of Tears. The last started November 4. The improvement in weather awaited during the tedious summer months in the stockades did not materialize. The spring migration had been cursed by oppressive heat and drought. The fall migration encountered deluges of rain followed by excessive cold. To the hundreds of deaths from heat-induced diseases were now added new hundreds of deaths from prolonged exposure.

The most vivid general account of the 1838 migration is again that of James Mooney, assembled from the recollections of participants:

. . . in October, 1838, the long procession of exiles was set in motion. A very few went by the river route; the rest, nearly all of the 13,000, went overland. Crossing to the north side of the Hiwassee at a ferry above Gunstocker creek, they proceeded down along the river, the sick, the old people, and the smaller children, with the blankets, cooking pots, and other belongings in wagons, the rest on foot or on horses. The number of wagons was 645. It was like the march of an army, regiment after regiment, the wagons in the center, the officers along the line and the horsemen on the flanks and at the rear. Tennessee river was crossed at Tucker (?) ferry, a short distance above Jollys island, at the mouth of the Hiwassee. Thence the route lay south of Pikeville, through McMinnville and on to Nashville, where the Cumberland was crossed. Then they went on to Hopkinsville, Kentucky, where the noted chief Whitepath, in charge of a detachment, sickened and died. His people buried him by the roadside, with a box over the grave and poles with streamers around it, that the others coming on behind might note the spot and remember him. Somewhere also along that march of death—for the exiles died by tens and twenties every day of the journey—the devoted wife of John Ross sank down, leaving him to go on with the bitter pain of bereavement added to heartbreak at the ruin of his nation. The Ohio was crossed at a ferry near the mouth of the Cumberland, and the army passed on through southern Illinois until the great Mississippi was reached opposite Cape Girardeau, Missouri. It was now the middle of winter, with the river running full of ice, so that several detachments were obliged to wait some time on the eastern bank for the channel to become clear. In talking with old men and women at Tahlequah the author found that the lapse of over half a century had not sufficed to wipe out the memory of the miseries of that halt beside the frozen river, with hundreds of sick and dying penned up in wagons or stretched upon the ground, with only a blanket overhead to keep out the January blast. The crossing was made at last in two divisions, at Cape Girardeau and at Green's Ferry, a short distance below, whence the march was made on through Missouri to Indian Territory, the later detachments making a northerly circuit by Springfield, because those who had gone before had killed off all the game along the direct route. At last their destination was reached. They had started in October, 1838, and it was now March, 1839, the journey having occupied barely six months of the hardest part of the year.

President Van Buren in his December 1838 message to Congress announced the administration's view of the event:

> . . . It affords me sincere pleasure to apprise the Congress of the entire removal of the Cherokee Nation of Indians to their new homes west of the Mississippi. The measures authorized by Congress at its last session have had the happiest effects. By an agreement concluded with them by the commanding general in that country, their removal has been principally under the conduct of their own chiefs, and they have emigrated without any apparent reluctance.

A traveler who had encountered the Indians en route was moved by the President's words to write his own eyewitness report which was published in the January 26, 1839 *New York Observer* under the heading "A Native of Maine, traveling in the Western Country":

> . . . On Tuesday evening we fell in with a detachment of the poor Cherokee Indians . . . about eleven hundred Indians—sixty wagons, six hundred horses, and perhaps forty pairs of oxen. We found them in the

forest camped for the night by the road side . . . under a severe fall of
rain accompanied by heavy wind. With their canvas for a shield from
the inclemency of the weather, and the cold wet ground for a resting
place, after the fatigue of the day, they spent the night . . . many of the
aged Indians were suffering extremely from the fatigue of the journey,
and the ill health consequent upon it . . . several were then quite ill,
and one aged man we were informed was then in the last struggles of
death. . . . The last detachment which we passed on the seventh embraced rising two thousand Indians with horses and mules in proportion. The forward part of the train we found just pitching their tents
for the night, and notwithstanding some thirty or forty wagons were
already stationed, we found the road literally filled with the procession
for about three miles in length. The sick and feeble were carried in
wagons—about as comfortable for traveling as a New England ox cart
with a covering over it—a great many ride on horseback and multitudes
go on foot—even aged females, apparently nearly ready to drop into
the grave, were traveling with heavy burdens attached to the back—on
the sometimes frozen ground, and sometimes muddy streets, with
no covering for the feet except what nature had given them. . . . We
learned from the inhabitants on the road where the Indians passed,
that they buried fourteen or fifteen at every stopping place, and they
make a journey of ten miles per day only on an average. One fact which
to my own mind seemed a lesson indeed to the American nation is, that
they will not travel on the Sabbath. . . . The Indians as a whole carry on
their countenances every thing but the appearance of happiness. Some
carry a downcast dejected look bordering upon the appearance of
despair others a wild frantic appearance as if about to burst the chains
of nature and pounce like a tiger upon their enemies. . . . When I past
[sic] the last detachment of those suffering exiles and thought that my
native countrymen had thus expelled them from their native soil and
their much-loved homes, and that too in this inclement season of the
year in all their suffering, I turned from the sight with feelings which
language cannot express. . . . I felt that I would not encounter the
secret silent prayer of one of these sufferers armed with the energy that
faith and hope would give it (if there be a God who avenges the wrongs
of the injured) for all the lands of Georgia. . . . When I read in the
President's message that he was happy to inform the Senate that the
Cherokees were peaceably and without reluctance removed—and remember that it was on the third day of December when not one of the
detachments had reached their destination; and that a large majority
had not made even half their journey when he made that declaration, I
thought I wished the President could have been there that very day in

Kentucky with myself, and have seen the comfort and the willingness with which the Cherokees were making their journey.

The first migrants reached their destination on the plains beyond the western border of Arkansas on January 4, 1839. Other contingents continued to straggle in until late in March. Examination of all available records by Grant Foreman, outstanding authority on Indian removal, led him to conclude 4,000 Cherokee had died either during confinement in the stockades or on their 800-mile journey west.

While the Cherokee were traversing their Trail of Tears their fellow southern Indians were committed to afflictions as dismal. The processes of removal were grinding out the cumulative calamities that had been visited upon a race by governmental fiat.

The Chickasaw had at length embarked upon their self-governed migration. They were the aristocrats of the Indian world, long noted for the prowess of their warriors, the beauty of their women and the speed of their horses. They had bargained shrewdly until they had wrung every possible advantage from federal authorities, including uninterrupted control over their affairs and a good price for their lands in western Tennessee and northwestern Mississippi. When finally they started west it was a movement under their own leadership undertaken at a time of their own choosing after repeated inspections of their new territory and the route to it by their own representatives. They traveled in comfort, well supplied with equipment, food and money. It might have been expected that were removal ever to be conducted under acceptable conditions it might prove so in their case. But it did not. Their relative prosperity became one of the major causes of their undoing. Sensing unusual profits, contractors gathered stockpiles of supplies along the way in such quantities that the food spoiled before it could be eaten. The travelers were charged exorbitantly for transportation and their every other requirement. They picked up smallpox en route and the disease reached epidemic proportions after their arrival. Most had arrived too late to get in an 1838 crop and they were soon as hungry as their poorer fellow colonists. The move west had made plaintive beggars of the once proud and warlike Chickasaw.

Nearly 2,000 Seminole, rounded up by various devices, pseudo-agreements and military pressures, were also on the way west in 1838. Having suffered so much more than other migrants before their start, they continued to suffer more en route. Many had scarcely emerged from their swampland refuges before they were crowded, naked and undernourished, aboard ship. Others had already endured long periods of imprisonment by which they had been weakened. Most were detained for weeks and months en route in noisome concentration camps in Tampa, Mobile and New Orleans. In addition to all their other privations and afflictions they were continually harassed at every stop and in every new state jurisdiction by the claims of slave dealers to the ownership of Seminole prisoners who showed evidence of Negro blood. A considerable proportion of Seminole were Negroes who had for generations been considered members of the tribe and even though they were closely guarded prisoners each group of exiles fiercely resisted every attempt to single out any of their number for delivery into slavery. The problem of identification had been complicated by the flight to the Seminole of many actual slaves during the war. Some of the slave traders' claims were thus clothed with a species of legitimacy which made adjudication of every dispute more difficult. As one controversial example, among the Seminole prisoners of war taken by the Creek auxiliaries in 1837 had been 90 black Seminole whom they had sold to traders. In all these disputes federal and state authorities, except for the attendant army officers, in their anxiety to expedite the removal tended to support the traders' claims to an extent that provoked a congressional investigation. Meanwhile, in Florida the war went on, with American troops now under the command of Brigadier General Zachary Taylor, later President of the United States, continuing their attempts to run to earth the some 2,000 Seminole still in hiding.

The year 1838 also witnessed the initiation of a companion Indian removal in an adjoining country. Bowl's band of Cherokee, the first recorded migrants who had fled their homeland in 1794, had eventually settled on the Texas side of the Red River in what was then Mexican territory. Joined by other Cherokee and other Indians, the colony had increased to some 8,000. At the outbreak of the Texas revolution Sam Houston had negotiated a treaty of friendship with Bowl's Cherokee which saved the Americans in Texas from possible attack by Indians at the precarious moment they were being assaulted by Santa Anna in return for a Texan recognition of Cherokee title to the land on which they had settled. But in 1838 Mirabeau Lamar, upon succeeding Houston as President of Texas, immediately proclaimed his intention of expelling all Indians from the republic. In the ensuing 1839 campaign the aged Bowl was killed, still clutching the tin box containing the documents and deeds relating to the 1836 treaty of friendship with Texas. The Texas Cherokee were driven across the Red River to share the fortunes of the West and newly arrived East Cherokee on the upper Arkansas.

Indian removal had now been accomplished. Aside from a few scattered remnants, such as the Seminole fugitives in the Florida swamps, the few mountain Cherokee in North Carolina, the Choctaw residue in Mississippi and an occasional tiny enclave in the north, every Indian nation which had originally occupied the immense expanse of woodland extending across the eastern half of the United States had been compelled to seek new homes on the plains beyond that woodland's western margin. It had required a persisting effort over a period of 15 years, distinguished not only by the sufferings inflicted upon Indians but by the virulent disagreements excited among Americans, to give effect to the outwardly plausible policy announced by Monroe and Calhoun in 1825. Removal had been a contemporary success in the sense that the national government had proved able to impose its will and the states concerned had been rid of unwanted

Indian inhabitants. But for the Indians and for the larger interests of the United States it had been a deplorable failure. The opportunity for Indians to become useful and valued members of American society, an achievement many had seemed on the verge of attaining in 1825, had been heedlessly postponed for more than a century.

Most informed Indians had long realized that such an assimilation represented the one lingering hope that Indians might ever regain comfort and security. The mass of Indians, less aware of the economic and political realities, had as long clung despairingly to the more appealing hope that they might yet contrive some escape from the white incubus. Removal dealt crushing blows to both hopes. In the west progressive Indians were compelled to begin again, under far greater handicaps, the painful climb toward citizenship and all Indians were subjected to white exactions more distracting than any they had known in the east. It was only after decades of miraculously patient struggle that Indians were finally to gain recognition of the principle that the rights of the conquered are even more precious than the prerogatives of their conquerors.

During the three centuries Indians had been retreating before the inexorable advance of alien invaders they had been bitterly conscious that they were suffering greater deprivations than the loss of their lands and lives. Their entire way of life, their whole world as they had known it, was in the course of obliteration. They understood, as could nobody else, by how wide a margin their post-invasion opportunities to pursue happiness failed to match the opportunities they had known before invasion. There was little enough comfort in the reflection that these opportunities were being denied them by a force physically too strong for them to resist.

In their despair Indians had sought consolation in resort to the supernatural. Native prophets, such as those who had inspired the followers of Pontiac and Tecumseh, had emerged again and again to preach the doctrine of original blessedness. They had exhorted Indians to eschew every compromise with white influence, especially by forswearing the use of white tools, weapons and alcohol, so that by a return to their ancient purity they might regain the strength to regain their former freedoms. These movements had been frustrated by their adherents' realization that obedience left Indians even more defenseless than before. By the time of the removal Indians were increasingly addicted to more extravagant religious phantasies. A favorite conceit, intermittently erupting for generation after generation until its final resurgence as the Ghost Dance excitement among the Plains Indians in the late 1880's, envisioned the evocation, by appropriate prayers, dances and rites, of the innumerable spirits of all Indian dead who would return to earth as a mighty host capable of expelling the white invaders and thus restoring the land of peace and plenty Indians had once enjoyed.

Even so superior an intellect as Sequoyah's was subject to wishful fancies. He had from his youth believed that the one Indian hope to retain their identity as a people was to withdraw from white contamination. He had himself moved west nearly twenty years before removal and all his life had sought by advice and example to persuade Indians to shun intercourse with whites. In his declining years he became obsessed with the possibility that the Lost Cherokee, reputed by tribal legend to have disappeared into the farthest west in the forgotten past, still lived in innocence, freedom and security in some distant land. In his frail old age, still in pursuit of this relic of the Indian golden age, he set out on a two-year journey in search of a remote Cherokee colony reported to have found sanctuary in the mountains of Mexico. His 1843 death in a Mexican desert was giving ultimate poignancy to the discovery all Indians were being required to make. For them there was no way back. There was only the way ahead.

16. The Cult of True Womanhood, 1820–1860

Barbara Welter

Men and women today still confront sexual stereotyping. There is still a double standard in American society, and it is reflected in expectations concerning sex to the issue of "equal pay, equal work." The root of this problem is centuries old. In this article, Barbara Welter looks at the antebellum decades of the nineteenth century and describes an important stage in the public expression of sexual stereotypes. American culture hoped to promote industrialization while preserving some premodern values. As a result, women were expected to possess the virtues of piety, purity, submissiveness and domesticity while men were free to exhibit a much wider range of behaviors.

The nineteenth century American man was a busy builder of bridges and railroads, at work long hours in a materialistic society. The religious values of his forebears were neglected in practice if not in intent, and he occasionally felt some guilt that he had turned this new land, this temple of the chosen people, into one vast countinghouse. But he could salve his conscience by reflecting that he had left behind a hostage, not only to fortune, but to all the values which he held so dear and treated so lightly. Woman, in the cult of True Womanhood presented by the women's magazines, gift annuals and religious literature of the nineteenth century, was the hostage in the home. In a society where values changed frequently, where fortunes rose and fell with frightening rapidity, where social and economic mobility provided instability as well as hope, one thing at least remained the same—a true woman was a true woman, wherever she was found. If anyone, male or female, dared to tamper with the complex of virtues which made up True Womanhood, he was damned immediately as an enemy of God, of civilization and of the Republic. It was a fearful obligation, a solemn responsibility, which the nineteenth century American woman had—to uphold the pillars of the temple with her frail white hand.

The attributes of True Womanhood, by which a woman judged herself and was judged by her husband, her neighbors and society could be divided into four cardinal virtues—piety, purity, submissiveness and domesticity. Put them all together and they spelled mother, daughter, sister, wife—woman. Without them, no matter whether there was fame, achievement or wealth, all was ashes. With them she was promised happiness and power.

Religion or piety was the core of woman's virtue, the source of her strength. Young men looking for a mate were cautioned to search first for piety, for if that were there, all else would follow. Religion belonged to woman by divine right, a gift of God and nature. This "peculiar susceptibility" to religion was given her for a reason: "the vestal flame of piety, lighted up by Heaven in the breast of woman" would throw its beams into the naughty world of men. So far would its candle power reach that the "Universe might be Enlightened, Improved, and Harmonized by WOMAN!!" She would be another, better, Eve, working in cooperation with the Redeemer, bringing the world back "from its revolt and sin." The world would be reclaimed for God through her suffering, for "God increased the cares and sorrows of woman, that she might be sooner constrained to accept the terms of salvation." A popular poem by Mrs. Frances Osgood, "The Triumph of the Spiritual Over the Sensual" expressed just this sentiment, woman's purifying passionless love bringing an erring man back to Christ.

Dr. Charles Meigs, explaining to a graduating class of medical students why women were naturally religious, said that "hers is a pious mind. Her confiding nature leads her more readily than men to accept the proffered grace of the Gospel." Caleb Atwater, Esq., writing in *The Ladies' Repository*, saw the hand of the Lord in female piety: "Religion is exactly what a woman needs, for it gives her that dignity that best suits her dependence." And Mrs. John Sandford, who had no very high opinion of her sex, agreed throughly: "Religion is just what woman needs. Without it she is ever restless or unhappy. . . ." Mrs. Sandford and the others did not speak only of that restlessness of the human heart, which St. Augustine notes, that can only find its peace in God. They spoke rather of religion as a kind of tranquilizer for the many undefined longings which swept even the most pious young girl, and about which it was better to pray than to think.

One reason religion was valued was that it did not take a woman away from her "proper sphere," her home. Unlike participation in other societies or movements, church work would not make her less domestic or submissive, less a True Woman. In religious vineyards, said the *Young Ladies' Literary and Missionary Report*, "you may labor without the apprehension of detracting from the charms of feminine delicacy." Mrs. S. L. Dagg, writing from her chapter of the Society in Tuscaloosa, Alabama, was equally reassuring: "As no sensible woman will suffer her intellectual pursuits to clash with her domestic duties" she should concentrate on religious work "which promotes these very duties."

The women's seminaries aimed at aiding women to be religious, as well as accomplished. Mt. Holyoke's catalogue promised to make female education "a handmaid to the Gospel and an efficient auxiliary in the great task of renovating the world." The Young Ladies' Seminary at Bordentown, New Jersey, declared its most important function to be "the forming of a sound and virtuous character." In Keene, New Hampshire, the Seminary tried to instill a "consistent and useful character" in its students, to enable them in this life to be "a good friend, wife and mother" but more important, to qualify them for "the enjoyment of Celestial Happiness in the life to come." And Joseph M. D. Mathews, Principal of Oakland Female Seminary in Hillsborough, Ohio, believed that "female education should be preeminently religious."

If religion was so vital to a woman, irreligion was almost too awful to contemplate. Women were warned not to let their literary or intellectual pursuits take them away from God. Sarah Josepha Hale spoke darkly of those who, like Margaret Fuller, threw away the "One True Book" for others, open to error. Mrs. Hale used the unfortunate Miss Fuller as fateful proof that "the greater the intellectual force, the greater and more fatal the errors into which women fall who wander from the Rock of Salvation, Christ the Saviour. . . ."

One gentleman, writing on "Female Irreligion" reminded his readers that "Man may make himself a brute, and does so very often, but can woman bruitfy herself to his level—the lowest level of human nature—without exerting special wonder?" Fanny Wright, because she was godless, "was no woman, mother thigh she be," A few years ago, he recalls, such women would have been whipped. In any case, "woman never looks lovelier than in her reverence for religion" and, conversely, "female irreligion is the most revolting feature in human character."

Purity was as essential as piety to a Young woman, its absence as unnatural and unfeminine. Without it she was, in fact, no woman at all, but a member of some lower order. A "fallen woman" was a "fallen angel," unworthy of the celestial company of her sex. To contemplate the loss of purity brought tears; to be guilty of such a crime, in the women's magazines at least, brought madness or death. Even the language of the flowers had bitter words for it: a dried white rose symbolized "Death Preferable to Loss of Innocence." The marriage night was the single great event of a woman's life, when she bestowed her greatest treasure upon her husband, and from that time on was completely dependent upon him, an empty vessel, without legal or emotional existence of her own.

Therefore all True Women were urged, in the strongest possible terms, to maintain their virtue, although men, being by nature more sensual than they, would try to assault it. Thomas Branagan admitted in *The Excellency of the Female Character Vindicated* that his sex would sin and sin again, they could not help it, but woman, stronger and purer, must not give in and let man "take liberties incompatible with her delicacy." "If you do," Branagan addressed his gentle reader, "You will be left in silent sadness to bewail your credulity, imbecility, duplicity, and premature prostitution."

Mrs. Eliza Farrar, in *The Young Lady's Friend* gave practical logistics to avoid trouble: "Sit not with another in a place that is too narrow; read not out of the same book; let not your eagerness to see anything induce you to place your head close to another person's."

If such good advice was ignored the consequences were terrible and inexorable. In *Girlhood and Womanhood: Or Sketches of My Schoolmates*, by Mrs. A. J. Graves (a kind of mid-nineteenth century *The Group*), the bad ends of a boarding school class of girls are scrupulously recorded. The worst end of all is reserved for "Amelia Dorrington: The Lost One." Amelia died in the almshouse "the wretched victim of depravity and intemperance" and all because her mother had let her be "high-spirited not prudent." These girlish high spirits had been misinterpreted by a young man, with disastrous results. Amelia's thoughtless levity" was "followed by a total loss of virtuous principle" and Mrs. Graves editorializes that "the coldest reserve is more admirable in a woman a man wishes to make his wife, than the least approach to undue familiarity.

A popular and often-reprinted story by Fanny Forester told the sad tale of "Lucy Dutton." Lucy with the seal of innocence upon her heart, and a rose-leaf on her cheek" came out of her vine-covered cottage and ran into a city slicker. "And Lucy was beautiful and trusting, and thoughtless: and he was gay, selfish and profligate. Needs the story to be told?. . . Nay, censor, Lucy was a child— consider how young, how very untaught—oh! her innocence was no match for the sophistry of a gay, city youth! Spring came and shame was stamped upon the cottage at the foot of the hill." The baby died; Lucy went mad at the funeral and finally died herself. "Poor, poor Lucy Dutton! The grave is a blessed couch and pillow to the wretched. Rest thee there, poor Lucy!" The frequency with which derangement follows loss of virtue suggests the exquisite sensibility of woman, and the possibility that, in the women's magazines at least, her intellect was geared to her hymen, not her brain.

If, however, a woman managed to withstand man's assaults on her virtue, she demonstrated her superiority and her power over him. Eliza Farnham, trying to prove this female superiority, concluded smugly that "the purity of women is the everlasting barrier against which the tides of man's sensual nature surge."

A Story in *The Lady's Amaranth* illustrates this dominance. It is set, improbably, in Sicily, where two lovers, Bianca and Tebaldo, have been separated because her family insisted she marry a rich old man. By some strange circumstance the two are in a shipwreck and cast on a desert island, the only survivors. Even here, however, the rigid standards of True Womanhood prevail. Tebaldo unfortunately forgets himself slightly, so that Bianca must warn him: "We may not indeed gratify our fondness by caresses, but it is still something to bestow our kindest language, and looks and prayers, and all lawful and honest attentions on each other." Something, perhaps, but not enough, and Bianca must further remonstrate: "It is true that another man is my husband, but you are my guardian angel." When even that does not work she says in a voice of sweet reason, passive and proper to the end, that she wishes he wouldn't but "still, if you insist, I will become what you wish; but I beseech you to consider, ere that decision, that debasement which I must suffer in your esteem." This appeal to his own double standards holds the beast in him at bay. They are rescued, discover that the old husband is dead, and after "mourning a decent season" Bianca finally gives in, legally.

Men could be counted on to be grateful when women thus saved them from themselves. William Alcott, guiding young men in their relations with the opposite sex, told them that "Nothing is better calculated to preserve a young man from contamination of low pleasures and pursuits than frequent intercourse with the more refined and virtuous of the other sex." And he added, one assumes in equal innocence, that youths should "observe and learn to admire, that purity and ignorance of evil which is the characteristic of well educated young ladies, and which, when we are near them, raises us above those sordid and sensual considerations which hold such sway over men in their intercourse with each other."

The Rev. Jonathan F. Steams was also impressed by female chastity in the face of male passion, and warned woman never to compromise the source of her power: "Let her lay aside delicacy, and her influence over our sex is gone."

Women themselves accepted, with pride but suitable modesty, this priceless virtue. *The Ladies' Wreath*, in "Woman the Creature of God and the Manufacturer of Society" saw purity as her greatest gift and chief means of discharging her duty to save the world: "Purity is the highest beauty—the true pole-star which is to guide humanity aright in its long, varied, and perilous voyage."

Sometimes, however, a woman did not see the dangers to her treasure. In that case, they must be pointed out to her, usually by a male. In the nineteenth century any form of social change was tantamount to an attack on woman's virtue, if only it was correctly understood. For example, dress reform seemed innocuous enough and the bloomers worn by the lady of that name and her followers were certainly modest attire. Such was the reasoning only of the ignorant. In another issue of *The Ladies' Wreath* a young lady is represented in dialogue with her "Professor." The girl expresses admiration for the bloomer costume—it gives freedom of motion, is healthful and attractive. The "Professor" sets her straight. Trousers, he explains, are "only one of the many manifestations of that wild spirit of socialism and agrarian radicalism which is at present so rife in our land." The young lady recants immediately: "If this dress has any connexion with Fourierism or Socialism, or fanaticism in any shape whatever, I have no disposition to wear it at all. . . no true woman would so far compromise her delicacy as to espouse, however unwittingly, such a cause."

America could boast that her daughters were particularly innocent. In a poem on "The American Girl" the author wrote proudly:

> *Her eye of light is the diamond bright,*
> *Her innocence the pearl,*
> *And these are ever the bridal gems*
> *That are worn by the American girl.*

Lydia Maria Child, giving advice to mothers, aimed at preserving that spirit of innocence. She regretted that "want of confidence between mothers and daughters on delicate subjects" and suggested a woman tell her daughter a few facts when she reached the age of twelve to "set her mind at rest." Then Mrs. Child confidently hoped that a young lady's "instinctive modesty" would "prevent her from dwelling on the information until she was called upon to use it."

In the same vein, a book of advice to the newly-married was titled *Whisper to a Bride*. As far as intimate information was concerned, there was no need to whisper, since the book contained none at all.

A masculine summary of this virtue was expressed in a poem "Female Charms":

I would have her as pure as the snow on the
    mount—
   As true as the smile that to infamy's given—
As pure as the wave of the crystalline fount,
    Yet as warm in the heart as the sunlight of
    heaven.
With a mind cultivated, not boastingly wise,
    I could gaze on such beauty, with exquisite
    bliss,
With her heart on her lips and her soul in her
    eyes—
What more could I wish in dear woman than
    this.

Man might, in fact, ask no more than this in woman, but she was beginning to ask more of herself, and in the asking was threatening the third powerful and necessary virtue, submission. Purity, considered as a moral imperative, set up a dilemma which was hard to resolve. Woman must preserve her virtue until marriage and marriage was necessary for her happiness. Yet marriage was, literally, an end to innocence. She was told not to question this dilemma, but simply to accept it.

Submission was perhaps the most feminine virtue expected of women. Men were supposed to be religious, although they rarely had time for it, and supposed to be pure, although it came awfully hard to them, but men were the movers, the doers, the actors. Women were the passive, submissive responders. The order of dialogue was, of course, fixed in Heaven. Man was "woman's superior by God's appointment, if not in intellectual dowry, at least by official decree." Therefore, as Charles Elliott argued in *The Ladies' Respository*, she should submit to him "for the sake of good order at least." In *The Ladies Companion* a young wife was quoted approvingly as saying that she did not think woman should "feel and act for herself" because "When, next to God, her husband is not the tribunal to which her heart and intellect appeals—the golden bowl of affection is broken." Women were warned that if they tampered with this quality they tampered with the order of the Universe.

The Young Lady's Book summarized the necessity of the passive virtues in its readers' lives: "It is, however, certain, that in whatever situation of life a woman is placed from her cradle to her grave, a spirit of obedience and submission, pliability of temper, and humility of mind, are required from her."

Woman understood her position if she was the right kind of woman, a true woman, "She feels herself weak and timid. She needs a protector," declared George Burnap, in his lectures on *The Sphere and Duties of Woman*. "She is in a measure dependent. She asks for wisdom, constancy, firmness, perseverance, and she is willing to repay it all by the surrender of the full treasure of her affections. Woman despises in man every thing like herself except a tender heart. It is enough that she is effeminate and weak; she does not want another like herself." Or put even more strongly by Mrs. Sandford: "A really sensible woman feels her dependence. She does what she can, but she is conscious of inferiority, and therefore grateful for support."

Mrs. Sigourney, however, assured young ladies that although they were separate, they were equal. This difference of the sexes did not imply inferiority, for it was part of that same order of Nature established by Him "who bids the oak brave the fury of the tempest, and the alpine flower lean its cheek on the bosom of eternal snows." Dr. Meigs had a different analogy to make the same point, contrasting the anatomy of the Apollo of the Belvedere (illustrating the male principle) with the Venus de Medici (illustrating the female principle). "Woman," said the physician, with a kind of clinical gallantry, "has a head almost too small for intellect but just big enough for love."

This love itself was to be passive and responsive. "Love, in the heart of a woman," wrote Mrs. Farrar, "should partake largely of the nature of gratitude. She should love, because she is already loved by one deserving her regard."

Woman was to work in silence, unseen, like Wordsworth's Lucy. Yet, "working like nature, in secret" her love goes forth to the world "to regulate its pulsation, and send forth from its heart, in pure and temperate flow, the life giving current." She was to work only for pure affection, without thought of money or ambition. A poem, "Woman and Fame," by Felicia Hemans, widely quoted in many of the gift books, concludes with a spirited renunciation of the gift of fame:

Away! to me, a woman, bring
  Sweet flowers from affection's spring.

"True feminine genius," said Grace Greenwood (Sara Jane Clarke) "is ever timid, doubtful, and clingingly dependent; a perpetual childhood." And she advised literary ladies in an essay on "The Intellectual Woman"—"Don't trample on the flowers while longing for the stars." A wife who submerged her own talents to work for her husband was extolled as an example of a true woman. In *Women of Worth: A Book for Girls*, Mrs. Ann Flaxman, an artist of promise herself, was praised because she "devoted herself to sustain her husband's genius and aid him in his arduous career."

Caroline Gilman's advice to the bride aimed at establishing this proper order from the beginning of a marriage: "Oh, young and lovely bride, watch well the first moments when your will conflicts with his to whom God and society have given the control. Reverence his *wishes* even when you do not his *opinions*."

Mrs. Gilman's perfect wife in *Recollections of a Southern Matron* realizes that "the three golden threads with which domestic happiness is woven" are "to repress a harsh answer, to confess a fault, and to stop (right or wrong) in the midst of self-defense, in gentle submission." Woman could do this, hard though it was, because in her heart she knew she was right and so could afford to be forgiving, even a trifle condescending. "Men are not unreasonable," averred Mrs. Gilman. "Their difficulties lie in not understanding the moral and physical nature of our sex. They often wound through ignorance, and are surprised at having offended." Wives were advised to do their best to reform men, but if they couldn't, to give up gracefully. "If any habit of his annoyed me, I spoke of it once or twice, calmly, then bore it quietly."

A wife should occupy herself "only with domestic affairs—wait till your husband confides to you those of a high importance—and do not give your advice until he asks for it," advised the *Lady's Token*. At all times she should behave in a manner becoming a woman, who had "no arms other than gentleness." Thus "if he is abusive, never retort." *A Young Lady's Guide to the Harmonious Development of a Christian Character* suggested that females should "become as little children" and "avoid a controversial spirit." *The Mother's Assistant and Young Lady's Friend* listed "Always Conciliate" as its first commandment in "Rules for Conjugal and Domestic Happiness." Small wonder that these same rules ended with the succinct maxim: "Do not expect too much."

As mother, as well as wife, woman was required to submit to fortune. In *Letters to Mothers* Mrs. Sigourney sighed: "To bear the evils and sorrows which may be appointed us, with a patient mind, should be the continual effort of our sex. . . . It seems, indeed, to be expected of us; since the passive and enduring virtues are more immediately within our province." Of these trials "the hardest was to bear the loss of children with submission" but the indomitable Mrs. Sigourney found strength to murmur to the bereaved mother: "The Lord loveth a cheerful giver." *The Ladies' Parlor Companion* agreed thoroughly in "A Submissive Mother," in which a mother who had already buried two children and was nursing a dying baby saw her sole remaining child "probably scalded to death. Handing over the infant to die in the arms of a friend, she bowed in sweet submission to the double stroke." But the child "through the goodness of God survived, and the mother learned to say 'Thy will be done.'"

Woman then, in all her roles, accepted submission as her lot. It was a lot she had not chosen or deserved. As *Godey's* said, "the lesson of submission is forced upon woman." Without comment or criticism the writer affirms that "To suffer and to be silent under suffering seems the great command she has to obey." George Burnap referred to a woman's life as "a series of suppressed emotions."

She was, as Emerson said, "more vulnerable, more infirm, more mortal than man." The death of a beautiful woman, cherished in fiction, represented woman as the innocent victim, suffering without sin, too pure and good for this world but too weak and passive to resist its evil forces. The best refuge for such a delicate creature was the warmth and safety of her home.

The true woman's place was unquestionably by her own fireside—as daughter, sister, but most of all as wife and mother. Therefore domesticity was among the virtues most prized by the women's magazines. "As society is constituted," wrote Mrs. S. E. Farley, on the "Domestic and Social Claims on Woman," "the true dignity and beauty of the female character seem to consist in a right understanding and faithful and cheerful Performance of social and family duties." Sacred Scripture re-enforced social pressure: "St. Paul knew what was best for women when he advised them to be domestic," said Mrs. Sandford. "There is composure at home; there is something sedative in the duties which home involves. It affords security not only from the world, but from delusions and errors of every kind."

From her home woman performed her great task of bringing men back to God. *The Young Ladies' Class Book* was sure that "the domestic fireside is the great guardian of society against the excesses of human passions." *The Lady at Home* expressed its convictions in its very title and concluded that "even if we cannot reform the world in a moment, we can begin the work by reforming ourselves and our households—It is woman's mission. Let her not look away from her own little family circle for the means of producing moral and social reforms, but begin at home."

Home was supposed to be a cheerful place, so that brothers, husbands and sons would not go elsewhere in search of a good time. Woman was expected to dispense comfort and cheer. In writing the biography of Margaret Mercer (every inch a true woman) her biographer (male) notes: "She never forgot that it is the peculiar province of woman to minister to the comfort, and promote the happiness, first, of those most nearly allied to her, and then of those, who by the Providence of God are placed in a state of dependence upon her." Many other essays in the women's journals showed woman as comforter: "Woman, Man's Best Friend," "Woman, the Greatest Social Benefit," "Woman, A Being to Come Home To," "The Wife: Source of Comfort and the Spring of Joy."

One of the most important functions of woman as comforter was her role as nurse. Her own health was probably, although regrettably, delicate. Many homes had "little sufferers," those pale children who wasted away to saintly deaths. And there were enough other illnesses of youth and age, major and minor, to give the nineteenth century American woman nursing experience. The sickroom called for the exercise of her higher qualities of patience, mercy and gentleness as well as for her housewifely arts. She could thus fulfill her dual feminine function—beauty and usefulness.

The cookbooks of the period offer formulas for gout cordials, ointment for sore nipples, hiccough and cough remedies, opening pills and refreshing drinks for fever, along with recipes for pound cake, jumbles, stewed calves head and currant wine. *The Ladies' New Book of Cookery* believed that "food prepared by the kind hand of a wife, mother, sister, friend" tasted better and had a "restorative power which money cannot purchase."

A chapter of *The Young Lady's Friend* was devoted to woman's privilege as "ministering spirit at the couch of the sick." Mrs. Farrar advised a soft voice, gentle and clean hands, and a cheerful smile. She also cautioned against an excess of female delicacy. That was all right for a young lady in the parlor, but not for bedside manners. Leeches, for example, were to be regarded as "a curious piece of mechanism . . . their ornamental stripes should recommend them even to the eye, and their valuable services to our feelings." And she went on calmly to discuss their use. Nor were women to shrink from medical terminology, since "If you cultivate right views of the wonderful structure of the body, you will be as willing to speak to a physician of the bowels as the brains of your patient."

Nursing the sick, particularly sick males, not only made a woman feel useful and accomplished, but increased her influence. In a piece of heavy-handed humor in *Godey's* a man confessed that some women were only happy when their husbands were ailing that they might have the joy of nursing him to recovery "thus gratifying their medical vanity and their love of power by making him more dependent upon them." In a similar vein a husband sometimes suspected his wife "almost wishes me dead—for the pleasure of being utterly inconsolable."

In the home women were not only the highest adornment of civilization, but they were supposed to keep busy at morally uplifting tasks. Fortunately most of housework, if looked at in true womanly fashion, could be regarded as uplifting. Mrs. Sigourney extolled its virtues: "The science of housekeeping affords exercise for the judgment and energy, ready recollection, and patient self- possession, that are the characteristics of a superior mind." According to Mrs. Farrar, making beds was good exercise, the repetitiveness of routine tasks inculcated patience and perseverance, and proper management of the home was a surprisingly complex art: "There is more to be learned about pouring out tea and coffee than most young ladies are willing to believe." Godey's went so far as to suggest coyly, in "Learning vs. Housewifery" that the two were complementary, not opposed: chemistry could be utilized in cooking, geometry in dividing cloth, and phrenology in discovering talent in children.

Women were to master every variety of needlework, for, as Mrs. Sigourney pointed out. "Needle-work, in all its forms of use, elegance, and ornament, has ever been the appropriate occupation of woman." Embroidery improved taste; knitting promoted serenity and economy. Other forms of artsy-craftsy activity for her leisure moments included painting on glass or velvet, Poonah work, tussymussy frames for her own needlepoint or water colors, stands for hyacinths, hair bracelets or baskets of feathers.

She was expected to have a special affinity for flowers. To the editors of *The Lady's Token* "A Woman never appears more truly in her shpere, than when she divides her time between her domestic avocations and the culture of flowers." She could write letters, an activity particularly feminine since it had to do with the outpourings of the heart, or practice her drawingroom skills of singing and playing an instrument. She might even read.

Here she faced a bewildering array of advice. The female was dangerously addicted to novels, according to the literature of the period. She should avoid them, since they interfered with "serious piety." If she simply couldn't help herself and read them anyway, she should choose edifying ones from lists of morally acceptable authors. She should study history since it "showed the depravity of the human heart and the evil nature of sin." On the whole, "religious biography was best."

The women's magazines themselves could be read without any loss of concern for the home. *Godey's* promised the husband that he would find his wife "no less assiduous for his reception, or less sincere in welcoming his return" as a result of reading their magazine. *The Lily of the Valley* won its right to be admitted to the boudoir by confessing that it was "like its namesake humble and unostentatious, but it is yet pure, and, we trust, free from moral imperfections."

No matter what later authorities claimed, the nineteenth century knew that girls *could* be ruined by books. The seduction stories regard "exciting and dangerous books as contributory causes of disaster. The man without honorable intentions always provides the innocent maiden with such books as a prelude to his assault on her virtue. Books which attacked or seemed to attack woman's accepted place in society were regarded as equally dangerous. A reviewer of Harriet Martineau's *Society in America* wanted it kept out of the hands of American women. They were so susceptible to persuasion, with their "gentle yielding natures" that they might listen to "the bold ravings of the hard-featured of their own sex." The frightening result: "such reading will unsettle them for their true station and pursuits, and they will throw the world back again into confusion."

The debate over women's education posed the question of whether a "finished" education detracted from the practice of housewifely arts. Again it proved to be a case of semantics, for a true woman's education was never "finished" until she was instructed in the gentle science of homemaking. Helen Irving, writing on "Literary Women," made it very clear that if women invoked the muse, it was as a genie of the household lamp. "If the necessities of her position require these duties at her hands, she will perform them nonetheless cheerfully, that she knows herself capable of higher things." The literary woman must conform to the same standards as any other woman: "That her home shall be made a loving place of rest and joy and comfort for those who are dear to her, will be the first wish of every true woman's heart." Mrs. Ann Stephens told women who wrote to make sure they did not sacrifice one domestic duty. "As for genius, make it a domestic plant. Let its roots strike deep in your house. . . ."

The fear of "blue stockings" (the eighteenth century male's term of derision for educated or literary women) need not persist for nineteenth century American men. The magazines presented spurious dialogues in which bachelors were convinced of their fallacy in fearing educated wives. One such dialogue took place between a young man and his female cousin. Ernest deprecates learned ladies ("A *Woman* is far more lovable than a *philosopher*") but Alice refutes him with the beautiful example of their Aunt Barbara who "although she *has* perpetrated the heinous crime of writing some half dozen folios" is still a model of "the spirit of feminine gentleness." His memory prodded, Ernest concedes that, by George, there was a woman: "When I last had a cold she not only made me a bottle of cough syrup, but when I complained of nothing new to read, set to work and wrote some twenty stanzas on consumption."

The magazines were filled with domestic tragedies in which spoiled young girls learned that when there was a hungry man to feed French and china painting were not helpful. According to these stories many a marriage is jeopardized because the wife has not learned to keep house. Harriet Beecher Stowe wrote a sprightly piece of personal experience for *Godey's*, ridiculing her own bad housekeeping as a bride. She used the same theme in a story "The Only Daughter," in which the pampered beauty learns the facts of domestic life from a rather difficult source; her mother-in-law. Mrs. Hamilton tells Caroline in the sweetest way possible to shape up in the kitchen, reserving her rebuke for her son: "You are her husband—her guide—her protector— now see what you can do," she admonishes him. "Give her credit for every effort: treat her faults with tenderness; encourage and praise whenever you can, and depend upon it, you will see another woman in her." He is properly masterful, she properly domestic and in a few months Caroline is making lumpless gravy and keeping up with the darning. Domestic tranquillity has been restored and the young wife moralizes: "Bring up a girl to feel that she has a responsible part to bear in promoting the happiness of the family, and you make a reflecting being of her at once, and remove that lightness and frivolity of character which makes her shrink from graver studies." These stories end with the heroine drying her hands on her apron and vowing that *her* daughter will be properly educated, in piecrust as well as Poonah work.

The female seminaries were quick to defend themselves against any suspicion of interfering with the role which nature's God had assigned to women. They hoped to enlarge and deepen that role, but not to change its setting. At the Young Ladies' Seminary and Collegiate Institute in Monroe City, Michigan, the catalogue admitted few of its graduates would be likely "to fill the learned professions." Still, they were called to "other scenes of usefulness and honor." The average woman is to be "the presiding genius of love" in the home, where she is to "give a correct and elevated literary taste to her children, and to assume that influential station that she ought to possess as the companion of an educated man."

At Miss Pierce's famous school in Litchfield, the students were taught that they had "attained the perfection of their characters when they could combine their elegant accomplishments with a turn for solid domestic virtues." Mt. Holyoke paid pious tribute to domestic skills: "Let a young lady despise this branch of the duties of woman, and she despises the appointments of her existence." God, nature and the Bible "enjoin these duties on the sex, and she cannot violate them with impunity." Thus warned, the young lady would have to seek knowledge of these duties elsewhere, since it was not in the curriculum at Mt. Holyoke. "We would not take this privilege from the mother."

One reason for knowing her way around a kitchen was that America was "a land of precarious fortunes," as Lydia Maria Child pointed out in her book *The Frugal Housewife: Dedicated to Those Who Are Not Ashamed of Economy*. Mrs. Child's chapter "How To Endure Poverty, prescribed a combination of piety and knowledge—the kind of knowledge found in a true woman's education, "a thorough religious *useful* education." The woman who had servants today might tomorrow, because of a depression or panic, be forced to do her own work. If that happened she knew how to act, for she was to be the same cheerful consoler of her husband in their cottage as in their mansion.

An essay by Washington Irving, much quoted in the gift annuals, discussed the value of a wife in case of business reverses: "I have observed that a married man falling into misfortune is more apt to achieve his situation in the world than a single one . . . it is beautifully ordained by Providence that woman, who is the ornament of man in his happier hours, should be his stay and solace when smitten with sudden calamity."

A story titled simply but eloquently "The Wife" dealt with the quiet heroism of Ellen Graham during her husband's plunge from fortune to poverty. Ned Graham said of her: "Words are too poor to tell you what I owe to that noble woman. In our darkest seasons of adversity, she has been an angel of consolation—utterly forgetful of self and anxious only to comfort and sustain me." Of course she had a little help from "faithful Dinah who absolutely refused to leave her beloved mistress," but even so Ellen did no more than would be expected of any true woman.

Most of this advice was directed to woman as wife. Marriage was the proper state for the exercise of the domestic virtues. "True Love and a Happy Home," an essay in *The Young Ladies' Oasis*, might have been carved on every girl's hope chest. But although marriage was best, it was not absolutely necessary. The women's magazines tried to remove the stigma from being an "Old Maid." They advised no marriage at all rather than an unhappy one contracted out of selfish motives. Their stories showed maiden ladies as unselfish ministers to the sick, teachers of the young, or moral preceptors with their pens, beloved of the entire village. Usually the life of single blessedness resulted from the premature death of a fiancé, or was chosen through fidelity to some high mission. For example, in "Two Sisters," Mary devotes herself to Ellen and her abandoned children, giving up her own chance for marriage. "Her devotion to her sister's happiness has met its reward in the consciousness of having fulfilled a sacred duty." Very rarely, a "woman of genius" was absolved from the necessity of marriage, being so extraordinary that she did not need the security or status of being a wife. Most often, however, if girls proved "difficult," marriage and a family were regarded as a cure. The "sedative quality" of a home could be counted on to subdue even the most restless spirits.

George Burnap saw marriage as "that sphere for which woman was originally intended, and to which she is so exactly fitted to adorn and bless, as the wife, the mistress of a home, the solace, the aid, and the counsellor of that ONE, for whose sake alone the world is of any consequence to her." Samuel Miller preached a sermon on women: "How interesting and important are the duties devolved on females as WIVES . . . the counsellor and friend of the husband; who makes it her daily study to lighten his cares, to soothe his sorrows, and to augment his joys; who, like a guardian angel, watches over his interests, warns him against dangers, comforts him under trials; and by her pious, assiduous, and attractive deportment, constantly endeavors to render him more virtuous, more useful, more honourable, and more happy." A woman's whole interest should be focused on her husband, paying him "those numberless attentions to which the French give the title of *petits soins* and which the woman who loves knows so well how to pay . . . she should consider nothing as trivial which could win a smile of approbation from him."

Marriage was seen not only in terms of service but as an increase in authority for woman. Burnap concluded that marriage improves the female character "not only because it puts her under the best possible tuition, that of the affections, and affords scope to her active energies, but because it gives her higher aims, and a more dignified position." *The Lady's Amaranth* saw it as a balance of power: "The man bears rule over his wife's person and conduct. She bears rule over his inclinations: he governs by law; she by persuasion. . . . The empire of the woman is an empire of softness . . . her commands are caresses, her menaces are tears."

Woman should marry, but not for money. She should choose only the high road of true love and not truckle to the values of a materialistic society. A story "Marrying for Money" (subtlety was not the strong point of the ladies' magazines) depicts Gertrude, the heroine, rueing the day she made her crass choice: "It is a terrible thing to live without love. . . . A woman who dares marry for aught but the purest affection, calls down the just judgments of heaven upon her head."

The corollary to marriage, with or without true love, was motherhood, which added another dimension to her usefulness and her prestige. It also anchored her even more firmly to the home. "My Friend," wrote Mrs. Sigourney, "If in becoming a mother, you have reached the climax of your happiness, you have also taken a higher place in the scale of being . . . you have gained an increase of power." The Rev. J. N. Danforth pleaded in *The Ladies' Casket*, "Oh, mother, acquit thyself well in thy humble sphere, for thou mayest affect the world." A true woman naturally loved her children; to suggest otherwise was monstrous.

America depended upon her mothers to raise up a whole generation of Christian statesmen who could say "all that I am I owe to my angel mother." The mothers must do the inculcating of virtue since the fathers, alas, were too busy chasing the dollar. Or as *The Ladies' Companion* put it more effusively, the father "weary with the heat and burden of life's summer day, or trampling with unwilling foot the decaying leaves of life's autumn, has forgotten the sympathies of life's joyous springtime.... The acquisition of wealth, the advancement of his children in worldly honor—these are his self-imposed tasks." It was his wife who formed "the infant mind as yet untainted by contact with evil.... like wax beneath the plastic hand of the mother."

The Ladies' Wreath offered a fifty-dollar prize to the woman who submitted the most convincing essay on "How May An American Woman Best Show Her Patriotism." The winner was Miss Elizabeth Wetherell who provided herself with a husband in her answer. The wife in the essay of course asked her husband's opinion. He tried a few jokes first—Call her eldest son George Washington," "Don't speak French, speak American"—but then got down to telling her in sober prize-winning truth what women could do for their country. Voting was no asset, since that would result only in "a vast increase of confusion and expense without in the smallest degree affecting the result." Besides, continued this oracle, "looking down at their child," if "we were to go a step further and let the children vote, their first act would be to vote their mothers at home." There is no comment on this devastating male logic and he continues: "Most women would follow the lead of their fathers and husbands," and the few who would "fly off on a tangent from the circle of home influence would cancel each other out."

The wife responds dutifully: "I see all that. I never understood so well before." Encouraged by her quick womanly perception, the master of the house resolves the question—an American woman best shows her patriotism by staying at home, where she brings her influence to bear "upon the right side for the country's weal." That woman will instinctively choose the side of right he has no doubt. Besides her "natural refinement and closeness to God" she has the "blessed advantage of a quiet life" while man exposed to conflict and evil. She stays home with "her Bible and a well-balanced mind" and raises her sons to be good Americans. The judges rejoiced in this conclusion and paid the prize money cheerfully, remarking "they deemed it cheap at the price."

If any woman asked for greater scope for her gifts the magazines were sharply critical. Such women were tampering with society, undermining civilization. Mary Wollstonecraft, Frances Weight and Harriet Martineau were condemned in the strongest possible language—they were read out of the sex. "They are only semi-women, mental hermaphrodites." The Rev. Harrington knew the women of America could not possibly approve of such perversions and went to some wives and mothers to ask if they did want a "wider sphere of interest" as these nonwomen claimed. The answer was reassuring. "NO!" they cried simultaneously, "Let the men take care of politics, *we will take care of the children!*" Again female discontent resulted only from a lack of understanding: women were not subservient, they were rather "chosen vessels." Looked at in this light the conclusion was inescapable: "Noble, sublime is the task of the American mother."

"Women's Rights" meant one thing to reformers, but quite another to the True Woman. She knew her rights,

> *The right to love whom others scorn,*
> *The right to comfort and to mourn,*
> *The right to shed new joy on earth,*
> *The right to feel the soul's high worth. . .*
> *Such women's rights, and God will bless*
> *And crown their champions with success.*

The American woman had her choice—she could define her rights in the way of the women's magazines and insure them by the practice of the requisite virtues, or she could go outside the home, seeking other rewards than love. It was a decision on which, she was told, everything in her world depended. "Yours it is to determine the Rev. Mr. Stearns solemnly warned from the pulpit, "whether the beautiful order of society . . . shall continue as it has been" or whether "society shall break up and become a chaos of disjointed and unsightly elements." If she chose to listen to other voices than those of her proper mentors, sought other rooms than those of her home, she lost both her happiness and her power—"that almost magic power, which, in her proper sphere, she now wields over the destinies of the world."

But even while the women's magazines and related literature encouraged this ideal of the perfect woman, forces were at work in the nineteenth century which impelled woman herself to change, to play a more creative role in society. The movements for social reform, westward migration, missionary activity, utopian communities, industrialism, the Civil War—all called forth responses from woman which differed from those she was trained to believe were hers by nature and divine decree. The very perfection of True Womanhood, moreover, carried within itself the seeds of its own destruction. For if woman was so very little less than the angels, she should surely take a more active part in running the world, especially since men were making such a hash of things.

Real women often felt they did not live up to the ideal of True Womanhood: some of them blamed themselves, some challenged the standard, some tried to keep the virtues and enlarge the scope of womanhood. Somehow through this mixture of challenge and acceptance, of change and continuity, the True Woman evolved into the New Woman—a transformation as startling in its own way as the abolition of slavery or the coming of the machine age. And yet the sterotype, the "mystique" if you will, of what woman was and ought to be persisted, bringing guilt and confusion in the midst of opportunity.

The women's magazines and related literature had feared this very dislocation of values and blurring of roles. By careful manipulation and interpretation they sought to convince woman that she had the best of both worlds—power and virtue—and that a stable order of society depended upon her maintaining her traditional place in it. To that end she was identified with everything that was beautiful and holy.

"Who Can Find a Valiant Woman?" was asked frequently from the pulpit and the editorial pages. There was only one place to look for her—at home. Clearly and confidently these authorities proclaimed the True Woman of the nineteenth century to be the Valiant Woman of the Bible, in whom the heart of her husband rejoiced and whose price was above rubies.

17. Hindrances to Revivals

Charles G. Finney

Charles Grandison Finney (1792–1875) was one of the most significant figures in the Second Great Awakening. His revivals were highly successful. Hundreds of thousands of persons professed a conversion experience during his revivals in New York. Vast numbers of Rochester citizens fell under Finney's influence in 1832; thousands of persons in New York City professed conversion experiences in the famous Great Revival of 1858–1859.

Finney was born in Connecticut but would spend most of his years in two states, New York and Ohio. Trained as a lawyer, Finney became a revivalist in 1824 and then a Presbyterian pastor in New York City. In 1835, Finney moved to Oberlin College in Ohio where he was professor of theology; in 1852 he became its president.

Finney changed American evangelicalism. His ideas about revival were new in antebellum America. He broke with traditional Calvinistic thought about revival and promoted revivalistic "methods" and the agency of free will. He was not without opposition. Yet his ideas became the standard for evangelical revivalists in the 19th and 20th centuries. Evangelists from Dwight L. Moody to Billy Sunday to Billy Graham used his ideas and techniques. Finney linked the conversion experience with social reform. He believed that Christians were to be active in changing society, especially in the area of abolitionism. Finney argued that it was the responsibility of the "church" to rid America of slavery. If the "church" did not do its part in destroying slavery, war would come. In this sermon, preached in 1835 at the Chatham Chapel in New York City, Finney was prophetic.

> I am doing a great work, so that I cannot come down: why should the work cease, whilst I leave it, and come down to you.? - Nehemiah. 6:3.

II. THINGS WHICH OUGHT TO BE DONE.

I proceed to mention some things which ought to be done to continue this great and glorious revival of religion, which has been in progress for the last ten years.

1. There should be great and deep repentings on the part of ministers. WE, my brethren, must humble ourselves before God. It will not do for us to suppose that it is enough to call on the people to repent. We must take the lead in repentance, and then call on the Churches to follow.

Especially must those repent who have taken the lead in producing feelings of opposition and distrust in regard to revivals. Some ministers have confined their opposition against revivals and revival measures to their own congregations, and have created such suspicions among their own people as to prevent the work from spreading and prevailing among them. Such ministers will do well to consider the remarks of President Edwards on this subject:

"If ministers preach never so good doctrine, and are never so painful and laborious in their work, yet, if at such a day as this, they show to their people that they are not well-affected to this work, but are very doubtful and suspicious of it, they will be very likely to do their people a great deal more hurt than good; for the very fame of such a great and extraordinary work of God, if their people were suffered to believe it to be His work, and the example of other towns, together with what preaching they might hear occasionally, would be likely to have a much greater influence upon the minds of their people, to awaken and animate them in religion, than all their labors with them. And besides, their minister's opinion would not only beget in them a suspicion of the work they hear of abroad, whereby the mighty hand of God that appears in it loses its influence upon their minds, but it will also tend to create a suspicion of everything of the like nature, that shall appear among themselves, as being something of the same distemper that has become so epidemical in the land; and that is, in effect, to create a suspicion of all vital religion, and to put the people upon talking against it, and discouraging it, wherever it appears, and knocking it on the head as fast as it rises. And we that are ministers, by looking on this work, from year to year, with a displeased countenance, shall effectually keep the sheep from their pasture, instead of doing the part of shepherds to them by feeding them; and our people had a great deal better be without any settled minister at all at such a day as this." Others have been more public, having aimed at exerting a wider   influence.

Some have written pieces for the public papers. Some men, in high standing in the Church, have circulated letters which were never printed; others have had their letters printed and circulated. There seems to have been a system of letter-writing about the country calculated to create distrust. In the days of President Edwards, substantially the same course was pursued, in view of which he says, in his work on Revivals:

"Great care should be taken that the press should be improved to no purpose contrary to the interest of this work. We read that when God fought against Sisera, for the deliverance of His oppressed Church, they that handled the pen of the writer came to the help of the Lord (Judges 5:14). Whatever class of men in Israel they were that are intended, yet as the words were indicted by a Spirit that had a perfect view of all events to the end of the world, it is not unlikely that they have respect to authors, those that should fight against the kingdom of Satan with their pens.

Those, therefore, that publish pamphlets to the disadvantage of this work, and tending either directly or indirectly to bring it under suspicion, and to discourage or hinder it, would do well thoroughly to consider whether this be not indeed the work of God; and whether, if it be, it is not likely that God will go forth as fire, to consume all that stand in His way, and so burn up those pamphlets; and whether there be not danger that the fire that is kindled in them will scorch the authors."

All these must repent. God never will forgive them, nor will they ever enjoy His blessing on their preaching, or be honored to labor in revivals, till they repent. This duty President Edwards pressed upon ministers in his day, in the most forcible terms. There doubtless have been now, as there were then, faults on both sides. And there must be deep repentance, and mutual confessions of faults on both sides.

"There must be a great deal done at confessing of faults on both sides: for undoubtedly many and great are the faults that have been committed, in the jangling and confusions, and mixtures of light and darkness, that have been of late. There is hardly any duty more contrary to our corrupt dispositions and mortifying to the pride of man; but it must be done.

Repentance of faults is, in a peculiar manner, a proper duty, when the kingdom of heaven is at hand, or when we especially expect or desire that it should come; as appears by John the Baptist's preaching. And if God does now loudly call upon us to repent, then He also calls upon us to make proper manifestations of our repentance.

"I am persuaded that those who have openly opposed this work, or have from time to time spoken lightly of it, cannot be excused in the sight of God, without openly confessing their fault therein: especially if they be ministers. If they have in any way, either directly or indirectly, opposed the work, or have so behaved in their public performances or private conversation as to prejudice the minds of their people against the work; if, hereafter, they shall be convinced of the goodness and divinity of what they have opposed, they ought by no means to palliate the matter, and excuse themselves, and pretend that they always thought so, and that it was only such and such imprudences that they objected against; but they ought openly to declare their conviction, and condemn themselves for what they have done; for it is   Christ that they have spoken against, in speaking lightly of, and prejudicing others against, this work. And though they have done it ignorantly and in unbelief, yet when they find out Who it is that they have opposed, undoubtedly God will hold them bound publicly to confess it.

"And on the other hand, if those who have been zealous to promote the work have, in any of the aforementioned instances, openly gone much out of the way, and done that which was contrary to Christian rules, whereby they have openly injured others or greatly violated good order, and so done that which has wounded religion, they must publicly confess it, and humble themselves, as they would gather out the stones, and prepare the way of God's people. They who have laid great stumbling-blocks in others' way by their open transgression, are bound to remove them by their open repentance."

There are ministers in our day, I say it not in unkindness, but in faithfulness, and I would that I had them all here before me while I say it, who seem to have been engaged much of their time, for years, in doing little else than acting and talking and writing in such a way as to create suspicion in regard to revivals. And I cannot doubt that their Churches would, as President Edwards says, be better with no minister at all, unless they will repent and regain God's blessing.

2. Those Churches which have opposed revivals must humble themselves and repent. Churches which have stood aloof, or hindered the work, must repent of their sin, or God will not go with them. Look at those Churches which have been throwing suspicion upon revivals. Do they enjoy revivals? Does the Holy Ghost descend upon them, to enlarge them and build them up? There is one of the Churches in this city, where the Session has been publishing in the newspapers what it calls its "Act and Testimony," calculated to excite an unreasonable and groundless suspicion against many ministers who are laboring successfully to promote revivals.

And what is the state of that Church? Have they had a revival? Why, it appears from the official report, that it has dwindled in one year twenty-seven per cent. And all such Churches will continue to dwindle, in spite of everything else that can be done, unless they repent and have a revival. They may pretend to be mighty pious, and jealous for the honor of God, but God will not believe they are sincere. And He will manifest His displeasure by not pouring out His Spirit. If I had a voice loud enough, I should like to make all those Churches and ministers that have slandered revivals, hear me, when I say that I believe they have helped to bring the pall of death over the Church, and that the curse of God is on them already, and will remain unless they repent. God has already sent leanness into their souls, and many of them know it.

3. Those who have been engaged in promoting the work must also repent.

Whenever a wrong spirit has been manifested, or they have got irritated and provoked at the opposition, and lost their temper, or mistaken Christian faithfulness for hard words and a wrong spirit, they must repent.

Those who are opposed can never stop a revival alone, unless those who promote it get wrong. So we must repent if we have said things that were censorious, or proud, or arrogant, or severe. Such a time as this is no time to stand justifying ourselves. Our first call is to repent. Let each one repent of his own sins, and not fall out about who is most to blame.

4. The Church must take right ground in regard to politics. Do not suppose that I am going to preach a political sermon, or that I wish to have you join in getting up a Christian party in politics. No, you must not believe that. But the time has come that Christians must vote for honest men, and take consistent ground in politics. They must let the world see that the Church will uphold no man in office who is known to be a knave, or an adulterer, or a Sabbath-breaker, or a gambler, or a drunkard. Such is the spread of intelligence and the facility

of communication in our country, that every man can know for whom he gives his vote. And if he will give his vote only for honest men, the country will be obliged to have upright rulers. All parties will be compelled to put up honest men as candidates. Christians have been exceedingly guilty in this matter. But the time has come when they must act differently. As on the subjects of Slavery and Temperance, so on this subject the Church must act rightly or the country will be ruined. God cannot sustain this free and blessed country, which we love and pray for, unless the Church will take right ground. Politics are a part of a religion in such a country as this, and Christians must do their duty to the country as a part of their duty to God.

It seems sometimes as if the foundations of the nation are becoming rotten, and Christians seem to act as if they think God does not see what they do in politics. But I tell you He does see it, and He will bless or curse this nation, according to the course they take.

5. The Churches must take right ground on the subject of Slavery. Here the question arises, What is right ground?

(a) I will state some of the things that should be avoided.

(1) First of all, a bad spirit should be avoided. Nothing is more calculated to injure religion, and to injure the slaves themselves, than for Christians to get into an angry controversy on the subject. It is a subject upon which there needs to be no angry controversy among Christians. Slave-holding professors, like rum-selling professors, may endeavor to justify themselves, and may be angry with those who press their consciences, and call upon them to give up their sins. Those proud professors of religion, who think a man to blame, or think it is a shame to him, to have a black skin, may allow their prejudices so far to prevail, as to shut their ears and be disposed to quarrel with those who urge the subject upon them. But I repeat it, the subject of Slavery is a subject upon which Christians, praying men, need not and must not differ.

(2) Another thing to be avoided is an attempt to take neutral ground on this subject. Christians can no more take neutral ground on this subject, since it has come up for discussion, than they can take neutral ground on the subject of the sanctification of the Sabbath. It is a great national sin. It is a sin of the Church. The Churches, by their silence, and by permitting shareholders to belong to their communion, have been consenting to it. All denominations have been more or less guilty, although the Quakers have of late years washed their hands of it. It is in vain for the Churches to pretend it is merely a political sin. I repeat, it is the sin of the Church, to which all denominations have consented. They have virtually declared that it is lawful. The very fact of suffering slave-holders quietly to remain in good standing in their Churches, is the strongest and most public expression of their view that it is not sin. For the Church, therefore, to pretend

to take neutral ground on the subject, is perfectly absurd. The fact is that she is not on neutral ground at all. While she tolerates slave-holders in her communion SHE JUSTIFIES THE PRACTICE:. And as well might an enemy of God pretend that he was neither a saint nor a sinner, that he was going to take neutral ground, and pray, "good Lord and good devil," because he did not know which side would be the most popular!

(3) Great care should be taken to avoid a censorious spirit on either side. It is a subject on which there has been, and probably will be for some time to come, a difference of opinion among Christians, as to the best method of disposing of the question: and it ought to be treated with great forbearance.

(b) I will mention several things that, in my judgment, the Church is imperatively called upon to do, on this subject:

(1) Christians, of all denominations, should lay aside prejudice, and inform themselves on this subject, without any delay. Vast multitudes of professors of religion have indulged prejudice to such a degree, as to be unwilling to read and hear, and come to a right understanding of the subject. But Christians cannot pray in this state of mind. I defy any one to possess the spirit of prayer while he is too prejudiced to examine this or any other question of duty. If the light did not shine, Christians might remain in the dark upon this point, and still possess the spirit of prayer.

But if they refuse to come to the light, they cannot pray. Where ministers, individual Christians, or whole Churches, resist truth upon this point, when it is so extensively diffused and before the public mind, I do not believe they will or can enjoy a revival of religion.

(2) Writings, containing temperate and judicious discussions on this subject, and such developments of facts as are before the public, should be quietly and extensively circulated, and should be carefully and prayerfully examined by the whole Church. I do not mean by this, that the attention of the Church should be so absorbed by this as to neglect the main question of saving souls in the midst of them; I do not mean that such premature movements on this subject should be made, as to astound the Christian community, and involve them in a broil; but that praying men should act judiciously, and that, as soon as sufficient information can be diffused through the community, the Churches should meekly, but firmly, take decided ground on the subject, and express, before the whole nation and the world, their abhorrence of this sin.

The anti-Masonic excitement which prevailed a few years since made such desolations in the Churches, and produced so much alienation of feeling and ill-will among ministers and people, and the introduction of this subject has been attended with such commotions, that many good ministers, who are themselves entirely opposed to slavery, dread to introduce the subject, through fear that their people have not religion enough to consider it calmly, and decide upon it in the spirit of the Gospel. I know there is danger of this. But still, the subject must be presented to the Churches. Let there be no mistake here. William Morgan's expose of freemasonry was published in 1826; the subsequent discussion continued until 1830. In the meantime the Churches had very generally borne testimony against freemasonry, and resolved that they could not have adhering masons in fellowship. As a consequence, the Masonic lodges generally disbanded. There was a general stampede of Christians from the lodges. This prepared the way, and in 1830 the greatest revival the world had then seen commenced in the center of the anti-Masonic region, and spread over the whole field where the Church action had been taken.

Perhaps no Church in this country has had a more severe trial upon this subject, than this, which was a Church of young, and for the most part, inexperienced Christians. And many circumstances conspired, in my absence, to produce confusion and wrong-feeling among them. But so far as I am now acquainted with the state of feeling in this Church, I know of no ill-will among the members on this subject. There are doubtless those who feel upon this subject, in very different degrees: and yet I can honestly say that I am not aware of the least difference in sentiment among them. We have from the beginning taken the same ground on the subject of Slavery that we have on Temperance. We have excluded slave-holders, and all concerned in the traffic, from our communion. By some, out of this Church, this course has been censured as unwarrantable and uncharitable, and I would by no means make my own judgment, or the example of this Church, a rule for the government of other ministers and Churches. Still, I conscientiously believe that the time is not far distant, when the Churches will be united in this expression of abhorrence against this sin. If I do not baptize slavery by some soft and Christian name, if I call it SIN, both consistency and conscience conduct to the inevitable conclusion, that while this sin is persevered in, its perpetrators cannot be fit subjects for Christian communion and fellowship.

To this it is objected that there are many ministers in the Presbyterian Church who are slaveholders. And it is said to be very inconsistent that we should refuse to suffer slave-holders to come to our Communion, and yet belong to the same Church with them, sit with them in ecclesiastical bodies, and acknowledge them as ministers. To this I answer, that I have not the power to deal with those ministers, and certainly I am not to withdraw from the Church because some of its ministers or members are slave-holders. My duty is to belong to the Church, even if the devil should belong to it. When I have authority, I exclude slave-holders from the Communion, and I always will as long as I live. But where I have no authority, if the table of Christ be spread, I will sit down to it in obedience to His commandment, whoever else may sit down or stay away.

I do not mean, by any means, to denounce all those slave-holding ministers and professors as hypocrites, and to say that they are not Christians. But this I say, that while they continue in this attitude, the cause of Christ and of humanity demands that they should not be recognized as such, unless we mean to be partakers of other men's sins. It is no more inconsistent to exclude shareholders because they belong to the Presbyterian Church, than it is to exclude persons who drink or sell ardent spirit. For there are many rum-sellers belonging to the Presbyterian Church.

I believe the time has come - although I am no prophet, I believe it will be found to have come, that the revival in the United States will prevail no further and no faster than the Church takes right ground upon this subject.

The Church is God's witness. The fact is, that Slavery is, pre-eminently, the sin of the Church. It is the very fact that ministers and professors of religion of different denominations hold slaves, which sanctifies the whole abomination, in the eyes of ungodly men. Who does not know that on the subject of Temperance, every drunkard in the land will skulk behind some rum-selling deacon, or wine-drinking minister? It is the most common objection and refuge of the intemperate, and of moderate drinkers, that it is practiced by professors of religion. It is this that creates the imperious necessity for excluding traffickers in ardent spirit, and rum-drinkers, from the Communion. Let the Churches of all denominations speak out on the subject of Temperance; let them close their doors against all who have anything to do with the death-dealing abomination, and the cause of Temperance is triumphant. A few years would annihilate the traffic. Just so with Slavery.

It is the Church that mainly supports this sin. Her united testimony upon the subject would settle the question. Let Christians of all denominations meekly, but firmly, come forth, and pronounce their verdict; let them wash their hands of this thing; let them give forth and write on the head and front of this great abomination, "SIN," and in three years, a public sentiment would be formed that would carry all before it, and there would not be a shackled slave, nor a bristling, cruel slavedriver, in this land.

Still it may be said, that in many Churches, this subject cannot be introduced without creating confusion and ill-will. This may be. It has been so on the subject of Temperance, and upon the subject of revivals too. In some Churches, neither Temperance nor revivals can be introduced without producing dissension. Sabbath Schools, and missionary operations, and everything of the kind, have been opposed, and have produced dissensions in many Churches. But is this a sufficient reason for excluding these subjects? And where Churches have excluded these subjects for fear of contention, have they been blessed with revivals?

Everybody knows that they have not. But where Churches have taken firm ground on these subjects, although individuals, and sometimes numbers, have opposed, still they have been blessed with revivals. Where any of these subjects are carefully and prayerfully introduced; where they are brought forward with a right spirit, and the true relative importance is attached to each of them; if in such cases, there are those who will make disturbance and resist, let the blame fall where it ought.

There are some individuals, who are themselves disposed to quarrel with this subject, who are always ready to exclaim: "Do not introduce these things into the Church, they will create opposition." And if the minister and praying people feel it their duty to bring the matter forward, they will themselves create a disturbance and then say: "There, I told you so; now see what your introducing this subject has done; it will tear the Church all to pieces." And while they are themselves doing all they can to create a division, they are charging the division upon the subject, and not upon themselves. There are some such people in many of our Churches. And neither Sabbath Schools, nor Missions, nor Antislavery, nor anything else that honors God or benefits the souls of men, will be carried on in the Churches, without these careful souls being offended by it.

There might infinitely better be no Church in the world, than that she should attempt to remain neutral, or give a false testimony on a subject of such importance as Slavery, especially since the subject has come up, and it is impossible, from the nature of the case, that her testimony should not be in the scale, on the one side or the other.

Do you ask: "What shall be done? Shall we make it the all-absorbing topic of conversation, and divert attention from the all-important subject of the salvation of souls in the midst of us?" I answer: "No." Let a Church express its opinion upon the subject, and be at peace. So far as I know, we are entirely at peace upon this subject.

We have expressed our opinion; we have closed our Communion against slave-holders, and are attending to other things. I am not aware of the least unhealthy excitement among us on this subject. And where it has become an absorbing topic of conversation in places, in most instances, I believe, it has been owing to the pertinacious and unreasonable opposition of a few individuals against even granting the subject a hearing.

6. If the Church wishes to promote revivals, she must sanctify the Sabbath. There is a vast deal of Sabbath breaking in the land. Merchants break it, travelers break it, the Government breaks it. A few years ago an attempt was made in the western part of this State, to establish and sustain a Sabbath-keeping line of boats and coaches. But it was found that the Church would not sustain the enterprise. Many professors of religion would not travel in these coaches, and would not have their goods forwarded in canal-boats that would be detained from traveling on the Sabbath. At one time, Christians were much engaged in petitioning Congress to suspend the Sabbath mails, and now they seem to be ashamed of it. But one thing is most certain, that unless something is done, and done speedily, and done effectually, to promote the sanctification of the Sabbath by the Church, the Sabbath will go by the board, and we shall not only have our mails running on the Sabbath, and post-offices open, but, by and by, our courts of justice, and halls of legislation, will be kept open on the Sabbath. And what can the Church

do, what will this nation do, without any Sabbath?

7. The Church must take right ground on all the subjects of practical morality which come up for discussion from time to time.

There are those in the Churches who are standing aloof from the subject of moral reform, and who are afraid to have anything said in the pulpit against lewdness. On this subject, the Church need not expect to be permitted to take neutral ground. In the providence of God, it is up for discussion. The evils have been exhibited; the call has been made for reform. And what is to reform mankind but the truth? And who shall present the truth if not the Church and the ministry? Away with the idea, that Christians can remain neutral, and yet enjoy the approbation and blessing of God!

In all such cases, the minister who holds his peace is counted among those on the other side. Everybody knows that it is so in a revival. It is not necessary for a person to rail out against the work. If he will only keep still and take neutral ground, the enemies of the revival will all consider him as on their side. So on the subject of Temperance. It is not needful that a person should rail at the Coldwater Society, in order to be on the best terms with drunkards and moderate drinkers. Only let him plead for the moderate use of wine, only let him continue to drink it as a luxury, and all the drunkards account him on their side. On all these subjects, when they come up, the Churches and ministers must take the right ground, and take it openly, and stand to the cause, and carry it through, if they expect to enjoy the blessing of God in revivals. They must cast out from their communions such members as, in contempt of the light that is shed upon them, continue to drink or traffic in ardent spirit.

8. There must be more done for all the great objects of Christian benevolence. There must be much greater effort for the cause of Missions, and Education, and the Bible, and all other branches of religious enterprise, or the Church will displease God. Look at it. Think of the mercies we have received, of the wealth, numbers, and prosperity of the Church. Have we rendered unto God according to the benefits we have received, so as to show that the Church is bountiful, and willing to give money, and to work for God? No. Far from it. Have we multiplied our means and enlarged our plans, in proportion as the Church has increased? Is God satisfied with what has been done, or has He reason to be? After such a revival as has been enjoyed by the Churches of America for the last ten years, we ought to have done ten times as much as we have for Missions, Bibles, Education, Tracts, Churches, and for all causes that are designed to promote religion and save souls. If the Churches do not wake up on this subject, and lay themselves out on a larger scale, they may expect that the revival in the United States will cease.

9. If Christians expect revivals to spread and prevail, till the world is con-

verted, they must give up writing letters and publishing pieces calculated to excite suspicion and jealousy in regard to revivals, and must take hold of the work themselves. If the whole Church, as a body, had gone to work ten years ago, and continued it as a few individuals, whom I could name, have done, there might not now have been an impenitent sinner in the land. The millennium would have fully come into the United States before this day. Instead of standing still, or writing letters, let ministers who think we are going wrong, just buckle on the harness and go forward, and show us a more excellent way. Let them teach us by their example how to do better. I do not deny that some may have made mistakes and committed errors. I do not deny that many things which are wrong have been done in revivals. But is that the way to correct them, brethren? So did not Paul. He corrected his brethren by telling them kindly that he would show them a more excellent way. Let our brethren take hold and go forward. Let us hear the cry from all their pulpits: "To the work!"

Let them lead on where the Lord will go with them and make bare His arm, and I, for one, will follow. Only let them GO ON, and let us have the people converted to God, and let all minor questions cease.

If not, and if revivals do cease in this land, the ministers and Churches will be guilty of all the blood of all the souls that shall go to hell in consequence of it. There is no need that the work should cease. If the Church will do all her duty, the millennium may come in this country in three years. But if it is to be always so, that in the time of revival, two-thirds of the Church will hang back and do nothing but find fault, the curse of God will be on this nation, and that before long.

REMARKS.

1. It is high time there should be great searchings of heart among Christians and ministers. Brethren, this is no time to resist the truth, or to cavil and find fault because the truth is spoken out plainly. It is no time to recriminate or to strive, but we must search our own hearts, and humble ourselves before God.

2. We must repent and forsake our sins, and amend our ways and our doings, or the revival will cease. Our ecclesiastical difficulties MUST CEASE, and all minor differences must be laid aside and given up, to unite in promoting the great interests of religion. If not, revivals will cease from among us, and the blood of lost millions will be found on our skirts.

3. If the Church would do all her duty, she would soon complete the triumph of religion in the world. But if a system of insinuation and denunciation is to be kept up, not only will revivals cease, but the blood of millions who will go to hell before the Church will get over the shock, will be found on the skirts of the men who have got up and carried on this dreadful contention.

4. Those who have circulated slanderous reports in regard to revivals, must repent. A great deal has been said about heresy, and about some men's denying the Spirit's influence, which is wholly groundless, and has been made up out of nothing. And those who have made up the reports, and those who have circulated them against their brethren, must repent and pray to God for His forgiveness.

5. We see the constant tendency there is in Christians to declension and backsliding. This is true in all converts of all revivals. Look at the revival in President Edwards' day. The work went on till thirty thousand books and pamphlets, on one side and the other, that they carried all by the board, and the revival ceased. Those who had opposed the work grew obstinate and violent, and those who promoted it lost their meekness, and got ill-tempered, and were then driven into the very evils that had been falsely charged upon them.

And now, what shall we do? This great and glorious work of God seems to be indicating a decline. The revival is not dead—blessed be God for that—it is not dead!

Now, we hear from all parts of the land that Christians are reading on the subject, and inquiring about the revival. In some places there are now powerful revivals. And what shall we do, to lift up the standard, to move this entire nation and turn all this great people to the Lord? We must DO RIGHT. We must all have a better spirit, we must get down in the dust, we must act unitedly, we must take hold of this great work with all our hearts, and then God will bless us, and the work will go on.

What is the condition of this nation? No doubt God is holding the rod of WAR over the heads of this nation. He is waiting, before He lets loose His judgments, to see whether the Church will do right. The nation IS under His displeasure, because the Church has acted in such a manner with respect to revivals. And now suppose war should come, where would be our revivals? How quickly would war swallow up the revival spirit. The spirit of war is anything but the spirit of revival Who will attend to the claims of religion when the public mind is engrossed by the all absorbing topic of war. See now how this nation is, all at once, brought upon the brink of war.

God brandishes His blazing sword over our heads. Will the Church repent? It is THE CHURCH that God chiefly has in view. How shall we avoid the curse of war?

Only by a reformation in the Church. It is in vain to look to politicians to avert war. Perhaps they would generally be in favor of war. Very likely the things they would do to avert it would run us right into it. If the Church will not feel, will not awaken, will not act, where shall we look for help? If the Church absolutely will not move, will not tremble in view of the just judgments of God hanging over our heads, we are certainly nigh unto cursing, as a nation.

6. Whatever is done must be done quickly. The scales are on a poise. If we do

not go forward, we must go back. Things cannot remain as they are. If we do not have a more powerful revival than we have had, very soon we shall have none at all. We have had such a great revival that now small revivals do not interest the public mind.

7. It is common, when things get all wrong in the Church, for each individual to find fault both with the Church, and with his brethren, and to overlook his own share of the blame. But, as individual members of the Church of Christ, let each one act rightly, and get down in the dust, and never speak proudly, or censoriously. GO FORWARD. Who would leave such a work, and go down into the plain of Ono? Let us mind our work, and leave the issue with God.

18. The Liberator

Inaugural Editorial by William Lloyd Garrison

1 January 1831

TO THE PUBLIC

In the month of August, I issued proposals for publishing "The Liberator" in Washington City; but the enterprise, though hailed in different sections of the country, was palsied by public indifference. Since that time, the removal of the *Genius of Universal Emancipation* to the Seat of Government has rendered less imperious the establishment of a similar periodical in that quarter.

During my recent tour for the purpose of exciting the minds of the people by a series of discourses on the subject of slavery, every place that I visited gave fresh evidence of the fact, that a greater revolution in public sentiment was to be effected in the free States -- and particularly in New-England -- than at the South. I found contempt more bitter, opposition more active, detraction more relentless, prejudice more stubborn, and apathy more frozen, than among slave-owners themselves. Of course, there were individual exceptions to the contrary. This state of things afflicted, but did not dishearten me. I determined, at every hazard, to lift up the standard of emancipation in the eyes of the nation, within sight of Bunker Hill and in the birthplace of liberty. That standard is now un-furled; and long may it float, unhurt by the spoliations of time or the missiles of a desperate foe -- yea, till every chain be broken, and every bondman set free! Let Southern oppressors tremble -- let their secret abettors tremble -- let their Northern apologists tremble -- let all the enemies of the persecuted blacks tremble.

I deem the publication of my original Prospectus unnecessary, as it has ob-tained a wide circulation. The principles therein inculcated will be steadily pur-sued in this paper, excepting that I shall not array myself as the political partisan of any man. In defending the great cause of human rights, I wish to derive the assistance of all religions and of all parties.

Assenting to the "self-evident truth" maintained in the American Declaration of Independence, "that all men are created equal, and endowed by their Creator with certain inalienable rights -- among which are life, liberty and the pursuit of happiness," I shall strenuously contend for the immediate enfranchisement of our slave population. In Park-Street Church, on the Fourth of July, 1829, I unre-flectingly assented to the popular but pernicious doctrine of gradual abolition. I seize this moment to make a full and unequivocal recantation, and thus publicly to ask pardon of my God, of my country, and of my brethren the poor slaves, for having uttered a sentiment so full of timidity, injustice, and absurdity. A similar recantation, from my pen, was published in the Genius of Universal Emancipation at Baltimore, in September, 1829. My conscience is now satisfied.

I am aware that many object to the severity of my language; but is there not cause for severity? I will be as harsh as truth, and as uncompromising as justice. On this subject, I do not wish to think, or to speak, or write, with moderation. No! no! Tell a man whose house is on fire to give a moderate alarm; tell him to moderately rescue his wife from the hands of the ravisher; tell the mother to gradually extricate her babe from the fire into which it has fallen; -- but urge me not to use moderation in a cause like the present. I am in earnest -- I will not equivocate -- I will not excuse -- I will not retreat a single inch -- AND I WILL BE HEARD. The apathy of the people is enough to make every statue leap from its pedestal, and to hasten the resurrection of the dead.

It is pretended, that I am retarding the cause of emancipation by the coarseness of my invective and the precipitancy of my measures. The charge is not true. On this question of my influence, -- humble as it is,-- is felt at this moment to a considerable extent, and shall be felt in coming years -- not perniciously, but beneficially -- not as a curse, but as a blessing; and posterity will bear testimony that I was right. I desire to thank God, that he enables me to disregard "the fear of man which bringeth a snare," and to speak his truth in its simplicity and power. And here I close with this fresh dedication:

> "Oppression! I have seen thee, face to face,
> And met thy cruel eye and cloudy brow,
> But thy soul-withering glance I fear not now --
> For dread to prouder feelings doth give place
> Of deep abhorrence! Scorning the disgrace
> Of slavish knees that at thy footstool bow,
> I also kneel -- but with far other vow
> Do hail thee and thy herd of hirelings base: --
> I swear, while life-blood warms my throbbing veins,
> Still to oppose and thwart, with heart and hand,
> Thy brutalising sway -- till Afric's chains
> Are burst, and Freedom rules the rescued land, --
> Trampling Oppression and his iron rod:
> Such is the vow I take -- SO HELP ME GOD!"
> [by the Scottish poet Thomas Pringle]

19. Civil Disobedience

Henry David Thoreau

*This essay was first published in 1849 with the title "Resistance to Civil Govern-
ment". Thoreau was extremely disappointed with government's role in maintaining
slavery and promoting the Mexican War. He believed that conscientious
citizens could do their part in resisting a corrupt government and changing unjust laws. Individuals should not "resign" their consciences to the "legislator".
People could even resist being an agent of injustice by breaking the law. Thoreau's emphasis on personal involvement in attempting to correct the problems
of society had an impact for future reformers, inspiring Mahatma Ghandi and
Martin Luther King, Jr. in their attempts to bring about social change.*

I heartily accept the motto—"That government is best which governs least;" and
I should like to see it acted up to more rapidly and systematically. Carried out,
it finally amounts to this, which also I believe,—"That government is best which
governs not at all;" and when men are prepared for it, that will be the kind of
government which they will have. Government is at best but an expedient; but
most governments are usually, and all governments are sometimes, inexpedient.
The objections which have been brought against a standing army, and they are
many and weighty, and deserve to prevail, may also at last be brought against a
standing government. The standing army is only an arm of the standing government. The government itself, which is only the mode which the people have
chosen to execute their will, is equally liable to be abused and perverted before
the people can act through it. Witness the present Mexican war, the work of
comparatively a few individuals using the standing government as their tool; for,
in the outset, the people would not have consented to this measure.

This American government,—what is it but a tradition, though a recent one,
endeavoring to transmit itself unimpaired to posterity, but each instant losing
some of its integrity? It has not the vitality and force of a single living man; for
a single man can bend it to his will. It is a sort of wooden gun to the people
themselves; and, if ever they should use it in earnest as a real one against each
other, it will surely split. But it is not the less necessary for this; for the people
must have some complicated machinery or other, and hear its din, to satisfy that
idea of government which they have. Governments show thus how successfully
men can be imposed on, even impose on themselves, for their own advantage. It
is excellent, we must all allow; yet this government never of itself furthered any
enterprise, but by the alacrity with which it got out of its way. *It* does not keep

the country free. *It* does not settle the West. *It* does not educate. The character inherent in the American people has done all that has been accomplished; and it would have done somewhat more, if the government had not sometimes got in its way. For government is an expedient by which men would fain succeed in letting one another alone; and, as has been said, when it is most expedient, the governed are most let alone by it. Trade and commerce, if they were not made of india rubber, would never manage to bounce over the obstacles which legislators are continually putting in their way; and, if one were to judge these men wholly by the effects of their actions, and not partly by their intentions, they would deserve to be classed and punished with those mischievous persons who put obstructions on the railroads.

But, to speak practically and as a citizen, unlike those who call themselves no-government men, I ask for, not at once no government, but *at once* a better government. Let every man make known what kind of government would command his respect, and that will be one step toward obtaining it.

After all, the practical reason why, when the power is once in the hands of the people, a majority are permitted, and for a long period continue, to rule, is not because they are most likely to be in the right, nor because this seems fairest to the minority, but because they are physically the strongest. But a government in which the majority rule in all cases cannot be based on justice, even as far as men understand it. Can there not be a government in which majorities do not virtually decide right and wrong, but conscience?—in which majorities decide only those questions to which the rule of expediency is applicable? Must the citizen ever for a moment, or in the least degree, resign his conscience to the legislator? Why has every man a conscience, then? I think that we should be men first, and subjects afterward. It is not desirable to cultivate a respect for the law, so much as for the right. The only obligation which I have a right to assume, is to do at any time what I think right. It is truly enough said, that a corporation has no conscience; but a corporation of conscientious men is a corporation *with* a conscience. Law never made men a whit more just; and, by means of their respect for it, even the well-disposed are daily made the agents of injustice. A common and natural result of an undue respect for law is, that you may see a file of soldiers, colonel, captain, corporal, privates, powder-monkeys and all, marching in admirable order over hill and dale to the wars, against their wills, aye, against their common sense and consciences, which makes it very steep marching indeed, and produces a palpitation of the heart. They have no doubt that it is a damnable business in which they are concerned; they are all peaceably inclined. Now, what are they? Men at all? or small moveable forts and magazines, at the service of some unscrupulous man in power? Visit the Navy Yard, and behold a marine, such a man as an American government can make, or such as it can make a man with its black arts, a mere shadow and reminiscence of humanity, a man laid out alive and standing, and already, as one may say, buried under arms with funeral accompaniments, though it may be

"Not a drum was heard, nor a funeral note,
As his corse to the ramparts we hurried;
Not a soldier discharged his farewell shot
O'er the grave where our hero we buried."

The mass of men serve the State thus, not as men mainly, but as machines, with their bodies. They are the standing army, and the militia, jailers, constables, *posse comitatus, &c.* In most cases there is no free exercise whatever of the judgment or of the moral sense; but they put themselves on a level with wood and earth and stones; and wooden men can perhaps be manufactured that will serve the purpose as well. Such command no more respect than men of straw, or a lump of dirt. They have the same sort of worth only as horses and dogs. Yet such as these even are commonly esteemed good citizens. Others, as most legislators, politicians, lawyers, ministers, and office-holders, serve the State chiefly with their heads; and, as they rarely make any moral distinctions, they are as likely to serve the devil, without intending it, as God. A very few, as heroes, patriots, martyrs, reformers in the great sense, and *men* serve the State with their consciences also, and so necessarily resist it for the most part; and they are commonly treated by it as enemies. A wise man will only be useful as a man, and will not submit to be "clay," and "stop a hole to keep the wind away," but leave that office to his dust at least:—

"I am too high-born to be propertied,
To be a secondary at control,
Or useful serving-man and instrument
To any sovereign state throughout the world."

He who gives himself entirely to his fellow-men appears to them useless and selfish; but he who gives himself partially to them is pronounced a benefactor and philanthropist.

How does it become a man to behave toward this American government to-day? I answer that he cannot without disgrace be associated with it. I cannot for an instant recognize that political organization as *my* government which is the *slave's* government also.

All men recognize the right of revolution; that is, the right to refuse allegiance to and to resist the government, when its tyranny or its inefficiency are great and unendurable. But almost all say that such is not the case now. But such was the case, they think, in the Revolution of '75. If one were to tell me that this was a bad government because it taxed certain foreign commodities brought to its ports, it is most probable that I should not make an ado about it, for I can do without them: all machines have their friction; and possibly this does enough good to counterbalance the evil. At any rate, it is a great evil to make a stir about it. But when the friction comes to have its machine, and oppression and robbery are organized, I say, let us not have such a machine any longer. In other words, when a sixth of the population of a nation which has undertaken to be the refuge of liberty are slaves, and a whole country is unjustly overrun and conquered by a foreign army, and subjected to military law, I think that it is not too soon for honest men to rebel and revolutionize. What makes this duty the more urgent is the fact, that the country so overrun is not our own, but ours is the invading army.

Paley, a common authority with many on moral questions, in his chapter on the "Duty of Submission to Civil Government," resolves all civil obligation into expediency; and he proceeds to say, "that so long as the interest of the whole society requires it, that is, so long as the established government cannot be resisted or changed without public inconveniency, it is the will of God that the established government be obeyed,—and no longer. This principle being admitted, the justice of every particular case of resistance is reduced to a computation of the quantity of the danger and grievance on the one side, and of the probability and expense of redressing it on the other." Of this, he says, every man shall judge for himself. But Paley appears never to have contemplated those cases to which the rule of expediency does not apply, in which a people, as well as an individual, must do justice, cost what it may. If I have unjustly wrested a plank from a drowning man, I must restore it to him though I drown myself. This, according to Paley, would be inconvenient. But he that would save his life, in such a case, shall lose it. This people must cease to hold slaves, and to make war on Mexico, though it cost them their existence as a people.

In their practice, nations agree with Paley; but does any one think that Massachusetts does exactly what is right at the present crisis?

"A drab of state, a cloth-o'-silver slut,
To have her train borne up, and her soul trail in the dirt."

Practically speaking, the opponents to a reform in Massachusetts are not a hundred thousand politicians at the South, but a hundred thousand merchants and farmers here, who are more interested in commerce and agriculture than they are in humanity, and are not prepared to do justice to the slave and to Mexico, *cost what it may.* I quarrel not with far-off foes, but with those who, near at home, co-operate with, and do the bidding of those far away, and without whom the latter would be harmless. We are accustomed to say, that the mass of men are unprepared; but improvement is slow, because the few are not materially wiser or better than the many. It is not so important that many should be as good as you, as that there be some absolute goodness somewhere; for that will leaven the whole lump. There are thousands who are *in opinion* opposed to slavery and to the war, who yet in effect do nothing to put an end to them; who, esteeming themselves children of Washington and Franklin, sit down with their hands in their pockets, and say that they know not what to do, and do nothing; who even postpone the question of freedom to the question of free-trade, and quietly read the prices-current along with the latest advices from Mexico, after dinner, and, it may be, fall asleep over them both. What is the price-current of an honest man and patriot to-day? They hesitate, and they regret, and sometimes they petition; but they do nothing in earnest and with effect. They will wait, well disposed, for others to remedy the evil, that they may no longer have it to regret. At most, they give only a cheap vote, and a feeble countenance and God-speed, to the right, as it goes by them. There are nine hundred and ninety-nine patrons of virtue to one virtuous man; but it is easier to deal with the real possessor of a thing than with the temporary guardian of it.

All voting is a sort of gaming, like chequers or backgammon, with a slight moral tinge to it, a playing with right and wrong, with moral questions; and betting naturally accompanies it. The character of the voters is not staked. I cast my vote, perchance, as I think right; but I am not vitally concerned that that right should prevail. I am willing to leave it to the majority. Its obligation, therefore, never exceeds that of expediency. Even voting *for the right* is *doing* nothing for it. It is only expressing to men feebly your desire that it should prevail. A wise man will not leave the right to the mercy of chance, nor wish it to prevail through the power of the majority. There is but little virtue in the action of masses of men. When the majority shall at length vote for the abolition of slavery, it will be because they are indifferent to slavery, or because there is but little slavery left to be abolished by their vote. *They* will then be the only slaves. Only *his* vote can hasten the abolition of slavery who asserts his own freedom by his vote.

I hear of a convention to be held at Baltimore, or elsewhere, for the selection of a candidate for the Presidency, made up chiefly of editors, and men who are politicians by profession; but I think, what is it to any independent, intelligent, and respectable man what decision they may come to, shall we not have the advantage of his wisdom and honesty, nevertheless? Can we not count upon some independent votes? Are there not many individuals in the country who do not attend conventions? But no: I find that the respectable man, so called, has immediately drifted from his position, and despairs of his country, when his country has more reason to despair of him. He forthwith adopts one of the candidates thus selected as the only *available* one, thus proving that he is himself *available* for any purposes of the demagogue. His vote is of no more worth than that of any unprincipled foreigner or hireling native, who may have been bought. Oh for a man who is a *man,* and, as my neighbor says, has a bone in his back which you cannot pass your hand through! Our statistics are at fault: the population has been returned too large. How many *men* are there to a square thousand miles in this country? Hardly one. Does not America offer any inducement for men to settle here? The American has dwindled into an Odd Fellow,—one who may be known by the development of his organ of gregariousness, and a manifest lack of intellect and cheerful self-reliance; whose first and chief concern, on coming into the world, is to see that the almshouses are in good repair; and, before yet he has lawfully donned the virile garb, to collect a fund for the support of the widows and orphans that may be; who, in short, ventures to live only by the aid of the mutual insurance company, which has promised to bury him decently.

It is not a man's duty, as a matter of course, to devote himself to the eradication of any, even the most enormous wrong; he may still properly have other concerns to engage him; but it is his duty, at least, to wash his hands of it, and, if he gives it no thought longer, not to give it practically his support. If I devote myself to other pursuits and contemplations, I must first see, at least, that I do not pursue them sitting upon another man's shoulders. I must get off him first, that he may pursue his contemplations too. See what gross inconsistency is tolerated. I have heard some of my townsmen say, "I should like to have them order me out to help put down an insurrection of the slaves, or to march to Mexico,—see if I would go;" and yet these very men have each, directly by their allegiance, and so indirectly, at least, by their money, furnished a substitute. The soldier is applauded who refuses to serve in an unjust war by those who do not refuse to sustain the unjust government which makes the war; is applauded by those whose own act and authority he disregards and sets at naught; as if the State were penitent to that degree that it hired one to scourge it while it sinned, but not to that degree that it left off sinning for a moment. Thus, under the name of order and civil government, we are all made at last to pay homage to and support our own meanness. After the first blush of sin, comes its indifference; and from immoral it becomes, as it were, *un*moral, and not quite unnecessary to that life which we have made.

The broadest and most prevalent error requires the most disinterested virtue to sustain it. The slight reproach to which the virtue of patriotism is commonly liable, the noble are most likely to incur. Those who, while they disapprove of the character and measures of a government, yield to it their allegiance and support are undoubtedly its most conscientious supporters, and so frequently the most serious obstacles to reform. Some are petitioning the State to dissolve the Union, to disregard the requisitions of the President. Why do they not dissolve it themselves,—the union between themselves and the State,—and refuse to pay their quota into its treasury? Do not they stand in the same relation to the State that the State does to the Union? And have not the same reasons prevented the State from resisting the Union, which have prevented them from resisting the State?

How can a man be satisfied to entertain an opinion merely, and enjoy *it*? Is there any enjoyment in it, if his opinion is that he is aggrieved? If you are cheated out of a single dollar by your neighbor, you do not rest satisfied with knowing that you are cheated, or with saying that you are cheated, or even with petitioning him to pay you your due; but you take effectual steps at once to obtain the full amount, and see that you are never cheated again. Action from principle,—the perception and the performance of right,—changes things and relations; it is essentially revolutionary, and does not consist wholly with any thing which was. It not only divides states and churches, it divides families; aye, it divides the *individual*, separating the diabolical in him from the divine.

Unjust laws exist: shall we be content to obey them, or shall we endeavor to amend them, and obey them until we have succeeded, or shall we transgress them at once? Men generally, under such a government as this, think that they ought to wait until they have persuaded the majority to alter them. They think that, if they should resist, the remedy would be worse than the evil. But it is the fault of the government itself that the remedy *is* worse than the evil. *It* makes it worse. Why is it not more apt to anticipate and provide for reform? Why does it not cherish its wise minority? Why does it cry and resist before it is hurt? Why does it not encourage its citizens to be on the alert to point out its faults, and *do* better than it would have them? Why does it always crucify Christ, and ex-communicate Copernicus and Luther, and pronounce Washington and Franklin rebels?

One would think, that a deliberate and practical denial of its authority was the only offence never contemplated by government; else, why has it not assigned its definite, its suitable and proportionate penalty? If a man who has no property re-fuses but once to earn nine shillings for the State, he is put in prison for a period unlimited by any law that I know, and determined only by the discretion of those who placed him there; but if he should steal ninety times nine shillings from the State, he is soon permitted to go at large again.

If the injustice is part of the necessary friction of the machine of govern-ment, let it go, let it go: perchance it will wear smooth,—certainly the machine will wear out. If the injustice has a spring, or a pulley, or a rope, or a crank, ex-clusively for itself, then perhaps you may consider whether the remedy will not be worse than the evil; but if it is of such a nature that it requires you to be the agent of injustice to another, then, I say, break the law. Let your life be a counter friction to stop the machine. What I have to do is to see, at any rate, that I do not lend myself to the wrong which I condemn.

As for adopting the ways which the State has provided for remedying the evil, I know not of such ways. They take too much time, and a man's life will be gone. I have other affairs to attend to. I came into this world, not chiefly to make this a good place to live in, but to live in it, be it good or bad. A man has not every thing to do, but something; and because he cannot do *every thing*, it is not neces-sary that he should do *something* wrong. It is not my business to be petitioning the governor or the legislature any more than it is theirs to petition me; and if they should not hear my petition, what should I do then? But in this case the State has provided no way: its very Constitution is the evil. This may seem to be harsh and stubborn and unconciliatory; but it is to treat with the utmost kind-ness and consideration the only spirit that can appreciate or deserves it. So is all change for the better, like birth and death which convulse the body.

I do not hesitate to say, that those who call themselves abolitionists should at once effectually withdraw their support, both in person and property, from the government of Massachusetts, and not wait till they constitute a majority of one, before they suffer the right to prevail through them. I think that it is enough if they have God on their side, without waiting for that other one. Moreover, any man more right than his neighbors constitutes a majority of one already.

I meet this American government, or its representative the State govern-ment, directly, and face to face, once a year, no more, in the person of its tax-gatherer; this is the only mode in which a man situated as I am necessarily meets it; and it then says distinctly, Recognize me; and the simplest, the most effectual, and, in the present posture of affairs, the indispensablest mode of treating with it on this head, of expressing your little satisfaction with and love for it, is to deny it then. My civil neighbor, the tax-gatherer, is the very man I have to deal with,—for it is, after all, with men and not with parchment that I quarrel,—and he has voluntarily chosen to be an agent of the government. How shall he ever know well what he is and does as an officer of the government, or as a man, until he is obliged to consider whether he shall treat me, his neighbor, for whom he has respect, as a neighbor and well-disposed man, or as a maniac and disturber of the peace, and see if he can get over this obstruction to his neighborliness without a ruder and more impetuous thought or speech corresponding with his action? I know this well, that if one thousand, if one hundred, if ten men whom I could name,—if ten *honest* men only,—aye, if *one* HONEST man, in this State of Massachusetts, *ceasing to hold slaves*, were actually to withdraw from this copartnership, and be locked up in the county jail therefor, it would be the abolition of slavery in America. For it matters not how small the beginning may seem to be: what is once well done is done for ever. But we love better to talk about it: that we say is our mission. Reform keeps many scores of newspapers in its service, but not one man. If my esteemed neighbor, the State's ambassador, who will devote his days to the settlement of the question of human rights in the Council Chamber, instead of being threatened with the prisons of Carolina, were to sit down the prisoner of Massachusetts, that State which is so anxious to foist the sin of slavery upon her sister,—though at present she can discover only an act of inhospitality to be the ground of a quarrel with her,—the Legislature would not wholly waive the subject the following winter.

Under a government which imprisons any unjustly, the true place for a just man is also in prison. The proper place to-day, the only place which Massachusetts has provided for her freer and less desponding spirits, is in her prisons, to be put out and locked out of the State by her own act, as they have already put themselves out by their principles. It is there that the fugitive slave, and the Mexican prisoner on parole, and the Indian come to plead the wrongs of his race, should find them; on that separate, but more free and honorable ground, where the State places those who are not *with* her, but *against* her,—the only house in a slave-state in which a free man can abide with honor. If any think that their influence would be lost there, and their voices no longer afflict the ear of the State, that they would not be as an enemy within its walls, they do not know by how much truth is stronger than error, nor how much more eloquently and effectively he can combat injustice who has experienced a little in his own person. Cast your whole vote, not a strip of paper merely, but your whole influence. A minority is powerless while it conforms to the majority; it is not even a minority then; but it is irresistible when it clogs by its whole weight. If the alternative is to keep all just men in prison, or give up war and slavery, the State will not hesitate which to choose. If a thousand men were not to pay their tax-bills this year, that would not be a violent and bloody measure, as it would be to pay them, and enable the State to commit violence and shed innocent blood. This is, in fact, the definition of a peaceable revolution, if any such is possible. If the tax-gatherer, or any other public officer, asks me, as one has done, "But what shall I do?" my answer is, "If you really wish to do any thing, resign your office." When the subject has refused allegiance, and the officer has resigned his office, then the revolution is accomplished. But even suppose blood should flow. Is there not a sort of blood shed when the conscience is wounded? Through this wound a man's real manhood and immortality flow out, and he bleeds to an everlasting death. I see this blood flowing now.

I have contemplated the imprisonment of the offender, rather than the sei-zure of his goods,—though both will serve the same purpose,—because they who assert the purest right, and consequently are most dangerous to a corrupt State, commonly have not spent much time in accumulating property. To such the State renders comparatively small service, and a slight tax is wont to appear exorbitant particularly if they are obliged to earn it by special labor with their hands. If there were one who lived wholly without the use of money, the State itself would hesitate to demand it of him. But the rich man—not to make any invidious comparison—is always sold to the institution which makes him rich. Absolutely speaking, the more money, the less virtue; for money comes between a man and his objects, and obtains them for him; and it was certainly no great virtue to obtain it. It puts to rest many questions which he would otherwise be taxed to answer; while the only new question which it puts is the hard but super-fluous one, how to spend it. Thus his moral ground is taken from under his feet. The opportunities of living are diminished in proportion as what are called the "means" are increased. The best thing a man can do for his culture when he is rich is to endeavour to carry out those schemes which he entertained when he was poor. Christ answered the Herodians according to their condition. "Show me the tribute-money," said he;—and one took a penny out of his pocket;—if you use money which has the image of Caesar on it, and which he has made current and valuable, that is, *if you are men of the State*, and gladly enjoy the advantages of Caesar's government, then pay him back some of his own when he demands it. "Render therefore to Caesar that which is Caesar's, and to God those things which are God's,"—leaving them no wiser than before as to which was which; for they did not wish to know.

When I converse with the freest of my neighbors, I perceive that, whatever they may say about the magnitude and seriousness of the question, and their regard for the public tranquillity, the long and the short of the matter is, that they cannot spare the protection of the existing government, and they dread the consequences of disobedience to it to their property and families. For my own part, I should not like to think that I ever rely on the protection of the State. But, if I deny the authority of the State when it presents its tax-bill, it will soon take and waste all my property, and so harass me and my children without end. This is hard. This makes it impossible for a man to live honestly, and at the same time comfortably in outward respects. It will not be worth the while to accumulate property; that would be sure to go again. You must hire or squat somewhere, and raise but a small crop, and eat that soon. You must live within yourself, and depend upon yourself, always tucked up and ready for a start, and not have many affairs. A man may grow rich in Turkey even, if he will be in all respects a good subject of the Turkish government. Confucius said,—"If a State is governed by the principles of reason, poverty and misery are subjects of shame; if a State is not governed by the principles of reason, riches and honors are the subjects of shame." No: until I want the protection of Massachusetts to be extended to me in some distant southern port, where my liberty is endangered, or until I am bent solely on building up an estate at home by peaceful enterprise, I can afford to refuse allegiance to Massachusetts, and her right to my property and life. It costs me less in every sense to incur the penalty of disobedience to the State than it would to obey. I should feel as if I were worth less in that case.

Some years ago, the State met me in behalf of the church, and commanded me to pay a certain sum toward the support of a clergyman whose preaching my father attended, but never I myself. "Pay it," it said, "or be locked up in the jail." I declined to pay. But, unfortunately, another man saw fit to pay it. I did not see why the schoolmaster should be taxed to support the priest, and not the priest the schoolmaster; for I was not the State's schoolmaster, but I supported myself by voluntary subscription. I did not see why the lyceum should not present its tax-bill, and have the State to back its demand, as well as the church. However, at the request of the selectmen, I condescended to make some such statement as this in writing:—"Know all men by these presents, that I, Henry Thoreau, do not wish to be regarded as a member of any incorporated society which I have not joined." This I gave to the townclerk; and he has it. The State, having thus learned that I did not wish to be regarded as a member of that church, has never made a like demand on me since; though it said that it must adhere to its original presumption that time. If I had known how to name them, I should then have signed off in detail from all the societies which I never signed on to; but I did not know where to find a complete list.

I have paid no poll-tax for six years. I was put into a jail once on this account, for one night; and, as I stood considering the walls of solid stone, two or three feet thick, the door of wood and iron, a foot thick, and the iron grating which strained the light, I could not help being struck with the foolishness of that institution which treated me as if I were mere flesh and blood and bones, to be locked up. I wondered that it should have concluded at length that this was the best use it could put me to, and had never thought to avail itself of my services in some way. I saw that, if there was a wall of stone between me and my townsmen, there was a still more difficult one to climb or break through, before they could get to be as free as I was. I did not for a moment feel confined, and the walls seemed a great waste of stone and mortar. I felt as if I alone of all my townsmen had paid my tax.

They plainly did not know how to treat me, but behaved like persons who are underbred. In every threat and in every compliment there was a blunder; for they thought that my chief desire was to stand the other side of that stone wall. I could not but smile to see how industriously they locked the door on my meditations, which followed them out again without let or hinderance, and *they* were really all that was dangerous. As they could not reach me, they had resolved to punish my body; just as boys, if they cannot come at some person against whom they have a spite, will abuse his dog. I saw that the State was half-witted, that it was timid as a lone woman with her silver spoons, and that it did not know its friends from its foes, and I lost all my remaining respect for it, and pitied it.

Thus the State never intentionally confronts a man's sense, intellectual or moral, but only his body, his senses. It is not armed with superior wit or honesty, but with superior physical strength. I was not born to be forced. I will breathe after my own fashion. Let us see who is the strongest. What force has a multitude? They only can force me who obey a higher law than I. They force me to become like themselves. I do not hear of *men* being *forced* to live this way or that by masses of men. What sort of life were that to live? When I meet a government which says to me, "Your money or your life," why should I be in haste to give it my money? It may be in a great strait, and not know what to do: I cannot help that. It must help itself; do as I do. It is not worth the while to snivel about it. I am not responsible for the successful working of the machinery of society. I am not the son of the engineer. I perceive that, when an acorn and a chestnut fall side by side, the one does not remain inert to make way for the other, but both obey their own laws, and spring and grow and flourish as best they can, till one, perchance, overshadows and destroys the other. If a plant cannot live according to its nature, it dies; and so a man.

The night in prison was novel and interesting enough. The prisoners in their shirt-sleeves were enjoying a chat and the evening air in the doorway, when I entered. But the jailer said, "Come, boys, it is time to lock up;" and so they dispersed, and I heard the sound of their steps returning into the hollow apartments. My room-mate was introduced to me by the jailer, as "a first-rate fellow and a clever man." When the door was locked, he showed me where to hang my hat, and how he managed matters there. The rooms were whitewashed once a month; and this one, at least, was the whitest, most simply furnished, and probably the neatest apartment in the town. He naturally wanted to know where I came from, and what brought me there; and, when I had told him, I asked him in my turn how he came there, presuming him to be an honest man, of course; and, as the world goes, I believe he was. "Why," said he, "they accuse me of burning a barn; but I never did it." As near as I could discover, he had probably gone to bed in a barn when drunk, and smoked his pipe there; and so a barn was burnt. He had the reputation of being a clever man, had been there some three months waiting for his trial to come on, and would have to wait as much longer: but he was quite domesticated and contented, since he got his board for nothing, and thought that he was well treated.

He occupied one window, and I the other; and I saw, that, if one stayed there long, his principal business would be to look out the window. I had soon read all the tracts that were left there, and examined where former prisoners had broken out, and where a grate had been sawed off, and heard the history of the various occupants of that room; for I found that even here there was a history and a gossip which never circulated beyond the walls of the jail. Probably this is the only house in the town where verses are composed, which are afterward printed in a circular form, but not published. I was shown quite a long list of verses which were composed by some young men who had been detected in an attempt to escape, who avenged themselves by singing them.

I pumped my fellow-prisoner as dry as I could, for fear I should never see him again; but at length he showed me which was my bed, and left me to blow out the lamp.

It was like travelling into a far country, such as I had never expected to behold, to lie there for one night. It seemed to me that I never had heard the town-clock strike before, nor the evening sounds of the village; for we slept with the windows open, which were inside the grating. It was to see my native village in the light of the middle ages, and our Concord was turned into a Rhine stream, and visions of knights and castles passed before me. They were the voices of old burghers that I heard in the streets. I was an involuntary spectator and auditor of whatever was done and said in the kitchen of the adjacent village-inn,—a wholly new and rare experience to me. It was a closer view of my native town. I was fairly inside of it. I never had seen its institutions before. This is one of its peculiar institutions; for it is a shire town. I began to comprehend what its inhabitants were about.

In the morning, our breakfasts were put through the hole in the door, in small oblong-square tin pans, made to fit, and holding a pint of chocolate, with brown bread, and an iron spoon. When they called for the vessels again, I was green enough to return what bread I had left; but my comrade seized it, and said that I should lay that up for lunch or dinner. Soon after, he was let out to work at haying in a neighboring field, whither he went every day, and would not be back till noon; so he bade me good-day, saying that he doubted if he should see me again.

When I came out of prison,—for some one interfered, and paid the tax,—I did not perceive that great changes had taken place on the common, such as he observed who went in a youth and emerged a tottering and gray-headed man; and yet a change had to my eyes come over the scene,—the town, and State and country,—greater than any that mere time could effect. I saw yet more distinctly the State in which I lived. I saw to what extent the people among whom I lived could be trusted as good neighbors and friends; that their friendship was for summer weather only; that they did not greatly purpose to do right; that they were a distinct race from me by their prejudices and superstitions, as the China-men and Malays are; that, in their sacrifices to humanity, they ran no risks, not even to their property; that, after all, they were not so noble but they treated the thief as he had treated them, and hoped, by a certain outward observance and a few prayers, and by walking in a particular straight though useless path from time to time, to save their souls. This may be to judge my neighbors harshly; for I believe that most of them are not aware that they have such an institution as the jail in their village.

It was formerly the custom in our village, when a poor debtor came out of jail, for his acquaintances to salute him, looking through their fingers, which were crossed to represent the grating of a jail window, "How do ye do?" My neighbors did not thus salute me, but first looked at me, and then at one another, as if I had returned from a long journey. I was put into jail as I was going to the shoemaker's to get a shoe which was mended. When I was let out the next morning, I proceeded to finish my errand, and, having put on my mended shoe, joined a huckleberry party, who were impatient to put themselves under my conduct; and in half an hour,—for the horse was soon tackled,—was in the midst of a huckleberry field, on one of our highest hills, two miles off; and then the State was nowhere to be seen.

This is the whole history of "My Prisons."

I have never declined paying the highway tax, because I am as desirous of being a good neighbor as I am of being a bad subject; and as for supporting schools, I am doing my part to educate my fellow-countrymen now. It is for no particular item in the tax-bill that I refuse to pay it. I simply wish to refuse allegiance to the State, to withdraw and stand aloof from it effectually. I do not care to trace the course of my dollar, if I could, till it buys a man, or a musket to shoot one with,—the dollar is innocent,—but I am concerned to trace the effects of my allegiance. In fact, I quietly declare war with the State, after my fashion, though I will still make what use and get what advantage of her I can, as is usual in such cases.

If others pay the tax which is demanded of me, from a sympathy with the State, they do but what they have already done in their own case, or rather they abet injustice to a greater extent than the State requires. If they pay the tax from a mistaken interest in the individual taxed, to save his property or prevent his going to jail, it is because they have not considered wisely how far they let their private feelings interfere with the public good.

This, then, is my position at present. But one cannot be too much on his guard in such a case, lest his action be biassed by obstinacy or an undue regard for the opinions of men. Let him see that he does only what belongs to himself and to the hour.

I think sometimes, Why, this people mean well; they are only ignorant; they would do better if they knew how: why give your neighbors this pain to treat you as they are not inclined to? But I think, again, this is no reason why I should do as they do, or permit others to suffer much greater pain of a different kind. Again, I sometimes say to myself, When many millions of men, without heat, without ill-will, without personal feeling of any kind, demand of you a few shillings only, without the possibility, such is their constitution, of retracting or altering their present demand, and without the possibility, on your side, of appeal to any other millions, why expose yourself to this overwhelming brute force? You do not resist cold and hunger, the winds and the waves, thus obstinately; you quietly submit to a thousand similar necessities. You do not put your head into the fire. But just in proportion as I regard this as not wholly a brute force, but partly a human force, and consider that I have relations to those millions as to so many millions of men, and not of mere brute or inanimate things, I see that appeal is possible, first and instantaneously, from them to the Maker of them, and, secondly, from them to themselves. But if I put my head deliberately into the fire, there is no appeal to fire or to the Maker of fire, and I have only myself to blame. If I could convince myself that I have any right to be satisfied with men as they are, and to treat them accordingly, and not according, in some respects, to my requisitions and expectations of what they and I ought to be, then, like a good Mussulman and fatalist, I should endeavor to be satisfied with things as they are, and say it is the will of God. And, above all, there is this difference between resisting this and a purely brute or natural force, that I can resist this with some effect; but I cannot expect, like Orpheus, to change the nature of the rocks and trees and beasts.

I do not wish to quarrel with any man or nation. I do not wish to split hairs, to make fine distinctions, or set myself up as better than my neighbors. I seek rather, I may say, even an excuse for conforming to the laws of the land. I am but too ready to conform to them. Indeed I have reason to suspect myself on this head; and each year, as the tax-gatherer comes round, I find myself disposed to review the acts and position of the general and state governments, and the spirit of the people, to discover a pretext for conformity. I believe that the State will soon be able to take all my work of this sort out of my hands, and then I shall be no better a patriot than my fellow-countrymen. Seen from a lower point of view, the Constitution, with all its faults, is very good; the law and the courts are very respectable; even this State and this American government are, in many respects, very admirable and rare things, to be thankful for, such as a great many have described them; but seen from a point of view a little higher, they are what I have described them; seen from a higher still, and the highest, who shall say what they are, or that they are worth looking at or thinking of at all?

However, the government does not concern me much, and I shall bestow the fewest possible thoughts on it. It is not many moments that I live under a government, even in this world. If a man is thought-free, fancy-free, imagination-free, that which *is not* never for a long time appearing *to be* to him, unwise rulers or reformers cannot fatally interrupt him.

I know that most men think differently from myself; but those whose lives are by profession devoted to the study of these or kindred subjects, content me as little as any. Statesmen and legislators, standing so completely within the institution, never distinctly and nakedly behold it. They speak of moving society, but have no resting-place without it. They may be men of a certain experience and discrimination, and have no doubt invented ingenious and even useful systems, for which we sincerely thank them; but all their wit and usefulness lie within certain not very wide limits. They are wont to forget that the world is not governed by policy and expediency. Webster never goes behind government, and so cannot speak with authority about it. His words are wisdom to those legislators who contemplate no essential reform in the existing government; but for thinkers, and those who legislate for all time, he never once glances at the subject. I know of those whose serene and wise speculations on this theme would soon reveal the limits of his mind's range and hospitality. Yet, compared with the cheap professions of most reformers, and the still cheaper wisdom and eloquence of politicians in general, his are almost the only sensible and valuable words, and we thank Heaven for him. Comparatively, he is always strong, original, and, above all, practical. Still his quality is not wisdom, but prudence. The lawyer's truth is not Truth, but consistency or a consistent expediency. Truth is always in harmony with herself, and is not concerned chiefly to reveal the justice that may consist with wrongdoing. He well deserves to be called, as he has been called, the Defender of the Constitution. There are really no blows to be given by him but defensive ones. He is not a leader, but a follower. His leaders are the men of '87. "I have never made an effort," he says, "and never propose to make an effort; I have never countenanced an effort, and never mean to countenance an effort, to disturb the arrangement as originally made, by which the various States came into the Union." Still thinking of the sanction which the Constitution gives to slavery, he says, "Because it was a part of the original compact,—let it stand." Notwithstanding his special acuteness and ability, he is unable to take a fact out of its merely political relations, and behold it as it lies absolutely to be disposed of by the intellect,—what, for instance, it behoves a man to do here in America today with regard to slavery, but ventures, or is driven, to make some such desperate answer as the following, while professing to speak absolutely, and as a private man,—from which what new and singular code of social duties might be inferred?—"The manner," says he, "in which the governments of those States where slavery exists are to regulate it, is for their own consideration, under their responsibility to their constituents, to the general laws of propriety, humanity, and justice, and to God. Associations formed elsewhere, springing from a feeling of humanity, or any other cause, have nothing whatever to do with it. They have never received any encouragement from me, and they never will."[1]

They who know of no purer sources of truth, who have traced up its stream no higher, stand, and wisely stand, by the Bible and the Constitution, and drink at it there with reverence and humility; but they who behold where it comes trickling into this lake or that pool, gird up their loins once more, and continue their pilgrimage toward its fountainhead.

---

[1] These extracts have been inserted since the Lecture was read.

No man with a genius for legislation has appeared in America. They are rare in the history of the world. There are orators, politicians, and eloquent men, by the thousand; but the speaker has not yet opened his mouth to speak, who is capable of settling the much-vexed questions of the day. We love eloquence for its own sake, and not for any truth which it may utter, or any heroism it may inspire. Our legislators have not yet learned the comparative value of free-trade and of freedom, of union, and of rectitude, to a nation. They have no genius or talent for comparatively humble questions of taxation and finance, commerce and manufactures and agriculture. If we were left solely to the wordy wit of legislators in Congress for our guidance, uncorrected by the seasonable experience and the effectual complaints of the people, America would not long retain her rank among the nations. For eighteen hundred years, though perchance I have no right to say it, the New Testament has been written; yet where is the legislator who has wisdom and practical talent enough to avail himself of the light which it sheds on the science of legislation?

The authority of government, even such as I am willing to submit to,—for I will cheerfully obey those who know and can do better than I, and in many things even those who neither know nor can do so well,—is still an impure one: to be strictly just, it must have the sanction and consent of the governed. It can have no pure right over my person and property but what I concede to it. The progress from an absolute to a limited monarchy, from a limited monarchy to a democracy, is a progress toward a true respect for the individual. Is a democracy, such as we know it, the last improvement possible in government? Is it not possible to take a step further towards recognizing and organizing the rights of man? There will never be a really free and enlightened State, until the State comes to recognize the individual as a higher and independent power, from which all its own power and authority are derived, and treats him accordingly. I please myself with imagining a State at last which can afford to be just to all men, and to treat the individual with respect as a neighbor; which even would not think it inconsistent with its own repose, if a few were to live aloof from it, not meddling with it, nor embraced by it, who fulfilled all the duties of neighbors and fellowmen. A State which bore this kind of fruit, and suffered it to drop off as fast as it ripened, would prepare the way for a still more perfect and glorious State, which also I have imagined, but not yet anywhere seen.

20. Stephen F. Austin: Political and Cultural Mediator

Gregg Cantrell

The Anglo-American colonists who came to Mexican Texas brought with them some heavy cultural baggage. Most came from slaveholding states and subscribed to southern notions of white supremacy—notions that might easily be applied to dark-skinned Mexicans as well as to African Americans. Many undoubtedly embodied the other forms of ethnocentrism peculiar to the Jacksonian era, such as a strident prejudice against Catholics and an intense hatred of Indians. Moreover, few settlers would have questioned the basic tenets of the ideology that would someday be called "Manifest Destiny:" the belief that the United States would inevitably spread American-style democracy and cultural institutions westward across the continent. Given these realities, many recent scholars have viewed the Anglo settlement of Texas as little more than an American invasion, a racist land grab of Mexico's northern frontier in which Mexicans and Indians were the chief victims.

At first glance, the foremost leader of this "invasion" seems to sustain these interpretations. Stephen Fuller Austin was a Virginia native who had grown up mostly on the Missouri frontier, where he utilized slave labor on a large scale in his family's lead-mining operation. In Texas, he worked repeatedly to ensure that slavery would be protected by the government. He had also served in the Missouri militia during the War of 1812, participating in a military campaign that burned Indian villages in Illinois. His credentials as a white supremacist seemed secure.

The same might be said for his standing as a proponent of Manifest Destiny. In an Independence Day speech in 1818, he delivered an address extolling the virtues of American civilization and the Founding Fathers. Near the end of the oration, he alluded to Mexico's ongoing independence struggle:

> ...the same spirit that unsheathed the sword of Washington and sacrificed servitude and slavery in the flames of the Revolution, will also flash across the Gulph of Mexico and over the western wilderness that separates independent America from the enslaved colonies of Spain, and darting the beams of intelligence into the benighted souls of their inhabitants awake them from the stupor of slaves to the energy of freemen, from the degradation of vassals to the dignity of sovereigns.

Essay by Gregg Cantrell, written for this volume. Reprinted with permission of the author.

After emigrating to Texas, he frequently defined his mission as that of "[spreading] over it North American population, enterprise, and intelligence."

In addition to his racial beliefs and his pro-American chauvinism, Austin also seemed typically American in his attitudes toward Mexican Catholicism. On his first trip through the interior of Mexico, he wrote that "the people are bigoted and superstitious to an extreem, and indolence appears to be the general order of the day." And in another, oft-quoted passage, he added, "to be candid the majority of the people of the whole nation as far as I have seen them want nothing but tails to be more brutes than the apes…Fanaticism reigns with a power that equally astonishes and grieves a man of common sense."

Austin's words and deeds seemed to confirm his ethnocentrism when Texas began to wage war against Mexico. Not only did he publicly advocate independence several months before the actual declaration, but he justified the revolution on the grounds that "A war of extermination is raging in Texas, a war of barbarism and of despotic principles, waged by the mongrel Spanish-Indian and Negro race, against civilization and the Anglo-American race." He recounted the fifteen years in which he had labored "like a slave to *Americanize Texas*" so that the southwestern frontier of the United States would be safe. "But the Anglo-American foundation, this nucleus of republicanism, is to broken up," he declared, "and its place supplied by a population of Indians, Mexicans, and renegadoes, all mixed together, and all the natural enemies of white men and civilization:' In other statements he raised the cry of anti-Catholicism, claiming that the revolution was being fought for "religious liberty" and against the "banner of the inquisition." With such actions and statements coming from the man who initiated the Anglo-American colonization of Texas, who could doubt that racism, imperialism, cultural chauvinism, and greed were the main impulses behind the American occupation of Texas all along?

Despite all of this, the case of Stephen F. Austin—when considered in its entirety—actually tells a very different story. For the better part of fifteen years, the young Missourian served as a political and cultural mediator between Anglo Texans and Mexicans. When examined objectively, Austin's career demonstrates the very real potential for political, economic, and social cooperation across social and cultural lines. The history leading up to the Texas Revolution emerges as a far more complex story than it appears.

When Austin received permission in 1821 to introduce 300 American families into the region between the Brazos and Colorado, his timing was perfect. The newly independent government of Mexico, as well as the local Tejano leadership of Texas, recognized the need to populate the sparsely settled province with hardworking, taxpaying citizens who would contribute to the economic development of northern Mexico, help fight hostile Indians, and hopefully prevent the loss of Texas to the rapidly expanding United States. Austin's title was empresario, which meant that he was responsible for recruiting settlers, surveying and issuing land titles, enforcing the laws, and acting as liaison between his colonists and the Mexican government. From the start, Austin labored tirelessly and took his responsibilities as empresario seriously.

One of the first indications of that seriousness was his approach to the language barrier. Austin spoke little or no Spanish when he first arrived in Texas, but he dedicated himself to learning the language not just passably but fluently. Most of this effort took place in 1822 when he was forced to travel to Mexico City to secure confirmation of his grant from the new government of Mexico. Within a few weeks of his arrival there, Austin was conducting business in Spanish and even acting as spokesman for other Americans in their business with the government.

We get a glimpse of Austin's attitudes toward the language issue in his letters to his younger brother, Brown Austin. Stephen had left Brown, who was only nineteen, behind in Texas when he went to Mexico City. But rather than leave Brown with Anglo friends in the new colony, he placed Brown in the household of the prominent Tejano citizen Erasmo Seguín of San Antonio with instructions to spend every waking moment studying Spanish and learning Mexican ways. "Remember," Stephen lectured Brown, "that all your hopes of rising in this country depend on lear[n]ing to speak and write the language correctly. Without that, you will do nothing," Ten years later he would take a similar course with his teenage nephew, Moses Austin Bryan.

By the time Austin returned to Texas in 1823, he could speak Spanish and was personally acquainted with a host of major Mexican leaders. Arriving home, he issued a proclamation reminding the settlers of their obligation to the government. He instructed them "to remember that the Roman Catholic is the religion of this nation" and urged them to "respect the Catholic religion with all that attention due to its sacredness and to the laws of the land." Two years later, when the new national constitution was published, he summoned the colonists to San Felipe for a grand celebration of the new system of government. There, in the village he had laid out in a traditional Spanish pattern with streets named for Mexican statesmen, Austin raised the Mexican flag, read the constitution, and administered the oath of allegiance. Good order prevailed the entire day, and the people expressed "general enthusiasm in favor of the Government of our adopted Country." Austin made the phrase "fidelity to Mexico'" and for years preached it like gospel to the colonists, frequently reminding them that they lived under "the most liberal and munificent government on earth to emigrants."

Austin soon formed harmonious working relationships with important Tejanos as well as Mexicans from the interior. When the national congress combined Texas with Coahuila to form one state, he succeeded in forging an effective three-pronged political coalition between Anglo colonists, Tejanos, and a group of powerful Coahuilan politicians/businessmen headed by the Viesca brothers of Parras. Together, they dominated the politics of the vast frontier state for more than a decade, finding common ground on a wide range of issues.

Prominent Tejano José Antonio Navarro of San Antonio was one of Austin's key allies in this coalition. Navarro represented Texas in the 1828 state legislature, at a time when Austin, along with other Anglo colonists, feared that the state was on the verge of enforcing its prohibitions on slavery. Navarro came to the rescue, quietly securing the passage of a bill that allowed Americans to continue to bring their slaves into Texas. Modern sensibilities will condemn the purpose of Navarro's labors, but the point here is to show the close cooperation and identification of mutual interests between these two men who came from such different cultural backgrounds.

Equally telling is the *personal* relationship that apparently developed between Austin and Navarro. Stephen F. Austin was not the sort who formed intimate friendships easily, and he tended to be a very private and reserved man, rarely mentioning personal matters to business or political associates. But in 1829, he faced one of the greatest personal crises of his life when his beloved younger brother, Brown, suddenly died of yellow fever. The stress of this event triggered a severe attack of fever in Austin, who lingered near death for weeks. When he finally was able to sit up in bed and write a few letters, Navarro was one of the first people he contacted—and one of the few in whom he confided. Austin poured out his grief to his Tejano friend, poignantly writing of the "terrible blow" he had received. That Austin would share his anguish with Navarro (who would later sign the Texas Declaration of Independence) says much about the degree of trust and friendship that existed between the two men.

Similarly strong and enduring was Austin's relationship with the Seguín family. Erasmo Seguín was among a group of Tejanos who traveled to Louisiana in 1821 to escort Stephen F. Austin to the site of his grant. The men became friends, and Brown Austin apparently lived with the Seguíns for the entire year that Austin was gone. Several years later, Austin made efforts to purchase cotton ginning equipment for Erasmo in New Orleans because Erasmo had refused to accept any reimbursement for the time that Brown had boarded with him.

Like the Austin-Navarro relationship, the Austin-Seguín relationship extended into the period of the Revolution itself. In the fall of 1835, when Austin was commanding Texan troops in the field, into the camp galloped Juan Seguín— Erasmo's son—along with a company of Tejano cavalrymen, volunteering their services in the Texas cause. Austin welcomed them into the ranks, commissioning Seguín as a lieutenant colonel. Austin would later praise the Tejano troops, saying that "They uniformly acquitted themselves to their credit as patriots and soldiers."

But Austin did not simply cooperate with Mexicans when they were willing to take the side of Anglos in some conflict. There were also times when he stood by the Mexican government in conflicts with other Anglos. Perhaps the most famous case involved the Fredonian Rebellion of 1826–27. In 1825, an Anglo-American, Haden Edwards, received an empresario contract from the state government to introduce 800 settlers into the Nacogdoches area. Edwards, a reckless and undiplomatic man, soon angered both Anglo and Tejano settlers who had long predated him in the region, and finally the Mexican government canceled his contract and ordered him expelled from Texas. He responded by declaring the independence of the "Fredonian" republic, and he made an alliance with a portion of the local Cherokee Indian tribes who had failed in their attempts to gain land titles from the Mexican government. Political chief Jose Antonio Saucedo assembled Mexican troops from Goliad and San Antonio, marched to San Felipe where they were joined by Stephen F. Austin and his colony's militia, and together the mixed force marched to Nacogdoches and put down the rebellion with minimal difficulty.

In hindsight, the Fredonian rebellion resembles comic opera, but for those willing to read the lessons carefully, it indicates more about the real nature of the Texas frontier from 1821 to 1835 and of racial and ethnic relations than almost any other incident. The temptation is to look only at surface facts and to see the rebellion as a precursor of the 1836 revolution—a land grab by aggressive, ungrateful Anglos. But the realities are much more complex. Consider several points. Before the granting of the Edwards empresario contract, the Nacogdoches region was occupied by an incredibly diverse population of Tejanos and Anglos, with a sprinkling of other ethnic Europeans. The region was also home to a number of indigenous Texas Indian tribes, plus the semi-Europeanized Cherokees, who were themselves recent emigrants from the American southeast. Edwards's contract was granted by a state legislature in far-off Saltillo, by Mexican elites whose own financial interests depended on the economic development of Texas. Edwards antagonized both Anglos and Tejanos in Nacogdoches, and the actual fighting that took place there was by no means an Anglo vs. Mexican affair. When Austin learned of the revolt, he called the Fredonians "a party of infatuated madmen," and Austin's Anglo colonists turned out unhesitatingly to aid the Mexicans in putting down the rebellion. Furthermore, facts show that the Cherokees themselves were actually sharply divided over the affair, and a sizable portion of them repudiated their comrades who had sided with Edwards and instead aided the Tejanos and Anglos in opposing the rebels. When the revolt disintegrated, the Cherokee leaders who had joined with the Fredonians were condemned by a tribal council, hunted down and executed by their own people. In the aftermath of the rebellion Anastacio Bustamante, commandant general of Mexico's northern frontier states, wrote Stephen Austin a letter expressing his gratitude for Austin's colonists' support, saying he wanted personally to give Austin *"un Extrechisimo abrazo"*—a very strong embrace—for "the happy result of the Expedition to Nacogdoches."

Like so much Texas history during this period, the simple dichotomies break down. In the Fredonian episode, Austin and his Anglo colonists marched side by side with Mexican troops against other Anglo-Americans. Even the Indians were bitterly divided. At Austin's suggestion, the Mexicans later granted amnesty to all but the ringleaders of the revolt, and he remained in East Texas several weeks, traveling the region with the Mexican leaders to calm the fears of the inhabitants and restore peace and order. Brown Austin undoubtedly spoke for his brother when he wrote that the insurgents were "treated with a degree of lenity by the Mexicans they had no right to expect from the nature of their crimes—and which I vouchsafe would not have been shewn them in their native country for similar offences." The actions of Austin and his colonists, as well as the response of the Mexican authorities, suggest a degree of cooperation and identification of common interests that transcended cultural differences.

After the notorious Law of April 6, 1830 disrupted the empresario system and initiated a Mexican crackdown on Anglo Texas, Austin once again sought to act as mediator. Although he potentially had more to lose under the law than almost anyone else, he counseled calmness and continued loyalty toward Mexico, even pointing out to his colonists the beneficial aspects of the much-hated decree. Over the next four years, every time that Texans grew dissatisfied with the actions of the government in Mexico City, he tried to forge solidarity between the Tejanos and Anglos of Texas and to encourage the Tejanos to take the lead in petitioning the government for redress. Even after Austin's arrest and imprisonment in 1833, he continued to call for calm in Texas. Indeed, after four months in a dungeon, he was still asking friends in Texas to "Remember me to Ramón Músquíz [the Tejano political chief in San Antonio] particularly—I shall feel grateful to him as long as I live…"

Austin's friendship and respect for a long list of Mexican and Tejano leaders never faltered. His efforts to build a society in Mexican Texas where enterprising men of Anglo and Hispanic backgrounds might live in harmony and prosperity remained constant for fifteen years prior to the outbreak of revolution. He tried to avoid warfare against Indians, and he even accepted a few free blacks as settlers in his colony.

Given these efforts, how are the seemingly bigoted statements that he occasionally uttered to be explained? Take, for example, his famous 1823 complaint about Mexicans as being uncivilized apes. It is easy to take such a statement out of context, but if one continues reading that same letter, Austin predicts optimistically that the Mexican nation would soon "assume her rights in full, and bursting the chains of superstition declare that *man has a right to think for himself.*" In other words, Austin directed his criticism at the Church itself and what he perceived as its oppression of the Mexican people, not at Mexicans for any inherent defect of character. In 1833, he was even more explicit on this theme, actually defending Roman Catholicism as "a religion whose foundation is perfect harmony, a union of principles, & of action." But he condemned the *type* of Catholicism then being practiced in Mexico, saying it was "in theory divine, in practice infernal." These were not the words of a knee-jerk nativist.

But what about the harsh racial invective that he employed in 1835–1836? What are we to make of his support for independence, his 1836 outburst about the "war of barbarism" being "waged by the mongrel Spanish-Indian race, against civilization and the Anglo-American race," and his declaration that the non-Anglos of Texas were "the natural enemies of white men and civilization?" Was this the chauvinistic American finally showing his true colors? How do we reconcile such statements with his actions during the previous fifteen years?

Again, context is everything, and placing Austin's racist-sounding comments in context reveals the great tragedy of Anglo-Tejano relations in the Texas Revolutionary period. Austin wrote these words at a point in the Revolution when he was desperately trying to arouse sympathy and support from citizens of the United States. His main audience was made up of Jacksonian Democrats—and *southern* Democrats at that. His rhetorical transformation of the Texian struggle into a war agianst racially inferior Mexicans was carefully calculated to stir the deepest fears and emotions of southerners. One of the tragic consequences of this war—and of almost all others in which the enemy is of a different race, ethnicity, or culture—is that such wars almost inevitably generate this sort of propaganda. Portray your enemies as somehow less than human, and killing them becomes much easier. Recall how Germans were portrayed in American propaganda during World War I, or the Japanese during World War II, and the genesis of Austin's words can be understood. Was he wrong to resort to racist appeals when his actions over a fifteen-year period clearly contradicted such sentiments? Of course he was. In this one instance, Austin sacrificed his principles in a desperate attempt to reverse the tide of a war that by all appearances was about to be lost. We may wish that he had possessed the superhuman strength of character needed to resist such a sellout, but in the end he was only human.

Returning to his beloved Texas in the critical summer of 1836, Austin reverted to his tried-and-true philosophy of seeking reconciliation and national unity. He never had the opportunity to visit his old Tejano friends in San Antonio, but there is no indication that he would have treated them any differently than before. The harsh rhetoric was never repeated at home. Nothing from his short, ill-fated presidential campaign against Sam Houston that September suggests that he would have changed his longstanding policy of working to build a Texas in which Anglos and Tejanos could honorably cooperate and coexist. And his willingness to accept a cabinet appointment from his rival, Sam Houston, and to support Houston in all broad policy matters, further suggests that he, like Houston, would have resisted the movement toward persecution and recrimination against Tejanos that grew in intensity over the coming years.

However, Stephen F. Austin was a man of his times in one important respect. He believed that American-style democracy—flawed though it may have been by the stain of slavery—was the best system of government yet devised. He only gave up on Mexico when he became convinced that his adopted country had utterly failed to secure the blessings of democracy for its people, Anglo and Hispanic. Having reached that determination, he was willing to employ whatever necessary means to win the Revolution and bring Texas under a better government. That decision—and those means—could give the appearance that he was motivated by an unthinking bigotry against all things not American. But to arrive at such a conclusion, based on a selective reading of the evidence, is to overlook the fifteen-year reality of Austin as a genuine political and cultural mediator.

21. The Trial of Sam Houston

H.W. Brands

In March 1861, the governor of Texas sat quietly in the house the state had built for its chief executives in the city named for his only equal in the pantheon of Texas heroes. Night had fallen across Austin, but more than night was falling across America, and Sam Houston waited to hear the latest ill tidings. He had just passed his sixty-eighth birthday, and he felt every one of those years. His San Jacinto ankle had never healed properly, and it reminded him at each step of his day of triumph. His arrow wound from the Horseshoe Bend still suppurated, recalling his time with General Jackson. Between the ooze and the limp—the first a mark of his service to the United States, the second to Texas—he did better sitting than standing these days.

He had outlived most of his peers from those earlier times. Stephen Austin, of course, died in the year of Texas independence. Andrew Jackson died in the year of annexation. John Quincy Adams collapsed and died in the House in 1848, still declaiming against slavery, still convinced that Texas foretold the wreck of the Union. Santa Anna survived, but he had more lives than a cat.

Houston hadn't believed it then, and he hated to admit it now, but Adams—not Jackson—had been right about Texas and the Union. As soon as the American Congress offered annexation, Houston had thrown over the British. "Supposing a charming lady has two suitors," he explained to an audience wondering at his apparent change of heart.

> One of them she is inclined to believe would make the better husband, but is a little slow to make interesting propositions. Do you think if she was a skillful practitioner in Cupid's court she would pretend that she loved the other "feller" the best and be sure that her favorite would know it? [Laughter and applause.] If ladies are justified in making use of coquetry in securing their annexation to good and agreeable husbands, you must excuse me for making use of the same means to annex Texas to Uncle Sam. [Laughter and cheers.]

The laughter faded, however, when annexation and a consequent dispute over the boundary of Texas triggered the war with Mexico that Adams had predicted. The conflict suited James Polk, who employed it to acquire California and round out the American Southwest. It also suited Santa Anna, in a different way. In the year of Texas's annexation to the Union, the Mexican leader had again overreached himself and thereby united disparate elements of the opposition;

these combined to force him from power and from the country. "Mexicans!" he declared as he embarked for Cuba. "In my old age and mutilated, surrounded by a wife and innocent children, I am going into exile to seek a resting place among strangers. Mercifully forgive the mistakes I made unintentionally, and believe me, in God's name, that I have labored sincerely that you should be independent, free and happy."

He wasn't gone long, though, before Polk conspired to send him back to Mexico. On the theory previously endorsed by Houston and Jackson, Polk judged that Santa Anna would make mischief in Mexico upon reentry, and no sooner had the second war for Texas begun—with fighting along the Rio Grande—than the American president directed U.S. naval commanders in the Caribbean to let Santa Anna through their blockade of the Mexican coast.

Polk's thinking proved as wishful as Houston's and Jackson's on the same subject. Santa Anna rallied Mexican forces against the American invaders, dashing to meet Zachary Taylor at Buena Vista in the north, then racing to cut off Winfield Scott at Cerro Gordo on the road from Veracruz. The hero was again in his element defending Mexico from invasion, and between his battlefield bravery (he led from the front and had horses killed beneath him) and his stirring speeches ("Mexicans! You have a religion: protect it! You have honor: free yourselves from infamy! You love your wives, your children: liberate them from American brutality!") he inspired his countrymen to resist the invaders with surprising effectiveness. Yet he couldn't overcome the backbiting and suspicion that had characterized Mexican politics since 1810 (to which, of course, he had contributed his full share), and he couldn't keep Scott and the Americans from capturing the Mexican capital in the summer of 1847. He tried to arrange a surrender, but the Mexican congress couldn't bring itself to face defeat, and his efforts earned him another exile. He narrowly escaped capture by Texas Rangers serving under the American flag but bent on avenging the Alamo and Goliad; only a safe-conduct issued by the U.S. commander of the Jalapa district allowed him to pass through the Ranger ranks, while the Texans gnashed their teeth and longed for the days under Houston when they ignored orders at pleasure.

The war ended in what appeared a brilliant victory for the United States, with Mexico accepting American control of Texas and additionally ceding California and New Mexico to the United States.

And the victory seemed even more brilliant just months after the Treaty of Guadalupe Hidalgo, when word arrived that a carpenter in California digging a race for a sawmill had discovered gold. By 1848 the spirit of "manifest destiny" infused American politics, and many Americans found it easy to believe that heaven had anointed them to take and civilize the whole of North America. But nothing seemed such patent proof of the destinarian case as the gold discovery. For a quarter millennium the gold of California had been hidden from the Spanish, for a quarter century from the Mexicans; but it hadn't eluded the Americans for a quarter year. Polk and the expansionists had expected the Mexican War to pay for itself in the long run; to see it pay so soon—and in gold, no less—was enough to convince the most skeptical that God was an American.

Yet the golden lining came with a cloud. Although Texas had entered the Union as a slave state, the condition of the rest of the Mexican cession vis-à-vis the peculiar institution had to be determined. Until the gold discovery, most observers assumed that whatever arrangements needed to be made could be made slowly, as the newly acquired territory—mostly desert or mountains, and dauntingly distant from the populated areas of America—filled slowly with people. The Louisiana Purchase, to cite the obvious precedent, was still half empty a half century after Jefferson acquired it. But the gold rush to California overturned all expectations. By the middle of 1849 California had more than enough people to qualify for statehood; by the end of that year those people had written a constitution and sent it to Washington, with emissaries who demanded California's admission to the Union.

Sam Houston was there to greet them. To no one's surprise, Houston had been chosen to represent Texas in the U.S. Senate upon annexation. That he accepted the office, however, wasn't a foregone conclusion. Houston had remarried (after a belated divorce from Eliza), and his new wife, Margaret, didn't want him to leave Texas. She hoped his retirement from the Texas presidency in December 1844 would bring him home to her for good. A poet, she put in verse her vision for him and the family they were creating:

> This task is done. The holy shade
>   Of calm retirement waits thee now.
> The lamp of hope relit hath shed
>   Its sweet refulgence o'er thy brow.
>
> Far from the busy haunts of men,
>   Oh! may thy soul each fleeting hour
> Upon the breath of prayer ascend
>   To Him who rules with love and power.

It was a fond hope, but Margaret could have guessed her husband wouldn't find contentment communing with God. He heeded Margaret sufficiently not to seek public office, but he couldn't—or wouldn't—decline an office that sought him. When the people of Texas, speaking through the Texas legislature, insisted that he serve them in the Senate of the United States, he didn't say no.

Houston's return to Washington excited great comment. His appearance was more striking than ever. He walked with the limp from San Jacinto, but still he towered over ordinary men. His mane and side whiskers were silver now, topped by a white beaver hat and set against a multicolored Cherokee blanket draped over his dress coat. President Polk might have been the political heir of Jackson, but Houston was Old Hickory's spiritual heir and first scion in the line of democratic descent. It was Houston, rather than Polk, who had hastened to Jackson's deathbed in Nashville, only to arrive moments late. He instructed his young son, the eldest of eight children he would have with Margaret, to mark the moment. "My son," he said, "try to remember that you have looked upon the face of Andrew Jackson." As Polk's presidency wound down, many in Washington thought the magnificent Texan—the conqueror of Santa Anna, the George Washington of the Lone Star republic—ought to assume Jackson's political mantle. Returning from a White House reception that saw Polk off, Houston wrote to Margaret: "I suppose that not less than one hundred persons of both sexes spoke to me on the subject of bringing you to the White House, and living there! It may be so!!"

While Margaret prayed to be spared such a fate, Houston dreamed of this stunning conclusion to his remarkable career. But any aspirant to the American presidency in the mid-nineteenth century had to negotiate the narrowing channels of slavery politics, which tightened treacherously upon California's application to the Union. Henry Clay, returned to the Senate after losing the presidency to Polk, proposed to wrap California in a package acceptable to North and South alike. The North would get a free California (the California constitution barred slavery) and an end to the slave trade in the District of Columbia, while the South would get a stiffened fugitive slave law and the possibility of slavery in the rest of the Mexican cession. To sweeten the deal for Texas, the federal government would assume the former republic's crushing debts.

Clay's compromise bill elicited the greatest Senate debate in American history. Clay himself spoke for days on behalf of his measure. John Calhoun, too weak to address the Senate in his own voice, and coughing blood from the tuberculosis that would kill him before the debate ended, had an associate read a rebuttal that was as incendiary as anything the old nullifier had ever written. Daniel Webster riposted that such sentiments as Calhoun's were irresponsible and incipiently treasonous.

Sam Houston had special standing in the affair, hailing from the state that had set the whole crisis in motion. He sided with Calhoun and most of the South in holding that Congress had no right to speak on slavery in the admission of new states. Under the Constitution, Congress could—and must—insist that the states applying for admission have republican governments, but beyond that, Houston said, Congress could not go without trampling the rights of the people. "The Congress of the United States does not possess the power to legislate upon the subject of slavery, either within the Territories or in any other section of the Union. . . . In the formation of their constitutions, under which they ask admission, the people of the Territories have the right to give their own form to their own institutions, and in their own way."

Yet Houston's democratic faith in the people didn't prevent him from denouncing those people who spoke of extreme measures in the event their side didn't get everything it wanted in the present debate. Northern abolitionists were "a contemptible minority," he said, while southern secessionists were "ultras" blind to the danger of the course they advocated. This danger was nothing less than "a war of dissolution, the worst of all wars; a war not of race, a war not of language or of religion, but a war of brothers, the most sanguinary of mortal strife." Houston urged his colleagues to set aside sectionalism and seek the national interest. "I call upon the friends of the Union from every quarter to come forward like men and to sacrifice their differences upon the common altar of the country's good, and to form a bulwark around the Constitution that cannot be shaken." In the current climate, this was no small request. "It will require manly efforts, sir, and they must expect to meet with prejudices growing up around them that will assail them from every quarter. They must stand firm to the Union, regardless of all personal consequences." Houston acknowledged that he wasn't a religious man, but he almost wished he was, that he might request the aid of the Almighty. "I cannot offer the prayers of the righteous that my petition might be heard. But I beseech those whose piety will permit them reverently to petition, that they will pray for this Union and ask that He who buildeth up and pulleth down nations will, in mercy, preserve and unite us. For a nation divided against itself cannot stand." Beyond this, Houston's one request was that in the event that prayers and the wisdom of the people proved unavailing, he not live to see the result. "I wish, if this Union must be dissolved, that its ruins may be the monument of my grave and the graves of my family. I wish no epitaph to be written that I survive the ruin of this glorious Union."

He didn't get his wish. The decade after the Compromise of 1850, as Clay's ultimately successful omnibus measure was called, witnessed the fulfillment of the fears of every friend of the American Union. The Fugitive Slave Act outraged the North by compelling complicity in the return of escaped bondsmen (and others merely alleged by interested parties to have escaped), while the admission of free California continued to rankle the South. The Kansas-Nebraska Act of 1854 repealed the Missouri Compromise of 1820 and opened those two territories to slavery should settlers there choose it; in the process the act provoked a guerrilla war in "bleeding Kansas" and furnished recruits to the new, antislavery Republican party. The Supreme Court declared in the 1857 Dred Scott case that Congress had no authority to bar slavery from the territories, a decision that appeared to corroborate the slaveholder-conspiracy theories of abolitionists and other northerners, with slaveholding Chief Justice Roger B. Taney cast as arch-conspirator. John Brown's botched but bloody effort to start a slave rebellion at Harpers Ferry, Virginia, in 1859, and the reverence accorded the convicted murderer on his way to the gallows, convinced southerners that the real conspiracy was in the North. Abraham Lincoln's 1860 election, with solely northern support, made the perfection of the antislavery conspiracy seem merely a matter of time.

Houston watched the descent toward dissolution with sickening dread. He called the Kansas-Nebraska bill "an eminently perilous measure" and urged the South not to repeal the Missouri Compromise. Repeal, he said, would provoke the North and unsettle the Union. "Maintain the Missouri Compromise! Stir not up agitation! Give us peace!"

He stayed in the Senate another half decade but, as a southern Unionist, found himself increasingly isolated. His cachet in the country as a whole continued to be formidable; Democrat Andrew Johnson of Tennessee asserted, as his party surveyed its presidential prospects, "All agree that if Sam Houston could receive the nomination that he would be elected by a greater majority than any other person." But as the Democrats' center of gravity drifted from West to South, from the land of Jackson to that of Calhoun, an outspoken Unionist stood no chance of being nominated. In the late 1850s secessionist sentiment seized the Texas legislature, and in 1859 it forced Houston from the Senate.

Yet the ordinary people of Texas still responded to the hero of San Jacinto, and Houston had hardly returned from Washington before they elected him governor. Meanwhile his supporters outside the state persisted in hoping for a Houston presidency. After the Democratic party split in the summer of 1860, Houston's friends put his name forward at the convention of the Constitutional Union party. He narrowly lost the nomination to John Bell of Tennessee.

Passion drove politics that season, and the secessionist fever rose by the week. Houston tried to talk it down, with a passion of his own. To a crowd in Austin he spoke of what he had hoped to accomplish in his long public life, and what the secessionists endangered. "Upward of forty-seven years ago," he said of his service with Andrew Jackson, "I enlisted, a mere boy, to sustain the national flag and in defense of a harassed frontier." A belief in the Constitution and the Union had motivated him then, as it motivated all who joined him in those parlous times. "And when again, in 1836, I volunteered to aid in transplanting American liberty to this soil, it was with the belief that the Constitution and the Union were to be perpetual blessings to the human race, that the success of the experiment of our fathers was beyond dispute, and that whether under the banner of the Lone Star or that many starred banner of the Union, I could point to the land of Washington, Jefferson, and Jackson as the land blest beyond all other lands, where freedom would be eternal and the Union unbroken." Houston had watched the Union grow and prosper. "I have seen it extend from the wilds of Tennessee, then a wilderness, across the Mississippi, achieve the annexation of Texas, scaling the Rocky Mountains in its onward march, sweeping the valleys of California, and laving its pioneer footsteps in the waves of the Pacific." This empire of liberty and prosperity was what the secessionists were determined to destroy.

Houston summoned the spirit of Old Hickory to oppose the wreckers. "I invoke the illustrious name of Jackson and bid you not to prove recreant to his memory...To the national men of long service, to the young men who have been reared to love that name, I appeal. The same issue is upon you that was upon him. He stood with the Constitution at his back and defied disunion." Jackson's example should strengthen his followers against sectionalists of all parties.

"Let the people say to these abolition agitators of the North, and to the disunion agitators of the South, 'You cannot dissolve this Union. We will put you both down; but we will not let the Union go!'"

Houston hoped reason would prevail but feared it would not. And he wished again, if it did not, to be spared the sight of the rending of everything he had struggled to achieve. "It has been my misfortune to peril my all for the Union, so indissolubly connected is my life, my history, my hopes, my fortunes with it. And when it falls, I would ask that with it might close my career, that I might not survive the destruction of the shrine that I had been taught to regard as holy and inviolate since my boyhood. I have beheld it, the fairest fabric of government God ever vouchsafed to man, more than half a century. May it never be my fate to stand sadly by gazing on its ruin!"

And now, five months later, he awaited a delegate from the convention that had decreed Texas secession. The election of Lincoln had prompted several southern states to make good their threat to leave the Union. Texas moved more slowly than the rest, in no small part because Houston employed every device he could think of to frustrate what was clearly a majority sentiment among Texas voters. He refused to call a special session of the legislature or summon a convention to consider secession, as had been done in other states; when a convention gathered over his objection, he belatedly brought the legislature into session, to muddy the political waters. But his obstructive efforts failed. The convention endorsed secession, and a popular referendum ratified it. The convention then drafted a new constitution for Texas, attaching the state to the Confederacy and requiring Texas officials to swear allegiance to the Confederate government.

Houston watched all this from the governor's house on a hill across from the state capitol. Now he waited for the convention's emissary, who would formally notify him of the convention's action and of his new duty.

George Chilton arrived at eight. He advised the governor that the convention required his oath at once; should he fail to comply, he would be removed from office.

Chilton wasn't half Houston's age, having been a child at the time of San Jacinto. And his service to Texas paled beside the decades Houston had devoted to his adopted country and state. Consequently Chilton could hardly object when Houston requested more time to consider his response to the convention's demand. By noon the next day, Houston said, the convention would have its answer.

That night was the longest of Houston's life. Past twelve and far till dawn, he struggled with his conscience, with what was left of his ambition, and with history. The irony of his predicament must have forced a wry smile to his face even as it banished sleep from his brain. He, the man who had done more than any other to attach Texas to the Union, was now required to approve the severing of Texas from the Union. Each weary step as he paced the pine boards of the mansion recalled the personal price he had paid; his ankle hurt more on some steps, his thigh on others. To choose between Texas and the Union was to deny the meaning of half the pain he had suffered to bring them together.

The irony was personal, but it was more than that. Houston had fought a war, risking life and reputation, to free Texas from Mexico and make Texas part of the American Union; yet the very success of that war had taught Texas and the South how to dismantle the Union. The secession of Texas from Mexico in 1836 supplied a model for the secession of the South from the Union a quarter century later. In each case secession was defended in terms of states' rights, said to have been traduced by an overweening central authority. Santa Anna had destroyed the Mexican constitution of 1824 by a few swift blows; the North and the Republicans, southerners asserted, had been undermining the American constitution of 1787 for decades. In each case slavery played a role. In Texas in the 1830s slavery was one concern among several; in the South in the early 1860s it was the defining grievance of the Confederacy. Many southern secessionists in 1861 doubted that the North would fight, or if it did that its efforts would avail any better than those of Mexico against Texas in 1836. Hadn't a handful of Texans defeated the hosts of Santa Anna? With such inspiration, did it matter that the North outnumbered the South?

But there was a deeper irony. Houston, like Jackson and all who won political distinction in the age of democracy, placed his confidence in the people. "The people are always right: that is the dogma of the republic," Alexis de Tocqueville had scribbled in the same notebook in which he marveled at the election of David Crockett. Houston agreed, regarding both the phrase being the dogma and the people being right. The people could be unruly and intemperate, as his soldiers were unruly and intemperate during the retreat across Texas in 1836. But eventually the people got it right, as his men got it right at San Jacinto, and as the people of Texas got it right—if he did say so himself—in conferring on him the highest offices at their command.

The people were a tide nothing could resist for long. They had broken down the barriers to voting in the United States in the early nineteenth century. They had swarmed into Texas against the wishes of the Mexican government. They had made the independence of Texas inevitable, seizing that province in fact before they seized it in name. They had demanded the annexation of Texas to the United States and ultimately compelled Congress to take Texas in.

During all that time Houston had seen the people as a progressive force. Democracy could be rough; no one who knew Indians and loved many of them as Houston did could be other than dismayed at what American democracy had done to them. But on balance the expansion of democracy, the growth of the American Union, had been a blessed thing. Democracy delivered opportunity; it meant better lives for more ordinary men and women than had ever enjoyed such opportunity in other times or places.

Yet now democracy was destroying the Union. Houston had held out against secession until the people of Texas spoke; he had hoped against reason and evidence that they would see the error of their intended ways. He didn't doubt that secession would lead to war—and not a war like that against Santa Anna but a conflict so violent as to make the Alamo and San Jacinto seem mere skirmishes.

It was a bitter draft for Houston to swallow: that the people could be so wrong. And it left him at a loss. The people of Texas had chosen disunion, and the representatives of the people now demanded that he swear allegiance to the secessionist confederacy. During his sleepless night, hobbling on his Texas ankle, rubbing his Union wound, he pondered his alternatives. The voice of the people, or the voice of his conscience? Texas or the Union?

In the dark, cold hours of dawn he reached his decision. The convention wanted his answer; instead he addressed it to a higher authority: the people.

Fellow citizens:
In the name of your rights and liberties, which I believe have been trampled upon, I refuse to take this oath.
In the name of the nationality of Texas, which has been betrayed by this convention, I refuse to take this oath.
In the name of the constitution of Texas, which has been trampled upon, I refuse to take this oath.
In the name of my own conscience and manhood, which this convention would degrade by dragging me before it, to pander to the malice of my enemies . . . I refuse to take this oath.

Houston understood the consequences of his refusal. "I am ready to be ostracized sooner than submit to usurpation. Office has no charm for me, that it must be purchased at the sacrifice of my conscience and the loss of my self-respect."

It was the saddest moment of his life. "I have seen the patriots and statesmen of my youth, one by one, gathered to their fathers, and the government which they had created rent in twain; and none like them are left to unite it once again. I stand the last almost of a race, who learned from their lips the lessons of human freedom."

Houston died in 1863, in the month of the battle of Gettysburg. He lived long enough to see his dire forecasts of the horrors of civil war come true, but not long enough to see the Union survive its greatest trial, nor to see Texas rejoined to the land of his birth. Though he mourned the losses Texas suffered during the war (his son was gravely wounded at Shiloh), he would have believed that democracy won in the end, as the American people secured popular government against the forces of particularism and disunion. And he would have been gratified to know that the two causes closest to his heart—the Union and Texas—could cohabit again in peace.

He had always thought that Texas and the Union were cut from the same cloth, that the republican principles of 1836 were indeed those of 1776. The lesson of both fateful years was that people must govern themselves, even if—or especially if—self-government required rebellion against forms and institutions received from the past, and even if the people were far from saints. Houston couldn't speak from personal acquaintance of the patriots of '76, but he would have been the first to acknowledge the imperfect pedigrees and mixed motives of those who fought beside him in the Texas revolution. Stephen Austin might have been above reasonable reproach, having lived as a loyal citizen of Mexico till Santa Anna overturned the Mexican constitution and drove him to revolt, but nearly everyone else was an opportunist of one sort or another. William Travis had abandoned his debts and pregnant wife to come to Texas, where he made trouble for the Mexican authorities as a way of making the reputation he had always coveted. James Bowie, having swindled himself into a corner in Louisiana, crossed the Sabine to continue his swindling on Mexican soil. David Crockett hoped to recover in Texas the political career he had lost in Tennessee. And of course Houston himself, crushed by love and dazed by drink, had traveled to Texas to find the man he had been before Eliza broke his heart.

But none of these, nor even most of the latecomers who arrived in response to the bounties promised to volunteers in the Texan army, were merely opportunists. They believed in liberty, as they understood the term. They believed in the rule of law and the right of people to govern themselves. Their victory was a victory for democracy, in the dawning age of democracy. If it was also a victory for slavery, this aspect of the triumph proved passing when democracy defeated slavery in the Civil War.

Houston was not religious, placing his faith in the people rather than in heaven. Yet he was forced to concede that the people, no less than heaven, sometimes worked in mysterious ways. The events culminating in the Texas revolution transcended morality, in the ordinary sense. Tens of thousands of Americans came to Texas to seek a better life. Some came legally, many others illegally. No force short of an army at the Sabine could have stopped them, so long as the opportunities in Texas were far greater than those at home. Certainly few of them felt any compunction about bending or dodging Mexican law in pursuit of their dreams. And after making Texas theirs by occupation, they saw no reason not to make it theirs by revolution.

Were they justified in doing so? Sensitive souls—the John Quincy Adamses of the era—complained that they were stealing land from Mexico. And maybe they were. But these were Americans, a people who were in the process of taking far more land from the native peoples of North America than the Texans took from Mexico (which itself, of course, was trying to take Texas from the Indians). If the Texans were guilty of theft, the people from whom they sprang were much guiltier. In any event, the sensitive souls who fretted about such things didn't frequent the frontier, where questions of survival took precedence over nuances of law.

For better and worse, Texas was very much like America. The people ruled, and little could stop them. If they ignored national boundaries, if they trampled the rights of indigenous peoples and of imported bondsmen, if they waged war for motives that started from base self-interest, all this came with the territory of democracy, a realm inhabited by ordinarily imperfect men and women. The one saving grace of democracy—the one thing that made all the difference in the end—was that sooner or later, sometimes after terrible strife, democracy corrected its worst mistakes. For a generation after San Jacinto, even the most ardent supporters of the Texas revolution had difficulty contending that the victory of Houston's ragged band had actually enlarged the area of human liberty. But when the Civil War terminated slavery, and as the American Southwest filled with people pursuing their own versions of the democratic dream, it was hard not to accept Houston's faith that the people ultimately got things right, and that the victory of the Texans was a victory for America.

22. Dred Scott vs. Sandford

The Dred Scott *decision is one of the most controversial decisions the U.S. Supreme Court has ever made. It defined slaves as "property," declared that blacks could not be (and were never) American citizens, and argued that the U.S. government could not prohibit slavery in the territories, declaring the Missouri Compromise unconstitutional. As a result, the volatile sectional differences between the non-slaveholding north and the slaveholding south continued to widen. It was a direct challenge to Abraham Lincoln and the new Republican party and encouraged those Southerners who advocated the expansion of slavery.* Dred Scott vs. Sanford *fueled the fires of sectionalism.*

Dred Scott was a slave who was born in Virginia and had moved with his "master" to St. Louis, Missouri. In St. Louis he was sold to another man, who then moved Scott to various places, including Illinois and Wisconsin. In 1842, Scott was back in Missouri and soon filed suit for his freedom, claiming that he had been in "free" territory and therefore free when he came back to Missouri. After a series of legal maneuvers that lasted for many years, Scott's case was finally taken by the U.S. Supreme Court. The issues were critical – Did Dred Scott have the right to sue in court as a U.S. citizen? Could the United States government dictate the status of slavery in territories? On March 6, 1857, two days after the inauguration of President James Buchanan, Chief Justice Roger B. Taney announced the majority opinion. Unfortunately, the decision that President Buchanan thought would end the controversy over slavery in the territories had the opposite effect.

The question is simply this: Can a Negro, whose ancestors were imported into this country, and sold as slaves, become a member of the political community formed and brought into existence by the Constitution of the United States, and as such become entitled to all the rights, and privileges, and immunities, guarantied by that instrument to the citizen? One of which rights is the privilege of suing in a court of the United States in the cases specified in the Constitution?

It will be observed, that the plea applies to that class of persons only whose ancestors were Negroes of the African race, and imported into this country, and sold and held as slaves. The only matter in issue before the court, therefore, is, whether the descendants of such slaves, when they shall be emancipated, or who are born of parents who had become free before their birth, are citizens of a State, in the sense in which the word citizen is used in the Constitution of the United States. And this being the only matter in dispute on the pleadings, the court must be understood as speaking in this opinion of that class only, that is, of those persons who are the descendants of Africans who were imported into this country, and sold as slaves...

The words "people of the United States" and "citizens" are synonymous terms, and mean the same thing. They both describe the political body who, according to our republican institutions, form the sovereignty, and who hold the power and conduct the Government through their representatives. They are what we familiarly call the "sovereign people," and every citizen is one of this people, and a constituent member of this sovereignty. The question before us is, whether the class of persons described in the plea in abatement compose a portion of this people, and are constituent members of this sovereignty? We think they are not, and that they are not included, and were not intended to be included, under the word "citizens" in the Constitution, and can therefore claim none of the rights and privileges which that instrument provides for and secures to citizens of the United States. On the contrary, they were at that time considered as a subordinate and inferior class of beings, who had been subjugated by the dominant race, and, whether emancipated or not, yet remained subject to their authority, and had no rights or privileges but such as those who held the power and the Government might choose to grant them.

It is not the province of the court to decide upon the justice or injustice, the policy or impolicy, of these laws. The decision of that question belonged to the political or law-making power; to those who formed the sovereignty and framed the Constitution. The duty of the court is, to interpret the instrument they have framed, with the best lights we can obtain on the subject, and to administer it as we find it, according to its true intent and meaning when it was adopted.

In discussing this question, we must not confound the rights of citizenship which a State may confer within its own limits, and the rights of citizenship as a member of the Union. It does not by any means follow, because he has all the rights and privileges of a citizen of a State, that he must be a citizen of the United States. He may have all of the rights and privileges of the citizen of a State, and yet not be entitled to the rights and privileges of a citizen in any other State...

It is very clear, therefore, that no State can, by any act or law of its own, passed since the adoption of the Constitution, introduce a new member into the political community created by the Constitution of the United States. It cannot make him a member of this community by making him a member of its own. And for the same reason it cannot introduce any person, or description of persons, who were not intended to be embraced in this new political family, which the Constitution brought into existence, but were intended to be excluded from it.

The question then arises, whether the provisions of the Constitution, in relation to the personal rights and privileges to which the citizen of a State should be entitled, embraced the negro African race, at that time in this country, or who might afterwards be imported, who had then or should afterwards be made free in any State; and to put it in the power of a singe State to make him a citizen of the United States, and endue him with the full rights of citizenship in every other State without their consent? Does the Constitution of the United States act upon him whenever he shall be made free under the laws of a State, and raised there to the rank of a citizen, and immediately clothe him with all the privileges of a citizen in every other State, and in its own courts?

The court thinks the affirmative of these propositions cannot be maintained. And if it cannot, the plaintiff in error could not be a citizen of the State of Missouri, within the meaning of the Constitution of the United States, and, consequently, was not entitled to sue in its courts.

It is difficult at this day to realize the state of public opinion in relation to that unfortunate race, which prevailed in the civilized and enlightened portions of the world at the time of the Declaration of Independence, and when the Constitution of the United States was framed and adopted. But the public history of every European nation displays it in a manner too plain to be mistaken.

They had for more than a century before been regarded as beings of an inferior order, and altogether unfit to associate with the white race, either in social or political relations; and so far inferior, that they had no rights which the white man was bound to respect; and that the negro might justly and lawfully be reduced to slavery for his benefit. He was bought and sold, and treated as an ordinary article of merchandise and traffic, whenever a profit could be made by it. This opinion was at that time fixed and universal in the civilized portion of the white race. It was regarded as an axiom in morals as well as in politics, which no one thought of disputing, or supposed to be open to dispute; and men in every grade and position in society daily and habitually acted upon it in their private pursuits, as well as in matters of public concern, without doubting for a moment the correctness of this opinion.

And in no nation was this opinion more firmly fixed or more uniformly acted upon than by the English Government and English people. They not only seized them on the coast of Africa, and sold them or held them in slavery for their own use; but they took them as ordinary articles of merchandise to every country where they could make a profit on them, and were far more extensively engaged in this commerce than any other nation in the world.

The opinion thus entertained and acted upon in England was naturally impressed upon the colonies they founded on this side of the Atlantic. And, accordingly, a negro of the African race was regarded by them as an article of property, and held, and bought and sold as such, in every one of the thirteen colonies which united in the Declaration of Independence, and afterwards formed the Constitution of the United States. The slaves were more or less numerous in the different colonies, as slave labor was found more or less profitable. But not one seems to have doubted the correctness of the prevailing opinion of the time.

But there are two clauses in the Constitution which point directly and specifically to the negro race as a separate class of persons, and show clearly that they were not regarded as a portion of the people or citizens of the Government then formed.

One of these clauses reserves to each of the thirteen States the right to import slaves until the year 1808, if it thinks proper. And the importation which it thus sanctions was unquestionably of persons of the race of which we are speaking, as the traffic in slaves in the United States had always been confined to them. And by the other provision the States pledge themselves to each other to maintain the right of property of the master, by delivering up to him any slave who may have escaped from his service, and be found within their respective territories...

No one, we presume, supposes that any change in public opinion or feeling, in relation to this unfortunate race, in the civilized nations of Europe or in this country, should induce the court to give to the words of the Constitution a more liberal construction in their favor than they were intended to bear when the instrument was framed and adopted. Such an argument would be altogether inadmissible in any tribunal called on to interpret it. If any of its provisions are deemed unjust, there is a mode described in the instrument itself by which it may be amended; but while it remains unaltered, it must be construed now as it was understood at the time of its adoption. It is not only the same in words, but the same in meaning, and delegates the same powers to the Government, and reserves and secures the same rights and privileges to the citizen; and as long as it continues to exist in its present form, it speaks not only in the same words, but with the same meaning and intent with which it spoke when it came from the hands of its framers, and was voted on and adopted by the people of the United States. Any other rule of construction would abrogate the judicial character of this court, and make it the mere reflex of the popular opinion or passion of the day. This court was not created by the Constitution for such purposes. Higher and graver trusts have been confided to it, and it must not falter in the path of duty.

What the construction was at that time, we think can hardly admit of doubt. We have the language of the Declaration of Independence and of the Articles of Confederation, in addition to the plain words of the Constitution itself; we have the legislation of the different States, before, about the time, and since, the Constitution was adopted; we have the legislation of Congress, from the time of its adoption to a recent period; and we have the constant and uniform action of the Executive Department, all concurring together, and leading to the same result. And if anything in relation to the construction of the Constitution can be regarded as settled, it is that which we now give to the word "citizen" and the word "people."

The act of Congress, upon which the plaintiff relies, declares that slavery and involuntary servitude, except as a punishment for crime, shall be forever prohibited in all that part of the territory ceded by France, under the name of Louisiana, which lies north of thirty-six degrees thirty minutes north latitude, and not included within the limits of Missouri. And the difficulty which meets us at the threshold of this part of the inquiry is, whether Congress was authorized to pass this law under any of the powers granted to it by the Constitution; for if the authority is not given by that instrument, it is the duty of this court to declare it void and inoperative, and incapable of conferring freedom upon any one who is held as a slave under the laws of any one of the States.

The counsel for the plaintiff has laid much stress upon that article in the Constitution which confers on Congress the power "to dispose of and make all needful rules and regulations respecting the territory or other property belonging to the United States:" but, in the judgment of the court, that provision has no bearing on the present controversy, and the power there given, whatever it may be, is confined, and was intended to be confined, to the territory which at that time belonged to, or was claimed by, the United States, and was within their boundaries as settled by the treaty with Great Britain, and can have no influence upon a territory afterwards acquired from a foreign Government. It was a special provision for a known and particular territory, and to meet a present emergency, and nothing more.

But the power of Congress over the person or property of a citizen can never be a mere discretionary power under our Constitution and form of Government. The powers of the Government and the rights and privileges of the citizen are regulated and plainly defined by the Constitution itself. And when the Territory becomes a part of the United States, the Federal Government enters into possession in the character impressed upon it by those who created it. It enters upon it with its powers over the citizen strictly defined, and limited by the Constitution, from which it derives its own existence, and by virtue of which alone it continues to exist and act as a Government and sovereignty. It has no power of any kind beyond it; and it cannot, when it enters a Territory of the United States, put off its character, and assume discretionary or despotic powers which the Constitution has denied to it. It cannot create for itself a new character separated from the citizens of the United States, and the duties it owes them under the provisions of the Constitution. The Territory being a part of the United States, the Government and the citizen both enter it under the authority of the Constitution, with their respective right defined and marked out; and the Federal Government can exercise no power over his person or property, beyond that instrument confers, nor lawfully deny any right which is has reserved.

These powers, and others, in relation to rights of person, which it is not necessary here to enumerate, are, in express and positive terms, denied to the General Government; and the rights of private property have been guarded with equal care. Thus the rights of property are united with the rights of person, and placed on the same ground by the fifth amendment to the Constitution, which provides that no person shall be deprived of life, liberty, and property, without due process of law. And an act of Congress which deprives a citizen of the United States of his liberty or property, merely because he came himself or brought his property into a particular Territory of the United States, and who had committed no offence against the laws, could hardly be dignified with the name of due process of law.

So, too, it will hardly be contended that Congress could by law quarter a soldier in a house in a Territory without the consent of the owner, in time of peace;

nor in time of war, but in a manner prescribed by law. Nor could they by law forfeit the property of a citizen in a Territory who was convicted of treason, for a longer period than the life of the person convicted; nor take private property for public use without just compensation.

The powers over person and property of which we speak are not only not granted to Congress, but are in express terms denied, and they are forbidden to exercise them. And this prohibition is not confined to the States, but the words are general, and extend to the whole territory over which the Constitution gives it power to legislate, including those portions of it remaining under Territorial Government, as well as that covered by States. It is a total absence of power everywhere within the dominion of the United States, and places the citizens of a Territory, so far as these rights are concerned, on the same footing with citizens of the States, and guards them as firmly and plainly against any inroads which the General Government might attempt, under the plea of implied or incidental powers. And if Congress itself cannot do this – if it is beyond the powers conferred on the Federal Government – it will be admitted, we presume, that it could not authorize a Territorial Government to exercise them. It could confer no power on any local Government, established by its authority, to violate the provisions of the Constitution.

The powers of the Government, and the rights of the citizen under it, are positive and practical regulations plainly written down. The people of the United States have delegated to it certain enumerated powers, and forbidden it to exercise others. It has no power over the person or property of a citizen but what the citizens of the United States have granted. And no laws or usages of other nations, or reasoning of statesmen or jurists upon the relations of master and slave, can enlarge the powers of the Government, or take from the citizens the rights they have reserved. And if the Constitution recognizes the right of property of the master in a slave, and makes no distinction between that description of property and other property owned by a citizen, no tribunal, acting under the authority of the United States, whether it be legislative, executive, or judicial, has a right to draw such a distinction, or deny to it the benefit of the provisions and guarantees which have been provided for the protection of private property against the encroachments of the Government.

Upon these considerations, it is the opinion of the court that the act of Congress which prohibited a citizen from holding and owning property of this kind in the territory of the United States north of the line therein mentioned, its not warranted by the Constitution, and is therefore void; and that neither Dred Scott himself, nor any of his family, were made free by being carried into this territory; even if they had been carried there by the owner, with the intention of becoming a permanent resident.

We have so far examined the case, as it stands under the Constitution of the United States, and the powers thereby delegated to the Federal Government.

23. The Everyday Life of Enslaved People In the Antebellum South

Calvin Schermerhorn

Coming of age in a nation that hungered for black labor, antebellum America's slaves were driven relentlessly to toil in fields and factories. Their bodies weakened by fatigue and hunger, wracked by chronic illnesses and injury, and, in the case of women of childbearing age, strained by near constant pregnancy, daily existence often came down to an endless struggle of will and endurance. Yet that was not the sum of the challenges and tribulations that burdened black people's lives, for they lived in the shadow of an agricultural revolution. Beginning in the 1790s, short-staple cotton began a profitable commodity owing to the introduction of efficient cotton gins (which separated the sticky seeds from the valuable lint) and a growing demand from British textile mills. To take advantage of new economic opportunities, migrating masters forcibly moved hundreds of thousands of enslaved women, children, and men from the Upper South onto the cotton and sugar frontiers of Mississippi, Texas, Arkansas, Louisiana, and Alabama. This agricultural revolution rapidly changed the shape and face of a young nation. It also profoundly altered the lives of America's slaves as owners and traders separated families, parted friends, and orphaned children. Though enslaved women and men worked as hard to repair the damage done to their families and friendships as they worked for their owners—meeting, marrying, raising babies, and forming all sorts of social institutions—few could escape the human cost of agricultural and national expansion. As Virginia native Madison Jefferson later recalled, "we [had] dread constantly on our minds," never knowing "how long master" might keep us, "not into whose hands we may fall".

Such fears were especially acute among slaves who lived in the upper South states of Maryland and Virginia. In these areas where much of the domestic (or internal) migration originated, owners increasingly came to value their slaves not for the work they might perform but for the cash they could bring at auction. A decline in the profitability of tobacco, combined with a steady growth in the population of slaves, encouraged such recalculation. Between 1790 and 1860 some 1.1 million enslaved people—the majority of them between the ages of 15 and 30—found themselves forced onto the roads. Often plucked away by traders called "Georgia men" and bound together in coffles, black women and men marched south and west, footsore, forlorn, and often missing their families. Later, as the machinery of the slave market grew more elaborate, traders packed slaves into railroad cars and the holds of ships, reducing the duration of the journey thought not its harmful effects. The bulk of this traffic took place in the winter, a choice that would deliver fresh workers just in time for spring planting. Some would be dispatched at one of the many auction houses that sprang up in New Orleans, Natchez, and Memphis. Others would be marched through new neighborhoods and sold away in ones or twos by the trader. About 60 percent of America's forced migrants went that way, sold by traders ad mixed in with strangers. The remainder moved along with their owners, bundled together with horses, cattle, wagons, and supplies by men (and women) eagerly seeking their fortunes on the southern frontier.

Given the propensity of traders and free migrants to select the strongest, the healthiest, and the most fertile of slaves for transshipment to Deep South plantations—after all, what planters wanted were slaves who could both produce and reproduce—the impact on black families was extensive. Upper South slave communities in Virginia and Maryland were especially hard hit. There, in what amounted to the headwaters of a great forced migration, as many as one half of all sales separated parents from children. One-quarter took husbands from wives. Each season that passed without the sale of a friend or relative brought considerable relief, but slaves worried and prepared for the near inevitable arrival of a trader or his agent. In anticipation of such an eventuality, Henry "Box" Brown's mother took her son "upon her knee and, pointing to the forest trees which were then being stripped of their foliage by the winds of autumn, would say to me, my son, as yonder leaves are stripped from off the trees of the forest, so are the children of the slaves swept away from them by the hands of cruel tyrants". Other parents tried to delay the day of forced departure, hiding their children in the woods as did North Carolina native Moses Grandy's mother, in a heartbreaking and usually futile attempt "to prevent master selling us".

Planters and masters were quick to capitalize on black people's desperate efforts to keep their families intact. Recognizing a new means to wring obedience out of their labors, sale became a new way to "domesticate" those who, like Josiah Henson's father, proved immune to more conventional forms of slave discipline. Recounting how his father had been severely beaten for having intervened to protect his wife from an overseer's assault, Henson described a punishment that failed to achieve its intended effect. "My father became a different man," Henson later wrote, but not an obedient man. Despite a hundred lashes and the amputation of his right ear, he turned "morose, disobedient and intractable.: So mush so that the owner gave up on the more conventional modes of control and eventually rid himself of a difficult slave by selling Henson's father to "Alabama; and neither my mother nor I, ever heard of him again".

Sale as punishment was but just one of he many reasons slaves witnessed loved ones being bound away. Slave owners frequently balanced their personal accounts and paid off their debs by selling excess slaves. Others dismembered longstanding slave families and communities when they divided their property among heirs or gave away a slave t celebrate a child's marriage. These were practices that made enslaved women and men acutely conscious of the ambitions, health, and financial condition of those who claimed to own them. "A bankruptcy, a death, or a removal, may produce a score or two of involuntary divorces," recalled Virginia native Henry Goings. Husbands and wives who belonged to different owners and who had married "abroad" suffered disproportionately from owners' changing fortunes. Maria Perkins learned this first hand when her owner determined to sell away a number of his slaves. "Dear Husband," Maria opened her letter, "I write... to let you know of my distress. My master has sold [or son] Albert to trader on Monday court day and myself and another child is for sale also." "I don't want a trader to get me," Maria cried, before asking her husband to approach his own master about buying Maria and the couple's remaining child.

Slaves could do little, however, to slow the rushing tide of forced migration. Swept up in a current that would deposit 285,000 people on Deep South plantations in the 1830s alone, enslaved men and women soon found themselves hard at work in their new homes, creating cotton and sugar economies one field and furrow at a time. Sold away from his native Virginia, J. H. Banks arrived in Alabama by rail in the 1850s to find that his new owner "had purchased a new farm, and had taken a contract to finish three miles of railroad," which he intended his slaves to build before putting them to work making cotton. Viewing the fields from his drafty and ramshackle slave quarters—a cabin with "no chinking or daubing," Banks recalled seeing the toll the work took. Despite their location "in the midst of the cotton paradise," young men who were no more "than nineteen or twenty" looked easily twice their age. Along the Oconee and Savannah rivers in Georgia, the Coosa and Tombigbee rivers in Alabama, and along the banks of the Tennessee and Mississippi, conditions were no better. Young women and men labored from before dawn to after dark, usually under the supervision of overseers and horse-mounted patrollers. In places where "sugar wuz king," as one former Louisiana slave recalled it, the work regime pressed even harder, mirroring the volatile Caribbean slave societies that served as models for these factories in the fields. Because of the physically demanding nature of the work slaves performed on America's sugar estates, sex balances remained far out of balance. Men, planters believed, swung the heavy cane knives more effectively than did women. As a consequence, sugar plantations were characterized by disproportionately more men than women, fewer families, and birth rates that lagged behind those of other regions, where despite the trauma of forced migration, strangers gradually came to be friends, married, and had children.

Labor posed plenty of dangers, but it was not the only danger inherent to slavery. There was another side to daily life in bondage, one which women and girls especially confronted. The antebellum South was a landscape characterized by sexual violence against African American women. Harriet Jacobs knew this too well, having learned this particular terrain the day her owner "began to whisper foul words" into her ear. Some women tried to turn the tables and use their sexuality strategically. Though a few may have succeeded, failure could exact a deadly high price. Take Eliza, for example. The concubine of a Maryland planter, Eliza had borne the man a daughter named Emily. When jealous relatives intervened, the arrangement abruptly unraveled. Carried to Washington D.C. by her master's son-in-law, Eliza realized too late that she had been badly deceived. Rather than receiving her freedom as she had been promised, the finely attired and petted Eliza found herself lodged in a jail and discovered that her so called freedom paper was actually a bill of sale. Mary, too, suffered grievously when a vengeful mistress sold the Alabama woman away from the baby she had borne her master. The child, only eleven months old, went to a Kentucky owner while Mary ended up in the hands of a Maryland master. Sale did not end Mary's troubles. Subjected to the sexual harassment of her new owner's son, May fought back, as did the slave who had been courting her. In a rage, he murdered Mary's attacker. Neighborhood slaves were forced to watch the man who had defended Mary burned alive, and Mary—in a fit of desperation—ended her own life in the waters of the Chesapeake Bay.

Day-to-day life involved more than growing the South's staple crops. Besides constructing and maintaining miles of fence and outbuildings, tending owners' livestock, splitting firewood, and performing a near endless assortment of chores associated with antebellum agricultural enterprise, slaves grew a wide range of crops. In the cotton South, for example, Henry Goings recalled, "a good hand is supposed to cultivate 15 acres of cotton and 10 acres of corn," besides "potatoes and other vegetables," which were grown "for home consumption." After a day of sowing, weeding, chopping, or picking cotton, slaves would also often tend to their own garden patches where they would raise vegetables, keep chickens and small livestock, and sometimes even produce commodities or marginal land. In many corners of the South—particularly in or near urban centers—enslaved people became small property owners, accumulating small amounts of wealth by peddling extra eggs, homemade confections, and homegrown produce to townspeople. A few even sold small crops of cotton or tobacco back to their owner, some of whom occasionally found themselves in perpetual debt to their slaves. Others, however, promoted slaves' productive activities as a way to shift some of the burden of support from owners to the owned. Nevertheless, slaves' home enterprises produced some advantages. In creating informal economies, enslaved people developed their own concepts of property, and in rare cases, earned enough from their entrepreneurial and agricultural activities to finance their own freedom or that of a loved one.

Stretching the workday into the nights exposed slaves to a different kind of risk. Again, in the words of Henry Goings—who had been born a slave in Virginia before traveling much of the cotton South with a peripatetic owner—long work days and heavy work loads "often showed themselves in fevers and other miasmatic diseases"(18). Besides aging the nation's slaves before their time, the labor regimes that produced the South's great staples exposed workers to infectious diseases like hookworm, which was endemic on some plantations. Infected slaves grew anemic, lost weight, and succumbed to infections. The sufferers' symptoms began with a dermatitis, "ground itch" or "dew poison" when the hookworm larvae penetrated the skin en route to the small intestine. A raft of other diseases also plagued slaves. Mosquitoes spread yellow fever and malaria. Unwashed hands and undercooked meat introduced food poisoning and dysentery. Infections transmitted through exposure to soil and fecal matter (workers often went without shoes and babies went without diapers) were common and debilitating. To combat illness, enslaved people cultivated knowledge of folk remedies and sometimes used spiritual medicine. Enslaved women exchanged information on contraception and abortion and became expert midwives. But often even experienced doctors could do little. Outbreaks of viral hepatitis or cholera might tear through a neighborhood at any time, carried on occasion by coffles of the newly arrived slaves. Not surprisingly, the average life expectancy for slaves in antebellum America was just over thirty years.

In addition to being sick, enslaved people were perennially hungry and ill-clothed, especially infants, toddlers, and preteens who made up over 43 percent of the enslaved population in 1820. In the upper South, insufficient quantities of food complemented poor quality, as owners stinted children, reserving calories for slaves in their most productive years. Partly as a consequence, adult slaves tended to be shorter than other Americans. Fredrick Douglass recalled being "so pinched with hunger" as a child that he had "fought with the dog" for the "smallest crumbs" . Scanty clothing compounded children's problems. Virginia native John Brown recalled that youngsters "of both sexes usually run about quite naked, until they are from ten to twelve years of age". Young Moses Grandy was "compelled to go into the fields and woods to work, with my naked feet cracked and bleeding from extreme cold." To warm them he would "rouse an ox or hog, and stand on the place where it had lain".

Ill-health, hunger, and the raw winds of winter rarely excused slaves from their daily labors. Indeed, in a system as heavily dependent on slaves' labor as were the cotton, sugar, tobacco, and rice crops that enriched their owners—and the nation—any deviance brought summary and often severe punishment. Whips were the favored weapon of choice, falling on slaves' backs and gouging out flesh in retaliation for the smallest infractions. But virtually anything could become an instrument of discipline and control. Masters, mistresses, overseers, and agents routinely relied on sticks, pistols, knives, fists, feet, shovels, and tongs to terrorize and subdue their slaves. Hanna Fambro's mistress beat her mother to death with a broomstick. Ira Jones's aunt died of tetanus after her owner nailed her hands to a barrel. When a young mother arrived late to the fields one morning, fellow slave Charles Ball recalled, the overseer "compelled her to remove her old tow linen shift, the only garment she wore, so as to expose her hits," whereupon he "gave her ten lashes, with his long whip, every touch of which brought blood, and a shriek from the sufferer". Children were not spared their owners' rods. Determined that the youngest slaves mature into the most obedient slaves, masters and mistresses beat children for crying, for failing to do their chores, and sometimes for no reason at all. As one survivor recalled years after the Civil War, slavery "wuz hell".

Family—whether remembered or reconstructed—gave slaves the strength to continue. Whether calling on one another to stave off an overseer's blows, sharing their meals in the sooty darkness of a plantation cabin, or as Maria Perkins attempted to do, keeping a slave trader at bay, husbands and wives, parents and children, sisters and brothers found in their affective and domestic relations the means to deflect some of the worst slavery's impositions. For many of those who were transported out of the upper, older, and seaboard South and onto cotton and sugar's new plantations, this often meant starting their families anew. One of probably hundreds of thousands of enslaved women and men who attempted to bring order out of chaos through marriage, Virginia-born Philip Joiner met and wed Henrietta when both were enslaved in South Georgia. By the Civil War, the couple had two daughters, Lucy Ann and Mary Jane, named as so many enslaved children were after grandparents and their close kin.

Despite the calloused advice of owners who told grieving husbands and wives that if they wanted a spouse "so badly, stop your crying and go and find another," many resisted forming new families while their closet kin remained alive in old homes. Charles Ball, for example, joined an enslaved family on his master's South Carolina plantation—sharing a roof, helping out, and contributing food to a collective table—but he never forgot the woman and children he had been made to leave behind in Maryland. As he later explained, "a firm conviction settled upon my mind, that by some means, at present incomprehensible to me, I should yet again embrace my wife, and caress my children." At length Ball did, escaping and making his way back to Maryland, where he was recaptured and re-enslaved.

Countless others relied solely on memory, keeping alive in their minds those heartfelt affections. These images did little to shield slaves from owners' blows, but they did remind enslaved people that they were far more than mere tools of agricultural and industrial production. They belonged not only to masters and mistresses, but also to each other. Thus it was that when Hawkins Wilson was sold away from Virginia in 1843, he carried with him a rich set of memories that kept him in mental touch with a family he hoped to see again someday. After the Civil War and emancipation, that day seemed to be fast approaching and Wilson wrote home from Texas that he was "anxious to learn about my sisters, from whom I have been separated many years—I have never heard from them since I left Virginia twenty four years ago—I am in hopes that they are still living and I am anxious to hear how they are getting on." Lest the recipient (an agent of the Bureau of Refugees, Freedmen, and Abandoned Lands) deliver his letter into the wrong hands, Wilson offered a detailed description of his family as he had last known them"

One of my sisters belonged to Peter Coleman in Caroline County and her name was Jane—her husband's name was Charles and he belonged to Buck Haskin and lived near John Wright's store in the same county—She had three children, Robert, Charles and Julia, when I left—Sister Martha belonged to Dr. Jefferson, who lived two miles above Wright's store—Sister Matilda belonged to Mrs. Botts, in the same county—My dear uncle Jim had a wife at Jack Langley's and his wife was named Adie and his oldest son was named Buck and they all belonged to Jack Langley—These are all my own dearest relatives and I wish to correspond wit them with a view to visit them as soon as I can hear from them—My name is Hawkins Wilson and I am their brother, who was sold at Sheriff's sale.

Hawkins Wilson never reconnected with his family. Neither did hundreds of thousands of other slaves, men and women whose lives had been roughly transformed by cotton's and sugar's antebellum revolutions. Whether left behind in the upper South—unsure of where their loved ones went and how they fared–or deposited among strangers in a Deep South plantation, America's last generation of slaves experienced deep and wrenching change. Many, indeed, lived their lives in near perpetual motion. Subject to repeated sales and migrations, handed off from one owner to the next, burdened with heavy demands on their labor, and haunted by the chronic terror of losing a close friend or kinsman to a trader's coffle, America's enslaved women and men struggled continuously to maintain their health, their strength, and, above al, their humanity. Theirs were day-to-day experiences that involved a "hierarchy of concerns" for nourishment, for health, and for whatever security they could eke out of a system that repeatedly visited them with the incremental terrors of forced labor and enforced separations.

V

Civil War and Reconstruction: 1860–1877

24. Abraham Lincoln
and the Self-Made Myth

Richard Hofstadter

George Washington and Abraham Lincoln: One helped begin the nation, the other kept it from breaking apart. Historians routinely rank the two at the top of their list of great American presidents. Abraham Lincoln was president during the nations's deepest crisis. A complex man, he faced the challenges of the office with a mixture of intelligence, guile, melancholy humor and unparalleled political skill. James McPherson called him a "conservative revolutionary," for although he was a moderate on the question of slavery, and always one to keep his cards close to the vest, Abraham Lincoln oversaw the most momentous social and political upheaval in the nation's history.

Historian Richard Hofstadter details the political career of Lincoln He traces the evolution of Lincoln's views on slavery, and how the Civil War itself would force Lincoln to modify and finally reject previously held notions of federal law and slavery. In Hofstadter's view, did Lincoln shape events, or was he shaped by them? What is meant by "the self-made myth"?

What was Lincoln's political background? Where did he stand on the important issues of the day, i.e., The Mexican War, the Kansas-Nebraska Act, and the Fugitive Slave Law? Was Lincoln an abolitionist? Why or why not? Finally, what separates Abraham Lincoln, president, from presidents of the modern era?

> I happen, temporarily, to occupy this White House. I am a living witness that any one of your children may look to come here as my father's child has.
> —Abraham Lincoln to the 166th Ohio Regiment

> His ambition was a little engine that knew no rest.
> —William H. Herndon

The Lincoln legend has come to have a hold on the American imagination that defies comparison with anything else in political mythology. Here is a drama in which a great man shoulders the torment and moral burdens of a blundering and sinful people, suffers for them, and redeems them with hallowed christian virtues—"malice toward none and charity for all"—and is destroyed at the pitch of his success. The world-wise John Hay, who knew him about as well as he permitted himself to be known, called him "the greatest character since Christ," a comparison one cannot imagine being made of any other political figure of modern times.

If the Lincoln legend gathers strength from its similarity to the Christian theme of vicarious atonement and redemption, there is still another strain in American experience that it represents equally well. Although his métier was politics and not business, Lincoln was a pre-eminent example of that self-help which Americans have always so admired. He was not, of course, the first eminent American politician who could claim humble origins, nor the first to exploit them. But few have been able to point to such ascent from relative obscurity to high eminence; none has maintained so completely while scaling the heights the aspect of extreme simplicity; none has combined with the attainment of success and power such an intense awareness of humanity and moral responsibility. It was precisely in his attainments as a common man that Lincoln felt himself to be remarkable, and in this light that he interpreted to the world the significance of his career. Keenly aware of his role as the exemplar of the self-made man, he played the part with intense and poignant consistency that gives his performance the quality of a high art. The first author of the Lincoln legend and the greatest of Lincoln dramatist was Lincoln himself.

Lincoln's simplicity was very real. He called his wife "mother," received distinguished guests in shirtsleeves, and once during his presidency hailed a soldier out of the ranks with the cry: "Bub! Bub!" But he was also a complex man, easily complex enough to know the value of his own simplicity. With his morbid compulsion for honesty he was too modest to pose coarsely and blatantly as a Henry Clay or James C. Blaine might pose. (When an 1860 campaign document announced that he was a reader of Plutarch, he sat down at once to validate the claim by reading the Lives.) But he did develop a political personality by intensifying qualities he actually possessed.

Even during his early days in politics, when his speeches were full of conventional platform bombast, Lincoln seldom failed to strike the humble manner that was peculiarly his. "I was born and have ever remained" he said in his first extended campaign speech, "in the most humble walks of life. I have no popular relations or friends to recommend me." Thereafter he always resounded the theme. "I presume you all know who I am—I am humble Abraham Lincoln. If elected I shall be thankful; if not it will be all the same." Opponents at times grew impatient with his self-degradation ("my poor, lean, lank face") and a Democratic journal once called him a Uriah Heep. But self-conscious as the device was, and coupled even as it was with a secret confidence that Hay called "intellectual arrogance," there was still no imposture in it. It corresponded to Lincoln's own image of himself, which placed him with the poor, the aged, and the forgotten. In a letter to Herdon that was certainly not meant to impress any constituency, Lincoln, near his thirty-ninth birthday, referred to "my old, withered, dry eyes."

There was always this pathos in his plainness, his lack of external grace. "He is," said one of Mrs. Lincoln's friends, "the *ungodliest man* you ever saw." His colleagues, however, recognized in this a possible political asset and transmuted it into one of the most successful of all political symbols—the hard-fisted rail splitter. At a Republican meeting in 1860 John Hanks and another old pioneer appeared carrying fence rails labeled: "Two rails from a lot made by Abraham Lincoln and John Hanks in the Sangamon Bottom in the year 1830." And Lincoln, with his usual candor, confessed that he had no idea whether these were the same rails, but he was sure he had actually split rails every bit as good. The time was to come when little Tad could say: "Everybody in this world knows Pa used to split rails."

Humility belongs with mercy among the cardinal Christian virtues. "Blessed are the meek, for they shall inherit the earth." But the demands of Christianity and the success myth are incompatible. The competitive society out of which the success myth and the self-made man have grown may accept the Christian virtues in principle but can hardly observe them in practice. The motivating force in the mythology of success is ambition, which is closely akin to the cardinal Christian sin of pride. In a world that works through ambition and self-help, while inculcating an ethic that looks upon their results with disdain, how can an earnest man, a public figure living in a time of crisis, gratify his aspirations and yet remain morally whole? If he is, like Lincoln, a man of private religious intensity, the stage is set for high tragedy.

The clue to much that is vital in Lincoln's thought and character lies in the fact that he was thoroughly and completely the politician, by preference and by training. It is difficult to think of any man of comparable stature whose life was so fully absorbed into his political being. Lincoln plunged into politics almost at the beginning of his adult life and was never occupied in any other career except for a brief period when an unfavorable turn in the political situation forced him back to his law practice. His life was one of caucuses and conventions, party circulars and speeches, requests, recommendations, stratagems, schemes, and ambitions. "It was in the world of politics that he lived," wrote Herndon after his death. "Politics were his life, newspapers his food, and his great ambition his motive power."

Like his father, Lincoln was physically lazy ever as a youth, but unlike him had an active forensic mind. When only fifteen he was often on stumps and fences making political speeches, from which his father had to haul him back to his chores. He was fond of listening to lawyers' arguments and occupying his mind with them. Herndon testifies that "He read specially for a special object and thought things useless unless they could be of utility, use, practice, etc." When Lincoln read he preferred to read aloud. Once when Hendon asked him about it he answered: "I catch the idea by two senses, for when I read aloud I *hear* what is read and I see it . . . remember it better, if I do not understand it better." These are the reading habits of a man who was preparing for the platform.

For a youth with such mental habits—and one who had no business talents in the narrower sense—the greatest opportunities on the Illinois prairies were in the ministry, law, or politics. Lincoln, who had read Paine and Volney, was too unorthodox in theology for the ministry, and law and politics it proved to be. But politics was first: at twenty-three, only seven months after coming to the little Illinois community of New Salem, he was running for office. Previously he had worked only at odd jobs as ferryman, surveyor, postmaster, storekeeper, rail-splitter, farm hand, and the like; and now, without any other preparation, he was looking for election to the state legislature. He was not chosen, but two years later, in 1834, Sailgamon County sent him to the lower house. Not until his first term had almost ended was he sufficiently qualified as a lawyer to be admitted to the state bar.

From this time to the end of his life—except for the years between 1849 and 1854, when his political prospects were discouraging—Lincoln was busy either as officeholder or officeseeker. In the summer of 1860, for a friend who wanted to prepare a campaign biography, he wrote in the third person a short sketch of his political life up to that time: 1832—defeated in an attempt to be elected to the legislature; 1834—elected to the legislature "by the highest vote cast for any candidate"; 1836, 1838, 1840—re-elected; 1838 and 1840—chosen by his party as its candidate for Speaker of the Illinois House of Representatives, but not elected. 1840 and 1844—placed on Harrison and Clay electoral tickets "and spent much time and labor in both those canvasses"; 1846—elected to Congress; 1848—campaign worker for Zachary Taylor, speaking in Maryland and Massachusetts, and "canvassing quite fully his own district in Illinois, which was followed by a majority in the district of over 1500 for General Taylor"; 1852—Placed on Winfield Scott's electoral ticket, "but owing to the hopelessness of the cause in Illinois he did less than in previous presidential canvasses"; 1854—" . . . his profession had almost superseded the thought of politics in his mind, when the repeal of the Missouri Compromise aroused him as he had never been before"; 1856—"made over fifty speeches" in the campaign for Frémont; prominently mentioned in the Republican national convention for the vice-presidential nomination. . . .

The rest of the story is familiar enough. . . .

As an economic thinker, Lincoln had a passion for the great average. Thoroughly middle class in his ideas, he spoke for those millions of Americans who had begun their lives as hired workers—as farm hands, clerks, teachers, mechanics, flatboat men, and rail splitters—and had he passed into the ranks of landed farmers, prosperous grocers, lawyers, merchants, physicians, and politicians. Theirs were the traditional ideals of the Protestant ethic: hard work, frugality, temperance, and a touch of ability applied long and hard enough would lift a man into the propertied or professional class and give him independence and respect if not wealth and prestige. Failure to rise in the economic scale was generally viewed as a fault of the individual, not in society. It was the outward sign of an inward lack of grace—of idleness, indulgence, waste, or incapacity.

This conception of the competitive world was by no means so inaccurate in Lincoln's day as it has long since become; neither was it so conservative as time has made it. It was the legitimate inheritance of Jacksonian democracy. It was the belief not only of those who had arrived but also of those who were pushing their way to the top. If it was intensely and at times inhumanly individualistic, it also defied aristocracy and class distinction. Lincoln's life was a dramatization of it in the sphere of politics as, say, Carnegie's was in business. His own rather conventional version of the self-help ideology is expressed with some charm in a letter written to his feckless stepbrother, John D. Johnston, in 1851:

> Your request for eighty dollars I do not think it best to comply with now. At the various times when I have helped you a little you have said to me, "We can get along very well now"; but in a very short time I find you in the same difficulty again. Now, this can only happen by some defect in your conduct. What that defect is, I think I know. You are not lazy, and still you are an idler. I doubt whether, since I saw you, you have done a good whole day's work in any one day. You do not very much dislike to work, and still you do not work much, merely because it does not seem to you that you could get much for it. This habit of uselessly wasting time is the whole difficulty.

Lincoln advised Johnston to leave his farm in charge of his family and go to work for wages.

> I now promise you, that for every dollar you will, between this and the first of May, get for your own labor . . . I will then give you one other dollar. . . . Now if you will do this, you will soon be out of debt, and, what is better, you will have a habit that will keep you from getting in debt again. . . . You have always been kind to me, and I do not mean to be unkind to you. On the contrary, if you will but follow my advice, you will find it worth more than eighty times eighty dollars to you.

Given the chance for the frugal, the industrious, and the able—for the Abraham Lincolns if not the John D. Johnstons—to assert themselves, society would never be divided along fixed lines. There would be no eternal mud-sill class. "There is no permanent class of hired laborers among us," Lincoln declared in a public address. "Twenty-five years ago I was a hired laborer. The hired laborer of yesterday labors on his own account today, and will hire others to labor for him tomorrow. Advancement—improvement in condition—is the order of things in a society of equals." For Lincoln the vital test of a democracy was economic—its ability to provide opportunities for social ascent to those born in its lower ranks. This belief in opportunity for the self-made man is the key to his entire career; it explains his public appeal; it is the core of his criticism of slavery.

There is a strong pro-labor strain in all of Lincoln's utterances from the beginning to the end of his career. Perhaps the most sweeping of his words, and certainly the least equivocal, were penned in 1847. "Inasmuch as most good things are produced by labor," he began,

> it follows that all such things of right belong to those whose labor has produced them. But it has so happened, in all ages of the world, that some have labored, and others have without labor enjoyed a portion of the fruits. This is wrong and should not continue. To secure to each laborer the whole product of his labor, or as nearly as possible, is a worthy object of any good government.

This reads like a passage from a socialist argument. But its context is significant; the statement was neither a preface to an attack upon private property nor an argument for redistributing the world's goods—it was part of a firm defense of the protective tariff!

In Lincoln's day, especially in the more primitive communities of his formative years, the laborer had not yet been fully separated from his tools. The rights of labor still were closely associated in the fashion of Locke and Jefferson with the right of the laborer to retain his own product; when men talked about the sacredness of labor, they were often talking in veiled terms about the right to own. These ideas, which belonged to the age of craftsmanship rather than industrialism, Lincoln carried into the modern industrial scene. The result is a quaint equivocation, worth observing carefully because it pictures the state of mind of a man living half in one economy and half in another and wishing to do justice to every interest. In 1860, when Lincoln was stumping about the country before the Republican convention, he turned up at New Haven, where shoemakers were on strike. The Democrats had charged Republican agitators with responsibility for the strike, and Lincoln met them head-on:

> . . . I am glad to see that a system of labor prevails in New England under which laborers can strike when they want to, where they are not obliged to work under all circumstances, and are not tied down and obliged to labor whether you pay them or not! I like the system which lets a man quit when he wants to, and wish it might prevail everywhere. One of the reasons why I am opposed to slavery is just here. What is the true condition of the laborer? I take it that it is best for all to leave each man free to acquire property as fast as he can. Some will get wealthy. I don't believe in a law to prevent a man from getting rich; it would do more harm than good. So while we do not propose any war upon capital, we do wish to allow the humblest man an equal chance to get rich with everybody else. When one starts poor, as most do in the

race of life, free society is such that he knows he can better his condition; he knows that there is no fixed condition of labor for his whole life. . . . That is the true system.

If there was a flaw in all this, it was one that Lincoln was never forced to meet. Had he lived to seventy, he would have seen the generation brought up on self-help come into its own, build oppressive business corporations, and begin to close off those treasured opportunities for the little man. Further, he would have seen his own party become the jackal of the vested interests, placing the dollar far, far ahead of the man. He himself presided over the social revolution that destroyed the simple equalitarian order of the 1840s, corrupted what remained of its values, and caricatured its ideals. Booth's bullet, indeed, saved him from something worse than embroilment with the radicals over Reconstruction. It confined his life to the happier age that Lincoln understood—which unwittingly he helped to destroy—the age that gave sanction to the honest compromises of his thought.

A story about Abraham Lincoln's second trip to New Orleans when he was twenty-one holds an important place in the Lincoln legend. According to John Hanks, when Lincoln went with his companions to a slave market they saw a handsome mulatto girl being sold on the block, and "the iron entered his soul"; he swore that if he ever got a chance he would hit slavery "and hit it hard." The implication is clear: Lincoln was half abolitionist and the Emancipation Proclamation was a fulfillment of that young promise. But the authenticity of the tale is suspect among Lincoln scholars. John Hanks recalled it thirty-five years afterward as a personal witness, whereas, according to Lincoln, Hanks had not gone beyond St. Louis on the journey. Beveridge observes that Lincoln himself apparently never spoke of the alleged incident publicly or privately, and that for twenty years afterward he showed little concern over slavery. We know that he refused to denounce the Fugitive Slave Law, viciously unfair though it was, even to free Negroes charged as runaways. ("I confess I hate to see the poor creatures hunted down," he wrote to Speed, " . . . but I bite my lips and keep quiet.")

His later career as an opponent of slavery extension must be interpreted in the light of his earlier public indifference to the question. Always moderately hostile to the South's "peculiar institution," he quieted himself with the comfortable thought that it was destined very gradually to disappear. Only after the Kansas-Nebraska Act breathed political life into the slavery issue did he seize upon it as a subject for agitation; only then did he attack it openly. His attitude was based on justice tempered by expediency—or perhaps more accurately, expediency tempered by justice.

Lincoln was by birth a Southerner, a Kentuckian; both his parents were Virginians. His father had served on the slave patrol of Hardin County. The Lincoln family was one of thousands that in the early decades of the nineteenth century had moved from the Southern states, particularly Virginia, Kentucky, and Tennessee, into the valley of Democracy, and peopled the southern parts of Ohio, Indiana, and Illinois.

During his boyhood days in Indiana and Illinois Lincoln lived in communities where slaves were rare or unknown, and the problem was not thrust upon him. The prevailing attitude toward Negroes in Illinois was intensely hostile. Severe laws against free Negroes and runaway slaves were in force when Lincoln went to the Springfield legislature, and there is no evidence of any popular movement to liberalize them. Lincoln's experiences with slavery on his journeys to New Orleans in 1828 and 1831 do not seem to have made an impression vivid enough to change his conduct. Always privately compassionate, in his public career and his legal practice he never made himself the advocate of unpopular reform movements.

While Lincoln was serving his second term in the Illinois legislature the slavery question was discussed throughout the country. Garrison had begun his agitation, and petitions to abolish slavery in the District of Columbia had begun to pour in upon Congress. State legislatures began to express themselves upon the matter. The Illinois legislature turned the subject over to a joint committee, of which Lincoln and his Sangamon County colleague, Dan Stone, were members. At twenty-eight Lincoln thus had occasion to review the whole slavery question on both sides. The committee reported proslavery resolutions, presently adopted, which praised the beneficent effects of white civilization upon African natives, cited the wretchedness of emancipated Negroes as proof of the folly of freedom, and denounced abolitionists.

Lincoln voted against these resolutions. Six weeks later—the delay resulted from a desire to alienate no one from the cause that then stood closest to his heart, the removal of the state capital from Vandalia to Springfield—he and Stone embodied their own opinions in a resolution that was entered in the journal of the House and promptly forgotten. It read in part: "They [Lincoln and Stone] believe that the institution of slavery is founded on injustice and bad policy, but that the promulgation of abolition doctrines tends to increase rather than abate its evils." (Which means, the later Lincoln might have said, that slavery is wrong but that proposing to do away with it is also wrong because it makes slavery worse.) They went on to say that while the Constitution does not permit Congress to abolish slavery in the states, Congress can do so in the District of Columbia—but this power should not be exercised unless at "the request of the people of the District." This statement breathes the fire of an uncompromising insistence upon moderation. Let it be noted, however, that it did represent a point of view faintly to the left of prevailing opinion. Lincoln had gone on record as saying not merely that slavery was "bad policy" but even that it was unjust; but he had done so without jeopardizing his all-important project to transfer the state capital to Springfield.

In 1845, not long before he entered Congress, Lincoln again had occasion to express himself on slavery, this time in a carefully phrased private letter to a political supporter who happened to be an abolitionist.

> I hold it a paramount duty of us in the free States, due to the Union of the States, and perhaps to liberty itself (paradox though it may seem), to let the slavery of the other states alone; while, on the other hand, I hold it to be equally clear that we should never knowingly lend ourselves, directly or indirectly, to prevent that slavery from dying a natural death—to find new places for it to live in, when it can not longer exist in the old.

Throughout his political career he consistently held to this position.

After he had become a lame-duck Congressman, Lincoln introduced into Congress in January 1849 a resolution to instruct the Committee on the District of Columbia to report a bill abolishing slavery in the District. The bill provided that children born of slave mothers after January 1, 1850 should be freed and supported by their mothers' owners until of a certain age. District slaveholders who wanted to emancipate their slaves were to be compensated from the federal Treasury. Lincoln himself added a section requiring the municipal authorities of Washington and Georgetown to provide "active and efficient means" of arresting and restoring to their owners all fugitive slaves escaping into the District. (This was six years before he confessed that he hated "to see the poor creatures hunted down.") Years later, recalling this fugitive-slave provision, Wendell Phillips referred to Lincoln somewhat unfairly as "that slavehound from Illinois." The bill itself, although not passed, gave rise to a spirited debate on the morality of slavery, in which Lincoln took no part.

When Lincoln returned to active politics the slavery issue had come to occupy the central position on the American scene. Stephen Douglas and some of his colleagues in Congress had secured the passage of the Kansas-Nebraska Act, which, by opening some new territory, formally at least, to slavery, repealed the part of the thirty-four-year-old Missouri Compromise that barred slavery from territory north of 36° 30'. The measure provoked a howl of opposition in the North and split Douglas's party. The Republican Party, built on opposition to the extension of slavery, began to emerge in small communities in the Northwest. Lincoln's ambitions and interests were aroused, and he proceeded to rehabilitate his political fortunes.

His strategy was simple and forceful. He carefully avoided issues like the tariff, internal improvements, the Know-Nothing mania, or prohibitionism, each of which would alienate important groups of voters. He took pains in all his speeches to stress that he was not an abolitionist and at the same time to stand on the sole program of opposing the extension of slavery. On October 4, 1854, at the age of forty-five, Lincoln *for the first time in his life* denounced slavery in public. In his speech delivered in the Hall of Representatives at Springfield (and later repeated at Peoria) he declared that he hated the current zeal for the spread of slavery: "I hate it because of the monstrous injustice of slavery itself." He went on to say that he had no prejudice against the people of the South. He appreciated their argument that it would be difficult to get rid of the institution "in any satisfactory way." "I surely will not blame them for not doing what I should not know how to do myself. If all earthly power were given me, I should not know what to do as to the existing institution. My first impulse would be to free all the slaves and send them to Liberia, to their own native land." But immediate colonization, he added, is manifestly impossible. The slaves might be freed and kept "among us as underlings." Would this really better their condition?

> What next? Free them, and make them politically and socially our equals. My own feelings will not admit of this, and if mine would, we well know that those of the great mass of whites will not. Whether this feeling accords with justice and sound judgment is not the sole question, if indeed it is any part of it. A universal feeling, whether well or ill founded, cannot be safely disregarded.

And yet nothing could justify an attempt to carry slavery into territories now free, Lincoln emphasized. For slavery is unquestionably wrong. "The great mass of mankind" he said at Peoria, "consider slavery a great moral wrong. [This feeling] lies at the very foundation of their sense of justice, and it can not be trifled with. . . . No statesman can safely disregard it." The last sentence was the key to Lincoln's growing radicalism. As a practical politician he was naturally very much concerned about those public sentiments which no statesman can safely disregard. It was impossible, he had learned, to safely disregard either the feeling that slavery is a moral wrong or the feeling—held by an even larger portion of the public—that Negroes must not be given political and social equality.

He had now struck the core of the Republican problem in the Northwest: how to find a formula to reconcile the two opposing points of view held by great numbers of white people in the North. Lincoln's success in 1860 was due in no small part to his ability to bridge the gap, a performance that entitles him to a place among the world's great political propagandists.

To comprehend Lincoln's strategy we must keep one salient fact in mind: the abolitionists and their humanitarian sympathizers in the nation at large and particularly in the Northwest, the seat of Lincoln's strength, although numerous enough to hold the balance of power, were far too few to make a successful political party. Most of the white people of the Northwest, moreover, were in fact not only abolitionists, but actually—and here is the core of the matter—Negrophobes. They feared and detested the very thought of living side by side with large numbers of Negroes in their own states, to say nothing of competing with their labor. Hence the severe laws against free Negroes, for example in Lincoln's Illinois. Amid all the agitation in Kansas over making the territory a free state, the conduct of the majority of Republicans there was colored far more by self-interest than by moral principle. In their so-called Topeka Constitution the Kansas Republicans *forbade free Negroes even to come into the state*, and gave only to whites and Indians the right to vote. It was not bondage that troubled them—it was the Negro, free or slave. Again and again the Republican press of the Northwest referred to the Republican Party as the "White Man's Party." The motto of the leading Republican paper of Missouri, Frank Blair's *Daily Missouri Democrat*, was "White Men for Missouri and Missouri for White Men." Nothing could be more devastating to the contention that the early Republican Party in the Northwest was built upon moral principle. At the party convention of 1860 a plank endorsing the Declaration of Independence was almost hissed down and was saved only by the threat of a bolt by the antislavery element.

If the Republicans were to succeed in the strategic Northwest, how were they to win the support of both Negrophobes and antislavery men? Merely to insist that slavery was an evil would sound like abolitionism and offend the Negrophobes. Yet pitching their opposition to slavery extension on too low a moral level might lose the valued support of the humanitarians. Lincoln, perhaps borrowing from the old free-soil ideology, had the right formula and exploited it. He first hinted at it in the Peoria speech:

> The whole nation is interested that the best use shall be made of these Territories. *We want them for homes of free white people. This they cannot be, to any considerable extent, if slavery shall be planted within them.* Slave States are places for poor white people to remove from, not to remove to. New free States are the places for poor people to go to, and better their condition. For this use the nation needs these Territories.

The full possibilities of this line first became clear in Lincoln's "lost" Bloomington speech, delivered at a Republican state convention in May 1856. There, according to the report of one of his colleagues at the Illinois bar, Lincoln warned that Douglas and his followers would frighten men away from the very idea of freedom with their incessant mouthing of the red-herring epithet: "Abolitionist" "If that trick should succeed," he is reported to have said, "if free negroes should be made *things*, how long, think you, before they will begin to make *things* out of poor white men?"

Here was the answer to the Republican problem. Negrophobes and abolitionists alike could understand this threat; if freedom should be broken down they might themselves have to compete with the labor of slaves in the then free states—or might even be reduced to bondage along with the blacks! Here was an argument that could strike a responsive chord in the nervous system of every

Northern man, farmer or worker, abolitionist or racist: *if a stop was not put somewhere upon the spread of slavery, the institution would become nation-wide.* Here too, is the practical significance of the repeated statements Lincoln made in favor of labor at this time. Lincoln took the slavery question out of the realm of moral and legal dispute and, by dramatizing it in terms of free labor's self-interest, gave it a universal appeal. To please the abolitionists he kept saying that slavery was an evil thing; but for the material benefit of all Northern white men he opposed its further extension.

The importance of this argument becomes increasingly clear when it is realized that Lincoln used it in every one of his recorded speeches from 1854 until he became the President-elect. He once declared in Kansas that preventing slavery from becoming a nation-wide institution "is *the purpose* of this organization [the Republican Party]." The argument had a great allure too for the immigrants who were moving in such great numbers into the Northwest. Speaking at Alton, in the heart of a county where more than fifty percent of the population was foreign-born, Lincoln went out of his way to make it clear that he favored keeping the territories open not only for native Americans, "but as an outlet for *free white people* everywhere, the world over—in which Hans, and Baptiste, and Patrick, and all other men from all the world, may find new homes and better their condition in life."

During the debates with Douglas, Lincoln dwelt on the theme again and again, and added the charge that Douglas himself was involved in a Democratic "conspiracy . . . for the sole purpose of nationalizing slavery." Douglas and the Supreme Court (which a year before had handed down the Dred Scott decision) would soon have the American people "working in the traces that tend to make this one universal slave nation." Chief Justice Taney had declared that Congress did not have the constitutional power to exclude slavery from the territories. The next step, said Lincoln, would be:

> another Supreme Court decision, declaring that the Constitution
> of the United States does not permit a *State* to exclude slavery from
> its limits. . . . We shall lie down pleasantly, dreaming that the people
> of Missouri are on the verge of making their State free; and we shall
> awake to the reality instead, that the Supreme Court has made Illinois
> a slave State.

So also the theme of the "House Divided" speech:

> I do not expect the Union to be dissolved—I do not expect the
> House to fall—but I do expect it to cease to be divided. It will become
> all one thing or all the other. Either the opponents of slavery will arrest
> the further spread of it, and place it where the public mind shall rest in

the belief that it is in the course of ultimate extinction; or its advocates will push it forward, till it shall become alike lawful in all the States, old as well as new, North as well as South.

Have we no tendency to the latter condition?

The last sentence is invariably omitted when this passage is quoted, perhaps because from a literary standpoint it is anticlimactic. But in Lincoln's mind and, one may guess, in the minds' of those who heard him—it was not anticlimactic, but essential. Lincoln was *not* emphasizing the immediate "danger" that slavery would become a nation-wide American institution if its geographical spread were not severely restricted at once.

Once this "House Divided" speech had been made, Lincoln had to spend a great deal of time explaining it, proving that he was not an abolitionist. These efforts, together with his strategy of appealing to abolitionist and Negrophobes at once, involved him in embarrassing contradictions. In northern Illinois he spoke in one vein before abolition-minded audiences, but farther south, where settlers of Southern extraction were dominant, he spoke in another. It is instructive to compare what he said about the Negro in Chicago with what he said in Charleston.

Chicago, July 10, 1858:

> Let us discard all this quibbling about this man and the other man, this race and that race and the other race being inferior, and therefore they must be placed in an inferior position. Let us discard all these things, and unite as one people throughout this land, until we shall once more stand up declaring that all men are created equal.

Charleston, September 18, 1858:

> I will say, then, that I am not, nor ever have been, in favor of bringing about in any way the social and political equality of the white and black races [applause]: that I am not, nor ever have been, in favor of making voters or jurors of negroes, nor of qualifying them to hold office, nor to intermarry with white people. . . .
>
> And inasmuch as they cannot so live, while they do remain together there must be the position of superior and inferior, and I as much as any other man am in favor of having the superior position assigned to the white race.

It is not easy to decide whether the true Lincoln is the one who spoke in Chicago or the one who spoke in Charleston. Possibly the man devoutly believed each of the utterances at the time he delivered it; possibly his mind too was a house divided against itself. In any case it is easy to see in all this the behavior of a professional politician looking for votes.

Douglas did what he could to use Lincoln's inconsistency against him. At Galesburg, with his opponent sitting on the platform behind him, he proclaimed: "I would despise myself if I thought that I was procuring your votes by concealing my opinions, and by avowing one set of principles in one part of the state, and a different set in another." Confronted by Douglas with these clashing utterances from his Chicago and Charleston speeches, Lincoln replied: "I have not supposed and do not now suppose, that there is any conflict whatever between them."

But this was politics—the premium was on strategy, not intellectual consistency—and the effectiveness of Lincoln's campaign is beyond dispute. In the ensuing elections the Republican candidates carried a majority of the voters and elected their state officers for the first time. Douglas returned to the Senate only because the Democrats, who had skillfully gerrymandered the election districts, still, held their majority in the state legislature. Lincoln had contributed greatly to welding old-line Whigs and antislavery men into an effective party, and his reputation was growing by leaps and bounds. What he had done was to pick out an issue—the alleged plan to extend slavery, the alleged danger that it would spread throughout the nation—which would turn attention from the disintegrating forces in the Republican Party to the great integrating force. He was keenly aware that the party was built out of extremely heterogeneous elements, frankly speaking of it in his "House Divided" speech as composed of "strange, discordant, and even hostile elements." In addition to abolitionists and Negrophobes, it united high and low-tariff men, hard-and soft-money men, former Whigs and former Democrats embittered by old political fights, Maine-law prohibitionists and German tipplers, Know-Nothings and immigrants. Lincoln's was the masterful diplomacy to hold such a coalition together, carry it into power, and with it win a war. . . .

Lincoln was shaken by the presidency. Back in Springfield, politics had been a sort of game; but in the White House, politics was power, and power was responsibility. Never before had Lincoln held executive office. In public life he had always been a legislator whose votes were cast in concert with others and whose decisions in themselves had neither finalitly nor importance .As President he might consult others, but innumerable grave decisions were in the end his own, and with them came a burden of responsibility terrifying in its dimensions.

Lincoln's rage for personal success, his external and worldly ambition, was quieted when he entered the White House, and he was at last left alone to reckon with himself. To be confronted with the fruits of his victory only to find that it meant choosing between life and death for others was immensely sobering. That Lincoln should have shouldered the moral burden of the war was characteristic of the high seriousness into which he had grown since 1854; and it may be true, as Professor Charles W. Ramsdell suggested, that he was stricken by an awareness of his own part in whipping up the crisis. This would go far to explain the desperation with which he issued pardons and the charity that he wanted to extend to the conquered South at the war's close. In one of his rare moments of self-revelation he is reported to have said: "Now I don't know what the soul is, but whatever it is, I know that it can humble itself." The great prose of the presidential years came from a soul that had been humbled. Lincoln's lack of personal malice during these years, his humane detachment, his tragic sense of life, have no parallel in political history.

"Lincoln," said Herndon, "is a man of heart—aye, as gentle as a woman's and as tender . . . " Lincoln was moved by the wounded and dying men, moved as no one in a place of power can afford to be. He had won high office by means sometimes rugged, but once there, he found he could not quite carry it off. For him it was impossible to drift into the habitual callousness of the sort of officialdom that sees men merely as pawns to be shifted here and there and "expended" at the will of others. It was a symbolic thing that his office was so constantly open, that he made himself more accessible than any other chief executive in our history. "Men moving only in an official circle," he told Carpenter, "are apt to become merely official—not to say arbitrary—in their ideas, and are apter and apter with each passing day to forget that they only hold power in a representative capacity." Is it possible to recall anyone else in modern history who could exercise so much power and yet feel so slightly the private corruption that goes with it? Here, perhaps, is the best measure of Lincoln's personal eminence in the human calendar —that he was chastened and not intoxicated by power. It was almost apologetically that he remarked in response to a White House serenade after his re-election that "So long as I have been here, I have not willingly planted a thorn in any man's bosom."

There were many thorns planted in *his* bosom. The criticism was hard to bear (perhaps hardest of all that from the abolitionists, which he knew had truth in it). There was still in him a sensitivity that the years of knock-about politics had not killed, the remarkable depths of which are suddenly illumined by a casual sentence written during one of the crueler outbursts of the opposition press. Reassuring the apologetic actor James Hackett, who had unwittingly aroused a storm of hostile laughter by publishing a confidential letter, Lincoln added that he was quite used to it: "I have received a great deal of ridicule without much malice; and have received a great deal of kindness, not quite free from ridicule."

The presidency was not something that could be enjoyed. Remembering its barrenness for him, one can believe that the life of Lincoln's soul was almost entirely without consummation. Sandburg remarks that there were thirty-one rooms in the White House and that Lincoln was not at home in any of them. This was the house for which he had sacrificed so much!

As the months passed, a deathly weariness settled over him. Once when Noah Brooks suggested that he rest, he replied: "I suppose it is good for the body. But the tired part of me is *inside* and out of reach." There had always been a part of him, inside and out of reach, that had looked upon his ambition with detachment and wondered if the game was worth the candle. Now he could see the truth of what he had long dimly known and perhaps hopefully suppressed—that for a man of sensitivity and compassion to exercise great powers in a time of crisis is a grim and agonizing thing. Instead of glory, he once said, he had found only "ashes and blood." This was, for him, the end product of that success myth by which he had lived and for which he had been so persuasive a spokesman. He had had his ambitions and fulfilled them, and met heartache in his triumph.

25. Jefferson Davis's Farewell to the U.S. Senate

January 21, 1861

I rise, Mr. President, for the purpose of announcing to the Senate that I have satisfactory evidence that the State of Mississippi, by a solemn ordinance of her people, in convention assembled, has declared her separation from the United States. Under these circumstances, of course, my functions are terminated here. It has seemed to me proper, however, that I should appear in the Senate to announce that fact to my associates, and I will say but very little more. The occasion does not invite me to go into argument; and my physical condition would not permit me to do so, if it were otherwise; and yet it seems to become me to say something on the part of the State I here represent on an occasion as solemn as this.

It is known to Senators who have served with me here that I have for many years advocated, as an essential attribute of State sovereignty, the right of a State to secede from the Union. Therefore, if I had thought that Mississippi was acting without sufficient provocation, or without an existing necessity, I should still, under my theory of the Government, because of my allegiance to the State of which I am a citizen, have been bound by her action. I, however, may be permitted to say that I do think she has justifiable cause, and I approve of her act. I conferred with her people before that act was taken, counseled them then that, if the state of things which they apprehended should exist when their Convention met, they should take the action which they have now adopted.

I hope none who hear me will confound this expression of mine with the advocacy of the right of a State to remain in the Union, and to disregard its constitutional obligation by the nullification of the law. Such is not my theory. Nullification and secession, so often confounded, are, indeed, antagonistic principles. Nullification is a remedy which it is sought to apply within the Union, against the agent of the States. It is only to be justified when the agent has violated his constitutional obligations, and a State, assuming to judge for itself, denies the right of the agent thus to act, and appeals to the other states of the Union for a decision; but, when the States themselves and when the people of the States have so acted as to convince us that they will not regard our constitutional rights, then, and then for the first time, arises the doctrine of secession in its practical application.

A great man who now reposes with his fathers, and who has often been arraigned for want of fealty to the Union, advocated the doctrine of nullification because it preserved the Union. It was because of his deep-seated attachment to the Union -- his determination to find some remedy for existing ills short of a severance of the ties which bound South Carolina to the other States -- that Mr. Calhoun advocated the doctrine of nullification, which he proclaimed to be peaceful, to be within the limits of State power, not to disturb the Union, but only to be a means of bringing the agent before the tribunal of the States for their judgement.

Secession belongs to a different class of remedies. It is to be justified upon the basis that the states are sovereign. There was a time when none denied it. I hope the time may come again when a better comprehension of the theory of our Government, and the inalienable rights of the people of the States, will prevent any one from denying that each State is a sovereign, and thus may reclaim the grants which it has made to any agent whomsoever.

I, therefore, say I concur in the action of the people of Mississippi, believing it to be necessary and proper, and should have been bound by their action if my belief had been otherwise; and this brings me to the important point which I wish, on this last occasion, to present to the Senate. It is by this confounding of nullification and secession that the name of a great man whose ashes now mingle with his mother earth has been invoked to justify coercion against a seceded State. The phrase, "to execute the laws," was an expression which General Jackson applied to the case of a State refusing to obey the laws while yet a member of the Union. That is not the case which is now presented. The laws are to be executed over the United States, and upon the people of the United States. They have no relation to any foreign country. It is a perversion of terms -- at least, it is a great mis-apprehension of the case -- which cites that expression for application to a State which has withdrawn from the Union. You may make war on a foreign state. If it be the purpose of gentlemen, they may make war against a State which has withdrawn from the Union; but there are no laws of the United States to be executed within the limits of a seceded State. A State, finding herself in the condition in which Mississippi has judged she is -- in which her safety requires that she should provide for the maintenance of her rights out of the Union -- surrenders all the benefits (and they are known to be many), deprives herself of the advantages (and they are known to be great), severs all the ties of affection (and they are close and enduring), which have bound her to the Union; and thus divesting herself of every benefit -- taking upon herself every burden -- she claims to be exempt from any power to execute the laws of the United States within her limits.

I well remember an occasion when Massachusetts was arraigned before the bar of the Senate, and when the doctrine of coercion was rife, and to be applied against her, because of the rescue of a fugitive slave in Boston. My opinion then was the same that it is now. Not in a spirit of egotism, but to show that I am not influenced in my opinions because the case is my own, I refer to that time and that occasion as containing the opinion which I then entertained, and on which my present conduct is based. I then said that if Massachusetts -- following her purpose through a stated line of conduct -- chose to take the last step, which separates her from the Union, it is her right to go, and I will neither vote one dollar nor one man to coerce her back; but I will say to her, Godspeed, in memory of the kind associations which once existed between her and the other States.

It has been a conviction of pressing necessity -- it has been a belief that we are to be deprived in the Union of the rights which our fathers bequeathed to us -- which has brought Mississippi to her present decision. She has heard proclaimed the theory that all men are created free and equal, and this made the basis of an attack upon her social institutions; and the sacred Declaration of Independence has been invoked to maintain the position of the equality of the races. That Declaration is to be construed by the circumstances and purposes for which it was made. The communities were declaring their independence; the people of those communities were asserting that no man was born -- to use the language of Mr. Jefferson -- booted and spurred, to ride over the rest of mankind; that men were created equal -- meaning the men of the political community; that there was no divine right to rule; that no man inherited the right to govern; that there were no classes by which power and place descended to families; but that all stations were equally within the grasp of each member of the body politic. These were the great principles they announced; these were the purposes for which they made their declaration; these were the ends to which their enunciation was directed. They have no reference to the slave; else, how happened it that among the items of arraignment against George III was that he endeavored to do just what the North has been endeavoring of late to do, to stir up insurrection among our slaves? Had the Declaration announced that the negroes were free and equal, how was the prince to be arraigned for raising up insurrection among them? And how was this to be enumerated among the high crimes which caused the colonies to sever their connection with the mother-country? When our Constitution was formed, the same idea was rendered more palpable; for there we find provision made for that very class of persons as property; they were not put upon the equality of footing with white men -- not even upon that of paupers and convicts; but, so far as representation was concerned, were discriminated against as a lower caste, only to be represented in the numerical proportion of three-fifths. So stands the compact which binds us together.

Then, Senators, we recur to the principles upon which our Government was founded; and when you deny them, and when you deny us the right to withdraw from a Government which, thus perverted, threatens to be destructive of our rights, we but tread in the path of our fathers when we proclaim our independence and take the hazard. This is done, not in hostility to others, not to injure any section of the country, not even for our own pecuniary benefit, but from the high and solemn motive of defending and protecting the rights we inherited, and which it is our duty to transmit unshorn to our children.

I find in myself perhaps a type of the general feeling of my constituents towards yours. I am sure I feel no hostility toward you, Senators from the North. I am sure there is not one of you, whatever sharp discussion there may have been between us, to whom I cannot now say, in the presence of my God, I wish you well; and such, I feel, is the feeling of the people whom I represent toward those whom you represent. I, therefore, feel that I but express their desire when I say I hope, and they hope, for peaceable relations with you, though we must part. They may be mutually beneficial to us in the future, as they have been in the past, if you so will it. The reverse may bring disaster on every portion of the country, and, if you will have it thus, we will invoke the God of our fathers, who delivered them from the power of the lion, to protect us from the ravages of the bear; and thus, putting our trust in God and in our firm hearts and strong arms, we will vindicate the right as best we may.

In the course of my service here, associated at different times with a variety of Senators, I see now around me some with whom I have served long; there have been points of collision, but, whatever of offense there has been to me, I leave here. I carry with me no hostile remembrance. Whatever offense I have given which has not been redressed, or for which satisfaction has not been demanded, I have, Senators, in this hour of our parting, to offer you my apology for any pain which, in the heat of discussion, I have inflicted. I go hence unencumbered by the remembrance of any injury received, and having discharged the duty of making the only reparation in my power for any injured offered.

Mr. President and Senators, having made the announcement which the occasion seemed to me to require, it only remains for me to bid you a final adieu.

26. A War That Never Goes Away

James M. McPherson

"Americans just can't get enough of the Civil War." So says a man who should know, Terry Winschel, historian of the Vicksburg National Military Park. Millions of visitors come to Vicksburg and to more than a dozen other Civil War national battlefield and military parks every year. More than forty thousand Civil War reenactors spend hundreds of dollars each on replica weapons, uniforms, and equipment; many of them travel thousands of miles to help restage Civil War battles. Another two hundred and fifty thousand Americans describe themselves as Civil War buffs or "hobbyists" and belong to one of the hundreds of Civil War round tables or societies, subscribe to at least one of the half-dozen magazines devoted to Civil War history, or buy and sell Civil War memorabilia.

Above all, Americans buy books on the Civil War. This has always been true. More than fifty thousand separate books or pamphlets on the war have been published since the guns ceased firing 125 years ago. In recent years some eight hundred titles, many of them reprints of out-of-print works, have come off the presses annually. Nearly every month a new Civil War book is offered by the History Book Club or the Book-of-the-Month Club, often as the main selection. Many bookstore owners echo the words of Jim Lawson, general manager of the Book 'N Card shop in Falls Church, Virginia. "For the last two years," he said in 1988, "Civil War books have been flying out of here. It's not [just] the buffs who buy; it's the general public, from high school kids to retired people."

Although we are approaching the end of the 125th-anniversary commemorations of Civil War events, the boom shows no signs of fading. As a beneficiary of this popular interest in the Civil War, I am often asked to explain what accounts for it—in particular, to explain why my own recent contribution to the literature on the war and its causes, *Battle Cry of Freedom*, was on national best-seller lists for several months as a hardcover book in 1988 and again as a paperback in 1989. I have a few answers.

First, for Americans, the human cost of the Civil War was by far the most devastating in our history. The 620,000 Union and Confederate soldiers who lost their lives almost equaled the 680,000 American soldiers who died in all the other wars this country has fought combined. When we add the unknown but probably substantial number of civilian deaths—from disease, malnutrition, exposure, or injury—among the hundreds of thousands of refugees in the Confederacy, the toll of Civil War dead may exceed war deaths in all the rest of American history. Consider two sobering facts about the Battle of Antietam, America's single bloodiest day. The 25,000 casualties there were nearly four times the number of American casualties on D-day, June 6, 1944. The 6,500 men killed and mortally wounded in one day near Sharpsburg were nearly double the number of Americans killed and mortally wounded in combat in all the rest of the country's nineteenth-century wars combined—the War of 1812, the Mexican War, and the Spanish-American War.

This ghastly toll gives the Civil War a kind of horrifying but hypnotic fascination. As Thomas Hardy once put it, "War makes rattling good history; but Peace is poor reading." The sound of drum and trumpet, the call to arms, the clashing of armies have stirred the blood of nations throughout history. As the horrors and the seamy side of a war recede into the misty past, the romance and honor and glory forge into the foreground. Of no war has this been more true than of the Civil War, with its dashing cavaliers, its generals leading infantry charges, its diamond-stacked locomotives and paddle-wheeled steamboats, its larger-than-life figures like Lincoln, Lee, Jackson, Grant, and Sherman, its heroic and romantic women like Clara Barton and "Mother" Bickerdyke and Rose O'Neal Greenhow, its countless real-life heroines and knaves and heroes capable of transmutation into a Scarlett O'Hara, Rhett Butler, or Ashley Wilkes. If romance is the other face of horror in our perception of the Civil War, the poignancy of a brothers' war is the other face of the tragedy of a civil war. In hundreds of individual cases the war did pit brother against brother, cousin against cousin, even father against son. This was especially true in border states like Kentucky, where the war divided such famous families as the Clays, Crittendens, and Breckinridges and where seven brothers and brothers-in-law of the wife of the United States President fought for the Confederate States. But it was also true of states like Virginia, where Jeb Stuart's father-in-law commanded Union cavalry, and even of South Carolina, where Thomas F. Drayton became a brigadier general in the Confederate army and fought against his brother Percival, a captain in the Union navy, at the Battle of Port Royal. Who can resist the painful human interest of stories like these—particularly when they are recounted in the letters and diaries of Civil War protagonists, preserved through generations and published for all to read as a part of the unending stream of Civil War books?

Indeed, the uncensored contemporary descriptions of that war by participants help explain its appeal to modern readers. There is nothing else in history to equal it. Civil War armies were the most literate that ever fought a war up to that time, and twentieth-century armies censored soldiers' mail and discouraged diary keeping. Thus we have an unparalleled view of the Civil War by the people who experienced it. This has kept the image of the war alive in the families of millions of Americans whose ancestors fought in it. When speaking to audiences as diverse as Civil War buffs, Princeton students and alumni, and local literary clubs, I have sometimes asked how many of them are aware of forebears who fought in the Civil War. I have been surprised by the large response, which demonstrates not only a great number of such people but also their consciousness of events that happened so long ago yet seem part of their family lore today.

This consciousness of the war, of the past as part of the present, continues to be more intense in the South than elsewhere. William Faulkner said of his native section that the past isn't dead; it isn't even past. As any reader of Faulkner's novels knows, the Civil War is central to that past that is present; it is the great watershed of Southern history; it is, as Mark Twain put it a century ago after a tour through the South, "what A.D. is elsewhere; they date from it." The symbols of that past-in-present surround Southerners as they grow up, from the Robert E. Lee Elementary School or Jefferson Davis High School they attend and the Confederate battle flag that flies over their statehouse to the Confederate soldier enshrined in bronze or granite on the town square and the family folklore about victimization by Sherman's bummers. Some of those symbols remain highly controversial and provoke as much passion today as in 1863: the song "Dixie," for example, and the Confederate flag, which for many Southern whites continue to represent courage, honor, or defiance while to black Americans they represent racism and oppression.

This suggests the most important reason for the enduring fascination with the Civil War among professional historians as well as the general public: Great issues were at stake, issues about which Americans were willing to fight and die, issues whose resolution profoundly transformed and redefined the United States. The Civil War was a total war in three senses: It mobilized the total human and material resources of both sides; it ended not in a negotiated peace but in total victory by one side and unconditional surrender by the other; it destroyed the economy and social system of the loser and established those of the winner as the norm for the future.

The Civil War was fought mainly by volunteer soldiers who joined the colors before conscription went into effect. In fact, the Union and Confederate armies mobilized as volunteers a larger percentage of their societies' manpower than any other war in American history—probably in world history, with the possible exception of the French Revolution. And Civil War armies, like those of the French Revolution, were highly ideological in motivation. Most of the volunteers knew what they were fighting for, and why. What were they fighting for? If asked to define it in a single word, many soldiers on both sides would have answered: liberty. They fought for the heritage of freedom bequeathed to them by the Founding Fathers. North and South alike wrapped themselves in the mantle of 1776. But the two sides interpreted that heritage in opposite ways, and at first neither side included the slaves in the vision of liberty for which it fought. The slaves did, however, and by the time of Lincoln's Gettysburg Address in 1863, the North also fought for "a new birth of freedom, . . . " These multiple meanings of freedom, and how they dissolved and reformed in kaleidoscopic patterns during the war, provide the central meaning of the war for the American experience.

When the "Black Republican" Abraham Lincoln won the Presidency in 1860 on a platform of excluding slavery from the territories, Southerners compared him to George III and declared their independence from "oppressive Yankee rule." "The same spirit of freedom and independence that impelled our Fathers to the separation from the British Government," proclaimed secessionists, would impel the "liberty loving people of the South" to separation from the United States government. A Georgia secessionist declared that Southerners would be "either *slaves in the Union or freemen out of it*." Young men from Texas to Virginia rushed to enlist in this "Holy Cause of Liberty and Independence" and to raise "the standard of Liberty and Equality for white men" against "our Abolition enemies who are pledged to prostrate the white freemen of the South down to equality with negroes." From "the high and solemn motive of defending and protecting the rights which our fathers bequeathed to us," declared Jefferson Davis at the outset of war, let us "renew such sacrifices as our fathers made to the holy cause of constitutional liberty."

But most Northerners ridiculed these Southern professing to be fighting for the ideals of 1776. That was "a libel upon the whole character and conduct of the men of '76," said the antislavery poet and journalist William Cullen Bryant. The Founding Fathers had fought "to establish the rights of man . . . and principles of universal liberty." The South, insisted Bryant, had seceded "not in the interest of general humanity, but of a domestic despotism. . . . Their motto is not liberty, but slavery." Northerners did not deny the right of revolution in principle; after all, the United States was founded on that right. But "the right of revolution," wrote Lincoln in 1861, "is never a legal right. . . . At most, it is but a moral right, when exercised for a morally justifiable cause. When exercised without such a cause revolution is no right, but simply a wicked exercise of physical power." In Lincoln's judgment secession was just such a wicked exercise. The event that precipitated it was Lincoln's election by a constitutional majority. As Northerners saw it, the Southern states, having controlled the national government for most of the previous two generations through their domination of the Democratic party, now decided to leave the Union just because they had lost an election.

For Lincoln and the Northern people, it was the Union that represented the ideals of 1776. The republic established by the Founding Fathers as a bulwark of liberty was a fragile experiment in a nineteenth-century world bestridden by kings, emperors, czars, and dictators. Most republics through history had eventually been overthrown. Some Americans still alive in 1861 had seen French republics succumb twice to emperors and once to the restoration of Bourbon monarchy. Republics in Latin America came and went with bewildering rapidity. The United States in 1861 represented, in Lincoln's words, "the last, best hope" for the survival of republican liberties in the world. Would that hope also collapse? "Our popular government has often been called an experiment," Lincoln told Congress on July 4, 1861. But if the Confederacy succeeded in splitting the country in two, it would set a fatal precedent that would destroy the experiment. By invoking this precedent, a minority in the future might secede from the Union whenever it did not like what the majority stood for, until the United

States fragmented into a multitude of petty, squabbling autocracies. "The central idea pervading this struggle," said Lincoln, "is the necessity. . . of proving that popular government is not an absurdity. We must settle this question now, whether, in a free government, the minority have the right to break up the government whenever they choose."

Many soldiers who enlisted in the Union army felt the same way. A Missourian joined up as "a duty I owe my country and to my children to do what I can to preserve this government as I shudder to think what is ahead of them if this government should be overthrown." A New England soldier wrote to his wife on the eve of the First Battle of Bull Run: "I know . . . how great a debt we owe to those who went before us through the blood and sufferings of the Revolution. And I am willing—perfectly willing—to lay down all my joys in this life, to help maintain this government, and to pay that debt."

Freedom for the slaves was not part of the liberty for which the North fought in 1861. That was not because the Lincoln administration supported slavery; quite the contrary. Slavery was "an unqualified evil to the negro, to the white man . . . and to the State," said Lincoln on many occasions in words that expressed the sentiments of a Northern majority. "The monstrous injustice of slavery . . . deprives our republican example of its just influence in the world— enables the enemies of free institutions, with plausibility, to taunt us as hypocrites. . . . " Yet in his first inaugural address, Lincoln declared that he had "no purpose, directly or indirectly, to interfere with . . . slavery in the States where it exists." He reiterated this pledge in his first message to Congress, on July 4, 1861, when the Civil War was nearly three months old.

What explains this apparent inconsistency? The answer lies in the Constitution and in the Northern polity of 1861. Lincoln was bound by a constitution that protected slavery in any state where citizens wanted it. The republic of liberty for whose preservation the North was fighting had been a republic in which slavery was legal everywhere in 1776. That was the great American paradox—a land of freedom based on slavery. Even in 1861 four states that remained loyal to the Union were slave states, and the Democratic minority in free states opposed any move to make the war for the Union a war against slavery.

But as the war went on, the slaves themselves took the first step toward making it a war against slavery. Coming into Union lines by the thousands, they voted with their feet for freedom. As enemy property they could be confiscated by Union forces as "contraband of war." This was the thin edge of the wedge that finally broke apart the American paradox. By 1863 a series of congressional acts plus Lincoln's Emancipation Proclamation had radically enlarged Union war aims. The North henceforth fought not just to restore the old Union, not just to ensure that the nation born in 1776 "shall not perish from the earth," but to give that nation "a new birth of freedom."

Northern victory in the Civil War resolved two fundamental, festering issues left unresolved by the Revolution of 1776: whether this fragile republican experiment called the United States would survive and whether the house divided would continue to endure half-slave and half-free. Both these issues remained open questions until 1865. Many Americans doubted the Republic's survival; many European conservatives predicted its demise; some Americans advocated the right of secession and periodically threatened to invoke it; eleven states did invoke it in 1860 and 1861. But since 1865 no state or region has seriously threatened secession, not even during the "massive resistance" to desegregation from 1954 to 1964. Before 1865 the United States, land of liberty, was the largest slaveholding country in the world. Since 1865 that particular "monstrous injustice" and "hypocrisy" has existed no more.

In the process of preserving the Union of 1776 while purging it of slavery, the Civil War also transformed it. Before 1861 the words *United States* were a plural noun: "The United States are a large country." Since 1865 *United States* has been a singular noun. The North went to war to preserve the *Union*; it ended by creating a *nation*. This transformation can be traced in Lincoln's most important wartime addresses. The first inaugural address contained the word *Union* twenty times and the word *nation* not once. In Lincoln's first message to Congress, on July 4, 1861, he used *Union* forty-nine times and *nation* only three times. In his famous public letter to Horace Greeley of August 22, 1862, concerning slavery and the war, Lincoln spoke of the Union nine times and the nation not at all. But in the Gettysburg Address fifteen months later, he did not refer to the Union at all but used the word *nation* five times. And in the second inaugural address, looking back over the past four years, Lincoln spoke of one side's seeking to dissolve the Union in 1861 and the other side's accepting the challenge of war to preserve the nation. The old decentralized Republic, in which the post office was the only agency of national government that touched the average citizen, was transformed by the crucible of war into a centralized polity that taxed people directly and created an internal revenue bureau to collect the taxes, expanded the jurisdiction of federal courts, created a national currency and a federally chartered banking system, drafted men into the Army, and created the Freedman's Bureau as the first national agency for social welfare. Eleven of the first twelve amendments to the Constitution had limited the powers of the national government; six of the next seven, starting with the Thirteenth Amendment in 1865, radically expanded those powers at the expense of the states. The first three of these amendments converted four million slaves into citizens and voters within five years, the most rapid and fundamental social transformation in American history—even if the nation did backslide on part of this commitment for three generations after 1877.

From 1789 to 1861 a Southern slaveholder was President of the United States two-thirds of the time, and two-thirds of the Speakers of the House and presidents pro term of the Senate had also been Southerners. Twenty of the thirty-five Supreme Court justices during that period were from the South, which always had a majority on the Court before 1861. After the Civil War a century passed before another resident of a Southern state was elected President. For half a century after the war hardly any Southerners served as Speaker of the House or president pro tempore of the Senate, and only nine of the thirty Supreme Court justices appointed during that half-century were Southerners. The institutions and ideology of a plantation society and a caste system that had dominated half of the country before 1861 and sought to dominate more went down with a great crash in 1865 and were replaced by the institutions and ideology of free-labor entrepreneurial capitalism. For better or for worse, the flames of the Civil War forged the framework of modern America.

So even if the veneer of romance and myth that has attracted so many of the current Civil War camp followers were stripped away, leaving only the trauma of violence and suffering, the Civil War would remain the most dramatic and crucial experience in American history. That fact will ensure the persistence of its popularity and its importance as a historical subject so long as there is a United States.

March 1990

27. First Inaugural Address

Abraham Lincoln

This speech had its origins in the back room of a store in Springfield, Illinois. Lincoln, who lived in Springfield for nearly 25 years, wrote the speech shortly before becoming America's sixteenth President. As President-elect, he took refuge from hordes of office seekers at his brother-in-law's store in January 1861. There he used just four references in his writing: Henry Clay's 1850 Speech on compromise, Webster's reply to Hayne, Andrew Jackson's proclamation against nullification, and the U.S. Constitution. The desk Lincoln used has been preserved by the state of Illinois.

A local newspaper, the Illinois State Journal, secretly printed the first draft, which he took on his inaugural journey to Washington. He entrusted the speech to his son Robert, who temporarily lost the suitcase, causing a minor uproar until it was found. Once in Washington, Lincoln allowed a handful of people to read the speech before delivering it. William H. Seward, his Secretary of State, offered several suggestions which softened its tone and helped produce its famous closing. Although meant to allay the fears of Southerners, the speech did not dissuade them from starting the war, which broke out the following month.

Californians read the speech after it traveled via telegraph and Pony Express. It was telegraphed from New York to Kearney, Nebraska, then taken by Pony Express to Folsom, California, where it was telegraphed to Sacramento for publication. Today, you can see the First Inaugural Address manuscript and the Bible from the inaugural ceremony at the "American Treasures" exhibit, Library of Congress, Washington, D.C.

Washington, D.C.
March 4, 1861
Fellow-citizens of the United States:

In compliance with a custom as old as the government itself, I appear before you to address you briefly, and to take, in your presence, the oath prescribed by the Constitution of the United States, to be taken by the President "before he enters on the execution of this office."

I do not consider it necessary at present for me to discuss those matters of administration about which there is no special anxiety or excitement.

Apprehension seems to exist among the people of the Southern States, that by the accession of a Republican Administration, their property, and their peace, and personal security, are to be endangered. There has never been any reasonable cause for such apprehension. Indeed, the most ample evidence to the contrary has all the while existed, and been open to their inspection. It is found in nearly all the published speeches of him who now addresses you. I do but quote from one of those speeches when I declare that "I have no purpose, directly or indirectly, to interfere with the institution of slavery in the States where it exists. I believe I have no lawful right to do so, and I have no inclination to do so." Those who nominated and elected me did so with full knowledge that I had made this, and many similar declarations, and had never recanted them. And more than this, they placed in the platform, for my acceptance, and as a law to themselves, and to me, the clear and emphatic resolution which I now read:

Resolved, That the maintenance inviolate of the rights of the States, and especially the right of each State to order and control its own domestic institutions according to its own judgment exclusively, is essential to that balance of power on which the perfection and endurance of our political fabric depend; and we denounce the lawless invasion by armed force of the soil of any State or Territory, no matter what pretext, as among the gravest of crimes."

I now reiterate these sentiments; and in doing so, I only press upon the public attention the most conclusive evidence of which the case is susceptible, that the property, peace and security of no section are to be in any wise endangered by the now incoming Administration. I add too, that all the protection which, consistently with the Constitution and the laws, can be given, will be cheerfully given to all the States when lawfully demanded, for whatever cause -- as cheerfully to one section as to another.

There is much controversy about the delivering up of fugitives from service or labor. The clause I now read is as plainly written in the Constitution as any other of its provisions:

"No person held to service or labor in one State, under the laws thereof, escaping into another, shall, in consequence of any law or regulation therein, be discharged from such service or labor, but shall be delivered up on claim of the party to whom such service or labor may be due."

It is scarcely questioned that this provision was intended by those who made it, for the reclaiming of what we call fugitive slaves; and the intention of the law-giver is the law. All members of Congress swear their support to the whole Constitution -- to this provision as much as to any other. To the proposition, then, that slaves whose cases come within the terms of this clause, "shall be delivered," their oaths are unanimous. Now, if they would make the effort in good temper, could they not, with nearly equal unanimity, frame and pass a law, by means of which to keep good that unanimous oath?

There is some difference of opinion whether this clause should be enforced by national or by state authority; but surely that difference is not a very material one. If the slave is to be surrendered, it can be of but little consequence to him, or to others, by which authority it is done. And should any one, in any case, be content that his oath shall go unkept, on a merely unsubstantial controversy as to how it shall be kept?

Again, in any law upon this subject, ought not all the safeguards of liberty known in civilized and humane jurisprudence to be introduced, so that a free man be not, in any case, surrendered as a slave? And might it not be well, at the same time to provide by law for the enforcement of that clause in the Constitution which guarantees that "the citizens of each State shall be entitled to all privileges and immunities of citizens in the several States"?

I take the official oath to-day, with no mental reservations, and with no purpose to construe the Constitution or laws, by any hypercritical rules. And while I do not choose now to specify particular acts of Congress as proper to be enforced, I do suggest that it will be much safer for all, both in official and private stations, to conform to, and abide by, all those acts which stand unrepealed, than to violate any of them, trusting to find impunity in having them held to be unconstitutional.

It is seventy-two years since the first inauguration of a President under our national Constitution. During that period fifteen different and greatly distinguished citizens, have, in succession, administered the executive branch of the government. They have conducted it through many perils; and, generally, with great success. Yet, with all this scope for [of] precedent, I now enter upon the same task for the brief constitutional term of four years, under great and peculiar difficulty. A disruption of the Federal Union, heretofore only menaced, is now formidably attempted.

I hold, that in contemplation of universal law, and of the Constitution, the Union of these States is perpetual. Perpetuity is implied, if not expressed, in the fundamental law of all national governments. It is safe to assert that no government proper, ever had a provision in its organic law for its own termination. Continue to execute all the express provisions of our national Constitution, and the Union will endure forever -- it being impossible to destroy it, except by some action not provided for in the instrument itself.

Again, if the United States be not a government proper, but an association of States in the nature of contract merely, can it, as a contract, be peaceably unmade, by less than all the parties who made it? One party to a contract may violate it -- break it, so to speak; but does it not require all to lawfully rescind it?

Descending from these general principles, we find the proposition that, in legal contemplation, the Union is perpetual, confirmed by the history of the Union itself. The Union is much older than the Constitution. It was formed in fact, by the Articles of Association in 1774. It was matured and continued by the Declaration of Independence in 1776. It was further matured and the faith of all the then thirteen States expressly plighted and engaged that it should be perpetual, by the Articles of Confederation in 1778. And finally, in 1787, one of the declared objects for ordaining and establishing the Constitution, was "to form a more perfect Union." But if [the] destruction of the Union, by one, or by a part only, of the States, be lawfully possible, the Union is less perfect than before the Constitution, having lost the vital element of perpetuity.

It follows from these views that no State, upon its own mere motion, can lawfully get out of the Union,—that resolves and ordinances to that effect are legally void, and that acts of violence, within any State or States, against the authority of the United States, are insurrectionary or revolutionary, according to circumstances.

I therefore consider that in view of the Constitution and the laws, the Union is unbroken; and to the extent of my ability I shall take care, as the Constitution itself expressly enjoins upon me, that the laws of the Union be faithfully executed in all the States. Doing this I deem to be only a simple duty on my part; and I shall perform it, so far as practicable, unless my rightful masters, the American people, shall withhold the requisite means, or in some authoritative manner, direct the contrary. I trust this will not be regarded as a menace, but only as the declared purpose of the Union that will constitutionally defend and maintain itself.

In doing this there needs to be no bloodshed or violence; and there shall be none, unless it be forced upon the national authority. The power confided to me will be used to hold, occupy, and possess the property and places belonging to the government, and to collect the duties and imposts; but beyond what may be necessary for these objects, there will be no invasion -- no using of force against or among the people anywhere. Where hostility to the United States in any interior locality, shall be so great and so universal, as to prevent competent resident citizens from holding the Federal offices, there will be no attempt to force obnoxious strangers among the people for that object. While the strict legal right may exist in the government to enforce the exercise of these offices, the attempt to do so would be so irritating, and so nearly impracticable with all, that I deem it better to forego, for the time, the uses of such offices.

The mails, unless repelled, will continue to be furnished in all parts of the Union. So far as possible, the people everywhere shall have that sense of perfect security which is most favorable to calm thought and reflection. The course here indicated will be followed, unless current events and experience shall show a modification or change to be proper; and in every case and exigency my best discretion will be exercised according to circumstances actually existing, and with a view and a hope of a peaceful solution of the national troubles, and the restoration of fraternal sympathies and affections.

That there are persons in one section or another who seek to destroy the Union at all events, and are glad of any pretext to do it, I will neither affirm nor deny; but if there be such, I need address no word to them. To those, however, who really love the Union may I not speak?

Before entering upon so grave a matter as the destruction of our national fabric, with all its benefits, its memories, and its hopes, would it not be wise to ascertain precisely why we do it? Will you hazard so desperate a step, while there is any possibility that any portion of the ills you fly from have no real existence? Will you, while the certain ills you fly to, are greater than all the real ones you fly from? Will you risk the commission of so fearful a mistake?

All profess to be content in the Union, if all constitutional rights can be maintained. Is it true, then, that any right, plainly written in the Constitution, has been denied? I think not. Happily the human mind is so constituted, that no party can reach to the audacity of doing this. Think, if you can, of a single instance in which a plainly written provision of the Constitution has ever been denied. If by the mere force of numbers, a majority should deprive a minority of any clearly written constitutional right, it might, in a moral point of view, justify revolution -- certainly would, if such right were a vital one. But such is not our case. All the vital rights of minorities, and of individuals, are so plainly assured to them, by affirmations and negations, guaranties and prohibitions, in the Constitution, that controversies never arise concerning them. But no organic law can ever be framed with a provision specifically applicable to every question which may occur in practical administration. No foresight can anticipate, nor any document of reasonable length contain express provisions for all possible questions. Shall fugitives from labor be surrendered by national or by State authority? The Constitution does not expressly say. May Congress prohibit slavery in the territories? The Constitution does not expressly say. Must Congress protect slavery in the territories? The Constitution does not expressly say.

From questions of this class spring all our constitutional controversies, and we divide upon them into majorities and minorities. If the minority will not acquiesce, the majority must, or the government must cease. There is no other alternative; for continuing the government, is acquiescence on one side or the other. If a minority, in such case, will secede rather than acquiesce, they make a precedent which, in turn, will divide and ruin them; for a minority of their own will secede from them whenever a majority refuses to be controlled by such minority. For instance, why may not any portion of a new confederacy, a year or two hence, arbitrarily secede again, precisely as portions of the present Union now claim to secede from it? All who cherish disunion sentiments, are now being educated to the exact temper of doing this.

Is there such perfect identity of interests among the States to compose a new Union, as to produce harmony only, and prevent renewed secession?

Plainly, the central idea of secession, is the essence of anarchy. A majority, held in restraint by constitutional checks and limitations, and always changing easily with deliberate changes of popular opinions and sentiments, is the only true sovereign of a free people. Whoever rejects it, does, of necessity, fly to anarchy or to despotism. Unanimity is impossible; the rule of a minority, as a permanent arrangement, is wholly inadmissible; so that, rejecting the majority principle, anarchy or despotism in some form is all that is left.

I do not forget the position assumed by some, that constitutional questions are to be decided by the Supreme Court; nor do I deny that such decisions must be binding in any case, upon the parties to a suit; as to the object of that suit, while they are also entitled to very high respect and consideration in all parallel cases by all other departments of the government. And while it is obviously possible that such decision may be erroneous in any given case, still the evil effect following it, being limited to that particular case, with the chance that it may be over-ruled, and never become a precedent for other cases, can better be borne than could the evils of a different practice. At the same time, the candid citizen must confess that if the policy of the government upon vital questions, affecting the whole people, is to be irrevocably fixed by decisions of the Supreme Court, the instant they are made, in ordinary litigation between parties, in personal actions, the people will have ceased to be their own rulers, having to that extent practically resigned their government into the hands of that eminent tribunal. Nor is there in this view any assault upon the court or the judges. It is a duty from which they may not shrink, to decide cases properly brought before them; and it is no fault of theirs if others seek to turn their decisions to political purposes.

One section of our country believes slavery is right, and ought to be extended, while the other believes it is wrong, and ought not to be extended. This is the only substantial dispute. The fugitive slave clause of the Constitution, and the law for the suppression of the foreign slave trade, are each as well enforced, perhaps, as any law can ever be in a community where the moral sense of the people imperfectly supports the law itself. The great body of the people abide by the dry legal obligation in both cases, and a few break over in each. This, I think, cannot be perfectly cured, and it would be worse in both cases after the separation of the sections, than before. The foreign slave trade, now imperfectly suppressed, would be ultimately revived without restriction, in one section; while fugitive slaves, now only partially surrendered, would not be surrendered at all, by the other.

Physically speaking, we cannot separate. We can not remove our respective sections from each other, nor build an impassable wall between them. A husband and wife may be divorced, and go out of the presence, and beyond the reach of each other; but the different parts of our country cannot do this. They cannot but remain face to face; and intercourse, either amicable or hostile, must continue between them. Is it possible, then, to make that intercourse more advantageous or more satisfactory, after separation than before? Can aliens make treaties easier than friends can make laws? Can treaties be more faithfully enforced between aliens than laws can among friends? Suppose you go to war, you cannot fight always; and when, after much loss on both sides, and no gain on either, you cease fighting, the identical old questions, as to terms of intercourse, are again upon you.

This country, with its institutions, belongs to the people who inhabit it. Whenever they shall grow weary of the existing Government, they can exercise their constitutional right of amending it, or their revolutionary right to dismember or overthrow it. I cannot be ignorant of the fact that many worthy and patriotic citizens are desirous of having the national Constitution amended. While I make no recommendation of amendments, I fully recognize the rightful authority of the people over the whole subject to be exercised in either of the modes prescribed in the instrument itself; and I should, under existing circumstances, favor rather than oppose a fair opportunity being afforded the people to act upon it.

I will venture to add that to me the Convention mode seems preferable, in that it allows amendments to originate with the people themselves, instead of only permitting them to take or reject propositions, originated by others, not especially chosen for the purpose, and which might not be precisely such as they would wish to either accept or refuse. I understand a proposed amendment to the Constitution, which amendment, however, I have not seen, has passed Congress, to the effect that the federal government shall never interfere with the domestic institutions of the States, including that of persons held to service. To avoid misconstruction of what I have said, I depart from my purpose not to speak of particular amendments, so far as to say that holding such a provision to now be implied constitutional law, I have no objection to its being made express and irrevocable.

The Chief Magistrate derives all his authority from the people, and they have referred none upon him to fix terms for the separation of the States. The people themselves can do this if also they choose; but the executive, as such, has nothing to do with it. His duty is to administer the present government, as it came to his hands, and to transmit it, unimpaired by him, to his successor.

Why should there not be a patient confidence in the ultimate justice of the people? Is there any better or equal hope, in the world? In our present differences, is either party without faith of being in the right? If the Almighty Ruler of nations, with his eternal truth and justice, be on your side of the North, or on yours of the South, that truth, and that justice, will surely prevail, by the judgment of this great tribunal of the American people.

By the frame of the government under which we live, this same people have wisely given their public servants but little power for mischief; and have, with equal wisdom, provided for the return of that little to their own hands at very short intervals.

While the people retain their virtue and vigilance, no administration, by any extreme of wickedness or folly, can very seriously injure the government in the short space of four years.

My countrymen, one and all, think calmly and well, upon this whole subject. Nothing valuable can be lost by taking time. If there be an object to hurry any of you, in hot haste, to a step which you would never take deliberately, that object will be frustrated by taking time; but no good object can be frustrated by it. Such of you as are now dissatisfied still have the old Constitution unimpaired, and, on the sensitive point, the laws of your own framing under it; while the new administration will have no immediate power, if it would, to change either. If it were admitted that you who are dissatisfied, hold the right side in the dispute, there still is no single good reason for precipitate action. Intelligence, patriotism, Christianity, and a firm reliance on Him, who has never yet forsaken this favored land, are still competent to adjust, in the best way, all our present difficulty.

In your hands, my dissatisfied fellow countrymen, and not in mine, is the momentous issue of civil war. The government will not assail you. You can have no conflict without being yourselves the aggressors. You have no oath registered in Heaven to destroy the government, while I shall have the most solemn one to "preserve, protect, and defend it."

I am loath to close. We are not enemies, but friends. We must not be enemies. Though passion may have strained, it must not break our bonds of affection. The mystic chords of memory, stretching from every battle-field, and patriot grave, to every living heart and hearth-stone, all over this broad land, will yet swell the chorus of the Union, when again touched, as surely they will be, by the better angels of our nature.

28. The Gettysburg Address

November, 1863

Abraham Lincoln

Four score and seven years ago our fathers brought forth on this continent, a new nation, conceived in Liberty, and dedicated to the proposition that all men are created equal.

Now we are engaged in a great civil war, testing whether that nation or any nation so conceived and so dedicated, can long endure. We are met on a great battle-field of that war. We have come to dedicate a portion of that field, as a final resting place for those who here gave their lives that that nation might live. It is altogether fitting and proper that we should do this.

But, in a larger sense, we can not dedicate—we can not consecrate—we can not hallow—this ground. The brave men, living and dead, who struggled here, have consecrated it, far above our poor power to add or detract. The world will little note, nor long remember what we say here, but it can never forget what they did here. It is for us the living, rather, to be dedicated here to the unfinished work which they who fought here have thus far so nobly advanced. It is rather for us to be here dedicated to the great task remaining before us—that from these honored dead we take increased devotion to that cause for which they gave the last full measure of devotion—that we here highly resolve that these dead shall not have died in vain—that this nation, under God, shall have a new birth of freedom—and that government of the people, by the people, for the people, shall not perish from the earth.

Comments on Gettysburg Address by Henry Steele Commager

"I claim not to have controlled events," Abraham Lincoln admitted, "but confess plainly that events have controlled me." The firing on Fort Sumter, the steady stream of northern defeats while Lincoln searched for a winning general, the radical pressure which finally drove a reluctant President to issue the Emancipation Proclamation—all confirm Lincoln's assertion. But characteristically he was too modest in his analysis. His political skill kept the various factions of his own party working together; his shrewd intelligence enabled him, despite his lack of military experience, to perform ably as commander in chief; and his de-

termination to preserve the Union gave the northern cause a dignity and mean-
ing it desperately needed.

Lincoln's greatness is best revealed in his most famous wartime speech.
Shortly after the crucial battle at Gettysburg, Pennsylvania, a group of northern
governors created a commission to establish a national cemetery at the battle-
field. The trustees planned an impressive dedication ceremony and they asked
Edward Everett, the foremost orator of the time, to give the principal address.
They invited the President, members of his cabinet, and congressmen to attend;
and out of courtesy they asked Lincoln to make a few remarks. To the surprise
of his associates, Lincoln accepted the invitation and prepared two drafts of a
brief talk before he took the train to Gettysburg on November 18, 1863. The
next morning he made some minor changes in his speech, and then after lunch
he joined some fifteen thousand to listen for more than two hours as Everett
delivered his elaborate and eloquent formal address from memory. After a brief
pause, Lincoln spoke from his single folded page, adding one phrase extempora-
neously, and then sat down before many in the audience were aware he had be-
gun. The scattered applause came belatedly, a photographer took the President's
picture, and the event was over. Yet in less than 300 words Lincoln had given the
nation a perfect statement of what the war was all about.

29. Second Inaugural Address

Abraham Lincoln

On March 4, 1865, just over a month prior to his assassination on April 14, 1865, Lincoln delivered his second Inaugural Address. In this speech he tried to come to grips with the cause of the war and the suffering it had caused for both the North and the South. He made his final attempt to reconcile the different sec tions of the country and to restore the Union. It is considered by many histori ans to be one of the most important speeches in U.S. History.

Washington, D.C.

March 4, 1865

At this second appearing to take the oath of the presidential office, there is less occasion for an extended address than there was at the first. Then a statement, somewhat in detail, of a course to be pursued, seemed fitting and proper. Now, at the expiration of four years, during which public declarations have been constantly called forth on every point and phase of the great contest which still absorbs the attention, and engrosses the energies of the nation, little that is new could be presented. The progress of our arms, upon which all else chiefly depends, is as well known to the public as to myself; and it is, I trust, reasonably satisfactory and encouraging to all. With high hope for the future, no prediction in regard to it is ventured.

On the occasion corresponding to this four years ago, all thoughts were anxiously directed to an impending civil war. All dreaded it--all sought to avert it. While the inaugeral [sic] address was being delivered from this place, devoted altogether to saving the Union without war, insurgent agents were in the city seeking to destroy it without war--seeking to dissole [sic] the Union, and divide effects, by negotiation. Both parties deprecated war; but one of them would make war rather than let the nation survive; and the other would accept war rather than let it perish. And the war came.

One eighth of the whole population were colored slaves, not distributed generally over the Union, but localized in the Southern part of it. These slaves constituted a peculiar and powerful interest. All knew that this interest was, somehow, the cause of the war. To strengthen, perpetuate, and extend this interest was the object for which the insurgents would rend the Union, even by war;

while the government claimed no right to do more than to restrict the territorial enlargement of it. Neither party expected for the war, the magnitude, or the duration, which it has already attained. Neither anticipated that the cause of the conflict might cease with, or even before, the conflict itself should cease. Each looked for an easier triumph, and a result less fundamental and astounding. Both read the same Bible, and pray to the same God; and each invokes His aid against the other. It may seem strange that any men should dare to ask a just God's assistance in wringing their bread from the sweat of other men's faces; but let us judge not that we be not judged. The prayers of both could not be answered; that of neither has been answered fully. The Almighty has his own purposes. "Woe unto the world because of offences! for it must needs be that offences come; but woe to that man by whom the offence cometh!" If we shall suppose that American Slavery is one of those offences which, in the providence of God, must needs come, but which, having continued through His appointed time, He now wills to remove, and that He gives to both North and South, this terrible war, as the woe due to those by whom the offence came, shall we discern therein any departure from those divine attributes which the believers in a Living God always ascribe to Him? Fondly do we hope--fervently do we pray--that this mighty scourge of war may speedily pass away. Yet, if God wills that it continue, until all the wealth piled by the bond-man's two hundred and fifty years of unrequited toil shall be sunk, and until every drop of blood drawn with the lash, shall be paid by another drawn with the sword, as was said three thousand years ago, so still it must be said "the judgments of the Lord, are true and righteous altogether"

With malice toward none; with charity for all; with firmness in the right, as God gives us to see the right, let us strive on to finish the work we are in; to bind up the nation's wounds; to care for him who shall have borne the battle, and for his widow, and his orphan--to do all which may achieve and cherish a just and lasting peace, among ourselves, and with all nations.

30. Grant: Personal Memoirs of U.S. Grant Conclusion Chapter

Ulysses S. Grant published his "Memoirs" in 1885, several decades after the Civil War and a few years after his Presidency. But the war (or, as Grant called it, "the War of the Rebellion") was still vivid in his memory. Like Lincoln in his "Second Inaugural" Grant believed that the Civil War was caused by slavery and the issues concerning the preservation of the "institution". He was optimistic about the future, believing that it had made the country stronger. Like Lincoln, he believed that eventually there would be a reconciliation between North and South.

The cause of the great War of the Rebellion against the United States will have to attributed to slavery. For some years before the war began it was a trite saying among some politicians that "A state half slave and half free cannot exist." All must become slave or all free, or the state will go down. I took no part myself in any such view of the case at the time, but since the war is over, reviewing the whole question, I have come to the conclusion that the saying is quite true.

Slavery was an institution that required unusual guarantees for it security wherever it existed; and in a country like ours where the larger portion of it was free territory inhabited by an intelligent and well-to-do population, the people would naturally have but little sympathy with demands upon them for its protection. Hence the people of the South were dependent upon keeping control of the general government to secure the perpetuation of their favorite institution. They were enabled to maintain this control long after the States where slavery existed had ceased to have the controlling power, through the assistance they received from odd men here and there throughout the Northern States. They saw their power waning, and thus led them to encroach upon the prerogatives and independence of the Northern States by enacting such laws as the Fugitive Slave Law. By this law every Northern man was obliged, when properly summoned, to turn out and help apprehend the runaway slave of a Southern man. Northern marshals became slave-catchers, and Northern courts had to contribute to the support and protection of the institution.

This was a degradation which the North would not permit any longer than until they could get the power to expunge such laws from the statute books. Prior to the time of these encroachments the great majority of the people of the North had no particular quarrel with slavery, so long as they were not forced to have it themselves. But they were not willing to play the role of police for the South in the protection of this particular institution.

In the early days of the country, before we had railroads, telegraphs and steamboats—in a word, rapid transit of any sort—the States were each almost a separate nationality. At that time the subject of slavery caused but little or no disturbance to the public mind. But the country grew, rapid transit was established, and trade and commerce between the States got to be so much greater than before, that the power of the National government became more felt and recognized and, therefore, had to be enlisted in the cause of this institution.

It is probably well that we had the war when we did. We are better off now that we would have been without it, and have made more rapid progress than we otherwise should have made. The civilized nations of Europe have been stimulated into unusual activity, so that commerce, trade, travel, and thorough acquaintance among people of different nationalities, has become common; whereas, before it was but the few who had ever had the privilege of going beyond the limits of their own country or who knew anything about other people. Then, too, our republican institutions were regarded as experiments up to the breaking out of the rebellion, and monarchical Europe generally believed that our republic was a rope of sand that would part the moment the slightest strain was brought upon it. Now it has shown itself capable of dealing with one of the greatest wars that was ever made, and our people have proven themselves to be the most formidable in war of any nationality.

But this war was a fearful lesson, and should teach us the necessity of avoiding wars in the future.

The conduct of some of the European states during our troubles shows the lack of conscience of committees where the responsibility does not come upon a single individual. Seeing a nation that extended from the ocean to ocean, embracing the better part of a continent, growing as we were growing in population, wealth and intelligence, the European nations thought it would be well to give us a check. We might, possibly, after a while threaten their peace, or, at least, the perpetuity of their institutions. Hence, England was constantly finding fault with the administration at Washington because we were not able to keep an effective blockade. She also joined, at first, with France and Spain in setting up an Austrian prince upon the throne in Mexico, totally disregarding any rights or claims that Mexico had of being treated as an independent power. It is true they trumped up grievances as a pretext, but they were only pretexts which can always be found when wanted.

Mexico, in her various revolutions, had been unable to give that protection to the subjects of foreign nations which she would have liked to give, and some of her revolutionary leaders had forced loans from them. Under pretense of protecting their citizens, these nations seized upon Mexico as a foothold for establishing a European monarchy upon our continent, thus threatening our peace at home. I, myself, regarded this as a direct act of war against the United States by the powers engaged, and supposed as a matter of course that the United States would treat it as such when their hand were free to strike. I often spoke of the matter to Mr. Lincoln and the Secretary of War, but never heard any special views from them to enable me to judge what they thought or felt about it. I inferred that they felt a good deal as I did, but were unwilling to commit themselves while we had our own troubles upon our hands.

All of the powers except France very soon withdrew from the armed intervention for the establishment of an Austrian prince up on the throne of Mexico; but the governing people of these countries continued to the close of the war to throw obstacles in our way. After the surrender of Lee, therefore, entertaining the opinion here expressed, I sent Sheridan with a corps to the Rio Grande to have him where he might aid Juarez in expelling the French from Mexico. These troops got off before they could be stopped; and went to the Rio Grande, where Sheridan distributed them up and down the river much to the consternation of the troops in the quarter of Mexico bordering on that stream. This soon led to a request from France that we should withdraw our troops from the Rio Grande and to negotiations for the withdrawal of theirs. Finally Bazaine was withdrawn from Mexico by order of the French Government. From that day the empire began to totter. Mexico was then able to maintain her independence without aid from us. "

France is the traditional ally and friend of the United States. I did not blame France for her part in the scheme to erect a monarchy upon the ruins of the Mexican Republic. That was the scheme of one man, an imitator without genius or merit. He had succeeded in stealing the government of his country, and made a change in its form against the wishes and instincts of his people. He tried to play the part of the first Napoleon, without the ability to sustain that rôle. He sought by new conquests to add to his empire and his glory; but the signal failure of his scheme of conquest was the precursor of his own overthrow.

Like our own war between the States, the Franco-Prussian war was an expensive one; but it was worth to France all it cost her people. It was the completion of the downfall of Napoleon III. The beginning was when he landed troops on this continent. Failing here, the prestige of his name – all the prestige he ever had – was gone. He must achieve a success or fall. He tried to strike down his neighbor, Prussia – and fell.

I never admired the character of the first Napoleon; but I recognize his great genius. His work, too, has left its impress for good on the face of Europe. The third Napoleon could have no claim to having done a good or just act.

To maintain peace in the future it is necessary to be prepared for war. There can scarcely be a possible chance of a conflict, such as the last one, occurring among our own people again; but, growing as we are, in population, wealth and military power, we may become the envy of nations which led us in all these particulars only a few years ago; and unless we are prepared for it we may be in danger of a combined movement being some day made to crush us out. Now, scarcely twenty years after the war, we seem to have forgotten the lessons it taught, and are going on as if in the greatest security, without the power to resist an invasion by the fleets of fourth-rate European powers for a time until we could prepare for them.

We should have a good navy, and our sea-coast defenses should be put in the finest possible condition. Neither of these cost much when it is considered where the money goes, and what we get in return. Money expended in a fine navy, not only adds to our security and tends to prevent war in the future, but it is very material aid to our commerce with foreign nations in the meantime. Money spent upon sea-coast defenses is spent among our own people, and all goes back again among the people. The work accomplished, too, like that of the navy, gives us a feeling of security.

England's course towards the United States during the rebellion exasperated the people of this country very much against the mother country. I regretted it. England and the United States are natural allies, and should be the best of friends. They speak one language, and are related by blood and other ties. We together, or even either separately, are better qualified than any other people to establish commerce between all the nationalities of the world.

England governs her own colonies, and particularly those embracing the people of different races from her own, better than any other nation. She is just to the conquered, but rigid. She makes them self-supporting, but gives the benefit of labor to the laborer. She does not seem to look upon the colonies as outside possessions which she is at liberty to work for the support and aggrandizement of the home government.

The hostility of England to the United States during our rebellion was not so much real as it was apparent. It was the hostility of the leaders of one political party. I am told that there was no time during the civil war when they were able to get up in England a demonstration in favor of secession, while these were constantly being gotten up in favor of the Union, or, as they called it, in favor of the North. Even in Manchester, which suffered so fearfully by having the cotton cut off from her mills, they had a monster demonstration in favor of the North at the very time when their workmen were almost famishing.

It is possible that the question of a conflict between races may come up in the future, as did that between freedom and slavery before. The condition of the colored man within our borders may become a source of anxiety, to say the least. But he was brought to our shores by compulsion, and he now should be considered as having as good a right to remain here as any other class of our citizens. It was looking to a settlement of this question that led me to urge the annexation of Santo Domingo during the time I was President of the United States.

Santo Domingo was freely offered to us, not only by the administration, but by all the people, almost without a price. The island upon our shores, is very fertile, and is capable of supporting fifteen millions of people. The products of the soil are so valuable that labor in her fields would be so compensated as to enable those who wished to go there to quickly repay the cost of their passage. I took it that the colored people would go there in great numbers, so as to have independent states governed by their own race. They would still be States of the Union, and under protection of the General Government; but the citizens would be almost wholly colored.

By the war with Mexico, we had acquired, as we have seen, territory almost equal in extent to that we already possessed. It was seen that the volunteers of the Mexican war largely composed the pioneers to settle up the pacific coast country. Their numbers, however, were scarcely sufficient to be a nucleus for the population of the important points of the territory acquired by that war. After our rebellion, when so many young men were at liberty to return to their homes, they found they were not satisfied with the farm, the store, or the work-shop of the villages, but wanted larger fields. The mines of the mountains first attracted them; but afterwards they found that rich valleys and productive grazing and farming lands were there. This territory, the geography of which was not known to us at the close of the rebellion, is now as well mapped as any portion of our country. Railroads traverse it in every direction, north, south, east, and west. The mines are worked. The high lands are used for grazing purposes, and rich agricultural lands are found in many of the valleys. This is the work of the volunteer. It is probable that the Indians would have had control of these lands for a century yet but for the war. We must conclude, therefore, that wars are not always evils unmixed with some good.

Prior to the rebellion the great mass of the people were satisfied to remain near the scenes of their birth. In fact an immense majority of the whole people did not feel secure against coming to want should they move among entire strangers. So much was the country divided into small communities that localized idioms had grown up, so that you could almost tell what section a person was from by hearing him speak. Before, new territories were settled by a "class"; people who shunned contact with others; people who, when the country began to settle up around them, would push out farther from civilization. Their guns furnished meat, and the cultivation of a very limited amount of the soul, their bread and vegetables. All the streams abounded with fish. Trapping would furnish pelts to be brought into the States once a year, to pay for necessary articles which they could not raise—powder, lead, whiskey, tobacco and some store goods. Occasionally some little articles of luxury would enter into those purchases—a quarter of a pound of tea, two or three pounds of coffee, more of sugar, some playing cards, and if anything was left over of the proceeds of the sale, more whiskey.

Little was known of the topography of the country beyond the settlements of these frontiersmen. This is all changed now. The war begot a spirit of independence and enterprise. The feeling now is, that a youth must cut loose from his old surroundings to enable him to get up in the world. There is now such a commingling of the people that particular idioms and pronunciation are no longer localized to any great extent; the country has filled up "from the centre all around to the sea"; railroads connect the two oceans and all part of the interior; maps, nearly perfect, of every part of the country are now furnished the student of geography.

The war has made us a nation of great power and intelligence. We have but little to do to preserve peace, happiness and prosperity at home, and the respect of other nations Our experience ought to teach us the necessity of the first; our power secures the latter.

I feel that we are on the eve of a new era, when there is to be great harmony between the Federal and Confederate. I cannot stay to be a living witness to the correctness of this prophecy, but I feel it within me that it is to be so. The universally kind feelings expressed for me at a time when it was supposed that each day would prove my last, seemed to me the beginning of the answer to "Let us have peace."

The expressions of these kindly feelings were not restricted to a section of the country, nor to a division of the people. They came from individual citizens of all nationalities; from all denominations—the Protestant, the Catholic, and the Jew; and from the various societies of the land—scientific, educational, religious, or otherwise. Politics did not enter into this matter at all.

I am not egotist enough to suppose all this significance should be given because I was the object of it. But the war between the States was a very bloody and very costly war. One side or the other had to yield principles they deemed dearer than life before it could be brought to an end. I commanded the whole of the mighty host engage on the victorious side. I was, no matter whether deservedly so or not, a representative of that side of the controversy. It is a significant and gratifying fact that Confederates should have joined heartily in this spontaneous move. I hope the good feeling inaugurated may continue to the end.

31. The New View
of Reconstruction

Eric Foner

In the past twenty years, no period of American history has been the subject of a more thoroughgoing reevaluation than Reconstruction—the violent, dramatic, and still controversial era following the Civil War. Race relations, politics, social life, and economic change during Reconstruction have all been reinterpreted in the light of changed attitudes toward the place of blacks within American society. If historians have not yet forged a fully satisfying portrait of Reconstruction as a whole, the traditional interpretation that dominated historical writing for much of this century has irrevocably been laid to rest.

Anyone who attended high school before 1960 learned that Reconstruction was an era of unrelieved sordidness in American political and social life. The martyred Lincoln, according to this view, had planned a quick and painless re-admission of the Southern states as equal members of the national family. President Andrew Johnson, his successor, attempted to carry out Lincoln's policies but was foiled by the Radical Republicans (also known as Vindictives or Jacobins). Motivated by an irrational hatred of Rebels or by ties with Northern capitalists out to plunder the South, the Radicals swept aside Johnson's lenient program and fastened black supremacy upon the defeated Confederacy. An orgy of corruption followed, presided over by unscrupulous carpetbaggers (Northerners who ventured south to reap the spoils of office), traitorous scalawags (Southern whites who cooperated with the new governments for personal gain), and the ignorant and childlike freedmen, who were incapable of properly exercising the political power that had been thrust upon them. After much needless suffering, the white community of the South banded together to overthrow these "black" governments and restore home rule (their euphemism for white supremacy). All told, Reconstruction was just about the darkest page in the American saga.

Originating in anti-Reconstruction propaganda of Southern Democrats during the 1870s, this traditional interpretation achieved scholarly legitimacy around the turn of the century through the work of William Dunning and his students at Columbia University. It reached the larger public through films like *Birth of a Nation* and *Gone With the Wind* and that best-selling work of myth-making masquerading as history, *The Tragic Era* by Claude G. Bowers. In language as exaggerated as it was colorful, Bowers told how Andrew Johnson "fought the bravest battle for constitutional liberty and for the preservation of our institutions ever waged by an Executive" but was overwhelmed by the "poisonous propaganda" of the Radicals. Southern whites, as a result, "literally were put to the torture" by "emissaries of hate" who manipulated the "simple-minded" freedmen, "inflaming the negroes' egotism" and even inspiring "lustful assaults" by blacks upon white womanhood.

In a discipline that sometimes seems to pride itself on the rapid rise and fall of historical interpretations, this traditional portrait of Reconstruction enjoyed remarkable staying power. The long reign of the old interpretation is not difficult to explain. It presented a set of easily identifiable heroes and villains. It enjoyed the imprimatur of the nation's leading scholars. And it accorded with the political and social realities of the first half of this century. This image of Reconstruction helped freeze the mind of the white South in unalterable opposition to any movement for breaching the ascendancy of the Democratic party, eliminating segregation, or readmitting disfranchised blacks to the vote.

Nevertheless, the demise of the traditional interpretation was inevitable, for it ignored the testimony of the central participant in the drama of Reconstruction—the black freedman. Furthermore, it was grounded in the conviction that blacks were unfit to share in political power. As Dunning's Columbia colleague John W. Burgess put it, "A black skin means membership in a race of men which has never of itself succeeded in subjecting passion to reason, has never, therefore, created any civilization of any kind." Once objective scholarship and modern experience rendered that assumption untenable, the entire edifice was bound to fall.

The work of "revising" the history of Reconstruction began with the writings of a handful of survivors of the era, such as John R. Lynch, who had served as a black congressman from Mississippi after the Civil War. In the 1930s white scholars like Francis Simkins and Robert Woody carried the task forward. Then, in 1935, the black historian and activist W.E.B. Du Bois produced *Black Reconstruction* in America, a monumental reevaluation that closed with an irrefutable indictment of an historical profession that had sacrificed scholarly objectivity on the altar of racial bias. "One fact and one alone," he wrote, "explains the attitude of most recent writers toward Reconstruction; they cannot conceive of Negroes as men." Du Bois's work, however, was ignored by most historians.

It was not until the 1960s that the full force of the revisionist wave broke over the field. Then, in rapid succession, virtually every assumption of the traditional viewpoint was systematically dismantled. A drastically different portrait emerged to take its place. President Lincoln did not have a coherent "Plan" for Reconstruction, but at the time of his assassination he had been cautiously contemplating black suffrage. Andrew Johnson was a stubborn, racist politician who lacked the ability to compromise. By isolating himself from the broad currents of public opinion that had nourished Lincoln's career, Johnson created an impasse with Congress that Lincoln would certainly have avoided, thus throwing away his political power and destroying his own plans for reconstructing the South.

The Radicals in Congress were acquitted of both vindictive motives and the charge of serving as the stalking-horses of Northern capitalism. They emerged instead as idealists in the best nineteenth-century reform tradition. Radical leaders like Charles Sumner and Thaddeus Stevens had worked for the rights of blacks long before any conceivable political advantage flowed from such a commitment. Stevens refused to sign the Pennsylvania Constitution of 1838 because it disfranchised the state's black citizens; Sumner led a fight in the 1850s to integrate Boston's public schools. Their Reconstruction policies were based on principle, not petty political advantage, for the central issue dividing Johnson and these Radical Republicans was the civil rights of freedmen. Studies of congressional policy-making, such as Eric L. McKitrick's Andrew Johnson and Reconstruction, also revealed that Reconstruction legislation, ranging from the Civil Rights Act of 1866 to the Fourteenth and Fifteenth Amendments, enjoyed broad support from moderate and conservative Republicans. It was not simply the work of a narrow radical faction.

Even more startling was the revised portrait of Reconstruction in the South itself. Imbued with the spirit of the civil rights movement and rejecting entirely the racial assumptions that had underpinned the traditional interpretation, these historians evaluated Reconstruction from the black point of view. Works like Joel Williamson's *After Slavery* portrayed the period as a time of extraordinary political, social, and economic progress for blacks. The establishment of public school systems, the granting of equal citizenship to blacks, the effort to restore the devastated Southern economy, the attempt to construct an interracial political democracy from the ashes of slavery, all these were commendable achievements, not the elements of Bowers's "tragic era."

Unlike earlier writers, the revisionists stressed the active role of the freedmen in shaping Reconstruction. Black initiative established as many schools as did Northern religious societies and the Freedmen's Bureau. The right to vote was not simply thrust upon them by meddling outsiders, since blacks began agitating for the suffrage as soon as they were freed. In 1865 black conventions throughout the South issued eloquent, though unheeded, appeals for equal civil and political rights.

With the advent of Radical Reconstruction in 1867, the freedmen did enjoy a real measure of political power. But black supremacy never existed. In most states blacks held only a small fraction of political offices, and even in South Carolina, where they comprised a majority of the state legislature's lower house, effective power remained in white hands. As for corruption, moral standards in both government and private enterprise were at low ebb throughout the nation in the postwar years—the era of Boss Tweed, the Credit Mobilier scandal, and the Whiskey Ring. Southern corruption could hardly be blamed on former slaves.

Other actors in the Reconstruction drama also came in for reevaluation. Most carpetbaggers were former Union soldiers seeking economic opportunity in the postwar South, not unscrupulous adventurers. Their motives, a typically American amalgam of humanitarianism and the pursuit of profit, were no more insidious than those of Western pioneers. Scalawags, previously seen as traitors to the white race, now emerged as "Old Line" Whig Unionists who had opposed secession in the first place or as poor whites who had long resented planters' domination of Southern life and who saw in Reconstruction a chance to recast Southern society along more democratic lines. Strongholds of Southern white Republicanism like east Tennessee and western North Carolina had been the scene of resistance to Confederate rule throughout the Civil War; now, as one scalawag newspaper put it, the choice was "between salvation at the hand of the Negro or destruction at the hand of the rebels."

At the same time, the Ku Klux Klan and kindred groups, whose campaign of violence against black and white Republicans had been minimized or excused in older writings, were portrayed as they really were. Earlier scholars had conveyed the impression that the Klan intimidated blacks mainly by dressing as ghosts and playing on the freedmen's superstitions. In fact, black fears were all too real: the Klan was a terrorist organization that beat and killed its political opponents to deprive blacks of their newly won rights. The complicity of the Democratic party and the silence of prominent whites in the face of such outrages stood as an indictment of the moral code the South had inherited from the days of slavery.

By the end of the 1960s, then, the old interpretation had been completely reversed. Southern freedmen were the heroes, the "Redeemers" who overthrew Reconstruction were the villains, and if the era was "tragic," it was because change did not go far enough. Reconstruction had been a time of real progress and its failure a lost opportunity for the South and the nation. But the legacy of Reconstruction—the Fourteenth and Fifteenth Amendments—endured to inspire future efforts for civil rights. As Kenneth Stampp wrote in *The Era of Reconstruction,* a superb summary of revisionist findings published in 1965, "If it was worth four years of civil war to save the Union, it was worth a few years of radical reconstruction to give the American Negro the ultimate promise of equal civil and political rights."

As Stampp's statement suggests, the reevaluation of the first Reconstruction was inspired in large measure by the impact of the second—the modern civil rights movement. And with the waning of that movement in recent years, writing on Reconstruction has undergone still another transformation. Instead of seeing the Civil War and its aftermath as a second American Revolution (as Charles Beard had), a regression into barbarism (as Bowers argued), or a golden opportunity squandered (as the revisionists saw it), recent writers argue that Radical Reconstruction was not really very radical. Since land was not distributed to the former slaves, they remained economically dependent upon their former owners. The planter class survived both the war and Reconstruction with its property (apart from slaves) and prestige more or less intact.

Not only changing times but also the changing concerns of historians have contributed to this latest reassessment of Reconstruction. The hallmark of the past decade's historical writing has been an emphasis upon "social history"— the evocation of the past lives of ordinary Americans—and the downplaying of strictly political events. When applied to Reconstruction, this concern with the "social" suggested that black suffrage and officeholding, once seen as the most radical departures of the Reconstruction era, were relatively insignificant.

Recent historians have focused their investigations not upon the politics of Reconstruction but upon the social and economic aspects of the transition from slavery to freedom. Herbert Gutman's influential study of the black family during and after slavery found little change in family structure or relations between men and women resulting from emancipation. Under slavery most blacks had lived in nuclear family units, although they faced the constant threat of separation from loved ones by sale. Reconstruction provided the opportunity for blacks to solidify their preexisting family ties. Conflicts over whether black women should work in the cotton fields (planters said yes, many black families said no) and over white attempts to "apprentice" black children revealed that the autonomy of family life was a major preoccupation of the freedmen. Indeed, whether manifested in their withdrawal from churches controlled by whites, in the blossoming of black fraternal, benevolent, and self-improvement organizations, or in the demise of the slave quarters and their replacement by small tenant farms occupied by individual families, the quest for independence from white authority and control over their own day-to-day lives shaped the black response to emancipation.

In the post-Civil War South the surest guarantee of economic autonomy, blacks believed, was land. To the freedmen the justice of a claim to land based on their years of unrequited labor appeared self-evident. As an Alabama black convention put it, "The property which they [the planters] hold was nearly all earned by the sweat of *our* brows." As Leon Litwack showed in *Been in the Storm So Long*, a Pulitzer Prize-winning account of the black response to emancipation, many freedmen in 1865 and 1866 refused to sign labor contracts, expecting the federal government to give them land. In some localities, as one Alabama overseer reported, they "set up claims to the Plantation and all on it."

In the end, of course, the vast majority of Southern blacks remained propertyless and poor. But exactly why the South, and especially its black population, suffered from dire poverty and economic retardation in the decades following the Civil War is a matter of much dispute. In *One Kind of Freedom*, economists Roger Ransom and Richard Sutch indicted country merchants for monopolizing credit and charging usurious interest rates, forcing black tenants into debt and locking the South into a dependence on cotton production that impoverished the entire region. But Jonathan Wiener, in his study of postwar Alabama, argued that planters used their political power to compel blacks to remain on the plantations. Planters succeeded in stabilizing the plantation system, but only by blocking the growth of alternative enterprises, like factories, that might draw off black laborers, thus locking the region into a pattern of economic backwardness.

If the thrust of recent writing has emphasized the social and economic aspects of Reconstruction, politics has not been entirely neglected. But political studies have also reflected the postrevisionist mood summarized by C. Vann Woodward when he observed "how essentially nonrevolutionary and conservative Reconstruction really was." Recent writers, unlike their revisionist predecessors, have found little to praise in federal policy toward the emancipated blacks.

A new sensitivity to the strength of prejudice and laissez-faire ideas in the nineteenth-century North has led many historians to doubt whether the Republican party ever made a genuine commitment to racial justice in the South. The granting of black suffrage was an alternative to a long-term federal responsibility for protecting the rights of the former slaves. Once enfranchised, blacks could be left to fend for themselves. With the exception of a few Radicals like Thaddeus Stevens, nearly all Northern policy-makers and educators are criticized today for assuming that, so long as the unfettered operations of the marketplace afforded blacks the opportunity to advance through diligent labor, federal efforts to assist them in acquiring land were unnecessary.

Probably the most innovative recent writing on Reconstruction politics has centered on a broad reassessment of black Republicanism, largely undertaken by a new generation of black historians. Scholars like Thomas Holt and Nell Painter insist that Reconstruction was not simply a matter of black and white. Conflicts within the black community, no less than divisions among whites, shaped Reconstruction politics. Where revisionist scholars, both black and white, had celebrated the accomplishments of black political leaders, Holt, Painter, and others charge that they failed to address the economic plight of the black masses. Painter criticized "representative colored men," as national black leaders were called, for failing to provide ordinary freedmen with effective political leadership. Holt found that black officeholders in South Carolina mostly emerged from the old free mulatto class of Charleston, which shared many assumptions with prominent whites. "Basically bourgeois in their origins and orientation," he wrote, they "failed to act in the interest of black peasants."

In emphasizing the persistence from slavery of divisions between free blacks and slaves, these writers reflect the increasing concern with continuity and conservatism in Reconstruction. Their work reflects a startling extension of revisionist premises. If, as has been argued for the past twenty years, blacks were active agents rather than mere victims of manipulation, then they could not be absolved of blame for the ultimate failure of Reconstruction.

Despite the excellence of recent writing and the continual expansion of our knowledge of the period, historians of Reconstruction today face a unique dilemma. An old interpretation has been overthrown, but a coherent new synthesis has yet to take its place. The revisionists of the 1960s effectively established a series of negative points: the Reconstruction governments were not as bad as had been portrayed, black supremacy was a myth, the Radicals were not cynical manipulators of the freedmen. Yet no convincing overall portrait of the quality of political and social life emerged from their writings. More recent historians have rightly pointed to elements of continuity that spanned the nineteenth-century Southern experience, especially the survival, in modified form, of the plantation system. Nevertheless, by denying the real changes that did occur, they have failed to provide a convincing portrait of an era characterized above all by drama, turmoil, and social change.

Building upon the findings of the past twenty years of scholarship, a new portrait of Reconstruction ought to begin by viewing it not as a specific time period, bounded by the years 1865 and 1877, but as an episode in a prolonged historical process—American society's adjustment to the consequences of the Civil War and emancipation. The Civil War, of course, raised the decisive questions of America's national existence: the relations between local and national authority, the definition of citizenship, the balance between force and consent in generating obedience to authority. The war and Reconstruction, as Allan Nevins observed over fifty years ago, marked the "emergence of modern America." This was the era of the completion of the national railroad network, the creation of the modern steel industry, the conquest of the West and final subduing of the Native Americans, and the expansion of the mining frontier. Lincoln's America—the world of the small farm and artisan shop—gave way to a rapidly industrializing economy. The issues that galvanized postwar Northern politics—from the question of the greenback currency to the mode of paying holders of the national debt—arose from the economic changes unleashed by the Civil War.

Above all, the war irrevocably abolished slavery. Since 1619, when "twenty negars" disembarked from a Dutch ship in Virginia, racial injustice had haunted American life, mocking its professed ideals even as tobacco and cotton, the products of slave labor, helped finance the nation's economic development. Now the implications of the black presence could no longer be ignored. The Civil War resolved the problem of slavery but, as the Philadelphia diarist Sydney George Fisher observed in June 1865, it opened an even more intractable problem: "What shall we do with the Negro?" Indeed, he went on, this was a problem "*incapable* of any solution that will satisfy both North and South."

As Fisher realized, the focal point of Reconstruction was the social revolution known as emancipation. Plantation slavery was simultaneously a system of labor, a form of racial domination, and the foundation upon which arose a distinctive ruling class within the South. Its demise threw open the most fundamental questions of economy, society, and politics. A new system of labor, social, racial, and political relations had to be created to replace slavery.

The United States was not the only nation to experience emancipation in the nineteenth century. Neither plantation slavery, nor abolition were unique to the United States. But Reconstruction was. In a comparative perspective Radical Reconstruction stands as a remarkable experiment, the only effort of a society experiencing abolition to bring the former slaves within the umbrella of equal citizenship. Because the Radicals did not achieve everything they wanted, historians have lately tended to play down the stunning departure represented by black suffrage and officeholding. Former slaves, most fewer than two years removed from bondage, debated the fundamental questions of the polity: What is a republican form of government? Should the state provide equal education for all? How could political equality be reconciled with a society in which property was so unequally distributed? There was something inspiring in the way such men met the challenge of Reconstruction. "I knew nothing more than to obey my master," James K. Greene, an Alabama black politician later recalled. "But the tocsin of freedom sounded and knocked at the door and we walked out like free men and we met the exigencies as they grew up, and shouldered the responsibilities."

"You never saw a people more excited on the subject of politics than are the negroes of the south," one Planter observed in 1867. And there were more than a few Southern whites as well who in these years shook off the prejudices of the past to embrace the vision of a new South dedicated to the principles of equal citizenship and social justice. One ordinary South Carolinian expressed the new sense of possibility in 1868 to the Republican governor of the state: "I am sorry that I cannot write an elegant stiled letter to your excellency. But I rejoice to think that God almighty has given to the poor of S.C. a Gov. to hear to feel to protect the humble poor without distinction to race or color. . . . I am a native borned S.C. a poor man never owned a Negro in my life nor my father before me. . . . Remember the true and loyal are the poor of the whites and blacks, outside of these you can find none loyal."

Few modern scholars believe the Reconstruction governments established in the South in 1867 and 1868 fulfilled the aspirations of their humble constituents. While their achievements in such realms as education, civil rights, and the economic rebuilding of the South are now widely appreciated, historians today believe they failed to affect either the economic plight of the emancipated slave or the ongoing transformation of independent white farmers into cotton tenants. Yet their opponents did perceive the Reconstruction governments in precisely this way—as representatives of a revolution that had put the bottom rail, both racial and economic, on top. This perception helps explain the ferocity of the attacks leveled against them and the pervasiveness of violence in the post-emancipation South.

The spectacle of black men voting and holding office was anathema to large numbers of Southern whites. Even more disturbing, at least in the view of those who still controlled the plantation regions of the South, was the emergence of local officials, black and white, who sympathized with the plight of the black laborer. Alabama's vagrancy law was a "dead letter" in 1870, "because those who are charged with its enforcement are indebted to the vagrant vote for their offices and emoluments." Political debates over the level and incidence of taxation, the control of crops, and the resolution of contract disputes revealed that a primary issue of Reconstruction was the role of government in a plantation society. During presidential Reconstruction, and after "Redemption," with planters and their allies in control of politics, the law emerged as a means of stabilizing and promoting the plantation system. If Radical Reconstruction failed to redistribute the land of the South, the ouster of the planter class from control of politics at least ensured that the sanctions of the criminal law would not be employed to discipline the black labor force.

An understanding of this fundamental conflict over the relation between government and society helps explain the pervasive complaints concerning corruption and "extravagance" during Radical Reconstruction. Corruption there was aplenty; tax rates did rise sharply. More significant than the rate of taxation, however, was the change in its incidence. For the first time, planters and white farmers had to pay a significant portion of their income to the government, while propertyless blacks often escaped scot-free. Several states, moreover, enacted heavy taxes on uncultivated land to discourage land speculation and force land onto the market, benefiting, it was hoped, the freedmen.

As time passed, complaints about the "extravagance" and corruption of Southern governments found a sympathetic audience among influential Northerners. The Democratic charge that universal suffrage in the South was responsible for high taxes and governmental extravagance coincided with a rising conviction among the urban middle classes of the North that city government had to be taken out of the hands of the immigrant poor and returned to the "best men"—the educated, professional, financially independent citizens unable to exert much political influence at a time of mass parties and machine politics. Increasingly the "respectable" middle classes began to retreat from the very notion of universal suffrage. The poor were no longer perceived as honest producers, the backbone of the social order; now they became the "dangerous classes," the "mob." As the historian Francis Parkman put it, too much power rested with "masses of imported ignorance and hereditary ineptitude." To Parkman the Irish of the Northern cities and the blacks of the South were equally incapable of utilizing the ballot: "Witness the municipal corruptions of New York, and the monstrosities of negro rule in South Carolina." Such attitudes helped to justify Northern inaction as, one by one, the Reconstruction regimes of the South were overthrown by political violence.

In the end, then, neither the abolition of slavery nor Reconstruction succeeded in resolving the debate over the meaning of freedom in American life. Twenty years before the American Civil War, writing about the prospect of abolition in France's colonies, Alexis de Tocqueville had written, "If the Negroes have the right to become free, the [planters] have the incontestable right not to be ruined by the Negroes' freedom." And in the United States, as in nearly every plantation society that experienced the end of slavery, a rigid social and political dichotomy between former master and former slave, an ideology of racism, and

a dependent labor force with limited economic opportunities all survived abolition. Unless one means by freedom the simple fact of not being a slave, emancipation thrust blacks into a kind of no-man's land, a partial freedom that made a
mockery of the American ideal of equal citizenship.

Yet by the same token the ultimate outcome underscores the uniqueness of
Reconstruction itself. Alone among the societies that abolished slavery in the
nineteenth century, the United States, for a moment, offered the freedmen a
measure of political control over their own destinies. However brief its sway,
Reconstruction allowed scope for a remarkable political and social mobilization
of the black community. It opened doors of opportunity that could never be
completely closed. Reconstruction transformed the lives of Southern blacks in
ways unmeasurable by statistics and unreachable by law. It raised their expectations and aspirations, redefined their status in relation to the larger society, and
allowed space for the creation of institutions that enabled them to survive the
repression that followed. And it established constitutional principles of civil and
political equality that, while flagrantly violated after Redemption, planted the
seeds of future struggle.

Certainly, in terms of the sense of possibility with which it opened, Reconstruction failed. But as Du Bois observed, it was a "splendid failure." For its
animating vision—a society in which social advancement would be open to all
on the basis of individual merit, not inherited caste distinctions—is as old as
America itself and remains relevant to a nation still grappling with the unresolved legacy of emancipation.

October 1983